The Free-Market Family

The Free-Market Family

How the Market Crushed the American Dream (and How It Can Be Restored)

MAXINE EICHNER

OXFORD
UNIVERSITY PRESS

OXFORD
UNIVERSITY PRESS

Oxford University Press is a department of the University of Oxford. It furthers
the University's objective of excellence in research, scholarship, and education
by publishing worldwide. Oxford is a registered trade mark of Oxford University
Press in the UK and certain other countries.

Published in the United States of America by Oxford University Press
198 Madison Avenue, New York, NY 10016, United States of America.

CIP data is on file at the Library of Congress
ISBN 978–0–19–005547–9

1 3 5 7 9 8 6 4 2

Printed by Sheridan Books, Inc., United States of America

For Hannah, Abe, Eli, and, always, Eric.

CONTENTS

ACKNOWLEDGMENTS

I owe many people thanks for their help during this book's writing. Six won-derful friends and colleagues read the entire manuscript and met with me for extended discussions about it. My family law colleagues, Naomi Cahn, June Carbone, and Clare Huntington, together spent a day working through a draft with me, after which June sent me extended comments and Clare helped me restructure the draft. On the family policy side, my colleagues and comrades, Merike Blofield and Fernando Filgueira, spent two days poring over the draft with me (with Fernando flying in from Uruguay to do so) and giving me de-tailed comments, and both engaged in countless email discussions about inter-national comparisons. Fernando also gave me the benefit of his deep expertise in comparative welfare state data and helped construct several of the graphs in this book. Finally, Diane Kunz (whom, to my good fortune, I met by chance at our children's school) read the draft and then provided me with insightful comments. The book was immeasurably improved by all these colleagues' gen-erosity, and I'm forever grateful to them.

Other fine colleagues at the University of North Carolina and elsewhere read chapters or earlier drafts and gave me significant and helpful feedback, including Ray Boshara, Neil Buchanan, Nancy Dowd, Cynthia Edwards, Faith Eichner, Barb Fedders, Carissa Hessick, Melissa Jacoby, Alice Kessler-Harris, Holning Lau, Jared Make, Tamara Metz (who read the historical chapters several times in early iterations), Dana Remus, Michele Rivkin-Fish, Ziggy Rivkin-Fish, Melinda Ruley, Stephanie Schmit, Emily Stolzenberg, and Jonathan Weiler. Heather McCulloch, head of the Closing the Women's Wealth Gap Initiative, generously introduced me to people at several of the initiative's member organizations to help me find families to interview.

Several years of research assistants contributed to this project. A few re-quire special mention. Hanna Huffstetler, then an enormously talented under-graduate, set up the cite-checking system that moved this book to completion.

Caitlin Haff and Josh Renz were both critical in helping me nail down important issues, and Josh provided clutch assistance with the many graphs in this book. Caitlin Bell-Butterfield stepped in at the end and, calmly and efficiently, helped wrangle the last draft of the book. Last, but by no means least, I need to thank Jenna Mazzella, whose careful, tenacious, and intelligent research during the book's writing, and fact checking of the entire book after that, contributed far more to the final product than the title "research assistant" would suggest. "Collaborator" would be a more accurate term for the work she performed. This book would have been far tougher to finish without her and far worse as a result. Thanks as well to Tyla Olson for her sharp and careful proofreading and for her pristine corrections to the manuscript. The considerable help I received from all these colleagues prevented many errors; I take responsibility for any that remain.

I also owe a huge debt of gratitude to my husband, Eric Stein. From the first draft of the manuscript to the final page proofs, he tirelessly read and offered comments on every page of every draft, as well as talked through issue after issue with me as I thought the book through. I'm truly lucky to have him as a partner.

On the publishing side, I'm grateful for the sure hands of Dave McBride and Holly Mitchell at Oxford University Press during the editing and production process. And to Anna Stein, agent (and cousin-in-law) extraordinaire, for coaching me through how to write for a general audience, as well as her expertise and advice throughout the process. I'm also indebted to the fabulous production team at Newgen, including Cheryl Merritt for coordinating this project and Mary Becker for her intelligent (and opinionated!) copyediting.

Finally, I am fortunate to come from a large and wonderful family who supported me through the book's writing. I thank Vicky Eichner as well as my late father Arthur Eichner, Jane and Adam Stein, June Eichner and Barry Elman, Faith and Jeff Adler, Gerda Stein and Lee Norris, Josh and Anna Stein, Robert and Lisa Eichner, and all their children, for bearing with me through the years it took to write this book. I particularly thank my children, Hannah, Abe, and Eli Stein Eichner, and my husband, Eric, who continually teach me the importance of families, the joys they can bring, and the important ways they impart meaning to human lives.

INTRODUCTION

> The American Dream is that dream of a land in which life should be better and richer and fuller for everyone, with opportunity for each according to ability or achievement.... It is not a dream of motor cars and high wages merely, but a dream of social order in which each man and each woman shall be able to attain to the fullest stature of which they are innately capable, and be recognized by others for what they are, regardless of the fortuitous circumstances of birth or position.
>
> —James Truslow Adams (1931)[1]

All countries have myths that capture the identity and ambition of their citizens. The myth to which we Americans have long subscribed is known as the "American Dream." The writer James Truslow Adams, quoted in the epigraph, coined that term in 1931. But the ideal of our country that it stands for is far older. What sets America apart, as this myth has it, is that our society ensures every person, regardless of age, gender, and socioeconomic status, the opportunity to develop to their fullest potential. As Adams emphasized, our enduring myth doesn't mean only that we obtain material comforts. Rather, the American Dream stands for something more. It aspires to a society that allows each of us to achieve our full promise and to live rich, fulfilling lives.

In the past half-century, though, the American Dream has come to be interpreted as simply guaranteeing the right to compete for wealth in an ever more brutal market. As long as (an increasingly few) people can still rise from rags to riches, in this view, the Dream is still alive, regardless of the diminished quality of the lives of everyone else. During this same period, not coincidentally, Americans have had the growing sense that our country has gone off the rails. (That perception, by the way, began long before the election of Donald Trump as president. Given this, Trump's election should be seen not as the cause of where we've gone wrong but as a symptom of how wrong we've gone: many of the voters who pulled the lever for him were willing to roll the dice because of their view that we needed fundamental change.)

This book is not the first to explore how the American Dream has gone awry. Some of the subject's most insightful commentators have targeted our country's increasing economic inequality as the source of the problem. They muster good evidence of the mushrooming gaps in Americans' income and wealth in the past half-century and the fact that the overwhelming bulk of the economic gains during this period went to the wealthy. But this explanation doesn't tell the whole story: Even the college-educated, who are doing quite well economically, widely share the belief that our nation has gone down the wrong path. And even when Americans' incomes rise, that doesn't alter their views about our misdirection.

Those who argue that our problem is economic inequality, this book argues, do get it right, but only partly so. If we accept Adams's view of what the American project is fundamentally about—"a dream of social order in which each man and each woman shall be able to attain to the fullest stature of which they are innately capable"—the necessity of sound families for producing this society becomes obvious. Yet a range of harsh market forces are undercutting American families today. The problem driving American discontent is therefore broader than past commentators would have it, as economic forces besides inequality play a role. Yet the problem is also narrower in that our discontent stems not generally from the havoc caused by economic forces, but specifically from the damage these forces are wreaking on our family lives.[2]

In 1965, Daniel Patrick Moynihan, then Assistant Secretary of Labor for President Lyndon B. Johnson, released his report on the breakdown of African American inner-city families. Despite the report's significant flaws, Moynihan made a critical connection. He saw that the decline of manufacturing jobs in cities was the cause of the sharp upswing in single-parent black families in those areas. Unemployment at that time was regulated simply "as an economic phenomenon." What this missed, he argued, were the "social and personal consequences" of this job loss. More than half a century later, though, we are still ignoring the destructive effects that large-scale economic forces can have on the well-being of families. The result is that markets, rather than supporting sound family lives, are strangling the life out of them.

This matters so much because of the vital role that families play in our individual and collective well-being. Children need strong family relationships to build the stable foundation that will enable them to become sound adults. And it's through families that children will (or won't) get the economic support and caretaking they need to fulfill their potential. Family relationships are also central to most adults' life plans and moral commitments, as well as to their happiness and well-being. In addition, families play a key role in knitting adults into the social fabric of the community. Undermine families, and the rest of society topples down right along with them. Damage families, and you also undermine the American Dream as it was originally understood, before its meaning was narrowed solely to the right to compete for wealth. If the stress on American families interferes with their ability to raise their children well, as this book will show that it does on a daily basis, those children won't be able to develop the full potential that the Dream promises them. And if economic forces keep adults from fulfilling relationships, compel them to spend the bulk of their lives at work, and make combining work and family increasingly overwhelming, they, too, will be denied the Dream.

In the past several decades, families across the economic spectrum have seen the American Dream recede as a result of economic pressures. These pressures, to be sure, create problems that look very different for families of different classes. Low-income families, and particularly poor families, clearly have it worst of all.[3] Uncertain job prospects and low wages mean that many adults in this group won't ever form the stable partnerships they badly want. Because of this, a rising number of their children are born to unmarried parents, and most children from families toward the bottom of the income ladder will at some point be raised by single mothers. On top of that, low-income families' budgets are so tight that parents are constantly stressed about how to make ends meet, which harms their ability to parent. To make matters still worse, these parents have little chance of giving their children even the basics they need to have a solid start in life.

Take the situation of Wanda Johnson, a single mother from Charlotte, North Carolina.[4] Her son, Deonte, was born when she was eighteen and yet to graduate high school. Because she couldn't afford to pay for daycare, and the waitlist for childcare assistance was years long, she couldn't continue her job as a cashier or finish high school. That meant her only income was a monthly welfare check of $236, which left her family in deep poverty. The meager check wouldn't allow her to afford even the smallest apartment. She and her son wound up living with whichever relatives would have them in a series of overcrowded homes during most of Deonte's first five years. At one time, they shared a three-bedroom, one-bathroom house along with six other people. Wanda and Deonte slept in a den along with her grandmother because the bedrooms were full. At another time, they lived in a small home, again with six other people, with Wanda and Deonte sharing a twin bed in a room that also served as a passthrough. These situations were lousy, particularly for Deonte. The homes hadn't been childproofed, so he had little freedom to roam or play in his first years. He was repeatedly bullied by an older child in one home, was verbally abused and overdisciplined by an adult in another, and was raised in houses that reeked of tobacco and in which someone was screaming morning to night. But Wanda had no other way to put a roof over their heads.

At one point, Wanda found their situation so intolerable that the two moved out of the overcrowded, unpleasant house they were living in. When she couldn't find a new place to live, Child Protective Services took Deonte away and put him in foster care for an entire year before Wanda got him back. The only good thing to have come out of it was that Deonte was elevated to the top of the long waitlist for childcare subsidies because he was in foster care. He was allowed to keep the subsidy on his return to Wanda, which meant that, with his daycare paid for, Wanda could finally work full-time—at least when she could find full-time work. Working at a minimum-wage job with no welfare benefits by then, though, still meant living below the poverty line in overcrowded homes with many others. The difficulty of their situation kept Wanda on edge all the time, which made her a harsher parent to Deonte than she wanted to be. And Wanda stayed up late at night worrying about how to get Deonte the many things he needed. She could usually put food on the table, but when it occasionally ran out, she'd need to make a trip to the food bank during its sporadic weekend hours so she wouldn't miss work. There was no money for extras—not the recreational sports teams Deonte badly wanted to join (she couldn't afford the fees and gear) and not the birthday parties he saw other kids having. On top of all this, Wanda herself was, and is, lonely. She put all her energy and resources toward raising Deonte, and is now raising a younger son, Trevor, by herself. She never found the stable, responsible man she was looking for to be her partner.

Middle-income families don't often face the same struggles just to put food on the table (although rising financial insecurity means that an increasing number sometimes do) or to ensure decent conditions at home for their kids.[5] But they're still economically stressed. Most young couples with kids have fewer savings than parents did in the past because their basic expenses are much higher today. They're also often burdened with high mortgage payments, education loans, and out-of-pocket healthcare costs. What's left over from entry-level salaries isn't close to enough to give their kids what they need to thrive, particularly when it comes to good preschools and prekindergartens. On top of this, the cost of quality daycare is so high, and combining work with parenting and managing a household is so tough, that many mothers (and, increasingly, some fathers) wind up leaving their jobs to care for their kids, making family finances even tighter. And economic struggles mean that far more middle-income adults aren't marrying and, even when they do, are divorcing more often.

Annette Simmons, a married mother in Kansas City of two preschool-aged girls, Chloe and Sarah, lives with these pressures every day.[6] Her husband, Bob, earns about $58,000 a year including fringe benefits as a biologist with a nonprofit institute. Annette was a cook at local restaurants before she had kids. Even though she enjoyed her job, she didn't go back to work after she had her first child because good daycare would have cost as much as she earned, and daycare for two kids would have cost far more.

But staying home has required scrimping, saving, and virtually constant financial worry. Before the girls were born, Bob and Annette bought a modest house, with a little help from their parents. Once they had kids, between paying the mortgage, paying back Bob's college loans, and meeting the out-of-pocket medical expenses from complications during Annette's pregnancies and C-sections, they wound up with thousands of dollars of credit card debt. They have been digging their way out of that financial hole ever since, but it has meant a bare-bones life—no paid babysitters to give them a break or a night out, no vacations, and constant efforts to pare down costs. To help make ends meet, Annette has been babysitting two other children for a few hours Monday through Friday, earning another $150 or so a week. She doesn't know how much longer her family can afford to have her stay home with the girls, and she worries about it all the time. On the other hand, she doesn't know what she'll do when she goes back to work since they can't afford good daycare on her cook's wages. And on their budget, paying for prekindergarten when the girls are ready will be out of reach, let alone paying tuition when they're ready for college.

Finally, high-income families have all the money they need to support their families (although it may not always feel that way to them).[7] But the long hours demanded by their jobs, combined with the many hours they put in to make sure that their kids will be economically stable when they grow up, often make life a grinding slog. Their stress and exhaustion are aggravated by technology: these parents are never completely off-the-clock and are always checking for texts and emails from work, even at home. Meeting all these demands leaves them overwhelmed.

Amira Patel knows something about feeling overwhelmed.[8] She is a junior partner at a large Washington, DC law firm, where she represents workers in employment matters. Her husband works in public policy. They have two sons, one seven and the other four.

Amira gave birth to her first child while she was a senior associate at the firm. Professionals are the group most likely to get paid leave in the United States, where market power dictates benefits. Amira's firm's policy was generous even by the standards of US professionals—twelve weeks of paid maternity leave— although that's less than a quarter of the leave available to all families with a new child in some European countries. She turned out to need those twelve weeks, plus six weeks of paid sick leave that she had banked, and another six weeks of unpaid leave, due to pregnancy complications and a very difficult childbirth and recovery. Even then, when she returned to work at the time her son was six months old, she still wasn't feeling well as a result of symptoms of postpartum depression.

Once she returned to work, though, she had to resume the schedule expected of the firm's litigators. On the plus side, the hours weren't exceptionally long by the standards of American professionals—on average fifty to sixty hours a week—and she was allowed to work from home at least one day a week and sometimes two. But her hours fluctuated tremendously: some weeks she worked sixty-five or seventy hours; some weeks she needed to work eighty hours to meet pressing deadlines. That meant that she was constantly exhausted from lack of sleep and she saw her son far less than she wanted. Her exhaustion grew after her second child was born and he took a long time to start sleeping through the night. Amira was getting between five and six hours sleep a night, and being woken up at 3 a.m. every morning to boot—all while working long hours at her job. Her grueling work schedule meant she missed dinner with her kids three or four nights a week. She had little time to take care of herself. Looking after her own health and well-being fit nowhere into her life.

Amira says she worries about the long-term effects on her body of her years of constant stress combining work and raising young children. During some periods, her stress levels were so high that it felt like she was in a constant state of borderline panic attacks. Recently, she's been trying to exercise regularly and meditate to keep the stress under control. But of course that takes time, which has to come from somewhere. "You're constantly robbing Peter to pay Paul," she says of her life. In the last months, she's also been trying to work a schedule in which she gets to the office by 6:30 or 7 a.m. Although it means that she doesn't see her kids in the morning, this schedule lets her make it home for dinner with her family two or three weeknight evenings a week. The nights she misses dinner she works until late in the evening, often putting in fourteen-hour workdays, and she gets home after her husband and the boys are in bed.

Amira says she and her husband outsource far more than they'd like to save any time they can. They had nannies for their kids' first years. They get groceries delivered when they don't have time to shop. They have also pared their lives down significantly to make the time they need for family and work. Still, Amira has a continual sense of having too many balls up in the air, with one of them about to drop at any moment. The result is that she constantly feels like she's doing neither her paid work nor her parenting well.

Amira's a partner at her law firm now—couldn't she just work fewer hours and take a pay cut? Not with her job, she says. Although her firm is more reasonable than most, in the hard-charging world of American law firms, there's only so far you can buck the dominant culture of long work hours, which is almost totally unresponsive to the needs of families. The result, she says, is that "we make it all work at great personal expense."

Why not quit and work someplace with fewer hours? Amira says that she and her husband ask themselves the same question at least once a week. But she loves her job and the people she represents and thinks, in some small way, she's serving the cause of justice in the world. She just wishes the costs of doing a job like hers weren't so high. Despite this, she recognizes how privileged her family's situation is compared with many American families. She and her husband have jobs that mean that they don't have to worry about how to feed their kids, whether they can afford good caretaking, or where their next paycheck will come from. But that doesn't make the acute trade-offs between work and family any easier.

The struggles that low-, middle-, and high-income American families are having today look very different, but they are all manifestations of the same problem: the increasingly large toll that market forces have been taking on families during the past several decades. The harm inflicted on families, however, wasn't inevitable, and it wasn't the necessary result of the forces of globalization or technology. Instead, the defeat of American families by market forces was the product of a long-term failure of American public policy. That defeat occurred because, beginning in the 1970s, American policymakers began to sell families out to a misguided ideal of free markets. Before then, the idea that the government should buffer families from harmful market forces was an accepted part of Americans' vision of government (even if, as the Moynihan Report pointed out, some of the market's effects on families had been overlooked). But toward the end of the twentieth century, that vision was undermined by an increasingly widespread, albeit wrongheaded, view that insulating families from market forces made them weaker, and that all policymakers needed to do to ensure healthy families was to deregulate markets. Based on this view, our elected officials took the first steps away from protecting families. And policymakers' continued elevation of markets over families since then has deprived families of the conditions they need to flourish.

Consider the virtual absence of public policies that help Americans balance work and family. Most US adults work long hours on their jobs. This generally isn't because we are particularly enthusiastic about our work—in fact, about two-thirds of American workers *don't* feel engaged in their jobs.[9] Nor is it because we put a higher premium on earning a lot of money than on spending time with our families. In truth, most of us put our families at the top of our list of priorities; becoming well off is far lower down on that list.[10] And most of us would like to cut back our paid work hours, many of us desperately, in order to have saner, calmer family lives.[11] Despite all this, increased inequality and insecurity, combined with the lack of government help, have pushed families into working more and more hours of paid work.[12]

Yet although Americans are overworked and overwhelmed, politicians continue to enact policies that push adults, including parents of young children, into the workplace and keep them there for long hours. Meanwhile, they have passed almost no laws that make it easier for workers to leave work at the end of the day to get back to their families. The politicians say doing so would be bad policy because it would undercut free-market forces. Such measures would also, they argue, decrease our nation's gross domestic product (GDP), our politicians' main measure of market health. They say the same thing about passing paid family leave policies, policies that would allow parents with young children to work part-time or flextime, and other policies that support families. The consequence is that US families' total work hours have risen significantly in recent decades. In fact, two-earner families put in *twice* as many total hours of paid work than couples did two generations ago.

There's significant evidence that the free-market policies put in place in the last five decades fail on their proponents' own terms, actually causing GDP to grow more slowly than if we had enacted policies that support families.[13] Regardless, putting the interests of markets before families puts the cart before the horse. Whereas families are central to our individual and collective flourishing, there's nothing intrinsically good about markets that gives them a necessary place in fulfilling lives. Instead, we value markets instrumentally for what they can do for us. In particular, using markets to produce and distribute goods and services frequently improves well-being because it puts them in the hands of people who value them.

But unregulated markets don't always serve well-being in this way. Sometimes the operation of markets undercuts the health of families. When that's the case, as it is for Americans who must work long hours, choosing not to regulate markets to support families undermines well-being. This stands the proper goal of economic policy on its head: that goal should be enabling Americans to live good lives consistent with our values, not enabling free markets regardless of the consequences. Our high GDP matters not a whit if we can't translate it into the things in life that count the most to us, including time for our loved ones.

The result of five decades of policymakers' market-centric decisions is that market forces have crushed Americans' ability to have thriving family lives, as well as to raise strong, solid kids. While our GDP has increased three times over, the well-being of our families—the top item on Americans' list of priorities—has gone rapidly downhill. No institution has as much impact on how well people and society are doing as families. But instead of helping families get the things they need to thrive, policymakers just keep cheering the market on, telling families that, if they only work a little harder, they can achieve their dreams.

Republicans have sounded this message most loudly. Former Pennsylvania senator Rick Santorum stated the party line when he said that conservatives "believe in the power of markets more than they do in the power of government."[14] But mainstream Democrats support this free-market mentality as well. It was President Bill Clinton who announced that "the era of big government is over." Clinton's economic policies, as touted in a centrist Democratic publication, aimed for "rapid growth and low inflation" based on the principle "of limited government interference in markets." To the extent these economic policies sought to help families, it was largely by assuming that economic growth alone would help them. That assumption was badly wrong.[15] Nevertheless, public policy continues to rest on the flawed notion that all families need to flourish are healthy markets. And in the last few years, politicians' efforts to push people to work harder and longer seem to be ramping up rather than diminishing, while efforts to defund existing government programs that help families, which have already been stretched thin by years of budget cuts, are increasing.

It's time we lay to rest the misguided view that families can do it all by themselves if we just leave the market to work its supposed magic. Few ideas have caused as much harm as this one has. Markets do an excellent job of getting a broad range of goods and services that can be monetized into the hands of people who want them and who have the ability to pay for them. But many things that people need to flourish, like the nurturing that parents provide, aren't distributed through markets. And some things that can be distributed through markets, like high-quality daycare, aren't affordable for many families. These gaps in markets reveal the lie in the claim that markets alone can solve all our problems. They also reveal the importance of government.

Many—in fact, most—other wealthy countries recognize the importance of the government's role in supporting families. These countries, like ours, have market economies. Yet, unlike us, they have regulated their markets in ways that help families out. For example, they have taken gains in productivity during the last half-century and, through policies that allow workers to limit their work hours, helped them spend more time with their families without reducing their wages. They have also used market gains to pay for programs like paid family leave, subsidies for families with young children, and universal daycare. In contrast, we've funneled our gains in productivity during this time into the pockets of the wealthy. The result is that people in these countries work fewer hours, lead saner lives, and have healthier families. We have a higher GDP that does nothing to improve our lives, individually or collectively.

I write about these issues as an academic, but my experience with the family-market problems that virtually all Americans face is also intensely personal. During the year after my first child was born, more than twenty years ago, I struggled hard to balance my responsibilities as a lawyer at a law firm with being a mother, in addition to having some semblance of a sane life. I had difficulty with the messages I received about how committed lawyers should behave. One senior attorney told me of having to miss her child's birthday party because of a court deadline. Another told me that, after the many times that she had to work through the night, the way she pulled herself together to start the next day was to lie in bed, even if just for five minutes, before getting up, showering, and doing it all over again.

My struggle to juggle work and family came to a head one night after I had just finished a jury trial but still had a court brief to complete. I called my husband to tell him that I'd make it home for dinner, unlike the nights before. But a secretary left early, the copier failed, and I wound up needing to make an emergency trip to Kinko's. After each of these complications, I called my husband to push back dinner, then to eat without me, then finally to say I'd be there to put our daughter to bed. In the few blocks between Kinko's and my house, speeding to try to make it home for bedtime, I was stopped by a police officer. I burst into tears when he turned down my desperate request to write the ticket at my house, so I might see my daughter before she went to sleep. When I got home, post-ticket, still sobbing, I lifted my then-sleeping child out of her crib and rocked her while she slept. I made the decision to quit practicing law that night.

The dilemma that I confronted fundamentally changed my views about what mattered in life. At the top of my list of priorities was making sure that my daughter had what she needed to flourish. But I was surprised by how strongly I felt that *I* wanted to be there with my child—not just because I thought it would be better for her, but also because being a hands-on parent was really important to me. The virtues of leading a sane, at least somewhat well-ordered existence also loomed large when I thought about changing my career. That first year of massive exhaustion as a parent had driven home the costs of our hard-charging culture. Looking ahead at a future of combining parenthood with lawyering, I could see years of too little sleep, of too many meals prepared and eaten on the fly, of a home cluttered with piles of paper my husband and I never had the time or energy to sort. I badly wanted a saner existence than that. Having a challenging career was important to me, but so was having a life that included happy, thriving kids, being an involved parent, spending time with my partner, and having an at least somewhat ordered home. But even talking about these issues was difficult since in the United States we tend to laud long hours of hard work while paying little heed to basic issues about the texture of our lives.

Under our free-market system, I had to sacrifice some of the things I cared about to get others higher on my list. I wound up in academia, a job I love, and one that has the considerable upside of providing more flexible hours for raising kids. Teaching at a law school meant that the cruelest issues so many American families face—of job insecurity and not being able to put food on the table or a roof over one's head—were not problems for my family.

Nevertheless, few families altogether escape the serious downsides of our economic system, and ours was not among the lucky few. Academia still required long hours, even if the hours were flexible. As a mentor put it to one of my friends in graduate school: "It's a great job. You can work any sixty hours a week that you want." My husband's and my high work hours meant that we had to let go of a number of things that make life sane during the years our three kids were young—adequate sleep, an organized home, spending almost any time with friends, cooking anything beyond the basics ("I know this is the third night in a row we've had cheese quesadillas; I just haven't had time to shop"), and exercise. And like many American families who just manage to keep it all together when things are going well, ours came close to the brink when something went awry— including when one of our kids developed serious medical issues that took eight years to properly diagnose and when my husband commuted to a job in another state. Throughout this time, I often thought that there had to be a way to make it easier to raise families in a country that has as many advantages as our own. When I became a professor, I made that question central to my research agenda.

The goals of this book are twofold. First, it seeks to bring to light the ways that market forces today are increasingly undermining the well-being of American families. Much of the problem for families stems from the steep increases in economic insecurity and inequality in the past couple of generations. Individuals' responses to these forces can be likened to that of children competing in a game of "king of the hill" on a giant dirt pile, in which the size and shape of the pile have changed. In decades past, that dirt pile was a lot broader and a lot lower. Because of that, more of those playing made it to the top, but getting there didn't put them nearly as high. Today, this heightened insecurity and inequality have made the pile far taller than it used to be (since adults who achieve success are much wealthier than they used to be), but also far narrower (since fewer adults attain such success). The result is that many more Americans wind up at the bottom of the hill and can't provide their families with the resources they need to thrive. Just as a game of king of the hill would be much harder fought in these circumstances, so adults today are competing much more fiercely than they used to because they don't want their families to wind up at the bottom of the hill. This means they are spending more hours at paid work, and have little time and energy left to enjoy their lives. The same is true for their children, who spend so many hours preparing to compete in our brutal economy for when they reach adulthood that they too are stressed and overwhelmed.[16]

One point the dirt-pile metaphor makes clear is the flaw in the way today's economic competition among families is usually described. We often talk about this competition in zero-sum terms, as if the more families at the bottom lose, the more families at the top win. But this isn't at all correct: Market competition among families is better thought of as what might be called a "negative-sum game."[17] The competition is so fierce for everyone that it is sapping Americans' energy to spend time doing the things they want to do, including enjoying their families. That means that *all* families lose when they play by today's rules. Even those who make it to the top of the pile and do well financially wind up devoting so much of their time and energy to the competition that they have too little time left over for the things they really care about. It's just that some families lose more than others.

One of the many tolls of this system is how it affects the happiness of Americans. A recent study compared the "happiness gap" between parents and nonparents (this gap measures how much happier nonparents are than parents in a particular country) in twenty-two countries. The researchers found that our nation's happiness gap was by far the largest of all the countries considered—meaning that parents in the United States were *less* happy than nonparents, and to a greater degree, than parents in any other wealthy country. In eight of the countries surveyed, parents actually reported being happier than nonparents.[18] What was the key difference between countries with smaller or nonexistent gaps and countries like ours with large happiness gaps? The answer is the presence or absence of public policies that support families, which improved parents' happiness without reducing that of nonparents. Given that more than eight in ten Americans will become parents during their lives, the drain on happiness that accompanies US parenting will eventually drag most Americans down with it.

This brings us to the second goal of this book, which is to call attention to the role that government can play—but hasn't in recent decades—in regulating the economy to support families. We could be using our nation's great wealth and the force of its public policy to make life easier for families. But, unfortunately, there is little that individual families can do on their own to ease their predicaments. Families themselves can't reshape the size and slope of the dirt pile. In fact, individual families face big risks if they step back on their own from the intense economic competition. Workers who try to reduce their work hours risk losing their jobs and being unable to support their families. Parents who don't spend long hours driving their kids to resume-building activities worry they are risking their kids not getting into a good college that will give them a better chance of succeeding economically.

But there is a lot that government can do to make life easier for families. We Americans don't tend to recognize this, since we focus so much on individual solutions and personal responsibility. That's one reason Sheryl Sandberg's *Lean In* manifesto, in which she argued that women need to put more effort into their paid work and seek career advancement, struck a chord with so many women. The problem is that, in our current system, mothers who are expected to "lean in" to the long hours and high demands of paid work have little to nothing left over for the significant demands of parenthood and the rest of life. Lean in enough and you'll collapse from exhaustion.[19] Or as one *Lean In* critic put it, "We need to fight for our right to lean back and put our feet up."[20] Making our system more humane requires institutional rather than individual change. And that's where government comes in.

What can government do to support families? To begin with, it can put in place public programs that help funnel some part of our nation's great wealth to families at the times they need it most, particularly when they have young kids.

Government can also, through market regulation, reshape the size and shape of the dirt pile—meaning reduce the insecurity and inequality families face in our economic system. Furthermore, the state can enact laws that change the rules of economic competition in order to make life easier on families. For example, it can set reasonable limits on the hours that employees can be required to work. A helpful way to think about the state's role here is to imagine it as playing "traffic cop" to ensure that the market stays in its lane when it comes to the role of paid work in the lives of workers and families. As traffic cop, the state can also establish rules allowing parents of young children to work reduced schedules, employees to take flextime, and family members with caretaking responsibilities to take time off. Government actions like these would help all Americans lead saner, more satisfying family lives.[21]

Although I use the terms "free market" and "deregulated market" throughout this book, anyone who has paid attention to markets knows that the kinds of exchanges I'm discussing are never truly either. A market system couldn't exist in the absence of significant government regulation, including laws that establish a stable currency, enforce property rights, back contracts with the force of law, and so forth. What this means is that when people use the terms "free" or "deregulated" to apply to markets, they don't really mean markets aren't regulated at all. Instead, they mean that markets aren't regulated with nonmarket goals in mind, like promoting fairness, good family lives, or other social welfare goals. I'll use these terms in the same way.

Further, when I use the term "family," I define it expansively. A wide range of long-term relationships foster the well-being, caretaking, and human development that humans need to flourish. Accordingly, in my view, the relationships we as a community and a nation should seek to support extend well beyond the heterosexual marital family together with its minor children, the grouping that many used to think of as the "natural" family. Today's families include, among others, same-sex couples with or without kids, unmarried cohabiting couples, adults with aging parents, and adult siblings. The long-term relationships that benefit kids today also include single-parent families. Although stable two-parent families have particular advantages when it comes to rearing children, single-parent families can do an excellent job of raising kids, and many do—particularly when they have adequate government support. The state should therefore recognize and support single-parent families, while at the same time still facilitating the conditions that encourage two-parent families.

We can recognize the importance of families without viewing them through rose-colored glasses. All families are imperfect, many perpetuate harmful dynamics like gender inequality, and some are downright abusive. When families don't function well, they don't give their members the positive benefits that we, as a society, count on them to deliver. Seniors in bad marriages don't do better than single adults as they age; many of them do worse. And outcomes are terrible for children who are the victims of domestic abuse. Despite their many shortcomings and risks, though, we haven't developed other institutions that come close to meeting the attachment, caretaking, and developmental needs that families provide to their members. That means that most people will continue to get much of what they need through families, if they are to receive these things at all.

To keep the scope of the book within reasonable bounds, I focus on families with young children. A similar book could be written about parents of older children, adults with aging parents, or the many other family relationships that are inadequately supported today.[22] Also for reasons of scope, I focus on the programs for families with young children that are usually labeled "family programs," like parental leave, child benefits, daycare, prekindergarten, and work–family reconciliation policies. Because of that, I have largely excluded discussing policies relating to healthcare and housing, as important as these are.

Part I begins by looking at measures of well-being for children, adults, and families in the United States, many of which are plummeting. Why are we doing so poorly? Our free-market family policy helps answer that question. The defining feature of this policy is the expectation that families will deal with market forces on their own, without help from the government. United States policy diverges sharply from that of the many other wealthy countries with pro-family policies, which treat strong families as a joint responsibility of both families *and* government. Under a pro-family policy, the government enforces regulations that support the economic conditions families need to flourish.

The free-market family policy undermines American families from the bottom to the top of the economic ladder. At the low end, economic inequality and insecurity make it less likely that poor and working-class adults will enter stable partnerships. This cuts many loose from the social fabric of the community, increasing the incidence of "deaths of despair." These economic forces also mean that people are having children in fragile relationships likely to break up. In raising these kids, parents contend with rising economic insecurity that means they can't be sure whether they can put food on the table. Many must also work service jobs that make scheduling childcare hellish. At the higher end of the economic ladder, parents have it easier but are confronted by a different set of problems: they are so exhausted by their long hours of paid work, as well as the long hours it takes to parent kids to succeed in our system, that life becomes a stressful slog. The end result is that US families are more stressed and stretched than families in any other wealthy country and are the least stable of families in any wealthy country to boot.

Our free-market family system also means that few children raised in the United States will get the circumstances they need to develop their best. Children from poor and working-class families certainly get the rawest deal. Most won't come close to getting what they need because the system forces their parents to choose between putting food on the table and providing the care that helps children do their best. But even children from well-to-do families won't do as well as they might since they have to contend with the intense pressure of learning to compete on an increasingly steep and insecure economic slope. That pressure leaves most kids stressed and many completely overwhelmed.

Part II turns to the question of how American families got to this sorry place. Free-market proponents sometimes argue that unregulated markets have always been an accepted feature of the American landscape, in the same way that the Mississippi River has been.[23] But the claim that market distribution should be treated as sacrosanct, consequences be damned, is based on a warped account of American history. At the time of our country's founding, the great bulk of American families lived on farms that they used to sustain themselves and had little contact with the market. As the market economy developed in the nineteenth century, Americans were persuaded to enter it on the promise that it would support the well-being of their families. By the end of the nineteenth century, though, as industrialization picked up steam, it became clear that market forces were instead crushing working-class families, even as they were yielding unprecedented material benefits to others. The misery of working-class families eventually led to the widespread recognition that the government needed to step in to ensure that the market's promise for families was vindicated. For most of the twentieth century, the view that government had a responsibility to regulate markets in order to support families remained a fundamental part of the American social contract.

It was only toward the end of the twentieth century that this principle began to be undermined. At that time, women's increased entry into the workforce meant that our government's protections for families, which had been structured on the assumption of a male breadwinner and a female caregiver, badly needed updating. Other Western countries facing the same issue adapted their systems of family protections to these new family patterns, while still buffering families from the market. The United States was poised at the brink of doing the same, but veered off this path at the final minute. Some of the reasons it did so were sheer happenstance. But this shift away from government support of families was bolstered by the loudly sounded assertion that government action—even action aimed at helping families—undermined families' health. Free-market family policy, its advocates claimed, would better support the well-being of families. That claim was completely false, but it still persuaded policymakers. The result was that our nation scrapped existing family protections and adopted the harmful free-market family policy we still have today.

Finally, Part III considers how we can get American families out of this mess. To start, we need to move away from thinking that the goal of the economy is to increase the nation's wealth or, relatedly, to expand GDP, and instead to focus our attention on the economy's proper purpose: ensuring that all Americans have the resources they need to thrive. When we do this, we're really asking, "How can we make the American Dream a reality for every adult and child?" And once we ask this question, the importance of two major sectors of the economy other than markets—the family and the government—become clear. Mainstream economic theory, wrapped up in free-market mania, largely views families as consumers, relevant because of the things they buy. But once we pose the larger question we should be asking of the economy—how can we get people the resources they need to flourish?—the work that families do (raising kids, caring for aging parents, as well as grocery shopping, cooking, and cleaning the house) becomes vitally important to the larger economic picture.

This is where the government has an important role to play. Free-market advocates are openly derisive of the state's role in the economy. Government, they claim, improperly distorts market incentives when it acts in the economic sphere. But once we focus on ensuring that people get what they need to thrive— which also means ensuring that families get what they need to thrive—we can see both the virtues and limits of markets. Markets are a great means of distributing many things, but they can distribute only those goods and services that can be bought and sold, and then only to those who can afford to pay for them. That leaves significant gaps in the economic system in ensuring families have what they need to thrive. It is up to government to fill these gaps. That's where enacting pro-family policy comes in.

We already know which policies effectively support families in a market economy, as versions of them have been in place for decades in the many countries that have embraced pro-family policy. Can we afford these policies and programs? Certainly. Far less wealthy nations—including places like Estonia, whose per capita GDP is roughly a third of ours—have adopted many of them. And countries like Canada, our neighbor to the north, have increasingly adopted many of these programs in recent years. In fact, we Americans already spend as much money as other countries do on well-being throughout the course of our lives—we just spend it directly, through making out-of-pocket payments to daycare facilities, preschools, and others. Meanwhile, Finns, Danes, Canadians, and others with pro-family policy pay more of their money in the form of higher taxes, the proceeds of which the government uses to fund daycare facilities, preschools, and so forth. But relying so much on private spending skews American spending on well-being toward the end of life, when families have more money to spend, and means that different families spend wildly disparate amounts. Our social welfare payoffs would be much higher if we used public dollars to invest in children early on, when families need it most, and spent that money more equally on children. And all our lives would be richer if the government buffered families from the market forces that undercut them.

Given that policymakers have refused to put these policies in place so far, it's up to us to hold them to it. It's time that we voters ensure that our representatives are committed to regulating the market to support our families. Unless we do so, we and our children will continue to watch the ideal of the American Dream recede still further away.

THE EMBATTLED AMERICAN FAMILY

|| 1 ||

What Went Wrong with the American Dream?

Most Americans believe that our nation has veered badly off course, but they aren't clear about what exactly has gone wrong. We hear a steady drumbeat of bad news about the state of the nation—the mediocre school performance of our kids, the opioid crisis, skyrocketing rates of mental illness and teenage suicides, decreased lifespans—but it's difficult to figure out what the common thread is. This chapter brings these issues into clearer focus.

These problems, the rest of the book will show, are all tied to the collapse of the American Dream in the past five decades. I don't mean "American Dream" in the way the term is often used today, simply to describe people having the chance to get rich. The more generous version of the Dream that I'm talking about, sounded more loudly in the past, dreams much bigger: as articulated by James Truslow Adams in the introduction's epigraph, it envisions a country that doesn't stand passively by while fate or forces buffet its citizens. Instead it constructs (in Adams's words) a "social order" aimed at ensuring that all people attain "the fullest stature of which they are innately capable," regardless of where or to whom they're born. And, further, that social order allows everyone the opportunity for a "better and richer and fuller" life. This is a more ambitious way to think about the goals of society than we Americans generally think about them today. The Dream means that the social order is supposed to do much more than just allow people the opportunity to compete in the market: it's supposed to enable them to flourish. And it's the loss of this vision of our social order that is responsible for Americans' deep slide downward on so many measures, as well as their pessimistic view of our country.

One helpful way to think about this broader conception of the Dream's promise is to see it as setting up an infrastructure or scaffolding that supports Americans as they lead their lives.[1] For that promise to be fulfilled, that scaffolding needs to handle two projects particularly well. First, it needs to support kids' thriving and developing their potential so they achieve their full promise as adults. Second, it needs to support the basic well-being and soundness of adults, so that they have the opportunity to live their lives well.

This chapter pulls together indicators to consider how well America is faring on these two projects. The picture that emerges shows that we are failing radically on both counts. Children aren't thriving, and they're falling far short of achieving their potential. Meanwhile adults are, in increasing numbers, unhappy and anxious, and they feel cut off from the social fabric of the community.

These results are not surprising, the last section of the chapter suggests, when we turn to consider the health of the nation's families. American thinkers too often conceive of people as creatures who build their own lives from the ground up. But humans don't construct their lives from scratch. Instead, they are born into families and lead their lives as members of institutions—family, school, place of worship, work—that shape them and that, in turn, they negotiate and re-shape over time. The well-being of citizens is integrally related to the well-being of these institutions. When these institutions founder or citizens are distanced from them and find no suitable replacements, large holes are created in the social fabric. Of all these institutions, the one most closely associated with both children's well-being and potential and adults' flourishing is the family. Yet American families are in dismal shape because, as I'll show, our social order doesn't support them. It is no coincidence that, with our families in turmoil, the well-being of both children and adults are undermined.

THE STATE OF AMERICA'S CHILDREN

The American Dream should offer its greatest promise to our nation's children. Whether Americans will lead rich, full lives later on depends in large part on whether they get the support they need to flourish as children. To what extent does our social order today support getting children what they need?

A substantial portion of this book will link US kids' failure to flourish to the economic stress our system puts on families. That stress interferes with the ability of families to raise their children well, particularly in those crucial early years. Families need to serve several functions in order to raise sound children. To begin with, parents must satisfy children's needs for "attachment." The critical importance of the bond between parent and child was first recognized when researchers studied orphans during World War II. As the British psychologist John Bowlby observed, "[M]other-love . . . is as important for mental health as are vitamins and proteins for physical health."[2]

Beyond attachment, children need loving interactions with a parent. It turns out that whether children receive this loving care early on affects the most basic aspects of their development, including the way their brains are wired for the rest of their lives. The National Scientific Council on the Developing Child put it this way: "Young children experience their world as an environment of relationships, and these relationships affect virtually all aspects of their development—intellectual, social, emotional, physical, behavioral, and moral."[3] Kids' interactions with their parents are so important that neglect can be a bigger threat to children's development than abuse: young children who are severely neglected often wind up having more extreme cognitive and behavioral problems as they mature than children who were abused physically.[4]

Families serve other important functions for children as well. For one, they provide or arrange for the tens of thousands of hours of caretaking kids need before they are old enough to care for themselves. It turns out that the quality of caretaking kids receive is critical to both their academic achievement and their social and emotional development.[5] Families also provide or arrange for much of the human development necessary for children to gain the knowledge and skills they need to take their place in school, in the social world, and, later, in the workplace. Parents do this directly by reading to young kids, talking to them, taking them places, and playing games with them, as well as making sure they get their homework done in later years. Families also facilitate their kids' development indirectly through enrolling them in daycare and preschool programs and, later, in schools and aftercare programs.

And last, but every bit as important, families provide the income for many of the market goods and services that children depend on. Children need a constant stream of resources to do well—a roof over their heads, food, diapers, clothing, books, and at least a few toys. If children don't get the resources they need, it fundamentally and permanently interferes with their development.[6] While we don't expect families to provide all the goods and services that children require—for example, the government pays for public schooling during the K–12 years—in the United States today, we do expect families to pay for many of these resources.

There's no single indicator that, in and of itself, shows how well kids are doing or whether they're developing to their full potential. But four measures together can give us at least a strong preliminary sense: kids' reports of their levels of happiness, as well as measures of academic achievement, mental health outcomes, and economic mobility. In the United States, the picture of our children shown by these indicators is not a happy one. Our society is doing a disturbingly bad job of giving our next generation a sound start. On many measures, we are doing a much poorer job than in past decades. What's more, compared with those of kids from other countries, our kids' outcomes range from mediocre to downright subpar, depending on the measure.

Happiness

Let's start with children's own sense of satisfaction with their lives. You might think the United States would top the scale given our great national wealth. Not so. When children from developed countries are ranked on life satisfaction, US kids fall below the average. One recent United Nations study of twenty-seven industrialized countries ranked our country tied for fifteenth along with seven other countries, including the Slovak Republic and the Czech Republic. That puts us below not only wealthy countries like Sweden, the Netherlands, and Spain but also countries that are far poorer than our own such as Estonia and Slovenia.[7]

Academic Achievement

But if our kids aren't the happiest, at least they outperform students from other countries in academic achievement, right? Wrong. Despite the considerable pressure American kids feel to do well in school, as well as the comparatively long hours they put in studying, our kids' academic performance is stunningly mediocre compared with kids' performance in other wealthy countries.[8]

As Figure 1.1 shows, the United States ranked fortieth on the mathematics portion of the Programme for International Student Assessment (PISA), a test administered to fifteen-year-olds worldwide in 2015.[9] That's well below the average of our peers in the Organisation for Economic Co-operation and Development (OECD), a group of wealthy nations of which the United States is a member. We were beaten by, among others, Vietnam, Russia, the Czech Republic, Portugal, Spain, Latvia, Malta, and Lithuania. Almost three in ten US students didn't even reach the baseline level of competence on math, the level that enables students to participate fully in modern society.[10] Our students did somewhat better, but not well, in science and reading, finishing in the twenty-fifth and twenty-fourth places, respectively.[11] All this is in spite of the fact that many of the countries that left us in the dust on the PISA spend far less on primary and secondary education than we do.[12]

Mental Health

Our kids' mental health outcomes are even more troubling. According to the Centers for Disease Control and Prevention, up to one in five American children aged two to seventeen has a diagnosable mental, emotional, or behavioral disorder in a given year—and these rates are rising.[13] There's good

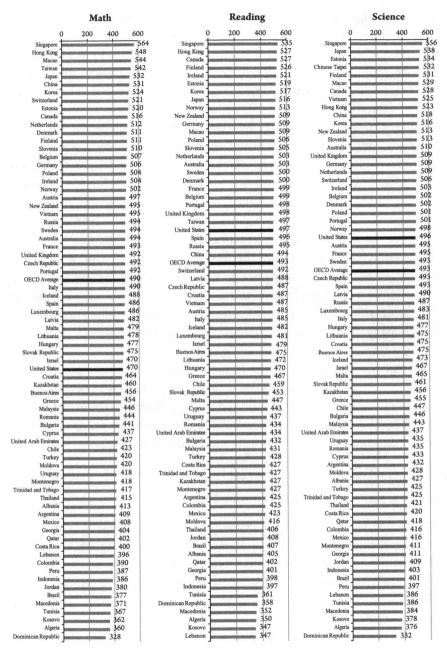

Figure 1.1. Student PISA Performance in Mathematics, Reading, and Science.
Source: Data from OECD (2016a), 44, fig. I.1.1.

reason to believe that these rates are far higher than those in the rest of the developed world.[14] Rates of serious depression, anxiety, and suicide are shooting up among our teens.[15] And five or more times as many US college students today meet diagnostic cutoffs for mental health disorders as met them during the Great Depression, even controlling for changes in diagnostic standards.[16]

Faith-Ann Bishop, a teen who lives outside Bangor, Maine, has lived these issues firsthand. When she was in eighth grade, late at night while her parents slept, she cut herself with a metal clip from a pen while sitting on the edge of the bathroom tub. The first cut was in her hand. The next sliced into the skin near her ribs. The act made her feel intense relief, dulling the throbbing intensity she felt the rest of the time—about grades, her future, school, and everything else. "It makes the world very quiet for a few seconds," said Faith-Ann. "For a while I didn't want to stop, because it was my only coping mechanism. I hadn't learned any other way." Her doctors eventually diagnosed Faith-Ann's cutting as the expression of deep-seated depression and anxiety—conditions she shares with millions of other US teens.[17] What they couldn't explain was why so many US teens suffer from these conditions today, and why their rates are still rising.

Perhaps unsurprisingly, youths from poor and low-income families have higher rates of anxiety and depression than the national averages. But it turns out that the rates among youths whose families are at the top of the income ladder are also far higher than average. If anything, the recent rise in anxiety and depression is concentrated among teens from well-to-do families.[18]

Economic Mobility

Last but not least when it comes to measures of our next generation's well-being is economic mobility. The American Dream suggests that each generation will do better than the last, as each generation raises its children to exceed its own level. The Dream also contemplates that children's potential won't be constrained by which family they happen to be born into. Sadly, neither of these promises holds for our nation's children today.

When the Harvard economist Raj Chetty and his colleagues calculated the proportion of US kids in a generation who, when they grew up, earned more than their parents had, a measure called "absolute economic mobility," they discovered the rate had fallen sharply in the past five decades. As Figure 1.2 shows, nine in ten children born in 1940 earned more at age thirty than their parents had at the same age. But only five in ten children born in the 1980s

Figure 1.2. Absolute Economic Mobility in the United States. Source: Chetty et al. (2017), 400.

did the same.[19] Put another way, generational progress on wages has flatlined; we're no longer providing our next generation with what it needs to exceed us economically.

When we turn to look at the extent to which young adults are constrained by their parents' place on the economic ladder, a measure known as "relative economic mobility," there's good news and bad news. The good news, again calculated by Chetty and his colleagues, is that our rate of relative mobility hasn't dropped in the past few generations. The bad news is that our rate is stuck at a disturbingly low level. Only one child in thirteen from a family in the bottom fifth of the income distribution will make it to the top fifth of the income distribution in adulthood. That's a far lower proportion than in many other countries. More than one in seven children born into the bottom fifth of the income distribution in Canada will do the same, as will more than one in nine children in Denmark. As Chetty bluntly put it, "[Y]our chances of achieving the 'American Dream' are almost two times higher if you're growing up in Canada relative to the United States."[20]

THE STATE OF AMERICA'S ADULTS

To what extent is our social order supporting adults in leading the rich, full lives that the American Dream promises? Here, as well, our indicators suggest that something has gone badly awry in our nation. In the next chapters, we'll see that the downturn in adults' well-being is linked to the stress our economic system is putting on family relationships. For now, let's briefly note the important role that these relationships play in the lives of adults. Families, of course, don't play the same formative role for adults that they do for children. Yet solid family ties—whether in a family of birth or of choice—are still critical to the well-being and happiness of adults. Humans need caretaking and are social by nature. So when the American Dream offers a life that is "better and richer and fuller for everyone," for most adults that's a life woven through with close family relationships.[21]

Robert Waldinger is the director of the Harvard Study of Adult Development, which has been following a group of more than seven hundred men for three-quarters of a century. When these men were first interviewed, as sophomores in college, they believed that having a good life required fame, wealth, and achievement—exactly the narrow interpretation of the American Dream that many hold today. They were wrong. As Waldinger put it:

> The clearest message that we get from this 75-year study is this: Good relationships keep us happier and healthier. Period. . . . We've learned . . . that social connections are really good for us, and that loneliness kills. It turns out that people who are more socially connected to family, to friends, to community, are happier, they're physically healthier, and they live longer than people who are less well connected. . . .
>
> Once we had followed our men all the way into their 80s, we wanted to look back at them at midlife and to see if we could predict who was going to grow into a happy, healthy octogenarian and who wasn't. And when we gathered together everything we knew about them at age 50, it wasn't their middle age cholesterol levels that predicted how they were going to grow old. It was how satisfied they were in their relationships. The people who were the most satisfied in their relationships at age 50 were the healthiest at age 80. And good, close relationships seem to buffer us from some of the slings and arrows of getting old. Our most happily partnered men and women reported, in their 80s, that on the days when they had more physical pain, their mood stayed just as happy. But for the people who were in unhappy relationships, on the days when they reported more physical pain, it was magnified by more emotional pain.[22]

Solid family ties are important for more than adults' happiness. As parents age, it's most often their adult children who step up to help with caretaking.[23]

When family members face serious illness, economic hardship, divorce, incarceration, or drug abuse, other family members play critical roles in helping them through—stepping in with caretaking, money, household upkeep, and driving.[24] In a world that is, in many ways, less stable than it used to be, families remain an important source of stability.[25]

When we consider a range of indicators relating to US adults—happiness, mental health, and life expectancy—just like the indicators relating to US children, it's clear that something has gone very wrong. Despite the promise of the American Dream, an increasingly large proportion of adults are not thriving, and many feel desperately removed from even the possibility of leading rich, full lives.

Happiness

As with our kids, our country's wealth hasn't helped adults' happiness much. Among the citizens of thirty-eight developed countries compared in one recent study, Americans reported that they were less satisfied with their lives than adults in fourteen other countries. That puts us far behind countries much less wealthy than our own.[26] What factors might be dragging down our happiness levels? In the words of Carol Graham, an economist who studies happiness: "A stable marriage, good health, and enough—but not too much—income are good for happiness. Unemployment, divorce, and economic instability are terrible for it."[27]

Mental Health

While we often think of depression and anxiety as stemming from a problem with brain chemistry, accumulating evidence suggests that they have as much or more to do with our social circumstances.[28] As the World Health Organization put it, "Mental health is produced socially: The presence or absence of mental health is above all a social indicator and therefore requires social, as well as individual, solutions."[29] How is our social order doing at supporting sound mental health? Badly. The United States has the third most depressed population in the world, as indicated by the number of quality years of life lost due to disability or death, a measure widely used to track the burden of disease. That's not just a comparison with other wealthy countries, but with *all* countries: we come in third behind China and India. When it comes to rates of anxiety, schizophrenia, and bipolar disorder, we also come in third place.[30] Overall, about one in five adults in the United States experiences a mental illness each year.[31]

Life Expectancy

Measures of life expectancy reveal an equally disturbing picture. In the three years between the beginning of 2015 and the end of 2017, American life expectancy declined each year. That made it the longest period of decline since the years between 1915 and 1918, a period that included World War I and a vicious flu pandemic that killed roughly 50 million people worldwide. Unlike a century ago, though, we have no major war or worldwide pandemic to explain this decline. And in other developed countries, life expectancy has continued to tick steadily upward for decades.[32] This decline is, in one expert's words, a "uniquely American pattern."[33]

Experts point to two causes of the drop in life expectancy. The first is the rise of drug overdoses, fueled by the opioid crisis. In 2017, the nation set a record of 70,000 fatal drug overdoses. Opioids alone took a total of 47,600 lives in that year, six times the number of opioid deaths as in 1999.[34]

The second factor in the drop in life expectancy is the suicide crisis gripping the nation. Our national suicide rate has risen 25 percent in the past twenty years.[35] Almost 45,000 Americans took their own lives in 2016 alone.[36] And this increase has occurred despite the fact that, during the same period, options for treating depression have multiplied. Experts don't think the wider availability of treatments for depression is somehow backfiring and causing more suicides. As one put it, "I think the increase in demand for the services is so huge that the expansion of treatment thus far is simply insufficient to make a dent in what is a huge social change."[37] Single Americans are particularly vulnerable. In 2005, single, middle-aged people were about three times as likely to take their own lives as were married people.[38]

How can we account for the opioid and suicide crises, and the accompanying drop in US life expectancy? In 2015, two Princeton economists, Angus Deaton and Anne Case, noted that death rates had begun to increase significantly at around the turn of the century for one particular group—middle-aged whites with no more than a high-school education—a group that used to be identified as the "white working class." That increase is especially shocking given that death rates have decreased in every other age group, every other racial and ethnic group, and every other wealthy country during those years.[39] Figure 1.3 charts the death rates since 1990 for people aged 50–54 in other developed countries compared with the death rates for US whites with no more than a high-school education in that age range.

When Deaton and Case sought the source for the increase in death rates among this group, they discovered that it came from a growing number of suicides, drug overdoses, and alcohol-related diseases, which they came to call "deaths of despair." They surmised that shrinking job opportunities for less-educated white

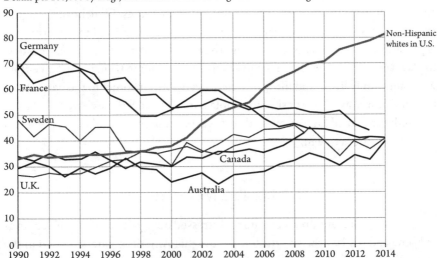

Deaths per 100,000 by drugs, alcohol and suicide among men and women ages 50–54

Figure 1.3. "Deaths of Despair" Rates across Countries. Source: Boddy (2017).

Americans have caused a cascade of changes, including changes in family life, that have contributed to patterns of risky behavior that cause early death. In their words:

> These changes left people with less structure when they came to choose their careers, their religion, and the nature of their family lives. When such choices succeed, they are liberating; when they fail, the individual can only hold him or herself responsible. In the worst cases of failure, this is a . . . recipe for suicide. We can see this as a failure to meet early expectations or, more fundamentally, as a loss of the structures that provide meaning to life.[40]

Key among the structures that lend stability and impart meaning to Americans' lives is a sound family. And in America today, that structure has become unsteady.

SOUND FAMILIES AND THE AMERICAN DREAM

Our country should have real advantages when it comes to maintaining sound families. For one thing, in the wealthiest country in the world, most families can afford labor-saving devices and services that lighten their workloads. For another, Americans still believe in strong marriages and stable families, and continue to put family at the top of their list of priorities. Somehow, though, a yawning gap has opened up between our desires and our lived reality. This gap is present between parents' desires and the way their families function on a day-to-day basis, with parents being constantly overwhelmed trying to balance their work and family lives. And the gap is there even when it comes to the basic structure of families, as adults' desires for stable partners and families have failed to be realized: the United States now leads the world in family *in*stability—a prize that no country hopes to win.[41]

Work–Family Conflict

American families are stretched thin and stressed out by the conflicting demands of home and paid work. Add the long hours that American parents spend in the workplace to the unpaid hours they spend parenting, and the sum is long days and crazy weeks. The total paid and unpaid workload in middle-class families where both parents work full-time is a stunning 135 hours a week—close to ten hours a day, seven days a week for each parent. And that workload increases for single parents.[42]

The result is that more than half of American parents find it difficult to balance work and family life, and more than a third always feel rushed, even just to do the things they *have* to do.[43] In one study, zero percent (*not* a typo) of mothers said they often had time to spare, and just 5 percent of fathers said the same.[44] To compensate, working parents empty out the other areas of their life beside work and children. Today's parents are far less likely than parents were two generations ago to spend time together with their spouses eating, socializing with friends, or working on projects around the house.[45] Sleep goes by the wayside—employed mothers get three fewer hours a week than those who don't work for pay. Another casualty is leisure time. Employed mothers have nine fewer hours of free time a week than women who don't work for pay.[46] Most full-time working mothers report that they have too little free time for themselves. Most married fathers say the same.[47]

A major consequence of this stress is that US parents are much less happy than grown-ups who don't have kids. As I described in the introduction, the "happiness gap" between parents and nonparents is much larger in the United States than in other developed countries. Figure 1.4 shows that the United States had the largest gap of the twenty-two countries compared by researchers, and by a substantial margin. In eight of the countries surveyed—Portugal, Hungary, Spain, Norway, Sweden, Finland, France, and Russia—parents reported being happier than nonparents.[48]

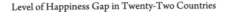

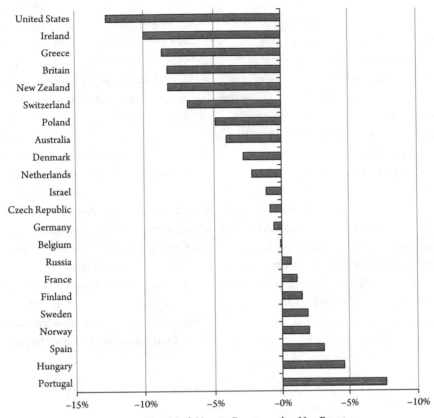

Level of Happiness Gap in Twenty-Two Countries

How Much Happier Parents are than Non-Parents

Figure 1.4. The Happiness Gap Between Parents and Nonparents across Countries.
Source: Data from Glass, Simon, and Andersson (2016).

Family Stability

It's not just how American families are functioning that is under stress; even the stability of our family structures is under siege. Americans still believe that marriage is the best form of family life. Those who marry believe that their marriages will last forever.[49] And most of those who haven't been married would like to be.[50] These beliefs, though, don't translate into stable relationships. After just five years, more than one-fifth of American married couples have either separated or divorced.[51] And cohabiting relationships, which are on the rise, are even less stable than marriages. Almost half of cohabitating couples break up within five years, and the breakup rates appear to be increasing.[52] The instability of these relationships means that a high proportion of American children will see their parents break up during childhood.[53]

How do we stack up against other countries on family stability? Poorly. Our divorce rates rank among the highest across wealthy nations.[54] For US children born to married parents, approximately 25 percent will see their parents break up by the time they're twelve, compared with less than 15 percent in Norway and France, and less than 10 percent in Belgium.[55] And while couples in other countries have more children outside of marriage, their cohabiting relationships are also far more stable than our own.[56] Compared with the almost half of American children born to cohabiting parents who will see their parents' union dissolve by age twelve, only about one in five children will see the same in France, Norway, and Belgium. And children in these other countries will experience far fewer familial transitions on average than US children.[57] In fact, Sweden's relationships generally are so much more stable than US relationships that a set of *unmarried parents* in Sweden is more likely to stay together than a set of *married parents* in the United States.[58] Overall, more than 21 percent of kids aged zero to five in the United States live with just their mother, the highest rate by far of any OECD country. By comparison, this value is 8 percent in Finland and 10 percent in France.[59]

The instability of American families, though, is concentrated among particular economic groups. To begin with, people's rung on the economic ladder has a lot to do with whether they'll get married. As Figure 1.5 shows, women with bachelor's degrees are far more likely to marry than their less-educated counterparts

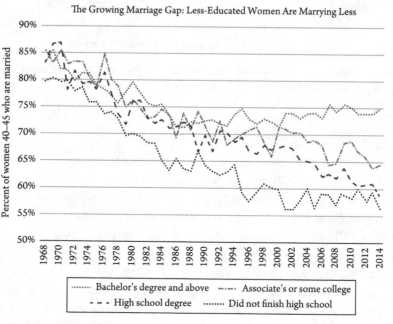

Figure 1.5. U.S. Marriage Rates by Education Over Time.

Source: Reeves, Sawhill, and Krause (2016). Reproduced with permission of the Brookings Institution.

(the same is true of men). Of college-educated women in their early forties, three-quarters are married. Women that age who have finished high school but not a four-year college trail behind by about 10 to 15 percentage points depending on whether they have some college education; women who haven't finished high school trail those with bachelor's degrees by almost 20 points.[60] This is a significant twist compared with the past. In the 1950s, those with high school but not college degrees—the group most identified with the working class—were the *most* likely to be married. Today, less-educated couples increasingly find themselves confined to the far less stable institution of cohabitation.[61]

A big divide exists as well when it comes to divorce. About half of first marriages in the United States survive at least twenty years. But women with a college education have a far higher chance of still being married: eight in ten. Meanwhile, women with some college have a five in ten chance of still being married. For women with a high school degree or less, that chance drops to four in ten.[62] In recent years divorce rates overall seem to be declining somewhat, but that's largely because less-educated Americans are marrying less often than they used to, thereby removing the least stable relationships from the pool of marriages that could end in divorce.[63]

The same massive disparity shows up when it comes to nonmarital births. In 2017, 52 percent of births to women without a high school degree occurred outside of marriage. That figure was only slightly reduced—50 percent—for women with high school degrees but no college education. But only 13 percent of women with college degrees gave birth outside of marriage.[64] The bottom line is that today few college-educated women will have children outside of marriage. Just the opposite is true for women without college degrees: only three in ten will have all their children *within* marriage.[65]

The growth in family instability toward the bottom of the economic ladder has created a huge divide in the family structures in which American kids are raised. If you were a child in the early 1980s, it didn't much matter which side of the tracks your family lived on; you were very likely to be raised by both your parents.[66] Today all that has changed. Eight in ten fourteen-year-old girls whose mothers are college graduates live with both parents. But this is true for just six in ten girls of mothers with high school but not college degrees, and just half of girls whose mothers haven't graduated from high school.[67] In terms of race and ethnicity, over half of black children and almost a third of Hispanic children live with a single parent. The same is true for less than a fifth of white children.[68]

As the law professors June Carbone and Naomi Cahn summed up the situation, "Marriage, once universal, . . . has emerged as a marker of the new class lines remaking American society. Stable unions have become a hallmark of privilege."[69] Marriage is still flourishing among the third of Americans with college degrees, even as it is increasingly unattainable for everyone else.[70] In the middle

of the twentieth century, stable families weren't confined to any particular portion of the economic spectrum. Today, though, families toward the bottom of
the economic ladder have far less chance of achieving stability than their more
well-heeled counterparts.

The steady stream of bad news about Americans' declining well-being is delivering the message loud and clear, if only we will listen, that our social order
is badly failing us. Children are unhappy, anxious, and aren't coming close to
achieving their full potential. Adults are in no better condition, and their despair
is reducing their lifespans. Meanwhile, the fragile state of the nation's families
leaves them unable to perform the tasks we need them to perform. The common
link connecting all these things is the expectation underpinning American
public policy that families will privately arrange the circumstances they need to
flourish without any help from government. I turn to this expectation and the
nation's public policy system built upon it in the next chapter.

2

America's Free-Market Family Policy

As all contemporary Western democracies are structured, thriving families are necessary to meet their people's needs for attachment, caretaking, human development, and affiliation. This raises the serious question of how market societies best ensure the conditions that families need to do their jobs well. There are two very different models of the role that government should play when it comes to families. Most policymakers in the United States support a vision that I'll call "free-market family policy," or just "free-market policy" for short.[1] The idea behind free-market family policy is that government should focus exclusively on supporting strong markets, which will in turn benefit families. The thinking is that people and families do better when they get what they need privately through markets. If markets are strong, then every family will get a big enough slice of the pie to privately satisfy its needs. In this model, it is the job of workers to bargain with employers privately over how much they'll work and when. Parents purchase the things their children need to do their best on the open market. They also provide caretaking for kids or arrange and pay for this caretaking.

Consider the emerging recognition by child development experts that most kids do better if a parent stays home with them for at least six months after birth, and perhaps most of their first year.[2] Under free-market family policy, this recognition doesn't lead to laws such as paid family leave that help parents get that time at home. Instead, policymakers focus on trying to increase the size of the economy by, for example, making it easy for companies to expand, or ensuring that all adults who can work get paid jobs. The theory is that individual workers in a booming economy will have more economic wherewithal to negotiate the leave they want with their employer. If they can't work out leave with their employer privately, their alternative under free-market family policy is either to find a new employer who will give them this leave or to quit and pay for time off out of their own savings.

Under free-market policy, government should support families only in the supposedly rare instances in which a family fails, usually meaning that it can't even minimally provide for its members through the market. As a result, government aid programs are often targeted at poor families, who have to prove financial need before they receive benefits. These benefits therefore come with the stigma of failure. Furthermore, they are generally supposed to terminate when families get back on their feet.

Free-market policy stands in stark contrast to another model of the government's relationship to families that I'll call "pro-family policy." This policy model, which has been adopted by many other countries, is built on the belief that families do better when the government actively supports them. Like free-market policy, pro-family policy recognizes the importance of work, markets, and a strong economy. Yet while it considers the market to be an important tool for distributing the resources that families need to thrive, it doesn't trust the market to do this on its own. To the contrary, pro-family policy insulates family life from many market pressures, and actively supports getting families what they need to succeed. In this model, the government helps people harmonize work and family. It also seeks to ensure that all families with kids have both the economic resources and conditions they need to raise their kids well. In this way, pro-family policy treats the imperative that families have the circumstances they need as a joint responsibility of both families *and* government.

As a result, pro-family policy would respond very differently than free-market policy to the research showing that most babies benefit from having a parent at home for much of their first year. The pro-family model would adopt public policies intended to make it easier for parents to spend that time at home. This might mean, for example, passing publicly subsidized leave programs to ensure that parents with newborns can take generous paid leaves from work. Under pro-family policy, programs to help families are generally available to all families regardless of income. Because of that, there is no stigma attached to taking part in these programs.

Pro-family policies can take a number of forms. Some seek to reduce market inequality and insecurity in ways that improve families' well-being, for example through laws setting a relatively high minimum wage. Others significantly "decommodify" services that benefit families, for example ensuring high-quality daycare for young children regardless of their family's income. Still others come from the state acting in its role as "traffic cop" to ensure that the market stays in its lane when it comes to paid work. These include laws that guarantee workers adequate time with their families by, for example, establishing the maximum number of hours employees can be made to work, requiring employers to give workers paid vacation and holiday time, and allowing reduced work hours for parents of young kids.

Countries with pro-family policy also regularly give cash to families with kids, subsidies often called "child benefits." They do so to make sure that kids' material needs are consistently met, taking into account the reality that parents' market earnings can be inconsistent and inadequate. That "making sure" is a critical piece of pro-family policy. While free-market policy believes that families should bear fundamental economic risks, pro-family policy believes that families do their jobs better when they can securely provide their members with what they need. This kind of security is often referred to as "social insurance." The idea behind it is to construct systems that ensure families get what they need *before* any damage is done to vulnerable people like children. Ensuring that kind of security is the reason many pro-family policy countries pay even greater child benefits each month to single-parent families than to couples: the state goes that extra mile to ensure that the families most at risk for not being able to meet their kids' material needs remain able to provide for them.

The distinctions I make between free-market and pro-family policies are between ideal types. In reality, there is no perfect model of either. However, the United States comes closer than any other wealthy country to having a system of pure free-market family policy. Our country has always fallen closer to the free-market end of the spectrum than many countries. In the past five decades, though, our nation has moved much further toward that end. Meanwhile, most wealthy European democracies cluster closer to the pro-family policy end of the spectrum. Finland is one of the countries that comes closest to the pro-family ideal. Many others, though, including Denmark, Germany, and France, also have strong pro-family policies. And even those wealthy countries that used to fall closer to the free-market policy end of the spectrum, like Canada and the United Kingdom, have in past decades adopted or enlarged a range of pro-family policies. We remain the lone outlier.

Comparing US public programs that support children with those of Finland fleshes out the real-world differences between free-market and pro-family policies. Finland explicitly seeks to support an environment in which children can thrive, as well as to provide parents with the resources and support they need to raise sound children.[3] A number of Finland's public programs interlock to help ensure that parents can secure the caretaking, education, and financial support that will serve their kids best from before birth through college. Pregnant Finnish women choose between receiving a onetime check for about $200 or the well-known "baby box," which not only serves as a bassinet but also contains infant essentials like a baby sleeping bag, mattress, toiletries, and clothing. Almost all Finnish parents choose the box. Then, families receive a child-benefit check from the government of about $110 each month following the birth of their first child and slightly more for each additional child (so that the total check for a family with two kids is more than double than for one child). Single parents receive an additional monthly stipend of roughly $60 and another $175 per month if the noncustodial parent is not paying child support. This means that a single parent of one child who does not receive child support would get $345 each month from the government for that child and more than double that for two kids.[4] And that's just the start of what Finland does to support families.

Finland also ensures parents the time they need with young kids, and pays them for it over and above their child benefits. Once a new child arrives, families get about a year's leave that can be split between parents, paid by the government at about two-thirds of their usual salary.[5] After that, children can be enrolled in universal daycare and then early childhood education, both of which coordinate with the schedules of working parents until grade school begins.[6] For most families, this early caretaking is free; for the rest, it is heavily subsidized.[7] And because the country enforces high teaching standards and low child–caregiver ratios, the care is of excellent quality.[8] Alternatively, parents can choose to stay at home until their child reaches the age of three in exchange for a caretaking stipend of roughly $390 each month, with the assurance that they can return to their job after that. Low-income families receive an added monthly payment for this caretaking that tops out at about $200.[9] Families who need still more financial help can fall back on Finland's safety-net programs, though given the public support all families receive, few need to. Finally, Finland provides free public education through high school and free tuition at college after that.

Beyond these benefits, public policies help all citizens balance market demands with the rest of life. Finnish law limits the workweek to an average of forty hours. To work more than that, employees have to voluntarily agree to overtime and be paid increasing amounts.[10] Workers also get thirty days of paid leave a year; comparable benefits go to most part-time workers.[11] Finally, by law, Finnish employers are prohibited from imposing less favorable employment terms on part-time employees due to their work schedules than on other employees.[12]

Finland is not alone in providing families with comprehensive support. In Germany, new mothers receive fourteen weeks of maternity leave at full pay.[13] After that, Germany provides parents with several different options to enable them to stay home with their child. Parents can choose to receive twelve to fourteen months of family leave, split between them, paid by the government at two-thirds of their normal annual income. Alternatively, parents can choose to receive up to twenty-four months of family leave paid at one-half of their normal annual income, also split between the parents. And if during the course of their family leave parents choose to work part-time for twenty-five to thirty hours a week concurrently over a period of four months, they can extend their family pay eligibility up to twenty-eight months.[14] As a result of these policies, few German children are cared for outside the home during their first year.

After their first year, German children have a legal right to placement in childcare partially subsidized by the government. As a result of these subsidies, prices for daycare are affordable, typically ranging from $80 to $170 per child per month—although prices vary by province. Some provinces have scrapped daycare fees altogether.[15] Once children reach the age of three, they attend free or heavily subsidized kindergarten, followed by free primary and secondary education and tuition-free tertiary education.[16] Additionally, every family receives a monthly child benefit of at least $215 per child until the child reaches age eighteen.[17] Furthermore, Germany ensures a reasonable work-life balance by limiting the workday to eight hours and providing all full-time workers with at least twenty paid vacation days annually.[18]

United States family policy provides for almost none of this. Forget about the year of paid leave that other countries provide: the United States is the only wealthy country that provides no paid parental leave whatsoever. Except in the few states that have passed their own paid leave laws, the only leave guaranteed to new parents is the twelve weeks provided by the federal Family and Medical Leave Act of 1993 (FMLA). Largely because the act excludes coverage of employees who work for small businesses, it covers just six in ten US workers. Further, because the leave is unpaid, the FMLA simply acts as a job guarantee for the employee during that period.[19]

Our country is also one of the few wealthy countries that doesn't give parents child benefit checks to help them cover the cost of raising kids. Through our largest domestic spending programs, Social Security and Medicare, we spend large amounts of public funds on older citizens toward the end of life. But we have no comparable spending programs that routinely help families at the beginning of life.[20] As a result, in 2019, we will have spent about 9 percent of the federal budget on the 22 percent of Americans who are eighteen or younger; meanwhile, we will have spent 45 percent of the federal budget on the 15 percent who are elderly.[21]

And we have no federal laws to help workers balance their jobs with the rest of life—no limits on mandatory work hours (although some employees must be paid overtime if they work long hours), no option to work part-time, no required paid (or even unpaid) vacation leave, and no parity of pay and benefits for part-time workers. Nothing.[22] Of course, our absence of laws doesn't mean that no US worker will get any of these things. Three-quarters of employees have access to some paid vacation—although only for about half the number of days that Finland requires as a minimum.[23] A few workers—one in seven—are given paid parental leave by their employer, although generally only for a period of weeks rather than the year or more that Finnish and German parents receive.[24] But while many US workers receive some of the benefits that other countries provide their workers by law, almost no one in the United States, even those with considerable market power, will get all of the benefits that *every* Finnish and German worker receives as a matter of course.

When it comes to education, our government does far more for families than it does in many other areas, but not until kids enter kindergarten. Despite experts' recognition that the years zero to five are critically important for children's learning, the United States hasn't developed any large-scale system to provide or even subsidize daycare. We don't even have a comprehensive system for regulating the quality of daycare.[25] Once kids reach kindergarten, though, our system provides public education through high school free of charge. After that, paying for college is largely a private responsibility, except that some state schools subsidize the cost for in-state students. The cost of many private colleges, meanwhile, is roughly the same as the median household income.[26]

Besides the provision of free public grade-school education, the largest exception to our lack of government support for families comes in the form of tax policy. Two large tax programs give some help to parents with kids. Unlike Finland's system of financial supports for parents, though, these two programs don't fit neatly together to provide good, stable financial scaffolding to parents with children. The Child Tax Credit (CTC) gives most US families besides the wealthiest a yearly tax credit of up to $1,000 (temporarily raised to $2,000 by tax reform in 2017).[27] Because the CTC is not fully refundable, though, the lowest-earning families—including 27 million children—can't get the full benefit of the credit.[28]

The Earned Income Tax Credit (EITC), on the other hand, is specifically aimed at low-income families. While this tax program is often compared to the child benefits that countries with pro-family policies provide, it actually serves a very different role. Child benefits are intended to ensure that all families with kids can securely provide the material resources their kids need. The EITC, in contrast, is designed to give low- to moderate-income earners an incentive to work. That means the program doesn't provide any benefits to the poorest American kids whose parents don't have earned income and who thus need that money the most.[29] But it does allow low-income families in which a parent works to get a refundable tax credit. To qualify for the maximum credit, a family's wages must be at about the amount that a minimum-wage worker would earn in a year.[30] Above that amount, the credit begins to decrease until it phases out entirely at about the point at which a family reaches the low end of middle-income status.[31] The goal is to ensure that the incomes of families of low-wage workers who work full-time will be raised (just slightly) above the federal poverty line and that those who earn somewhat higher wages will still get a (proportionately reduced) boost to give them the incentive to work and earn more.[32]

Even when US tax credits help parents, the type of aid they give is far more limited than parents receive under pro-family policy. Tax policy merely provides a potential tax refund, meaning cash. Unlike pro-family policy, tax cuts don't support parents in managing the realities of childrearing by, for example, allowing them to take leave to stay home with a new child, or giving their kids good daycare, or ensuring that they can get off work in time for dinner.

And of course the way tax policy provides cash is very different from the way child benefits provide families with cash under pro-family policy. Receiving a tax credit once a year doesn't provide the same consistent support that getting a child benefit check every month does. That leaves parents like Wanda Johnson, the single mother from Charlotte, North Carolina, that we met in the introduction, staying up late at night worrying how she'll meet her son's daily needs until her tax refund arrives, and making trips to the food bank to be sure she can feed him.

With that said, these tax programs still provide some financial help to a broad range of US families, including poor families. By one count, the CTC and EITC combined helped lift 4.7 million children out of poverty in 2016 and reduced the severity of poverty for 7.2 million more children.[33] Still, these two tax programs barely scratch the surface of the government help that countries with pro-family policies provide to families.

Finland's family policies are so comprehensive that its safety-net programs, meaning the programs geared specifically toward helping the poor, aren't often needed by families. Safety-net programs in the United States, on the other hand, have a much larger gap to fill. Our major safety-net program for families, Temporary Assistance for Needy Families (TANF), is a cash assistance program for families with children that was passed by Congress in 1996 as part of a major welfare overhaul.[34] That overhaul, which was designed to align the US safety net with free-market ideology, replaced the existing cash benefit program, Aid to Families with Dependent Children (AFDC), with TANF to ensure that government benefits to poor families are temporary and that parents in families receiving benefits perform paid work.

As such, TANF is structured less to ensure that poor children get the resources they need than to incentivize poor mothers to work for pay. The program has strict work requirements for adults, and most states require parents to take the first job offered to them, whether or not it falls within standard work hours. Finding childcare for nonstandard hours is difficult, and finding good and affordable childcare for these hours can be downright impossible. But unless a parent accepts an offered job, they're dropped from the TANF rolls. Ten states don't waive the work requirement even for parents of newborns; another twelve states waive it for only two to three months.[35] And although families receiving TANF benefits are supposed to have priority for childcare subsidies, these subsidies are underfunded, have long waitlists, and, even for the lucky few who receive them, are generally too small to pay for high-quality care.[36]

Even leaving aside these work requirements, by design state and federal governments have limited TANF eligibility so that families don't become too dependent on them. In order to qualify for benefits, it's not enough merely to be poor. A family needs to be *really* poor and, in most states, *really, really* poor to qualify for TANF. Thirty states require that a family of three have an income below 50 percent of the poverty line, or about $10,000 a year, just to be eligible for benefits; most of those require an even lower income—below 30 percent of the poverty line, or about $6,700.[37] On top of that, by federal law, every state must set a lifetime cap on the length of time a family can receive benefits, which cannot exceed five years; some states have set the cap at as few as twelve months. Roughly a third of states have also established policies that cap or reduce TANF benefits on the birth of a new child if the family was receiving TANF benefits when the child was born.[38]

The idea underlying past US cash assistance programs was that no child in America, the land of plenty, should have to grow up poor. That meant that all poor families, at least in theory, were entitled to benefits. That is far from the theory that animates TANF today. At the time that the welfare reform overhaul was passed in 1996, sixty-eight in one hundred poor families received cash benefits—already much lower than the eighty-two in one hundred poor families who received them in 1979. Today, only twenty-three in one hundred poor families nationally receive cash benefits.[39] In states that particularly dislike the idea of the government supporting families, this rate is even lower. Mississippi, for example, rejects almost all applications; among the more than 11,000 of Mississippi's low-income residents who applied for these benefits in 2016, only 167 applications were approved. That's an acceptance rate of well under 2 percent. Focus on that: only two in a hundred low-income Mississippi mothers who apply for these last-resort benefits get them.[40]

The few families lucky enough to be declared eligible for benefits won't get close to enough cash to pull them out of poverty. In fact, in every state, a family with no other income wouldn't get enough from TANF to pull itself up to even half of the poverty line. In two-thirds of states, the same family wouldn't get up to even a third of the poverty line.[41] A mother of two in Mississippi in 2016, for example, if she were one of the fortunate few to receive benefits, would receive a maximum monthly TANF benefit of only $170 for her whole family.[42] Compare this with the $345 a month that every Finnish single parent gets as a matter of course for *each* child. And that's *before* Finland's safety net kicks in for its poorest citizens.

In sum, Finland's policy comports with pro-family logic, which seeks to cushion families from the uncertainties associated with markets and to help ensure that parents can provide the circumstances that kids need to do their best. Family policy in the United States, on the other hand, is largely confined to providing financial help instead of taking a broad array of actions that might help parents balance work and home responsibilities and raise sound kids. Even then, the financial help government gives families is scant, and, for the most part, delivered in a manner meant to incentivize paid work rather than to meet children's needs for consistent support. In all these ways, US policy tracks free-market ideology's insistence that families be left to deal with market forces on their own.

PARENTS' EXPERIENCES IN THE UNITED STATES
AND FINLAND

Comparing the situations of middle-income families from the United States and Finland helps make the differences between free-market and pro-family policies concrete. Jessica and Zarni Zoladz are a married couple who live in upstate New York and have a four-month-old son.[43] The Zoladzes are in good financial shape for a young couple. Jessica is a senior medical science liaison for a genetic testing company, and Zarni works as a network administrator for a petroleum distributor. On their son's birth, Jessica was lucky for an American employee: she got eight weeks of paid leave from her employer. After Jessica's paid leave was up, she took another four weeks unpaid, the remaining amount granted by the FMLA. Zarni's company did not offer paternity leave, so he took only four days off, unpaid.

At the end of twelve weeks, Jessica had to return to work. She would have preferred to wait until their son was older to put him in daycare, for both his sake and hers—her job requires a lot of travel, and returning to work meant she had to use her breast pump in airports, airplanes, hotel rooms, and even taxis. The Zoladzes spent a lot of time considering the best caretaking arrangement for their son. They had little guidance in this matter, but used the internet to search for nearby daycare centers and then visited a range of them. Some seemed to provide good care, while others had too many kids with too few visible caretakers. They eventually settled on the one that they thought was best, but they couldn't afford it close to full-time, even though their household income is above the US average. Luckily, Jessica's seventy-two-year-old mother agreed to care for their son three days a week. That meant they could enroll him for the other two days in their preferred daycare program for a little more than $500 a month. In all this, except for the unpaid time off guaranteed by the FMLA, the Zoladzes received no government support—no publicly paid parental leave, no child benefits, no provision of or subsidies for daycare. At the end of each year, though, they'll be eligible for an annual tax credit of $1,000 (or $2,000 for the years Congress temporarily raised it, 2018–25) under the CTC, and up to about $1,000 under the Child and Dependent Care Tax Credit.

Kaisa and Tapani Ruohonen, who live in Tampere, Finland, had a very different experience raising their two daughters, now aged two and five. Like the Zoladzes, both Kaisa and Tapani are professionals who make above-average salaries: both work as engineers for a manufacturing company. Under Finland's pro-family policy system, after the birth of each child, Kaisa took nine months of parental leave, publicly paid at about 70 percent of her salary. Tapani took nine weeks of paid paternity leave after each birth, while Kaisa was on leave. He also took additional parental leave when Kaisa went back to work—three months with the first child and eight months (taking a caretaking stipend once parental leave ended) with the second, also publicly subsidized. That meant that neither child had to be placed in daycare until after her first birthday.

Once the Ruohonen parents returned to work, they enrolled their daughters full-time in their municipal daycare center, whose low caregiver–child ratios are set by the state and where their tuition is heavily subsidized. Based on their salaries, the family pays a total of about $600 a month for full-time care for both girls. Further, in addition to the "baby boxes" they received when Kaisa was pregnant, the Ruohonens have received a monthly check of about $106 since the birth of their first daughter, which they will continue to receive until her seventeenth birthday, along with an additional monthly check of $125 for their second daughter. These checks make things like diapers far more affordable.

As the experiences of the Zoladzes and Ruohonens make clear, whether a country adopts free-market or pro-family policy makes a big difference even for middle-class families. Finland's pro-family policy assists families with the costs of childrearing, regulates paid work to protect parents' time away from work, and ensures kids have high-quality paid caretaking during the time their parents work. Free-market policy in the United States is geared toward spurring parents to work paid jobs, after which it largely expects them to negotiate children's needs on their own.

SHIFTS IN THE US ECONOMY IN THE PAST FIVE DECADES

Free-market policy leaves every family to its own devices when it comes to arranging the resources and services they need. If families can't get what they need privately, which means largely through their earnings from work (or, for the very fortunate, from money passed down from the preceding generations), they're out of luck. This means that economic trends beyond families' control can have a big impact on their ability to provide for their members. Free-market policymakers sometimes ignore this. They hark back to the 1950s and 1960s, decades that were far easier economically on most US families.[44] Since then, though, two major shifts in economic forces—the dramatic increases in both economic inequality and economic insecurity—have made it far more difficult and, in many cases, downright impossible, for families to meet their bottom line.

America's Skyrocketing Economic Inequality

Free-market policy depends on parents having large enough slices of the economic pie to pay for what their families need. Those slices of pie, though, have become increasingly unequal in the past five decades. Economist Thomas Piketty and his colleagues Emmanuel Saez and Gabriel Zucman used individual US tax records to document the level of income inequality in the United States over time. Figure 2.1, based on their data, tracks the share of income going to the top 10 percent of households from 1910 to 2017. As you can see, that share climbed abruptly in the Roaring Twenties, declined precipitously in the decade and a half after the stock market crash in 1929, and then remained pretty level from the mid-1940s to the mid-1970s. Beginning the the last half of the 1970s, though, it began to climb again and, after getting knocked down a bit in the recession of 2008, hit new highs after that.[45] In the 1970s, the richest tenth of families took home one-third of the pie; today they take home half of it.[46] Bigger slices of the pie for them; smaller slices for the rest of us.

Our country's skyrocketing income inequality makes us an outlier among the Western democracies we usually consider our peers. In the 1970s, we were still well within the range of other advanced Western democracies when it came to inequality, even if we were somewhat more unequal than many. By the early 1990s, though, we had left our peers in the dust. Today we have to look outside North American and European democracies to find levels of inequality that are comparable to our own. We're now competing with capitalist oligarchies like Russia rather than representative democracies, and our level of inequality exceeds many Latin American countries—a region with some of the world's worst inequality.[47]

Free-market advocates would argue that even though the slices of the economic pie that families receive are more unequal than they were in the 1970s, the slices of most households aren't in absolute terms any smaller than they used

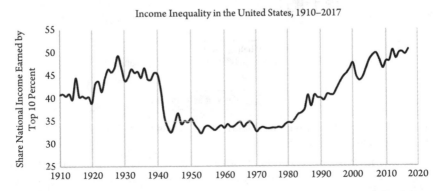

Income Inequality in the United States, 1910–2017

Figure 2.1. Share of National Income Earned by the Top 10 Percent of Earners.
Source: Data from Piketty and Saez (2019).

to be. That's because, they'd point out, the pie has grown a lot since the 1970s. Even though the richest Americans received almost all those gains, the income of most households didn't go down. In fact, even families in the bottom fifth of household incomes saw a small increase in their income in these decades.[48] So our slices, although smaller by comparison, are in absolute terms a little bit larger than they used to be.[49] That means, its advocates argue, the free-market system is still working to deliver benefits to Americans, and families can still go it alone.

Free-market proponents get some of their facts right here, but their conclusion is all wrong. The slight rise in household income among middle- and lower-income families during these past decades masks some crucial economic shifts that have undercut families' ability to support their children securely. To see this, we need to turn from household income data to individual wage data for workers. As Figure 2.2 shows, between 1979 and 2010, hourly wages dropped considerably for the two-thirds of men aged 25–39 without college diplomas.[50] Much of this decrease in wages came from the steep decline in US manufacturing jobs, for the most part, due both to improvements in technology as well as because some jobs moved overseas.[51] The drop in manufacturing jobs was largely offset by employment gains in the service industry, but those jobs don't pay nearly as well.[52]

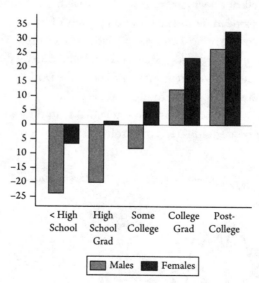

Figure 2.2. Percent Changes in Real Hourly Wage Levels 1979–2010, By Education and Sex, for Ages 25–39.

Source: Autor and Wasserman (2013), Fig. 2 (authors' calculations based on May/Outgoing Rotation Groups Current Population Survey data for years 1979–2010). This material was published by Third Way (www.thirdway.org).

How can we square the decreased wages that many Americans earn today with the fact that household incomes across the spectrum have grown at least slightly since the 1970s? The answer is that almost all of the gains for households in these decades come from women's increased hours of paid work during this time.[53] Women's increase in work hours caused household incomes to rise despite male partners' reduced wages because, taken as a whole, families now work many more hours than they did in the past. What that means is that the large increases in productivity that expanded our economic pie aren't what improved the balance sheets of American families; what did is largely the fact that families have been working longer hours.[54] Most of the remaining increase in household incomes comes from the rise of Medicare and Social Security benefits for middle- and low-income senior citizens during this era.[55]

But here's the important point when it comes to raising kids: While both of these changes—women's increasing hours of paid work and higher Medicare and Social Security benefits for seniors—improve the balance sheets of lower- and middle-income families compared with five decades ago, neither are of much help as families raise children. In families relying on two parents' wages to boost their household income, at least one parent almost always has to cut back on paid work when a child is born, which lowers household income. And insofar as both parents remain in paid jobs, they will also have to pay the high cost of daycare, which wasn't an expense for most families in the 1950s and 1960s when most women with kids stayed home.[56] Either choice—reducing hours spent on paid work or paying for daycare—eliminates the household gains from the second income, or at least pares them down significantly.[57] That's one reason that families with children under age five earn about $15,000 less a year than similar households without young kids.[58] And when it comes to increased Medicare and Social Security benefits, these are paid to families much further along in life than families with young children. The result is that families today have a much tougher time making ends meet while raising children, even if household income generally has increased slightly.

The fact that household gains in the last decades came from the increased hours worked by a second parent means that single-parent families shared in none of these gains. These parents have it even tougher in our free-market system because we expect them both to provide for their family financially and to ensure that kids are well cared for. Two-parent families can try to stretch a single salary so that they have a caretaker at home. Single-parent families have no such choice: not only must they support the family on just one income, they need to pay for caretaking from it as well. But the drop in the real value of the minimum wage over time and the large increase in the number of low-wage service jobs in our economy mean that far more jobs don't pay nearly enough to support a family. Almost a third of those in the workforce today make less than $12 an hour, and few in these low-wage jobs receive benefits.[59] Many of these workers have children, and no matter how hard or long they work, they simply won't earn enough to get their kids what they need to do their best.

Matthew Desmond, author of the Pulitzer Prize–winning book *Evicted*, more recently described the life of one working-poor family, Vanessa Solivan and her three kids, Taliya, age seventeen, Shamal, fourteen, and Tatiyana, twelve, in East Trenton, New Jersey. Vanessa is a home health nurse who earns between $10 and $14 an hour, depending on the client. But her wages and the tax breaks our system gives working families didn't bring her even close to the poverty line. In fact, she didn't even make enough for her to afford rent in the Trenton area. Because of that, she and her kids bounced between cheap motels, her mother's home, and sleeping in a car for three years before they finally got a place in public housing. Sleeping in the car, unsurprisingly, was an ordeal for her children, which Vanessa learned to manage as well as she could. As Desmond tells it, "So that the kids wouldn't run away out of anger or shame, Vanessa learned to park off Route 1, in crevices of the city that were so still and abandoned that no one dared crack a door until daybreak. Come morning, Vanessa would drive to her mother's home so the kids could get ready for school and she could get ready for work."[60]

America's problem of inequality looks even worse once we move from considering families' income to considering their wealth. (Income measures the money coming into the household. Wealth measures the total net worth of a household, calculated in terms of assets minus debts.) By this measure, even the median family is doing worse than it did in the 1970s. The share of national wealth held by just the top 1 percent of households rose from 30 to 40 percent in these decades. Meanwhile, the share of wealth held by the entire bottom 90 percent of households dropped from 33 to 23 percent. This means that families in just the top 1 percent now have roughly twice as much wealth as those in the entire bottom 90 percent.[61] Even as the net worth of the typical middle-class household has shrunk, the net worth of affluent households has hit the stratosphere.[62]

To make matters worse, the net worth of households headed by adults younger than thirty-five—the families most likely to have young kids—has dropped steeply. In 1984, the median net worth of these younger households was $11,500; in 2009, it was $3,500.[63] Some of this drop comes from the decreased wages of men without college degrees. But the ballooning of two types of costs in recent decades also play a major role. First, the large increase in housing costs has particularly affected younger couples just getting into the housing market, who must deal with the high cost of mortgages or rent. Second, young people have far more student loan debt than they used to, a product of mushrooming increases in the cost of higher education.[64] Buying a house and going to college are milestones in life that we generally associate with responsible adulthood.[65] Attaining them today, though, often depletes families' assets for two decades or longer, a period during which most will have young kids they must also pay for raise.

This decrease in wealth makes it tough to impossible for most young families to get their kids off to the best start possible in our free-market economy. The average wealth of $3,500 that most young households have is generally tied up in a house or a car. But even if that wealth were liquid and available, it would be almost completely depleted by the $3,400 average out-of-pocket fees that hospitals charge for a baby's delivery—and that's the cost for parents *with* health insurance.[66] That means most parents will have to scramble even to buy basics like diapers, formula, and baby food, which can cost almost $50 a week, or almost $2,500 a year.[67] Taking more than a few weeks of unpaid parental leave or paying for high-quality daycare on top of these expenses will be impossible for the average young family.

The economic situation is even tougher for African American families under free-market policy. The income gap between the median black and white household has lingered at just above 60 percent for decades.[68] That's partly because unemployment rates of black workers have remained roughly double those of white workers since 1970 for workers at every level of education and during both boom and bust economies.[69] And even when black workers find jobs, they are paid far less than white workers, and this wage gap has been widening in the last decades.[70] Some but not all of the increased wage disparity comes from the high cost of college in our free-market system. The disparate access to higher education between black and white families is one reason so many black workers wind up in low-wage jobs, like the home health aide position that Vanessa Solivan held.

Yet a large part of both the wage gap and the employment-rate gap between black and white Americans can't be explained by factors like education.[71] Experts attribute this part of the gap to our country's persistent racism. In one memorable experiment, researchers sent out nearly five thousand resumes in response to help-wanted ads for a broad range of positions advertised in Chicago and Boston newspapers, varying the resumes by using either black- or white-sounding names (for example, Lakisha Brown versus Emily Walsh) but keeping the credentials the same. Whether a black- or white-sounding name topped the resume made a big difference in the applicant's odds of being contacted about the job: it took sending out ten resumes with white-sounding names to get a callback; it took fifteen resumes with black-sounding names to get one. It turned out that having a white-sounding name on a resume led to the same number of callbacks as listing eight years of work experience.[72]

In another experiment, pairs of similarly attractive and articulate young men, one white and the other black, both with fake resumes, applied for jobs in

Milwaukee. One member of the pair was randomly assigned to report a criminal record. Young black men with supposedly clean records turned out to do worse in their job search than white men supposedly just out of prison. A white man with a record needed six applications to get a callback; a black man with no record needed seven.[73] Despite the far stronger economic headwinds they face, though, free-market policy holds black parents to the responsibility of supporting their parents through market earnings.

In sum, free-market family policy expects that families will pay for the things their children need and secure the circumstances that will enable them to thrive without government help. Yet changes in the economy have severely undermined the ability of families to accomplish these important tasks. Policymakers who point to families' ability in the 1950s and 1960s to raise children well, and who blame today's families for their failure to do the same, ignore our changed economic realities; when it comes to black families, they also ignore our nation's endemic racism.

Economic Insecurity

The other economic trend hurting families' ability to support themselves is the steep rise in economic insecurity among American families in the past five decades.[74] We know that young children need a baseline of reliable material support to thrive: a roof over their heads, square meals, clothing, diapers, and so forth. Yet increasingly families in the United States, including many working-class and middle-class families, can no longer deliver this support consistently.[75]

In 2006, political scientist Jacob Hacker was the first to call widespread notice to the skyrocketing economic insecurity in the United States. Hacker attributed most of this increase to private companies offloading risks they had once assumed onto American workers and their families.[76] In the 1970s, when companies needed work performed, they would have hired permanent employees. Today, they'd be more likely to use temporary employees or independent contractors.[77] So workers who would have had steady full-time jobs with stable income and benefits two generations ago now are less likely to have either. And even when employers do hire permanent workers today, they often use scheduling systems that shift employee staffing based on customer demand. One in six US employees works a shifting schedule, which helps employers maximize returns by enabling them to use the exact number of workers they need during a given hour.[78] But the savings for these companies come at the expense of their workers, whose erratic paychecks don't always cover their bills.[79] On top of that, companies are less likely to provide health insurance to employees than in the past, and when they do, they pass on more costs by providing policies with less generous terms.[80] Finally, companies are more likely to lay off workers when business is slow than in decades past.[81]

Rafael Sanchez of New Brunswick, New Jersey, has experienced firsthand the rising insecurity that results from this shift in employment practices. Rafael, who immigrated to the United States from Mexico, worked as a full-time employee at a window factory in New Brunswick for five years. After he was laid off in 2007, though, he wasn't able to find another permanent job. Instead, he's worked a series of stints through temp agencies, working in one manual labor job after another for $9 an hour. Although some positions have lasted months or even years, he doesn't work directly for the factories or warehouses. That means there's no career ladder he can climb to make a job permanent, let alone to get a raise or a promotion. He never knows how long he'll work at any given place or when a stint will end. Once it does, he'll be out of work until he manages to find the next temporary job at another business at the same low wage.[82]

Rising insecurity also comes from the dramatically inflated out-of-pocket costs that Americans increasingly pay when they need medical care. Out-of-pocket spending for healthcare has shot up by more than 50 percent just since 2010—and that's for those covered by health insurance. A major reason for this is that insurers are paying less or not at all for out-of-network doctors and services.[83] On top of that, employers are increasingly choosing health plans with deductibles of $1,000 or more per person—far more than most Americans can cover unexpectedly.[84] And as of 2017, more than 27 million nonelderly Americans had no insurance coverage.[85] The result is that, with or without coverage, one serious illness or significant chronic medical condition can destroy a family's budget. The bankruptcy law scholar Melissa Jacoby and her colleagues discovered that roughly half of personal bankruptcies in the United States have a medical component. Most of those filing for bankruptcy had health insurance. Despite this, more than three-quarters incurred medical expenses that weren't covered by insurance in the previous two years. For about one-third of these filers, out-of-pocket medical expenses totaled between $1,000 and $5,000. One in seven, though, had out-of-pocket medical expenses that exceeded $5,000; just under half of these had expenses of more than $10,000.[86]

Heather Bixler and her husband, of Bowling Green, Ohio, know how quickly medical bills can drain a family's budget. Heather is a professional violinist; her husband is a professor of music. Their son, Sean, developed seizures when he was seven that doctors diagnosed as epilepsy. Insurance covered 80 percent of the costs to diagnose the disorder, but that still left the Bixlers with out-of-pocket costs of about $1,500. And that was only the beginning. Sean began to have more frequent and severe seizures. Heather had to leave work to stay by his side so that he wouldn't hurt himself during the episodes.

Sometimes, when he turned blue and stopped breathing, she had to call an ambulance, which came with a significant price tag. The Bixlers tried neurologist after neurologist and medication after medication. As Sean's seizures worsened, his ability to communicate decreased. He could no longer answer basic questions that would have been easy for him just months before. In desperation, the couple took Sean to the Cleveland Clinic for an extensive workup. Although the visit gave them critical information, the Bixlers' insurance company rejected the $31,000 cost as unnecessary. "I've depleted my entire savings account, pretty much," Heather said. She estimates that between a third and a half of the family's income goes to Sean's care; most of the expenses have been out-of-pocket.[87]

The result of changes like these is that income insecurity has risen precipitously in the last five decades. It's not just poor folks whose income occasionally falls below the poverty line; an astounding 94 percent of people whose earnings are between 100 and 150 percent above the poverty line fall below that line for at least one month per year. Among all Americans, more than one-third—roughly 98 million people—were officially poor for at least two months between 2009 and 2012.[88] And many who don't fall below the poverty line are just one emergency away from that fate. In 2017, four in ten Americans reported that they wouldn't be able to cover an unexpected expense of $400.[89] It turns out that even hourly workers with middle-class incomes commonly have shifts in income of 30 percent per month.[90] Families of color bear the brunt of this insecurity.[91] Nearly two-thirds of African American families and half of Latino families live in a household with moderate or high levels of economic insecurity. The same is true for only a third of white families.[92]

While income volatility has increased for Americans generally, it is especially high for families with children.[93] Four in ten families with children fall below the poverty threshold for two consecutive months of the year.[94] What is the best predictor that a woman will file for bankruptcy? You guessed it—having kids. And this instability isn't just a problem for single-parent families. Senator Elizabeth Warren demonstrated when she was a Harvard law professor that two-parent families, which used to be the most economically stable families, are twice as likely to file for bankruptcy as single adults or childless couples.[95]

These increases in inequality and insecurity mean that far fewer families today can reliably support kids on their own than families could five decades ago. Even a common crisis, like a major car repair or a child's broken arm, can mean a family will have shortages of healthy food, lose its housing, or lack the money to pay for daycare.[96] As Professor Hacker summed up the situation: "[W]ages have basically flat-lined; the job market has become more uncertain; the difficulty of balancing work and family has increased; the costs of housing, education, health care, and child care have exploded. It is families that have borne the brunt of these larger changes, and it is families that falter when, as is too often the case, the strain proves too much."[97]

FREE-MARKET POLICY IN THE US ECONOMY TODAY

Let's take an initial look at what free-market family policy means for families with young kids in our increasingly insecure and unequal economy. Figure 2.3 illustrates in graphic detail the difference between pro-family and free-market policies on public spending for kids. Overall for children ages zero to five, the average level of Finland's public spending on family benefits per child, including spending on programs like parental leave, child benefits, daycare, and tax expenditures, clusters somewhere around $10,000 a year, calculated in purchasing power parity (PPP) adjusted dollars.[98] Most of that amount is for cash benefits for parental leave in the first year, transitioning to large amounts spent

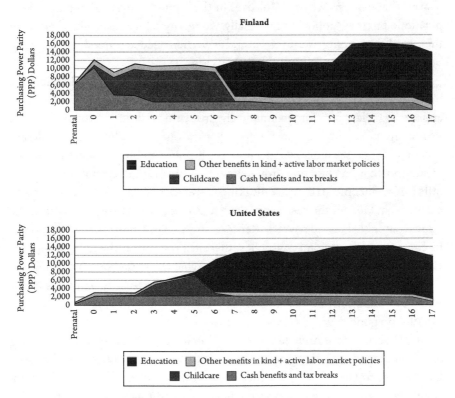

Figure 2.3. Public Spending on Family Benefits by Age. Source: Graph by Fernando Filgueira, based on the OECD Family database, 2017. Spending includes tax breaks for families with children, cash transfers (child benefits), paid maternity, paternity, and parental leaves, daycare and prekindergarten, and education.

for childcare after that. In contrast, the average level of US public spending per child in their first couple of years is less than a third of that amount. Most of that comes from tax breaks.[99] Public spending in the United States bumps up a little when kids reach ages three and four because of the (relatively limited) public funds spent on childcare programs like Head Start and prekindergarten at these ages. Then it bumps up far more when kids reach school age at five and six because of our high levels of public spending on grades kindergarten through twelfth grade. But by then, it is generally too late developmentally for kids to make up for what they didn't get in earlier years.

Pro-family policy raises the "ceiling" of support that all children get through funneling a consistent stream of cash and services to their families, which increases the funds that parents have available to spend on their children. That's why the parents in the Ruohonen family in Finland could afford to stay home with their daughters for an entire year and then put them in good daycare full-time when they returned to work. Meanwhile, under US free-market policy, the ceiling of support for middle-income children is limited by their parents' ability to pay. That explains why the Zoladzes in the United States, although similarly positioned to the Ruohonens financially, wound up taking just eight weeks with their son before going back to work, and even then needed a grandparent to help out because they couldn't afford full-time care.

Both the Ruohonen and the Zoladz families are not only middle-income but also fortunate to be economically stable. How do the two different policy approaches play out for economically insecure and low-income families? Pro-family policy and free-market policy turn out to produce vastly different outcomes for these families. Under pro-family policy, public funds act as a "floor" of support that no child will drop below. That means that, even if parents have little private income, or that income is inconsistent, or both, public spending still ensures that kids get the basics they need to do well, like a parent at home in the months after birth, good daycare after that, and some cash support every month. In contrast, under free-market policy, there is no floor on the level of support children receive if their parents can't pay. So what about the four in ten children whose families fall below the poverty threshold for at least two months of the year? Those kids just don't get what they need—no parent at home in the first months, no good daycare, no adequate material support.

The experiences of Anne Jespersen and her brother, Michael, who are raising their families in Copenhagen, cast into stark relief the differences between Denmark's pro-family policy system and our own. Anne married her high school sweetheart, Victor, when she was twenty. They had their first child, Sofia, the following year, while both were in college. In the United States, having to pay the expenses for both college and a kid would likely have knocked both Anne and Victor out of school, or at least made it very difficult to provide adequately for Sofia. Not in Denmark, where college tuition is free and comes with a stipend, healthcare is free, and parents receive a generous child benefit check every quarter to help offset the cost of kids. For the first months after Sofia was born, with some help from their parents, Anne and her husband traded off caring for the baby while the other went to class. When Sofia was one year old, they enrolled her in a municipal nursery around the corner, where her tuition was heavily subsidized. Their second child was born two years later, and entered the nursery at seven months. The nursery was open until 5 p.m., a schedule that allowed Anne and her husband to finish college and then her husband to finish medical school.

When each child turned three and was ready for what we would call prekindergarten, Anne and Victor enrolled them in a publicly subsidized Jewish preschool. By that time, Anne held a well-paying business job. Her high salary meant their kids' schooling was somewhat less subsidized than before, since tuition was based on a sliding-scale fee, but the fee still wasn't financially burdensome. When their third child came along, Anne and her husband took a year of publicly paid parental leave, split equally between them, and then sent him to the nursery and preschools that the older kids had attended. When each child entered grade school, they remained at the school, where their tuition, like kids' tuition at other private schools in the system, remained heavily subsidized (public schools are completely free). The Jewish school, like all Danish primary and secondary schools, made care before and after school available to accommodate working parents. Since most kids in Copenhagen are enrolled in aftercare, most want to stay for it so they can be with their friends. Through all that time, the family received a generous child benefit check for each child on a quarterly basis.

To Americans, one of the most interesting things about the circumstances in which Anne's kids were raised is how similar they were to that of their cousins, despite the differences in the families' financial situations. After college, Anne became a high-powered business executive; her husband became a high-profile academic physician in a medical school. Their career success (which Denmark's financial support helped them to achieve) placed them among Denmark's economic elite. In the meantime, Anne's brother, Michael, struggled financially. He never finished college, and although he ran a business as a general contractor for a while, the business didn't go well. He is now working as a carpenter. His wife, Dorthe, worked in a bowling alley before they had two kids. Despite the family's far lower and less consistent earnings, their children had most of the advantages that Anne's kids did. Dorthe took off almost a year for parental leave. Dorthe and Michael's kids, like Anne's, attended a high-quality nursery school in their neighborhood, again with their tuition heavily subsidized. When they were ready for prekindergarten, they went to the same high-quality Jewish school Anne's children went to and stayed there through grade school, with their tuition still heavily subsidized. While the kids were in school, Dorthe earned her nursing degree (free of cost and with a stipend). She now works as a nurse.

If Michael had lived in the United States, the difference between his and Anne's families' economic situations would have led to their raising their kids in very different circumstances. Michael's wife, Dorthe, couldn't have taken the long parental leaves she took, they couldn't have afforded to put their kids in a high-quality nursery and prekindergarten, and they wouldn't have had the re-sources to send their kids to a private school. Thanks to Denmark's pro-family policies, though, it's not only upper-income families that can afford to give their children these kinds of advantages; all parents can. In the United States, under free-market policy, meanwhile, only upper-income families can provide their children with this start in life.[100]

THE PRICE TAG OF FREE-MARKET AND PRO-FAMILY POLICY SYSTEMS

Some of you may now be thinking that even if pro-family policies like Finland's and Denmark's would help American families and increase Americans' well-being, they're just too expensive for the United States to adopt. But even leaving aside the fact that we're a far wealthier country than either Finland or Denmark, here's the thing: We *already* spend as much money to support people's well-being as these countries when you add America's public *and private* spending together. The eminent Danish sociologist Gøsta Esping-Andersen was the first to demonstrate this. What he showed was that the countries that rely most on markets to support people's well-being, of which the United States is the most extreme example, spend every bit as much of their income as countries that rely far more on government spending. We just spend most of it privately as consumers—paying it directly to doctors, hospitals, preschools, colleges, and private pension plans. In contrast, citizens of countries that rely more on public programs to support their people's well-being pay more taxes to the government, which then spends them on the same or equivalent goods and services.[101] In fact, when private spending and public spending on people's well-being in the United States are added together, the total—30 percent of our GDP in 2015—is sig-nificantly *higher* than what most other countries spend. In comparison, Finland spent 25.3 percent of its GDP on well-being, and Denmark spent 25.4 percent of its GDP on the same.[102]

But if we are already spending as much of our income on people's well-being as other countries, why is there any need to change what we do? Because of two huge differences with *how* we spend. First, as I mentioned earlier, our private and public spending on social welfare is skewed toward the end of life.[103] When it comes to our private spending, this is because families have more money available to spend privately on well-being at the end of life due to the fact that most families' earnings increase over time. Our public spending is also skewed toward the end of life because the largest public spending programs we have, Social Security and Medicare, serve the elderly. We enacted these programs because we've long known that relying only on markets to provide for well-being doesn't work well at the end of life. With the economic and social changes of the past five decades, though, it's now clear that the market alone also does a poor job at supporting well-being at the beginning of life.[104]

Second, the fact that the United States spends as much on its people's well-being as other countries doesn't mean that we spend this money in the same way as countries that spend more dollars publicly, and it sure doesn't mean that we reap the same social welfare payoffs. In a system geared toward private spending like our own, wealthy families spend much more on their children than do other families. For a child born in 2015, lower-income families are likely to spend $212,300 to raise that child through age seventeen. Higher-income families are likely to spend more than double that sum—$454,770.[105] Add a private college degree and that figure grows by close to another $200,000.[106] One recent *New York Times* headline succinctly describes how this affects the distribution of college education: "Some Colleges Have More Students from the Top 1 Percent Than the Bottom 60."[107] (And, as we've recently found out, if their children lack the credentials to get into an elite college legitimately, some very wealthy parents will spend up to $6.5 million to get them in illegitimately.[108]) The bottom line is that relying more on private funding means that a tremendous amount will be spent on some kids, while far less will be spent on many others. But more equitable spending on children would result in significantly higher social welfare payoffs overall. That hundredth book for a wealthy child would do far more good in the hands of a poor child with no books.

Our highly stratified social spending contrasts with that of countries with pro-family policy, where funds are distributed far more equally among children. For example, in many countries, including France, the United Kingdom, Italy, and Germany, high-quality prekindergarten, considered one of the most cost-effective programs to benefit children, is available to all and either free or heavily subsidized. The result is that virtually all children in these countries attend prekindergarten and experience the considerable benefits to be gained from it. In the United States, except in a few states, prekindergarten is generally available only privately (except for the minority of those poor families lucky enough to secure places in Head Start) and is therefore available only to those families who can pay. The result is that just two-thirds of US four-year-olds go to prekindergarten, causing us to place thirty-first among wealthy countries in enrollment numbers.[109] Similar things are true about the distribution of the rest of the goods and services kids need to do their best.

Every society faces the critical task of ensuring that families—the institution most directly linked to the well-being of both children and adults—have the circumstances they need for themselves and their members to flourish. In the past five decades, the United States has made itself an outlier among wealthy countries in the manner through which it seeks to accomplish this task. We have adopted free-market family policy, under which families are expected to arrange and pay privately for what they need, without the help of government. Other countries meanwhile have adopted pro-family policy, in which the government partners with families to ensure the circumstances in which families thrive. Which policy system better supports adults in living the richer, fuller lives promised by the American Dream?

The Overworked American Parent

In 1930, the economist John Maynard Keynes wrote an essay speculating about economic conditions a hundred years in the future. By then, he predicted, increases in economic productivity would allow societies to make everything they needed in a fraction of the time it took in his day. This would mean that the struggle for survival—the economic problem that had dominated human-kind since the dawn of time—would finally come to an end. Future adults would have higher living standards with lighter work schedules—at most fifteen hours a week. Human beings would instead, Keynes forecasted, begin grappling with a new and permanent problem: what to do with all their free time.[1]

Now, just slightly shy of this future date, Keynes's worry about how people would fill their free time seems laughable to most Americans. Our problem isn't filling the void left by too few hours at paid work. It's the opposite: trying desperately to squeeze family and personal life into the scant remaining hours after we finish work. Most American parents find it difficult to balance work and family life.[2] More than a third say they *always* feel rushed, and this number has been steadily rising since 1972.[3] One bestseller's title says it all: *Overwhelmed: Work, Love, and Play When No One Has the Time.*[4] Most of us are overtired and overworked, and finding the time to do even the things we really want to do feels impossible.

I raise Keynes's prediction not to ask how he got it so wrong, but to ask the more important question: How did *we* get it so wrong? Keynes's ulti-mate conclusion was faulty, but he was right on target with his underlying predictions: Productivity has increased steadily in the near century since he wrote. Americans today need to work about seventeen weeks a year to accom-plish the same amount of work that it would have taken a full year to perform a century ago.[5] And as Keynes predicted, our standard of living has increased five times over.[6] Further, Keynes could hardly have imagined the extent of US wealth today. So why, given our stellar productivity and tremendous wealth, do most families spend so much time in paid work? And what happened to the calm, leisurely lives that Keynes predicted we would have? Finally, why do parents in other wealthy countries do a much better job of striking a sane work–life balance than we do?

The answers to all these questions lie in our lawmakers' choice to favor markets over families. The simple fact that Americans have to balance paid work with caretaking responsibilities of course doesn't distinguish us from other countries with market economies. The difference is that US families have to strike this balance on their own, with no help from government, in an economy characterized by pervasive inequality and insecurity. Other countries regulate their markets to support families. They have passed laws that limit mandatory work hours, provide paid parental leave, and allow parents of young children to work part-time. They have also established measures to reduce economic inequality and insecurity. The United States, on the other hand, does none of these things. Not only haven't we passed protections to enable American workers to reconcile work with family, we've created economic incentives that encourage overwork and a culture in which work at the expense of all else is normal, even celebrated.

There's little that individual workers or families can do to keep work within reasonable bounds today. The result of almost five decades of free-market policy, in which policymakers have sought to increase GDP rather than families' well-being, is that American families are competing to succeed in a "king of the hill" game on a dirt pile that is a lot steeper and narrower than it used to be. This means that the rewards for making it to the top, as well as the penalties for falling down that slope, are far greater than they used to be. As a result, the competition is fierce. Any workers who try to withdraw unilaterally from the game by not working as hard as they can face the significant risk that their families will wind up at the bottom. Because of that, almost all play the game. Yet the amount of time and energy required to play takes a serious toll on all of us. That means that every family—whether it ultimately winds up at the top or the bottom of the hill—loses.

The heavy toll that the market takes on American families may seem inevitable to those of us who are slogging away in this system. But it doesn't have to be this hard. As Keynes reminds us, our economy could make life easier for every American family. Only the absence of the political will of our policymakers stands in the way.

AMERICAN FAMILIES' LONG HOURS AND DIFFICULT SCHEDULES IN THE WORKPLACE

Forget Keynes's worry about people having too much time to fill: Americans who work for pay increasingly wedge family time into what's left after exhausting days and weeks at work. Our supposedly standard forty-hour workweek is a fiction. Full-time US employees worked on average forty-seven hours per week in 2014—far more than people in any other wealthy country.[7] US hours haven't always been higher. As Figure 3.1 shows, in the 1970s, the average number of hours worked by full-time employees in the United States fell roughly in the middle of hours worked in wealthy countries. Since then, though, work hours have decreased in other countries while ours have remained roughly the same.

If American work hours have remained stable in the past five decades, why do we feel so much busier? There are two reasons. First, although the number of hours the average *worker* spends on the job has stayed about the same, the average number of hours that American *families* work has increased dramatically. That's because women entered the workplace in large numbers during this time and remained there even after they had kids.[8] In the early 1970s, most women with children stayed home to care for them. (These included the majority of African American women, although far more black women worked for pay than did white women.)[9] Today, the great majority of women work, even those with young kids.[10]

The workplace American women joined demands long hours. Fathers have cut back paid work by a few hours a week since their wives entered the workforce, but not by nearly as much as their wives have added work hours. All in all,

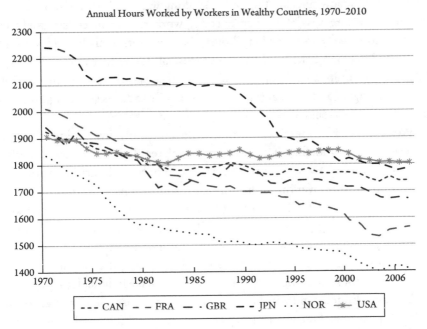

Annual Hours Worked by Workers in Wealthy Countries, 1970–2010

Figure 3.1. Annual Work Hours of Employees in Wealthy Countries, 1970–2010. Source: OECD (2009), 24, fig. 2.1.

two-earner families in the United States (six in ten of all married couples) spend a combined average of eighty-three hours a week at their jobs. This means that these families work for pay almost *twice* as many hours as their parents' families, despite the fact that most are little richer. Two-earner US parents spend more combined time in the workplace than their peers in any other wealthy country. At the low end of the scale, parents in the Netherlands work a combined average of twenty fewer hours a week than we do. There are countries in which two-earner couples work more hours than Americans, but these countries—Latvia, the Philippines, Mexico, and Hungary—are much poorer than the United States.[11]

Focusing only on the *average* family's work schedule, though, misses the second key reason so many of us today feel so much busier than in the past. It turns out that far fewer people now work an average schedule. Since the 1970s, market forces have increasingly divided workers and their families into two very different groups. One group—more educated, with higher incomes—is working far more hours than the average. The other group—less educated, with lower incomes—works fewer hours than average.[12] Today's economy is sorting winners from losers in the king of the hill game. And the price of winning is really long work hours.

The supposed winners in the American economy are working themselves silly. Thirty years ago, low-wage workers were likely to work more hours than the best-paid.[13] Breadwinners in the top jobs, along with their families, used to be called the "leisure class."[14] No longer. Today, workers who are college graduates are far more likely to work long hours than workers with less education.[15] A Harvard Business School survey of professionals found that almost all worked fifty hours or more a week; almost half worked sixty-five hours or more.[16] The cost of having a good job that supports your family today is spending a massive part of your life in paid work.

Work hours like these encroach heavily on family lives. Almost half of Americans who work fifty or more hours a week regularly work on weekends.[17] Even if an employee who worked at the low end of those hours performed five hours of paid work over the weekend, that would still leave forty-five hours of work during the week. This is a long workweek for parents with young kids. Assuming an average commute time of fifty minutes total and a half-hour for lunch, a parent would be gone for almost ten-and-a-half hours a day. When things go smoothly, this might be workable, assuming the parent could find childcare for these long hours. But that would still make it difficult to spend time with young children, and very little time to meet the rest of life's obligations or enjoy its pleasures. And when mishaps occur—a sick child, unscheduled travel, a school closure due to bad weather, car trouble—it would be completely overwhelming.

The fact that Americans are increasingly marrying partners socioeconomically similar to themselves means that the work-time gap between more- and less-educated employees is exaggerated when you compare work hours among different families.[18] Almost one in five US dual-earner couples work more than *one hundred* hours a week.[19] All told, US couples in the top fifth of the earnings scale work more than double the hours of couples in the bottom fifth.[20]

In truth, reasonably combining paid work with family life requires work schedules that allow parents to drop off kids at daycare or school in the morning and pick them up before daycare or aftercare ends. Taking into account time for an average commute and a quick lunch, that generally requires a work schedule of thirty-nine hours a week or less. Parents in countries with pro-family policies work a full but still manageable schedule like this far more often than US parents. As Figures 3.2 and 3.3 show, in the United States in 2016, only 16 percent of working mothers and 6 percent of working fathers with a child between the ages of zero and fourteen hit the sweet spot of thirty to thirty-nine hours a week of paid work. (Far more US mothers—67 percent—and even more fathers—90 percent—instead worked forty hours a week or more.) In contrast, in Denmark, 80 percent of mothers and 75 percent of fathers—five and twelve times as many as in the United States, respectively—worked between thirty and thirty-nine hours. Meanwhile, in Finland, 63 percent of mothers and 34 percent of fathers hit the sweet spot. In France, 58 percent of mothers and 50 percent of fathers did.[21]

The challenges of combining a family with a career are so formidable for US two-earner families that, in almost half of them, one parent winds up cutting back on paid work or leaving it altogether when they have children. That parent is almost always the mother, although this pattern is slowly changing.[22] A mother's retreat from paid work is often presented in the press as an

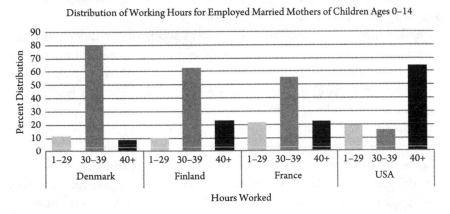

Figure 3.2. Employed Mothers by Weekly Working-Hour Bands. Source: Data from OECD 2016(c), 15–19, tables LMF2.2E and LFF2.2F.

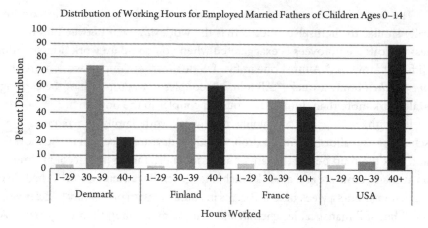

Figure 3.3. Employed Fathers by Weekly Working-Hour Bands. Source: Data from OECD 2016(c), 15–19, tables LMF2.2E and LFF2.2F.

empowering choice on her part. It is more likely, though, that the mother sees it as the best choice she can make for her family given she has no alternative that would let her sanely combine work and family.[23] The sociologist Pamela Stone, who studied women who step away from paid work, rejects the view that women quit "because" of the time demands of raising children. She asserts instead that they quit because their jobs required sixty-hour workweeks, and their efforts to negotiate a more reasonable deal for themselves and their families failed.[24] In contrast, in countries like Denmark and Sweden, where balanced combinations of work and family are truly possible, almost all women remain in paid work while raising a family.[25] One American sociologist talking to mothers in Sweden discovered that women in Stockholm were confused when she used the term "working mother." "I don't think that expression exists in Swedish," one mother told her. "It's not like there's a 'nonworking mother,'" she said. "I mean, what else would she do?"[26]

And, remember, the professional families working long hours are the supposed winners in our economic system—the ones who've made it close to the top of the economic hill. The less-educated families at the bottom have their own, more acute problems. An increasing number of workers without college degrees can't get enough work to pay the bills. More are working fewer than thirty hours a week, even while they are making much lower hourly pay than in years past.[27] On top of that, parents in these families often hold service jobs that require them to work nights and weekends, which makes finding steady childcare difficult and wreaks havoc on family schedules.[28] Many have their distinctly family-*un*friendly hours set by high-tech scheduling systems that maximize employer profits by moving workers from place to place and from shift to shift to match customer demand.[29]

Take Jannette Navarro, a San Diego single mother of a four-year-old. Jannette loved her job as a barista at Starbucks, where her $9 an hour pay was a step up from her past jobs. But her constantly fluctuating work schedule threw her family's life into a persistent state of crisis. Under the scheduling system Starbucks used, Jannette rarely learned her schedule more than three days before the start of a workweek. This meant she needed to scramble for childcare when she was scheduled outside normal daycare hours. Unlike professional families, Jannette couldn't afford to keep a nanny on call or to pay for babysitters beyond daycare. But that meant that she needed to rely on babysitting from family members when she had to work at times the daycare was closed. This created tension between Jannette and the aunt she lived with. The tension grew until Jannette eventually had to move out, which only made it harder for her to get help with her son. The two wound up moving into her boyfriend's place. The frantic tone that their lives took on because of Jannette's scheduling chaos then caused him to break up with her. He told her that he wanted a life that didn't revolve around last-minute scheduling logistics. This left her and her son with no place to live. Still, Jannette was afraid to ask her boss for a more stable schedule out of fear that she would be assigned fewer work hours.[30]

High-tech scheduling systems create other problems for low-wage workers' family lives, as well. Many put workers "on call" in case computers detect more last-minute demand than had been expected. Employees aren't paid unless they're called in, but they still have to have backup babysitters available. Martha Cadenas, a single mother from Apple Valley, Minnesota, had to be available to work any time she was called in by Walmart. She ultimately needed to have her mother move in with her to provide last-minute childcare. Other low-wage parents have the opposite problem: They book childcare for scheduled shifts but are dismissed hours early when computers detect slow sales. Work schedules like these shred family lives, weaken marriages, make planning for childcare a nightmare,[31] and interfere with breastfeeding.[32] Yet one in six US employees works irregular, on-call, or rotating shifts, with the lowest-income people working the most irregular schedules.[33]

We are the wealthiest country in the world, and our productivity is beyond what our nation's founders could possibly have imagined. This great good fortune could afford us balanced lives that combine a moderate amount of paid work with a high standard of living and generous time for our families. Yet few American workers actually lead such lives. Instead, the supposed winners in our economic system focus most of their waking hours and energy on paid work at the expense of time for the rest of their lives. The losers struggle to support their families with low wages, too few hours of work, and unpredictable schedules that ruin their family lives. Those who play the game by the current rules, winners and losers alike, are, to put it plainly, getting played.

EXPLAINING AMERICANS' LONG WORK HOURS

There's no rule of either nature or economics that requires us to spend the better part of our lives working. We could use our country's great wealth and high productivity to cut our work hours radically. That's what John Maynard Keynes expected would happen. Other wealthy countries have done just this. So how did our country get so off-track?

Let's take one explanation off the table right away: It's not because Americans *want* to work this much. Six in ten US workers today would prefer to work fewer hours. And still more of those who work more than fifty hours a week would like to cut back, with those working the longest hours wanting to cut back the most. So who does want to work more hours? Mainly male high school dropouts, the group that now works the fewest hours, and that has the greatest difficulty supporting their families.[34]

And it's not as though Americans are working so much because they're deeply engaged in their jobs. Half of US workers say they aren't even satisfied with their jobs.[35] And only a third say they are engaged in their work, meaning that they are involved, enthusiastic, and committed. The remaining two-thirds say that they are either not engaged or are actively disengaged in their work.[36]

In truth, Americans' hearts lie far more with their families than with their paid work. Almost all parents report that being a good parent is either one of the most important things or very important in their lives.[37] In contrast, only one in ten thinks that being wealthy is very important.[38] This doesn't mean that Americans don't care about their work—most see career success as important. But they see it as only one part of a rich, full life.[39]

Could it be that Americans work such long hours and under such difficult schedules because the value of hard work is so ingrained in our culture? Benjamin Franklin arguably captured the American spirit in counseling that it is "the working man who is the happy man. It is the idle man who is the miserable man."[40] But Americans didn't always work longer hours than people in other countries. As Figure 3.1 showed, it wasn't until the mid-1970s that American employees' hours began to outstrip those in the rest of the world. Before then, hours worked in the United States fell in the middle range of those in wealthy, developed countries.[41] The reasons that our work hours now diverge so sharply from those of other countries must therefore be found in more recent events, not in any long-held American work ethic.

We don't have to look far to come up with a better explanation for Americans' long work hours: our free-market family policy. Beginning in the 1970s, because more and more women were entering the workforce and staying there after having children, policymakers in all advanced countries began to reassess the way their governments supported families. Government programs for families in these countries had long been based on the assumption that breadwinning would be done by men and childrearing by women. As the way families organized their lives increasingly undermined this assumption, governments recognized these programs were outdated.[42]

Ultimately, all industrialized countries scrapped their outmoded programs, but from there, the United States went its own way. Other wealthy democracies held tight to the notion that government still had a fundamental role to play in ensuring that families had the conditions they needed to flourish, and they adopted a range of new laws that helped workers of both sexes balance work and family. By doing so, they accomplished what Keynes had predicted—they funneled market gains in productivity into reducing paid work hours, and they managed to do so without diminishing worker pay.[43] You can see their effects on reducing working hours in Figure 3.1.

The United States, in contrast, adopted public policies that funneled our market gains in productivity during these decades into the pockets of our top one percent. Although we scrapped our old public programs built on the assumption that women would stay at home, we didn't install new, updated protections for families. Instead, our policymakers insisted that unregulated markets alone would provide for American families. Accordingly, they required poor mothers to enter the workforce and suggested that struggling families just needed to work harder.[44] And they passed no laws that helped workers get home to their families. Instead, they left work hours to be settled by the market, through what Adam Smith called "the invisible hand." But it turns out that the invisible hand does a far worse job of allowing breadwinners to have sane family lives than public policies do.

Compare the regulation of work hours under pro-family versus free-market policy. Most European Union countries encourage adults to work for pay, just as the United States does. A key reason they do so is that the taxes these adults pay on their earned income helps defray the cost of these countries' generous public programs. But these countries also make it easy for adults to go home at the end of the workday, either by setting the number of hours in a standard workweek by law or by empowering collective-bargaining agreements between employees' unions and their companies. They also set a threshold (often, but not always, the same as the standard workweek) above which an employee must be paid overtime or receive compensatory time off. Even then, many of these countries allow overtime hours to be assigned only in certain conditions, such as when they are agreed to by the employee. Finally, these countries set a higher maximum cap, including overtime, on the total hours most employees can be assigned. This system allows for some individual variation based on the employer's needs at

particular times or the employee's own preferences, but the basic idea is to establish a baseline that allows employees a healthy work–life balance. For example, in
Finland, overtime pay is required after a forty-hour week or other standard week
set by a collective bargaining agreement, but the employee must agree to the
overtime. Furthermore, the amount of (consensual) overtime an employee can
be assigned is limited to 138 hours over a four-month period.[45]

In the United States, by contrast, our relevant law, the Fair Labor Standards
Act (FLSA), does far less. It simply requires that employees be paid time-and-a-
half wages when they work more than forty hours a week. Employees don't have
to agree to overtime in order to be assigned it, and there are no restrictions on
when it can be assigned. Nor is there a cap on how much overtime employers
can assign workers. Furthermore, while most countries exempt some professional and managerial employees from their work hour restrictions, the FLSA
exempts—well, pretty much everyone. It excludes employees classified as
executives, administrators, or professionals if they make more than $23,660 a
year. This income threshold, which hasn't been updated since 2004, falls below
the current poverty line for a family of four.[46] Not only do US laws not help
most salaried employees limit their hours, they have the opposite effect. Because
the FLSA makes it expensive for employers to have hourly workers but not
professionals work overtime, employers have an incentive to push their extra
work onto professionals.[47] Unsurprisingly, exempted employees are exactly the
people who work the most hours in our economy.[48]

Pro-family countries have also passed other laws that help employees balance
work with family life. These include measures requiring employers to provide
a minimum number of paid vacation days and national holidays. For example,
Spain requires that employees get thirty-nine paid days off a year, while Austria
requires thirty-eight. Portugal requires thirty-five paid days off a year. Denmark
requires thirty-four, and Germany requires thirty-three. The United Kingdom
requires twenty-eight days. Canada requires nineteen. The United States? Zero
days.[49]

Finally, countries with pro-family policies have put in place a range of programs
that support parents' taking time off to care for young children, as I outlined in
the preceding chapter. While pro-family policy tries to make it as easy as possible for workers to do the right thing by their kids, our country's free-market
regulations seem to bend over backward to make it difficult. According to the
United Nations International Labour Organization, we are one of two countries
in the entire world not to provide *any* paid maternity leave—the other country
is Papua New Guinea.[50] And even the twelve weeks of *unpaid* leave provided by
our Family and Medical Leave Act (FMLA) aren't available to almost half of the
private-sector workforce, including all those who work for employers with fewer
than fifty employees.[51] Parents who aren't covered can be fired for taking even a

day of leave after the birth of a baby. On top of that, most people protected by the FMLA can't take all the time it guarantees because it's unpaid. Given that most young families on the birth or adoption of a child will also be paying hospital bills—as well as for baby clothes and equipment, diapers, perhaps formula, and often moving to larger quarters—requiring parents to fund their own leave means that few can take this time off. Unsurprisingly, the vast majority of parents would prefer longer leaves, and most Americans think parents should be paid for leaves following the birth of a child.[52]

American families' experience with family leave is emblematic of our experience with free-market family policy generally. The period after a child's birth is a critical time for families—certainly one of the most major transitions they will ever make. Mothers need time to recuperate physically, to get breastfeeding on course if they are nursing, and for their hormones to adjust postpartum. Parents need time to bond with their baby. Infants have intense caretaking needs and their schedules are often highly irregular. Even in the best of circumstances, a new baby will mean months of interrupted sleep and round-the-clock caretaking for parents, not to mention adjustment to new parental roles. A generous period of paid parental leave helps enormously in this critical transition, both by keeping work demands at bay and by easing the significant economic pressures that a new child creates.

But under free-market family policy, most parents don't get anything close to that time with their babies. Tricia Olson of Rock Springs, Wyoming, works for a towing and U-Haul rental company with just four employees. Because she doesn't get any paid leave from work, before her baby was born she negotiated with her boss a period of between two and three weeks off, unpaid. In an audio diary of her first day back to work, Tricia describes drinking a pot of coffee earlier that morning to keep herself awake despite her exhaustion and stuffing her pockets with tissues to wipe away her tears. After dropping her baby off at a sitter, the new mother reports with relief that she "only lost it for a little bit, just as I was leaving." A little while later, though, she says, with her voice breaking, that she "just wish[es] I could be there, not here. But finances don't really give me that option. We have to work, have to have money. The house bill is not going to pay itself." She adds of her baby, "I'm just glad he gets to be with people who will take care of him and [crying now] make sure that he's okay 'til I can be there."[53]

Tricia's transition back to work was far harder than it would have been in any other wealthy country, but at least both the parents and the child involved were healthy. When things don't go as well during this transition to parenthood, the absence of the kind of protections other countries give can tip a family over the edge into significant hardship. For one young Durham, North Carolina, attorney and her family, it almost came to a tragic end. Before Maya Hall gave birth to her son, she and her husband knew that she would be able to take just two months of

unpaid maternity leave.[54] As an independent attorney who contracted for criminal cases, she had no one who would pay her for her time off or fill in for her on
her cases. Because of that, during her pregnancy, in her words:

> I worked every minute I could to leave my cases in a good place and to
> save money for the time I needed to take off to recover and to care for
> my newborn. I remember working through excruciating sciatic nerve
> pain that made it difficult to walk, and driving myself to the hospital [to
> give birth] after an important meeting. Even before my son was born,
> I was sleep deprived and emotionally exhausted.
>
> I gave birth by C-section. My beautiful baby was born and I was
> elated, and navigated my new challenges happily for a while. I strug-
> gled with breastfeeding, in part because of oversupply. This added to
> the usual sleep deprivation because I woke up each night in terrible
> pain even as my son was sleeping. I went back [to work] at around two
> months after I gave birth.
>
> Once I returned to the stress of my professional life, I began to un-
> ravel. My milk supply never regulated itself. I continued to wake up in
> pain at night. I often stayed awake worrying about my cases. And not
> to mention, I was still adjusting to having a new baby to care for when
> I wasn't working. My husband did everything in his power to be helpful,
> including taking nights with the baby.
>
> I reached my breaking point when we went to visit family to cele-
> brate Christmas. I had become increasingly disoriented. My insomnia
> worsened. I had panic attacks. I couldn't function. When I reached a
> point where I could no longer engage fully in conversation, my husband
> and some dear friends decided that I needed to be hospitalized. . . .
> I received inpatient treatment [for postpartum depression] at a local
> hospital that had a separate ward for perinatal women with psychiatric
> issues . . . for eight days before I was released. . . . In many ways we were
> fortunate. But we lived through a nightmare.[55]

Maya, like one in seven new mothers, suffered from postpartum depression.[56]
Mothers who return to work sooner after giving birth have a tougher time with
this condition than those who get more time at home. If Maya lived in a country
with pro-family policies, she could easily have taken much longer to recuperate,
breastfeed, and adapt to parenting before she had to return to work. Not under
free-market family policy, though.

Our hands-off attitude when it comes to helping families with children
stands in striking counterpoint to our nation's actively pro-natalist (often known
as "pro-life") policies, many of which are not at all hands-off when it comes to

families' decisions regarding whether to bear children. Ironically, the politicians who most oppose supports that would benefit families with children tend to be the same politicians most intent on banning access to contraceptives and abortion. Ultimately, our absence of support for families keeps Americans at paid work, which these politicians believe boosts the country's GDP. But it serves few American families well.

INTENSIVE WORK HOURS UNDER
FREE-MARKET FAMILY POLICY

Free-market proponents claim that employees could negotiate time off if they truly valued it. They say that letting markets work means that employees can shape their own lives and exercise their own freedom. But it isn't that simple in the real world. Many factors shape work hours beyond a worker's independent preferences about the trade-off between hours and salary. The most important of these may be economic inequality.

The British epidemiologists Richard Wilkinson and Kate Pickett in their international bestseller, *The Spirit Level*, demonstrated the strong association between high levels of economic inequality and long hours of work: the higher the level of economic inequality within a country, the longer people in that country tended to spend at paid work.[57] They left unexplained, though, exactly how large gaps between the rich and poor might cause people to work longer hours. One part of that answer is that high wage inequality, like the kind we have in the United States, increases the incentives for workers to work long hours in the hope of making it up the next rungs of the economic ladder.[58] This is particularly the case when pay disparities are large within a particular job category.[59] Consider the choices that confront young MBAs on Wall Street. The average pay of someone with an MBA is comparatively high, but success on Wall Street particularly can deliver stratospheric rewards—staggering salaries and huge annual bonuses for those in the top positions. The competition is intense among junior Wall Street employees precisely because the rewards are so high for the very few who make it to the top. As a result, many young investment bankers work virtually around the clock. As one young gun wryly put it, "[we work] bankers' hours: 9 to 5 (a.m.)." The pressure to work these grueling hours is so great that in the past few years there has been a spate of suicides, deaths from exhaustion, and hospitalizations from overwork.[60]

The problem here is what is sometimes called a "race to the bottom." Obviously, employees don't want to work themselves to death, but they do want to work just a little harder than the next person so that they'll excel. The rub is that the next person has exactly the same strategy. And so a cycle begins of each worker trying to work a little harder than the next. With the huge rewards granted to those at the top while those below earn so much less, the competition soon moves from the leisurely world that Keynes anticipated to a world that starts to look a lot more like the Hunger Games. And as in the Hunger Games, people compete in a fight to the death. This was literally the case at Goldman Sachs, where one first-year analyst committed suicide in connection with overwork and another first-year analyst was hospitalized with seizures after working seventy-two hours straight. After this, the firm established a new rule: junior employees would have to leave the building from 9 p.m. Friday evening to 9 a.m. on Sunday. Market incentives had been responsible for the excessive, damaging overwork among its employees; the company addressed the problem by implementing a centralized rule.

Although the wages within few job categories are as unequal as those of investment bankers, the pressure to work more hours generated by our mushrooming inequality has permeated all levels of the US labor market, particularly at the top. Meanwhile, the decrease in real wages at the middle and bottom of US income distribution gives those below an incentive to work long hours as well, if they can find the work. The result is that almost all employees work far more than they would otherwise choose to work.

Increases in economic insecurity also motivate longer hours. Employees who are insecure about their jobs are significantly more likely than others to allow work demands to encroach on their personal time.[61] Remember Jannette Navarro, the worker who accepted Starbucks' cruel scheduling practices without complaint, despite the havoc they wreaked on her family life, because she was concerned that she'd be scheduled for fewer hours if she objected? Even relatively small doubts about job security have this effect. This creates the motivation to work long hours among even highly educated workers, who have increasingly come to see their jobs as insecure.[62]

The fact that US families will lose their health insurance if workers lose their jobs, combined with skyrocketing healthcare costs, only adds to the pressure on employees, particularly if they have a family member with significant health problems. That pressure was responsible for the anger directed at a New Jersey congressman for spearheading the attempted repeal of the Affordable Care Act in 2017. In a speech that went viral, one constituent roared at his representative:

> My wife was diagnosed with cancer when she was 40 years old. She beat it. But every day, *every day*, she lives with it. She thinks about it. Every pain, every new something going on somewhere: "Is it coming back? Is this cancer? Do I have it again? Is it going to kill me this time? Is it going to take me away from my children?" . . .

You have been the single greatest threat to my family in the entire world. *You* are the reason that I stay up at night. *You* are the reason that I can't sleep. What happens if I lose my job? . . . I have really good health insurance. . . . But . . . if I lose my job, we can't afford . . . to get private insurance. . . . If I lose it, it's gone. If I lose my job on a Monday, if I'm lucky enough to find a job on Tuesday, which never happens, they won't have insurance ready for me, . . . I won't be eligible for three to six months. If I lapse my coverage, within 63 days, suddenly I'm in a high-risk pool.[63]

All of this—the mushrooming economic inequality combined with snowballing economic insecurity—creates, in the words of the Harvard economist Richard Freeman, both a carrot and a stick that push Americans to work long hours:

> The carrot is that Americans who work hard have a better chance of being promoted, moving up in the wide distribution of earnings, and experiencing substantial earnings increases. The stick is that Americans who lose their jobs suffer greatly because the United States has a minimal safety net for the unemployed.[64]

The pressure to work more hours shows up clearly in the amount of vacation time that US workers take. As I mentioned earlier, the United States is the only wealthy country that does not mandate that employers provide paid vacation time. About three-quarters of US employers still provide some paid time off—but even then, they offer only about half the number of paid days (on average sixteen) that employees receive in Austria, Finland, and France.[65] And yet, in 2010, almost half of American workers didn't even take all of their available leave. In France, by contrast, nine in ten workers took all of the much longer leave available to them.[66] Why do US workers leave the meager amount of paid vacation time that they do get on the table? Because of the powerful mix of economic inequality and insecurity we've been brewing in the United States for the past half-century. Research shows that employees are more likely to take less vacation time if they feel more insecure in their jobs.[67] Something similar happens when it comes to paternity leave. Fathers report that they would like to take more leave but don't for fear that they will be judged as insufficiently committed to their work.[68]

Economists call the kind of dynamic that is compelling US employees to put in so many work hours a "collective-action problem." By this, they mean a situation in which all the people involved would prefer a different outcome than the one that results. In the absence of joint action or agreement by the people involved, though, the choices available to individuals lead them to a less preferable outcome for everyone. The economist Thomas Schelling in the 1970s provided an illuminating example of a collective-action problem when he discussed the headgear that hockey players chose to wear. Schelling noticed that in the absence of rules about headgear, individual hockey players would never wear helmets. In situations in which they got to vote on a rule, though, they would uniformly vote in favor of a rule requiring such helmets. Why would they not simply wear helmets if they preferred to, even in the absence of the rule? Schelling explained that individual players can see and hear a little better without helmets. Because of this, in the absence of a rule, players wouldn't wear helmets in an effort to gain a comparative advantage over other players (as well as to avoid a comparative disadvantage from wearing a helmet). Yet not wearing a helmet made the game a lot more dangerous for the players. Because of this, when players were given the opportunity, they would adopt a collective rule in favor of helmets so that no one could gain a comparative advantage from not wearing one.[69]

In the case of most American workers, a similar collective-action dynamic is at play. Most workers would prefer to work fewer hours, yet those who scale back risk being seen as less committed than their co-workers. The safer option is to work a little harder than the next person.[70] And because each worker individually makes the same calculation, all wind up working far more than any of them would like. This problem can't be solved unilaterally. But as with the hockey players agreeing to pass a helmet rule, it could be solved collectively through laws that set limits on mandatory work hours. Just as a helmet rule makes competition in hockey games less dangerous, government regulation can change the rules of today's labor market competition to make it more humane. The vast majority of workers would prefer to reduce the hours they work in order to make more time for their families and the rest of their lives. But they need a collective rule to make this happen. Yet while other countries have adopted rules that keep work hours to reasonable amounts, our country hasn't.

Not only does free-market family policy perpetuate our culture of overwork by failing to set baseline rules that support families, it motivates it in another, more insidious way. Standard economic models treat people's preferences as if they are fixed—assuming that people rationally and autonomously determine how many hours they want to work a week and how much pay they would be willing to trade off to work fewer hours. This isn't how it works in real life, though. In reality, social scientists have discovered that people's preferences are deeply influenced by their social circumstances and culture. And our circumstances and culture, which include staggering levels of economic inequality combined with considerable conspicuous consumption, have persuaded Americans they need increasingly more money to live comfortably.

To begin with, an important way that people determine how much income they think they need is based on the spending patterns of people around them. In particular, we adjust our views about what makes for a comfortable standard of living on the basis of the spending patterns of people slightly above us on the economic ladder—the neighbor with a little bit bigger house, a colleague slightly ahead of us on our career track, a grown sibling who routinely eats at more expensive restaurants than we do.[71] So when economic inequality grows and the distance between the rungs of the economic ladder increases, our estimates of how much income we need to live comfortably also expand.[72] If you compare your lifestyle with that of your neighbors, you'll tend to want at least what they have. But as inequality grows, the gap between your neighbors and yourself will likely be larger than in the past, which means that the income you think you need will be higher than in the past. Only that could account for the bizarre fact that New Yorkers who earned more than $200,000 a year were the *most likely* of any income group to agree that "seeing other people with money" makes them feel poor.[73] Given the huge disparities in wealth at the top of New York society, these New Yorkers were most likely to feel economically left behind when they compared themselves with those above them. For similar reasons, another study found that married women were more likely to work in paid jobs if their sister's husband outearned their own husband.[74]

It doesn't help that the lifestyles of those at the top of the dirt pile in our increasingly unequal society are far more visible than they used to be. A proliferation of television shows, blogs, social media, and websites bring the sumptuous, well-appointed houses of the wealthy into middle-class living rooms with the message that this is what success looks like. These same messages are reinforced by our culture's obsession with celebrity. Once you see enough pictures of Ellen DeGeneres's gorgeous ranch, your own home starts looking pretty shabby. If you aren't quite sure how to translate those beautiful images into your middle-class life, the Pottery Barn catalog you receive in the mail will help you do that—for a price.

The effects of inequality are also exacerbated by the explosion of conspicuous consumption in the United States during the past decades. When I was growing up in the 1970s, the families of top business executives certainly had more money in the bank and lived in larger houses on the more exclusive side of town than middle-class families did. But the mothers drove the same beat-up station wagons with fake wood paneling on the outside as the middle-class mothers did. Their kids went to public school with us middle-class kids, even though they came dressed in the more expensive brands from our local department store. And their homes were usually the only residences they had. Today, the families of executives live very different lives from the middle class. They live in bigger homes in gated communities, they're more likely to drop off their kids at private school in a Lexus (if they don't have a driver), and their kids are dressed in designer clothes bought online or from tony designer stores instead of from the local department store. On top of that, they spend their weekends at second homes, and they sometimes summer at third homes in the Hamptons or on Nantucket.[75]

The increased consumption by wealthy families, combined with our increased awareness of this shift, has helped to boost the standard of living that middle-class Americans today associate with a comfortable life. Many of the children in my 1970s middle-class neighborhood shared bedrooms in homes geared toward functionality rather than attractiveness. These homes, including my own, had linoleum floors, fake wood paneling and cabinet fronts, Formica countertops, and a single black-and-white television with an antenna. The only other piece of electronics in these homes was a stereo system that consisted of a turntable with two attached speakers.

All that has changed. Although middle-class families now have fewer children, their houses are more than half again as large as they were in the 1970s.[76] And the aimed-for ambience of these homes is no longer utilitarian, it's designer. In place of the linoleum floors and Formica countertops, today's middle-class houses are likely to have real tile, granite countertops, and real wood cabinets, often with glass fronts. The single black-and-white television has been replaced by a proliferation of expensive electronics. Eight in ten households now have a computer. Almost a quarter have three or more. Almost seven in ten have at least one tablet. Four in ten have a streaming device like an Apple TV or Roku. And a third of households have three or more smartphones.[77]

When the sociologist Juliet Schor crunched the numbers, she found that the average American's spending increased somewhere between 30 and 70 percent just between 1979 and 1995.[78] Not all of that spending is a product of our raised expectations of living standards. Some comes from the higher cost of homes located near high-performing schools, as well as necessary costs associated with two-income households, like an extra car and daycare.[79] But all that increased spending raises the pressure on families to earn more. And that greater pressure to spend doesn't just put poor and working-class families in a bind. The Brookings Institution found that two-thirds of American families who lived from paycheck to paycheck are from the middle class or higher.[80]

It's not just our neighbor's lifestyles that affect our views of what constitutes an adequate standard of living. We're also heavily influenced by our own incomes. Schor points to one survey that asked people whether they would prefer more, fewer, or the same number of work hours, or instead choose a commensurate trade-off in income. Two-thirds responded that they'd choose their current arrangement. How do we know that this is truly a psychological "anchoring" process instead of their independent desire to work that number of hours? These same people were far more willing to trade income for time when it came to evaluating *future* income increases. Framed this way, 84 percent agreed to trade some income for more time, and almost half said they would prefer to trade all of a 10 percent raise for more free time.[81]

Economic incentives are the driving force here, but they certainly aren't the whole picture of why Americans work such long hours. Once economic incentives drive overwork, the forces of habit and routine then cause Americans to accept these long hours of work as both natural and normal. In turn, these patterns, as well as the public adulation conferred on those who succeed in this culture, reinforce and are reinforced by America's grinding culture of over-work.[82] The result is that our nation's economy is providing many of us with more material goods than we had a few generations ago—bigger houses and granite countertops. But in return we have sacrificed things we really care about, including time and energy for a rich life outside of work.

INTENSIVE PARENTING IN THE
FREE-MARKET FAMILY SYSTEM

You might assume that our long hours of paid work would cause American parents to spend less time with their children. This assumption, though, would be a hundred percent wrong. In fact, parents have substantially *increased* their time with their kids. Between 1965 and 2008, despite expanding their paid work time by an average of almost fourteen hours a week, mothers still managed to add three-and-a-half hours to the time they spent caring for their children. Mothers with full-time jobs today spend as many hours with their children as stay-at-home mothers did in the 1970s.[83] Meanwhile, fathers added four-and-a-half hours a week of time caring for kids.[84] At first glance, you could take this increase in parenting time as evidence that free-market policy is good for families: not only do families have more money to buy the material things they de-sire, but parents are spending larger chunks of time with their children. But this would miss the less than benign causes of this development, as well as its prob-lematic consequences. I'll discuss the causes of this phenomenon here, and then lay out its consequences for parents in the next section. Its consequences for children will be discussed in chapter 7.

The increased time parents are spending with kids today is a response to parents' growing anxiety about their children's futures, a product of our in-creasingly unequal and insecure economy. No longer is doing "pretty well" good enough to ensure kids' economic stability. Kids aren't likely to outearn their parents when they reach adulthood anymore, and even a college educa-tion doesn't guarantee success. Just between 2001 and 2012, the share of college graduates who wound up in jobs that don't require a college degree rose from

34 to 44 percent. Even more disconcerting, the share of noncollege jobs held by college graduates that are "good noncollege jobs" (meaning that they don't require a college degree but still pay at least $45,000 a year) has declined from more than half in 1990 to slightly over a third in 2012. Meanwhile, the share of "low-wage jobs" held by college graduates (defined as paying $25,000 a year or less) has risen from about 15 to 20 percent.[85] The result is that high school graduates who would have had steady jobs thirty years ago are now being displaced by underemployed college graduates and are forced to take dead-end service jobs.[86] In none of these jobs can young people be assured of benefits and an adequate pension for retirement.[87]

This high-risk economy for young people feeds a style of parenting that has come to be called "intensive parenting."[88] Parents are putting more time and energy into childrearing because of the growing perception that parental supervision is, in the Stanford sociologist's Sean Reardon's words, "central to winning a lifelong educational and economic competition."[89] Much of this intensive parenting is aimed at getting children into colleges (the more elite, the better) in order to secure their economic future.[90] Parents are spending more time parenting than they used to in order to ensure that their child has an edge on other children when it comes to attaining a secure place on the increasingly steep economic slope they'll have to climb as adults.[91] To give them a leg up, parents are constantly teaching and monitoring their kids, as well as enrolling them in music lessons and test preparation classes, taking them to sports practice, hiring math tutors, and seeing to it that they take part in the kind of community service that looks good on a resume. (One father told me that he tried not to be away from his kids when he wasn't working because that would mean he was missing the "opportunity to mold young minds." *That's* an intensive parent.)

Samuel Schram, a New York City architect who is the father of three boys, told me that he and his wife, despite living in the city itself—where public transportation is easy and parking is both complicated and expensive—each keep a car so that they can take their kids to play in baseball games in surrounding states. He said that this kind of "super fancy" travel baseball didn't exist when we were kids, and it seemed a little silly to him. It also certainly added to his and his wife's high stress stemming from their overly packed schedules. But he worried that if his kids didn't "play and get the right exposure, they'll never play in college." He added that "there's always pressure as a parent to not slip up and make sure that your kids get every opportunity they can get."[92]

The economists Fabrizio Zilibotti and Matthias Doepke make a powerful case that the rise of this mode of intensive parenting, as well as the growing number of hours that US parents spend caring for their children, are the products of increased economic inequality. This increase, they contend, has given parents strong incentives to push their children hard while closely monitoring them to be sure their efforts are successful. More permissive styles of parenting that promote children's independence and imagination, they argue, become "less attractive when the stakes are high, that is, when adult-style behavior is especially important for children's future success." That's why a far higher share of parents are permissive in more economically equal countries like Sweden and Norway.[93]

As with so much else in our society, the increase in parents' time with their kids has not been equal among families. Since 1975, the time parents spend actively parenting their children has grown twice as fast in high-income families as in families with lower incomes.[94] The greatest increase has taken place among college-educated fathers.[95] But recently, parents on the lower end of the socio-economic ladder have been ramping up the intensity of their parenting as well.[96] This means that the competitive arms race over time has heated up not just on the work side of the equation, but on the family side as well.

Perhaps no one has given as extreme an account of intensive parenting as Amy Chua in her bestselling memoir, *Battle Hymn of the Tiger Mother*. Chua struck a cultural nerve in the United States by contrasting her "Chinese mother" parenting style with "Western parenting." Chinese mothers, she claimed, groom their children for success. They demand straight As and supervise endless hours of study and other activities deemed sufficiently resume-worthy. And they banish sleepovers, playdates, and other activities that won't beef up a college application. In contrast, Western parents don't push their children nearly as hard, and they accept second-rate performances. "[M]y Western friends who consider themselves strict make their children practice their [musical] instruments 30 minutes every day," Chua writes. "An hour at most. For a Chinese mother, the first hour is the easy part. It's hours two and three that get tough."[97] *Tiger Mother* caused a national furor. An excerpt published in the *Wall Street Journal* provoked more than five thousand comments on the newspaper's website—a record—and set off a fiery debate in blogs and on editorial pages.[98]

Why did Americans react so strongly to this provocation? Because it stoked parents' anxieties about their children's futures in our hypercompetitive economy. Few if any parents could meet the ridiculously intense parenting standards that Chua (herself a full-time Yale Law School professor) claimed to follow, and many were outraged at the idea of sacrificing sleepovers, playdates, and recess for kids in favor of higher test scores. Still, Chua's book sold so many copies because it played on parents' worries that their own children would be among the many left at the bottom of the dirt pile in our economy.

The greater number of hours that American parents are spending with their kids isn't a collective-action issue in the same way that parents' increased work hours are: unlike work, parents see time with their kids as their highest priority, and a good many want even more of it. On top of this, most parents will go to great lengths to further the interests of their kids, and they engage in the hours that intensive parenting takes with a full heart. Nevertheless, we shouldn't overlook the likelihood that in an economic system in which the dirt pile was not as steep as our own and the competition more humane, parents would be less likely to parent in this way. Some would decrease the hours they spent with their kids somewhat—no longer schlepping them to violin lessons or out-of-state baseball tournaments. Others would spend as much time with their kids, but in a different way. Instead of taking them to SAT coaching sessions, they'd spend more time relaxing or playing board games with them. Or they'd spend time cooking and eating family dinners or baking the crunchy chocolate chip cookies with their kids that they remember from their own, slower-paced childhoods.[99]

THE TIME CRUNCH'S TOLL

When you add the long hours that American parents spend at their paid jobs to the long hours they spend on childrearing and housework, the sum total is exhausted families. Married middle-class mothers employed full-time spend an average of 68 hours a week between this paid and unpaid work. Employed fathers do less unpaid work than their wives, but they make up for it with more time at the office, committing a total of 67 hours a week between home and work. As discussed in chapter 1, this makes the total paid and unpaid workload in middle-class dual-earner families a shocking 135 hours a week—nearly 10 hours a day, seven days a week for each parent.[100] The hours are even higher for single parents.[101]

And remember: these are the *average* numbers of total hours. The hours are still higher for those parents in professional jobs. The impossibility of meshing those kinds of jobs with parenting in the United States is the reason that Anne-Marie Slaughter's *Atlantic* essay, "Why Women Still Can't Have It All," ignited such an intense national discussion. Slaughter argued that being an involved mother (a term she later amended to include parents of either gender) and holding a high-powered job in today's economy just can't be done. She cited her own experience working for the government in Washington, DC, for two years, while her family remained behind in Princeton, New Jersey. Her work-week began at 4:20 on Monday morning, when she woke up to catch the 5:30 train to Washington, and ended late Friday with the train ride home. In between, it was packed with nonstop meetings, memos, and reports. She never left the office in time to make it to the hair salon, the cleaners, or any shop that wasn't open twenty-four hours. This left only the weekend for those kinds of personal tasks, not to mention for things like grocery shopping. But weekends were her only family time, so she had to cram children's sporting events, music lessons, and family meals into her days off as well. Making this schedule work was difficult in the normal course of affairs, but when one of her sons entered a difficult period, Slaughter found that being both a good professional and an involved parent became impossible. In her words:

> In short, the minute I found myself in a job that is typical for the vast majority of working women (and men), working long hours on someone else's schedule, I could no longer be both the parent and the professional I wanted to be—at least not with a child experiencing a rocky adolescence. I realized what should have perhaps been obvious: having it all, at least for me, depended almost entirely on what type of job I had. The flip side is the harder truth: having it all was not possible in many types of jobs, including high government office—at least not for very long.[102]

In many ways, Slaughter's account of being unable to have it all is an updated, supercharged version of a story that American mothers have been telling for more than a generation. In 1989, soon after middle-class mothers started going back to the workplace after having kids, the sociologist Arlie Hochschild published her classic study of working mothers, *The Second Shift*, titled for the housework and caretaking that these women had to perform once they got home from their paid jobs. The book's power stemmed from its granular descriptions of the exhausting lives of these mothers as they accomplished the multitude of tasks needed to keep their work lives and families afloat. "These women talked about sleep the way a hungry person talks about food," she memorably wrote.[103] When Hochschild showed these mothers magazine ads of the era depicting a well-groomed working mother, smiling in a business suit, with a briefcase in one hand and a grinning child in the other, they could not connect that well-kempt figure with their own selves. As Hochschild tells it, "One daycare worker and mother of two, ages three and five, threw back her head: 'Ha! They've got to be *kidding* about her. Look at me, hair a mess, nails jagged, twenty pounds overweight. Mornings, I'm getting my kids dressed, the dog fed, the lunches made, the shopping list done.'"[104]

Thirty years after Hochschild's book was published, little has changed for American mothers. As Slaughter's account shows, they are still scrambling just to keep it together. Aimee Barnes, an employee of the California Environmental Protection Agency and the mother of a fifteen-month-old, described it this way: "You basically just always feel like you're doing a horrible job at everything. You're not spending as much time with your baby as you want, you're not doing the job you want to be doing at work, you're seeing your friends hardly ever."[105]

What *has* changed since Hochschild wrote is that men have joined in the scramble. Husbands have increasingly picked up a share of the unpaid domestic work, even if they still aren't doing half of it. Between this and their paid work, husbands too are exhausted.[106] Everyone today is working a second shift.

And life is made still more complicated by the fact that, even when parents are home with their kids, technology allows work demands to intrude on family life. More than seven in ten US workers check their work email account on weekends, almost four in ten check it after 11 p.m., and more than half keep on top of their work emails while on vacation. This means that even during the few hours they're home, Americans are never really off paid work.[107]

For many American parents raising children, the time crunch is exacerbated by the fact that they are in the "sandwich generation," and also have aging parents for whom they need to provide care.[108] One-quarter of Americans with a parent aged sixty-five or older report that the parent requires care or help handling affairs.[109] Most of the family members who provide this care are also employed,[110] and a third report that providing this assistance is stressful.[111]

American parents use a number of strategies to deal with the time overload. For one thing, they spend roughly eight fewer hours a week on housework than families did in 1965.[112] They also cut back on cooking: in the 1960s, American parents overall spent two-and-a-half hours a day cooking; today they devote fewer than two hours. (Most of that decrease comes from women spending less time cooking.) Further, today's parents multitask when they can, trying to clean or squeeze in a few emails while watching their children. Mothers tend to spend ten more extra hours per week multitasking than fathers do. Some researchers suspect this is the reason that mothers generally feel more rushed than fathers.[113]

Working parents also jettison other areas of their life outside work and children. This means they spend far less time with their partners eating together, socializing with friends, or working on projects around the house than they did in decades past.[114] They also cut back on sleep—working mothers get three fewer hours of sleep a week than mothers who don't work for pay.[115] And they have less leisure time. Working mothers get nine fewer hours a week than women who don't work for pay.[116] Unsurprisingly, most working mothers say they have too little spare time. The majority of married fathers say the same.[117]

But does the fact that parents feel overloaded really matter in the larger scope of their lives? All of us have had times when being busy and a little stressed nudged us to be more efficient but didn't really detract from our quality of life. Is that what's happening with our current overload? Unfortunately not. The constant rushing and scrambling take a significant toll on Americans' happiness.[118] And it undermines the joy parents feel from having kids.[119] As discussed in chapter 1, the "happiness gap" between parents and nonparents is much larger in the United States by a substantial margin than in other developed countries.

In some countries with pro-family policies, parents are happier than nonparents (and these policies increase parents' happiness without lowering nonparents' happiness).[120] In free-market countries like ours, though, with fewer or none of these policies, the boost in satisfaction that parents get from having children is overwhelmed by the strain they cause. As a result, parents are significantly less happy than adults who don't have children. That's particularly tragic given that we have both the knowledge and more than enough resources to do better.

We need to pay attention to the costs of having our lives so thoroughly dominated by the economic treadmill we're all running on. Among these costs are the toll that feeling constantly tired and stressed, and having little time to savor quiet moments and routines, takes on our lives. There are also the costs of every family paring its family life down to what it considers its most treasured moments—a bedtime ritual or an athletic game, for example—while having to abandon other activities like tromping off to a park together just to fill the time or planning a child's birthday rather than having a prepackaged party at a local party center.[121] Our civic lives also suffer, as added time at work and parenting leave us less time for community engagement, including PTA meetings, the bowling leagues that Robert Putnam made famous, or political engagement.[122] Yet the power exercised by the market and the competition associated with it make it difficult for people even to imagine living other kinds of lives besides the frenetic existences we lead today.

American parents' unhappiness is beginning to come home to roost. By the middle of 2017, US fertility rates had declined to their lowest level since the government began tracking these numbers in 1909.[123] Part of this reduction is a good thing, since it reflects a drop in births to teen mothers. But birth rates for all other age groups below age forty have fallen as well. All told, these shifts now put us well below the birth rate needed to maintain our population level.[124] Our nation had long been one of the few wealthy democracies with fertility rates high enough that we didn't have to worry about adequately reproducing our society. No longer. Raising kids has become so difficult that adults are simply having fewer of them.

Keynes failed to foresee Americans' overwork, not because his predictions about productivity were wrong, but because he didn't account for the collective-action problems that dominate Americans' lives today. Many American families are working longer and harder at their jobs so they don't fall off the increasingly steep dirt pile in the king of the hill game we're all playing. And when adults have finished those long hours at work, they intensively parent their kids in the hope that they too can maintain their place on the pile when they become adults. The intensity of the competition to stay up on that slope is interfering with the quality of Americans' lives up and down the dirt pile, not just those at the bottom. Playing this "negative-sum game," although some families do better than others, takes a serious toll on everyone.

The whole point about collective-action problems is that they can't be solved by individual action alone. And although policymakers could change the slope of our economic dirt pile or make the rules of the game more humane for families, they haven't done so. To make matters worse, as we'll see, free-market family policy doesn't just make American parents' daily lives stressful and overwhelming, it undermines the very structure and stability of American families.

The Economics of Disconnected Adults and Unstable Families

A photo posted on the Facebook page of the East Liverpool Police Department in East Liverpool, Ohio, went viral toward the end of 2016. In the picture, a couple is slumped in the front seat of a car, both unconscious from drug overdoses. Behind them, looking over their shoulders, is a four-year-old dressed in a dinosaur T-shirt, still strapped into his car seat. He is staring, expressionless, in the direction of the photographer.[1]

That picture circulated so widely because it hauntingly illustrates the opioid epidemic's damage to families. News coverage of the photo described the unstable family dynamics behind the picture. It turns out that it was the child's grandmother and her boyfriend who had overdosed in the front seat. (Both survived.) The child's parents, who had never married and were no longer together, had lost custody long before due to their own drug issues. The media reports that followed the picture's release recognized the link between the economic devastation to working-class communities and the opioid crisis.[2] "It's the old story," the child's great-aunt said of the parents. "No education. No jobs."[3]

Attention to the link between a broken economy and broken families represents progress of a sort: Stories of crack cocaine use back in the 1980s, and especially of "crack mothers" in that era, ignored the link between drug use and economic restructuring in favor of demonizing crack addicts as dangerous criminals. Media treatment of the opioid epidemic hasn't done the same. (And, yes, the skeptical reader will wonder how much this shift has to do with actual progress and how much it has to do with the perception that crack addicts are black and opioid addicts are white.) Yet even the more complicated story told today doesn't connect all the dots. In particular, it doesn't explain how economic inequality and instability create the family instability that is contributing to the opioid epidemic.

This chapter connects these dots. In doing so, it also explains how the damage to families caused by the market undermines the American Dream.[4] Children need stable family relationships to build the strong foundation that will enable them to become sound adults. Stable family relationships are also critical to adults' happiness and well-being, not to mention a key factor in knitting adults into the social fabric of their community. Unsettle the stability of families, and you undermine the basic structure of society.

Despite this, US policymakers continue to make decisions about economic policy based solely on their view of whether it would be good for the economy, ignoring the devastation that these decisions wreak on Americans and their families. Meanwhile, commentators treat the rise of nonmarital childbirth and single-parent families as a cultural rather than an economic problem, blaming parents' lack of personal responsibility. What is their solution to the rise of fragile families spurred on by free-market policy? More free-market policy! To counteract parents' supposed lack of personal responsibility, they must be re-quired to stand on their own financial feet and negotiate market forces on their own.[5] The result of our policy system is that our country now has the dubious honor of having the most unstable families of any of the world's developed na-tions.[6] Meanwhile US family instability continues to grow, at devastating costs to both grownups and children, as well as to our communities and the nation.

THE RISE OF FAMILY INSTABILITY

In 1965, Daniel Patrick Moynihan's report, "The Negro Family: The Case for National Action" (henceforth the Moynihan Report), cast a spotlight on the way that harsh market forces were undermining urban African American fam-ilies.[7] The Moynihan Report described an alarming increase in black, single-parent families. Nearly one in four African American wives living in cities were divorced, separated, or living apart, compared with one in twelve white women. The rate of nonmarital births among nonwhite women had also shot up to one in four. Meanwhile, the rate of nonmarital births among white women barely rose in the decades before, staying close to one in thirty-three.[8]

The report dramatically demonstrated the link between unemployment among African American men and changes in family structure. One particularly persuasive chart, reproduced here as Figure 4.1, superimposed a line graph of the rates of unemployed men from the previous year on top of a line graph of the annual rates of women who were separated the following year. The rates of marital separations closely tracked men's unemployment rates: the number of separations climbed when unemployment rose and dropped when unemploy-ment fell.[9] A similar graph showed that nonmarital births also closely tracked men's unemployment.[10] These negative effects of market forces needed to be

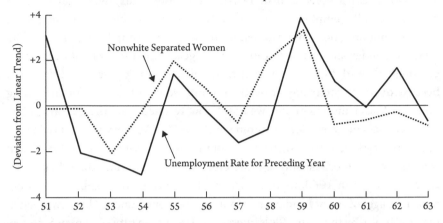

Figure 4.1. Unemployment Rate for Nonwhite Males Aged 14 and Older versus Percentage of Nonwhite Married Women Separated from Their Husbands. Source: Moynihan (1965).

taken into account in constructing public policy, the Moynihan Report argued. The market had to be regulated in order to support stable family structures.[11]

While the Moynihan Report made a crucial link between market forces and family instability, this critical revelation was eclipsed by the report's significant flaws. Most grievously, Moynihan's characterization of African American single-parent families was insulting and misleading. He described these families as a "tangle of pathologies," ignoring the fact that the single mothers he condemned were generally doing the best job possible under extremely difficult circumstances.[12] According to the report, these supposed pathologies were responsible for the children's bleak outcomes.[13] Critics justifiably asserted that this was a classic case of blaming the victims, given that racism had led to much of black men's unemployment in the first place, as well as to children's poor outcomes. As William Ryan's influential critique charged, "The Moynihan Report singled out 'the unstable Negro family' as the cause of Negro inequality. But the statistics reflect current effects of contemporary discrimination. They are results not causes."[14]

Ultimately, the controversy over the report's considerable flaws obscured its astute recognition of the relationship between unemployment and unstable families, as well as the need for market regulation to address this connection. The controversy also stifled nuanced discussion of the relationship between economics and family form for a generation. It was not until the sociologist William Julius Wilson released his 1987 book, *The Truly Disadvantaged*, that a more complex conversation about this relationship began.[15] In it, Wilson helped explain how men's diminished job prospects translated into unstable families. To do so, he constructed a "male marriageable pool index," which showed the number of fully employed—and therefore "marriageable"—nonwhite men for every hundred nonwhite women in the same age group.[16] Beginning in the 1950s, the index showed, the ratio of marriageable men to women became increasingly skewed, first as a result of rising male unemployment and then also because of young men's higher death and imprisonment rates. (The increasing number of black men in prison, we now know, resulted from the nation's public policy of mass incarceration beginning in the 1970s. At every stage of the criminal justice system—arrests, charges, sentencing, and time served—black men were treated far more harshly and therefore served more time than their white counterparts.[17]) In 1960, there were almost seventy employed black men between the ages of twenty and twenty-four for every one hundred black women in that age group. By the early 1980s, there were fewer than fifty such men for every one hundred women.[18] As these ratios grew more disproportionate, marriage rates fell, while nonmarital birth rates rose in tandem with the index. Black women weren't marrying, Wilson demonstrated, because there were too few economically stable men to marry.

Wilson's research undercut the widespread view that nonmarital births among black women had shot up because these women were having more children than in the past. In fact, Wilson showed, women in inner-city communities were having fewer children than they used to, not more. How could the rising number of kids born outside marriage be explained? While these women's overall birth rates had decreased, they'd fallen somewhat less than their marriage rates. That meant there were fewer children overall in these communities, but more nonmarital children.[19]

The Rise of Fragile Families among the Poor

In the decades since Wilson's book was published, we've learned still more about the relationship between economics and family form. For one thing, it has become clear that the poor black families that Moynihan and Wilson wrote about were the proverbial canaries in the coal mine. In the second third of the twentieth century, nonmarital births by white women in poor communities began to climb as well.[20] Instability in families, it became clear, has far more to do with class than with race.

Some of the most important research about the expanding group of nonmarital children and their parents comes from the Fragile Families and Child Wellbeing Study, undertaken by researchers at Princeton and Columbia Universities. That study has followed a broad cross-section of nearly five thousand children of all races from twenty large US cities who were born between

1998 and 2000, three-quarters of them to unmarried parents. Researchers interviewed mothers and fathers from the time of their children's birth through the years that followed, as well as periodically assessed the children's development, health, and home environment.[21]

The Fragile Families Study dispelled a number of common beliefs about the families of nonmarital children. Researchers learned that the reason for the increase in out-of-wedlock kids didn't stem from the fact that their mothers sought to bear and raise children by themselves. In fact, at the time of their child's birth, most of the mothers were in a relationship with the child's father, and the two were planning to raise the child together. What's more, most of these couples were cohabitating, although many had not started living together until the pregnancy was discovered. And most of the couples who weren't cohabiting were romantically involved. Further, whether they were living with the mother or not, most of the fathers were highly involved with their children in the period after birth. On top of all that, the unmarried parents generally held marriage in high esteem, wanted to be married themselves, and agreed that marriage is the best basis for family life. In fact, at the time of their child's birth, most couples believed they were likely to marry.[22]

Sadly, few of these couples' aspirations for their relationships came to pass. Fewer than one in four couples ever married. And by five years after their child's birth, only one in six of all couples unmarried at the time of birth were married. What's more, at that five-year mark, whether they had married or not, only about one-third of the nonmarital parents in the study were living together at all.[23]

Why did so few of these couples marry, given that they wanted and expected to marry, and thought it would be good for their child? The answer centered on economics. The unmarried parents associated marriage with economic stability and were waiting to marry until they achieved it. One young Latino father put it this way: "I want to be secure ... I don't want to get married and be like we have no money or nothing. . . . I want to get my little house in Long Island, you know, white-picket fence, and two-car garage, me hitting the garbage cans when I pull up in the driveway."[24] As the sociologists Kathryn Edin and Maria Kefalas, who spent five years talking to poor single mothers, described it in separate research, the low-income Americans who disproportionately have children outside of marriage "have embraced a set of surprisingly mainstream norms about marriage and the circumstances in which it should occur."[25] These parents want the American Dream. The problem is that they are "far less likely to reach their 'white picket fence dream'" than their more well-off peers.[26] Economic restructuring means that, for young people in poor communities, achieving economic stability is a long shot. But until they've achieved it, they don't want to marry.

Not all groups of young people put off marriage until they were financially stable. Mexican American fathers tended to marry their child's mother despite not being able to fulfill the breadwinner role. But African American and white parents generally waited to marry until a male partner, particularly, had a reasonably stable income.[27] (In focusing on the man as the breadwinner, these young people overlook the many families today *(in fact, three in ten households) in which women are the primary or coequal breadwinners.[28])

What should we make of the fact that young couples are postponing marriage until they are economically stable? The sociologist Andrew Cherlin makes the case that the role of marriage has changed for young adults. In the mid-twentieth century, marriage was thought of as a "cornerstone" of adult life, the first step toward adulthood.[29] Today, marriage has become the last step, the "capstone" of adult life—something that young adults do only after having acquired the other indicia of adulthood, including a stable job, a place to live, a partner with whom they cohabit, and sometimes even a child.[30] This "capstone" view of marriage holds for young people across the socioeconomic spectrum.[31] What differs across this spectrum is whether young people will be able to obtain a stable job. Those who are unlikely ever to achieve economic stability don't wait to marry before they have children.[32]

The Fragile Families researchers found that economics didn't just get in the way of marriage directly, by causing a mother not to marry her partner because he wasn't sufficiently stable economically. Skewed sex ratios between fully employed and therefore marriageable men and women also indirectly influenced whether couples got married by affecting other facets of their relationships. When marriageable men were in shorter supply, men were less likely to commit to relationships, probably because more potential partners were readily available to them. Skewed sex ratios also reduced the quality of the couples' relationships, making it less likely that women would characterize their partners as fair and willing to compromise, and more likely to report domestic violence.[33] The greater the difference in the sex ratios, the less likely it was that unmarried parents who had already had a child together would marry. In fact, an increase in ten marriageable men per one hundred women, the Fragile Families researchers found, was associated with a 16 percent increase in the chance that a couple with a non-marital child would marry. The differences in sex ratios between white, black, and Latino marriageable men and women turned out to explain much of black parents' lower marriage rates compared to parents of other groups.[34]

Beyond skewed sex ratios, researchers have shown that poverty and economic instability also depress marriage rates by encouraging behaviors like excessive drinking and use of drugs. Some experts have begun to talk about these behaviors as arising from the absence of "competing reinforcers." By this, they mean that people who live in poor communities often have few rewards in life.

One commentator put it this way: "If you're living in a poor neighborhood deprived of options, there's a certain rationality to keep taking a drug that will give you some temporary pleasure."[35] Mothers are less likely to stay with men, though, who develop problems with alcohol or drugs.[36]

But if members of poor communities don't marry for economic reasons, why don't they stop having kids as well? The explanation turns in part on shifting norms: The once-strict cultural prohibition on having a child outside of marriage has weakened significantly across Americans generally.[37] (A few groups, though, including Mexican Americans, have hung onto that prohibition more tightly.[38]) This shift, and the greater availability of and options for birth control, give young people today a larger range of choices when it comes to starting a family than past generations had. How unmarried young people respond to this less stringent prohibition on nonmarital births, though, is heavily influenced by their economic situation. Those who are college-bound generally wait until they are married to have children, likely because they believe that having a child would cause them to miss out on valuable education, job advancement, or a relationship that might lead to marriage. Poor youth don't make the same calculations, in large part because their prospects for rewarding education and careers are slim, and their chances of a successful marriage unlikely. Because of this, they increasingly come to focus on being a parent as a way of making their place in the world. Edin and Kefalas put it this way:

> For a lack of compelling alternatives, poor youth . . . often begin to eagerly anticipate children and the social role of parents at a remarkably tender age. While middle-class teens and twenty-somethings anticipate completing college and embarking on careers, their lower-class counterparts can only dream of such glories. . . . Visions of shared children stand in vivid, living color against a monochromatic backdrop of otherwise dismal prospects.[39]

This focus leads many young women in these communities, if they use birth control at all, to abandon it early in a romantic relationship, neither intentionally planning to get pregnant nor trying to prevent it. When they do get pregnant, many young men and women in the inner city see the pregnancy as a gift.[40]

While cultural commentators often depict poor women who give birth to children outside of marriage as dysfunctional and blame them for having ruined their own economic futures, Edin and Kefalas's work disputes these views. Poor women's assessments of their career and marriage prospects are correct, they assert; they are vastly grimmer than those of their middle-class counterparts in our free-market economy, even without kids.[41] Indeed, some economic analyses show that their prospects are so bleak that early childbearing doesn't hinder their lifetime earnings much. In fact, having children early may actually spur this group of women to earn more later on.[42] In the context of these young mothers' lives, early childbearing makes sense. All people, Edin and Kefalas point out, have a deep psychological need to create meaning in their lives. Barred from other opportunities for validation by their poverty, young women in poor communities come to focus on the one role left for them to succeed in: being a mother. Again, in Edin and Kefalas's words:

> Over the last half-century, new opportunities to gain esteem and valida-
> tion have opened for American women. But these new alternatives—
> the rewarding careers and professional identities—aren't equally
> available. While middle-class women are now reaching new heights of
> self-actualization, poor women are relegated to unstable, poorly paid,
> often mind-stultifying jobs with little room for advancement. Thus,
> for the poor, childbearing often rises to the top of the list of potential
> meaning-making activities from mere lack of competition.[43]

Those who disparage poor mothers who have had children out of wedlock as misguided, shortsighted, or welfare grifters, are therefore themselves misguided when it comes to what motivates these women. Brielle, a thirty-two-year-old African American mother of four children, notes that people outside her community don't understand why single mothers like herself have babies: "A lot of people . . . say [young girls have babies] for money from welfare. It's not for that. . . . It's not even to keep the *guy*. It's just to have somebody . . . to take *care* of, or somebody to *love* or whatever."[44] These single mothers recognize that being raised in a two-parent family is better for children than being raised in a single-parent family. But they badly want a child and understand that their likelihood of finding a partner to build a stable family with is low. And while they may hope the father of their child ends up being that stable partner down the road, few of the men are willing or able to stay the course.[45]

Which brings us to the men. After Kathryn Edin finished her research on why young women in the inner city got pregnant out of wedlock, she turned to focus on their male counterparts. With the sociologist Timothy Nelson, she spent seven years talking to fathers in inner cities. What they discovered was that these fathers' entry into parenthood was similarly driven by grim lives and blocked economic opportunities. Less-educated men have seen their work opportunities dwindle in the past several decades, largely as a result of the drop in manufacturing jobs. In the 1970s, two-thirds of men with less than a high school education worked full-time. Since the 1990s, their full-time employment has hovered at around 55 percent. The lack of steady employment for these men means that many wind up working part-time, taking on a succession of temporary jobs, or being unemployed. And when they do find work, their jobs are overwhelmingly menial, with little status or security.[46] With so many paths closed off to them, these young men, like their female counterparts, see children as giving them the rare opportunity for success. As Edin and Nelson put it, for many young men in the inner city, "a child—so pure and innocent—is a symbol, almost a magic wand that has the power to vanquish the oppressive sense of 'negativity' that quite literally surrounds those who come of age in the inner-urban core."[47]

Once their children are born, these men are committed to being there for them, and, to do so, seek to solidify their relationship with their baby's mother. Many obstacles, though, stand in the way.[48] For one thing, there is little that suggests that the parents, who often weren't seriously involved before the pregnancy, will be compatible over the long term.[49] And many causes of dissension are likely to arise. Some young men won't be able to resist behaviors they engaged in before their baby was born, like abusing drugs or alcohol or engaging in casual sex—behaviors more common to communities in distress, where social controls have been reduced.[50] In addition, many poor men attempt to assert patriarchal authority in the home, perhaps because they have lost it elsewhere. Their partners, though, resist, instead seeking the more equal gender bargain that most middle-class women have achieved.[51] Tensions over the father's financial contributions to the family are also common. Finally, few of the men who grow up in poor communities with bad schools and little paid work will have the kind of practice trading off short-term pleasures for long-term gain that successful relationships require.[52] Not many relationships between parents will survive all these perils.

Most fathers try to stay involved in their child's life after their relationship with the mothers ends, but this turns out to be hard. Our legal system, built on the free-market view that it is parents, not the state, who are financially responsible for kids, imposes child-support obligations that many men can't meet, meanwhile denying fathers legal help in spending time with their kids when mothers are unwilling to allow visitation. And despite their commitment to being there, few fathers have the wherewithal to follow through on doing half the hard work of caretaking. On top of all this, both mothers and fathers often move on to have children with other partners, which creates logistical issues and tensions that get in the way of a sustained father–child relationship. So do the drug and alcohol problems and the prison spells that many inner-city fathers experience. With these obstacles standing in the way, their goal of a long-term relationship with their child is likely to become one more failure in a life of failures. Fathers then move on to new relationships and new children for whom they hope to do better.[53]

The lesson in all this is that if a country regulates its economy in ways that provide young people with secure economic paths forward, they will tend to wait to have kids until they're in a better position to parent them. Because we don't, a far larger proportion of US teenagers give birth than teens in almost all other wealthy countries. By way of comparison, Denmark's, Finland's, and Sweden's teen birth rates are all one-third or less of our own.[54,55]

The Rise of Fragile Families among the Working Class

If you step back and think about the discussion so far, you can put together the pieces about where this discussion is headed. The instability in inner-city black families that the Moynihan Report charted in the 1950s and 1960s turned out to be less a problem of race than of class. This instability spread to poor families of all races and ethnicities by the 1980s. In that same decade, wages began to drop not just for men at the lowest income levels, but also for middle-income men. Meanwhile economic instability, which had been largely confined to the poor, expanded into the working class, and even made some gains in the middle class. As this economic precariousness made its way up the income ladder, so did fragile family patterns.[56] That's how we got from the black, inner-city, single-parent families that Moynihan focused on to the white four-year-old in East Liverpool, Ohio, in the photo described at the beginning of the chapter. And it's also how we came to top the list of wealthy countries when it comes to family instability.[57]

In the introduction to this book, I used income to distinguish socioeconomic positions among families. But several other indicators give us information about class in American society, including wealth and education. Because people generally get married and bear children when they're relatively young and haven't traveled far along their earning trajectory, researchers tend to use education completed as a measure of class when they look at issues of family structure. Because of that, in the rest of the discussion on family structure in this chapter, I'll do the same.

Americans with high school but not college degrees, the education level most identified with the working class, make up more than half of American adults. In the middle of the twentieth century, adults in this group were the most likely to be married. But since the late 1980s, this group's marriage rates have plummeted, divorce rates have risen, and rates of nonmarital births and single-parent families have skyrocketed.[58] The sociologist Bradford Wilcox sounded the alarm on this issue in 2010:

[T]he newest and perhaps most consequential marriage trend of our time concerns the broad center of our society, where marriage, that iconic middle-class institution, is foundering. Among Middle

Americans, defined here as those with a high-school but not a (four-year) college degree, rates of non-marital childbearing and divorce are rising, even as marital happiness is falling.... In these respects, the family lives of today's high-school graduates are beginning to resemble those of high-school dropouts—with all the attendant problems of economic stress, partner conflict, single parenting, and troubled children—rather than resembling the family lives they dreamed of when they threw their mortarboards into the air.[59]

Just like their more- and less-educated counterparts, young, working-class Americans still want to wed.[60] Yet the large drop in good, middle-wage jobs in recent decades means that the chances that these young people will marry are much lower than in the past. Decades ago, young men in this group would most likely have ended up in manufacturing jobs with stable wages, benefits, and a ladder to supervisory jobs. Today, they're far more likely to wind up in service jobs with lower pay, less stability, no benefits, and no ladder up. Because of this, women in this group are marrying less and have cut back on childbearing, just as less-educated women did. But like the poor women discussed earlier in the chapter, they haven't cut back on births as much as they have on marriages. The end result has been a steep rise in nonmarital births among the working class.[61]

And even when working-class couples do marry, which they do more often than their counterparts with less education, they often cycle through a pattern of divorce, remarriage, and blended families that sociologist Andrew Cherlin has dubbed "the marriage-go-round."[62] Compared with college-educated Americans, those in the working class have a much higher chance of divorce and are far less likely to consider themselves very happily married. What accounts for these differences? Law professors June Carbone and Naomi Cahn identify economic issues as the central driver. Working-class husbands' insecure jobs and wages create significant family stress. As a result, their wives more often need to work to support the family than in the past. But these wives are less likely to want to work for pay than professional women since the jobs open to them are usually less flexible and less personally rewarding. Further, these families can't afford the time-saving measures that professional families can to ease the time crunch of two-worker families, like good-quality takeout meals, professional house cleaning, and nannies. On top of this, perhaps because they feel disempowered in the workplace, the husbands in these families generally haven't adopted the more equal gender roles in the household that college-educated men have, and their tired wives resent this. All this creates significant strife in working-class families that leads to higher rates of divorce.[63]

FREE-MARKET FAMILY POLICY COMES HOME
TO ROOST: FAMILY INSTABILITY TODAY

The result of our policymakers' laissez-faire approach to the economy, as well as the inequality and insecurity it has fostered, is that stable families in America today are largely the province of the college-educated.[64] Chapter 1 presented a snapshot of the instability of American family structures. I return to these issues in more depth here to show the relationship between fragile families and the nation's free-market family policy.

Americans still believe in marriage as an institution more than adults in most wealthy countries, where cohabitation has gained more traction. Because of that, our marriage rates are higher than in other wealthy democracies.[65] Yet our marriages are also more prone to failure. By the five-year mark, more than one-fifth of married couples in the United States are either separated or divorced.[66] That makes our divorce rates higher than those of our peer countries.[67] In the United States, cohabiting relationships are even less stable.[68] Almost half of cohabiting couples break up within five years, and the breakup rates appear to be increasing.[69]

The instability of American couples means that significantly fewer American children will grow up with both parents than will children in other countries. Among US children born to married parents, approximately one-fourth will see their parents break up by the time they're twelve, compared with less than 15 percent in Norway and France and less than 10 percent in Belgium.[70] When it comes to cohabiting couples with children, 45 percent of US children born to these relationships will see their parents break up by age twelve, compared with only 21 percent in Norway, 16 percent in France, and 9 percent in the Netherlands. And US children will experience a greater number of family transitions, such as a parent's new partner moving in or out, than kids in other countries.[71] Further, more than 21 percent of kids aged zero to five in the United States live with just their mother, the highest rate by far of any OECD country. By comparison, this figure is 8 percent in Finland and 10 percent in France.[72] Overall, only 56 percent of US children are born to married or cohabiting parents who will still be together by the child's twelfth birthday.[73]

The widening relationship gap between the college-educated and other Americans relates to whether they'll enter marriage in the first place. As Figure 1.5 showed, those with college degrees are far more likely to marry than those with less education. Three-quarters of college-educated women in their early forties are married; that percentage drops almost twenty points for women who haven't finished high school.[74] Marriage is alive and well among college graduates. It's being crushed by the economy for everyone else.[75]

The chasm between the college-educated and other Americans also applies to divorce. Half of all first marriages last for two decades. But college-educated women's marriages have an eight in ten chance of lasting that long; those with high school degrees or less, meanwhile, have a chance just about half that large.[76] In recent years divorce rates overall seem to be declining somewhat, but that's largely because less-educated Americans are marrying less frequently than they used to, therefore removing the least stable relationships from the pool of marriages that could end in divorce.[77]

A growing gap has also opened up when it comes to nonmarital births. In 2017, of all births to women without a high school degree, slightly more than half—52 percent—were nonmarital. Similarly, of all births to women with high school degrees but no college education, 50 percent of births were nonmarital. In contrast, of all births to women with college degrees, only 13 percent were nonmarital. As June Carbone and Naomi Cahn point out, in the 1980s, working-class women's nonmarital birth rates were much closer to those of women with college degrees. Today, they are far closer to those of women without a high school degree.[78]

All this means that whether kids will be raised in a strong, stable family depends a great deal on whether they are fortunate enough to be born to parents who are college-educated.[79] In families headed by college-educated adults, eight in ten fourteen-year-olds live with both parents. In families headed by adults without high school degrees, just half of fourteen-year-olds do.[80] When it comes to inner-city kids born outside of marriage, the level of family instability is still higher. By the time they reach kindergarten, about four in five will have experienced a parental relationship change or a half-sibling added to the family.[81]

In sum, largely because of expanding inequality and insecurity, this generation of American kids will have had to deal with a more complicated and less stable set of family ties than any group of US kids before them. And under free-market policy, many will have to do this under extremely challenging economic circumstances.[82]

THE COSTS OF FAMILY INSTABILITY FOR ADULTS

Should we view the growing number of single-parent families and the high degree of family instability in the United States as problems that we should try to fix? Some of my closest family law colleagues argue no, contending that the upswing in the rate of single-parent families should be viewed neutrally, and treated as simply a normal variation in US family form. Their views are based on the best of motives: they want to avoid the narrow moralizing of past generations, as well as to ensure that they don't stigmatize families already burdened by inequality.

My colleagues are certainly right that the families who fit these patterns deserve our support. What is more, given the combined burdens of working the long hours needed to support a family and caring for children, most US single mothers deserve canonization rather than the vilification they too often receive from policymakers. Yet there are still strong reasons to be troubled by the rise of these patterns.

For one thing, the class divide in family forms is, for the most part, not the result of robust free choice by parents. Most of the adults in fragile families didn't shun stable marriages because they felt the institution was too confining.[83] To the contrary, most would prefer to be in a stable marriage. Treating these increasingly prevalent patterns as a simple cultural variation or a matter of free choice ignores the desires of most of the people involved. To be sure, there are single adults, including single parents, who more fully choose their lot. This isn't true for most, though. Approaching fragile families as simply a normal variation of family form also ignores the structural roots of the problem. Access to stable relationships, simply put, shouldn't depend on your economic class.

For another thing, the instability of their family ties disserves these adults' well-being. The economic changes of the past fifty years have loosened the ties of millions of Americans to work and family, the two institutions that generally provide the most structure to Americans' daily lives. Andrew Cherlin calls this shift the "casualization of the daily lives of the would-be working class."[84] By this, he means that many of these young people drift through their work lives taking on a succession of limited-term jobs with no prospects of advancement. They also cycle through one nonmarital relationship after another, with no firm sense of the commitment and stability that a long-term relationship could bring. The absence of a clear path forward at work or home means they have less sense of purpose than did their parents, as well as less sense that anything in life is worth investing significant time and energy in.[85]

Recall economist and happiness researcher Carol Graham's statement about what makes for a happy life: "A stable marriage, good health, and enough—but not too much—income are good for happiness. Unemployment, divorce, and economic instability are terrible for it."[86] Being deprived of purpose and meaning in both work and home life, as well as of the routine rhythms of life that give it structure like getting up for work and home for dinner, is a recipe for disaster— the opposite of the American Dream's promise of a rich, full life for adults. By regulating the economy without taking into account the well-being of families, our policymakers have consigned an increasingly large proportion of Americans to these diminished lives. This helps explain why the United States scored seventeenth of forty advanced countries in terms of how satisfied adults are with their lives, despite the fact that America is far richer than most of the countries that beat us out.[87] As the British economist Richard Layard observed in his classic discussion of happiness, "[I]n every study, family relationships (and our close private life) are more important than any single factor affecting our happiness."[88]

The circumstances that free-market family policy fosters—unstable families and jobs, and high levels of economic inequality and insecurity—also play a role in our nation's skyrocketing rates of anxiety and depression. Although we often think of both conditions as purely psychological disorders, remember the World Health Organization's observation, mentioned in chapter 1, that "[m]ental health is produced socially: The presence or absence of mental health is above all a social indicator and therefore requires social, as well as individual, solutions."[89] Richard Wilkinson and Kate Pickett have demonstrated the strong connection between the incidence of mental illness in a country and the extent of the country's economic inequality.[90] Why might mental health problems be more prevalent in free-market systems that foster inequality? We know that when people are disconnected—from other people, from meaningful work, from status, from a future that makes sense to them—they are far more prone to suffer anxiety and depression.[91] And all these circumstances are the consequence of free-market family policy in the United States.

Free-market policy also helps explain our growing opioid epidemic. When individuals have no driving purpose in life, when their work and family ties don't weave them tightly into the fabric of the community, and when they feel economically outmatched by others and financially insecure, many turn to self-medication.[92] To be sure, pharmaceutical companies have played a major role in this crisis. But it is no accident that the areas that have been hit hardest are places of high economic dislocation. This helps explain the rise in "deaths of despair" that the economists Angus Deaton and Anne Case discovered among less-educated middle-aged whites—the high rates of suicides, fatal drug overdoses, and alcohol-related deaths.[93] We can draw a straight line between free-market family policy and Deaton and Case's conclusions that these deaths are, at base, caused by "a loss of the structures that provide meaning to life."[94] This also helps to explain why suicides have gone up by 25 percent in the past generation, taking almost 45,000 American lives in 2016.[95] As noted in chapter 1, these suicides are related to family status: In 2005, single middle-aged women were almost three times as likely to commit suicide as married women. And single men were three-and-a-half times more likely than married men to take their own lives.[96]

The rending of the social fabric that spurred these deaths of despair represents not only a personal and social tragedy for the people and communities involved, but also a political tragedy in the making. White working-class Americans who grew up with visions of achieving the American Dream have had their hands pried away from the Dream finger by finger.[97] This explains their sense that the system is rigged against them, as well as their sense of anger and loss. Donald Trump largely traded on these emotions to get elected president. Those who voted for him were right in thinking that the system is rigged, even if many of them got it wrong in thinking that the problem lies with minorities or immigrants. The problem, instead, is our broken free-market system.

THE COSTS OF FAMILY INSTABILITY FOR CHILDREN

These fragile-family patterns are associated with problems for children as well as adults. Children raised by a single parent, particularly in an unstable household, tend to do worse than those raised in a stable, two-parent family. They are less likely than other children to finish high school, more likely to have lower earnings when they enter the workforce, and more likely to be poor in adulthood. That doesn't mean, of course, that single-parent and unstable families can't produce sound children. They can, and many of them do. But the chances they'll do so are lower than those of stable, two-parent families.[98] To understand why this is, and in what ways two-parent families make a difference, we need to know more about the effects of raising kids in different family forms.

One critical thing to know is that much of the difference between children's outcomes in single-parent and two-parent families aren't caused by family form at all. A significant portion of these differences are associated with what social scientists call "selection effects." By this, they mean that parents who raise kids in stable, two-parent families tend to have somewhat different characteristics from those who raise kids in single-parent families, and these different characteristics are causing much of kids' more positive outcomes rather than the fact that the child lives with both parents.[99] For example, we've already recognized that, in the United States today, better-educated parents are more likely to raise kids in two-parent homes than less-educated parents are. To the extent that it is parents' higher education that is causing kids from two-parent homes to do better than those from single-parent homes, that's a selection effect. Recognize that to the extent that children's better outcomes in two-parent families are driven by selection effects, policies that simply increase the rates of two-parent families wouldn't necessarily improve children's outcomes. For example, to the extent that better outcomes for children of two-parent families derive from the fact that more of them are being raised by parents in better mental health than are kids in single-parent families, persuading two unmarried adults with poor mental health to marry wouldn't improve outcomes for their children. Instead, good public policy that sought to improve children's outcomes would help get these parents the resources that actually caused improved outcomes for kids, like greater access to mental-health services.

In the United States, the single biggest factor responsible for kids' better outcomes in dual-parent families over single-parent families is money.[100]

Dual-parent families have more of it for three big reasons. The first is a selection effect: wealthier adults are more likely to enter and sustain relationships. (While some pro-marriage advocates tout how much wealthier married families are compared to single-parent families, suggesting that marriage *causes* wealth, to a considerable degree, they get the causation backward.) The second reason (and here's where the pro-marriage advocates' claims have some truth) is that, because it's cheaper for two adults to maintain one home rather than two, adults in partnered relationships will tend to have more money.[101] The third reason that dual-parent families are wealthier than single-parent families is one we've discussed for much of this book: our country's absence of public programs that support families who lack high market earnings, particularly when they have young children. The result is that nearly half of single-parent families in the United States—46 percent—are poor. A far lower rate of single-parent families are poor in Finland—12 percent.[102]

Good public policy would reduce the gap in outcomes between children raised in single-parent and dual-parent families through ensuring that all children have the economic support they need. Researchers who compared the gap in school achievement between single-parent and dual-parent families across twelve wealthy countries found that, of the countries compared, the gap was largest in the United States. Our absence of family policy supports, and particularly the absence of a child benefit program, they concluded, accounted for much of the size of our gap. In the researchers' words, "the detriment of single parenthood on children's education, so widely noted in the United States and elsewhere, is not a necessary consequence of single parenthood. Economic assistance to the children . . . can partially offset these detrimental consequences." [103]

There are, though, also ways that stable, two-parent households improve kids' outcomes beyond providing financial advantages, and which don't involve selection effects. Being raised in two-parent households often means that there are two extended families who can offer support.[104] Children in two-parent households on average also receive more parental engagement, more supervision, more support, and more discipline than children raised in households with a single parent.[105] This is partly because single mothers are more stressed than parents in two-parent households.[106] Some of this stress comes from the impossible economic burdens that free-market policy imposes on single-parent families, as well as the dearth of public support it offers, both of which could be eased by better public policies. But some of this stress is simply endemic to being a single parent trying to raise young kids on his or her own. (Even a small taste of solo caregiving can be stressful: The first time that my husband returned from a business trip after we had a second child, leaving me with a toddler and a baby, I was so shell-shocked and (irrationally) angry that I could barely speak to him.) And stressed parents have a tougher time providing the nurturing their kids need.[107]

Other real advantages for kids raised in two-parent homes arise from the fact that nonresident parents are, by and large, much less engaged with their children than parents who live with them. Some of this is a product of the logistical difficulties that come from coordinating parenting among different households. Some is caused by the tension that can result from parents having kids by multiple partners, a frequent occurrence in fragile families. While it's possible that some of these difficulties could be remedied by better public support to sustain the connection between nonresident parents and their children, a portion of the engagement gap between resident and nonresident parents is likely inevitable. Yet the time, attention, and nurturing kids get from both parents turn out to be really important in children's development.[108]

Finally, some preliminary evidence suggests that over and above the negative effects of being raised by a single parent compared with two parents, transitions in family structure, which are endemic to fragile families, may themselves cause children harm.[109] Children have a need for stability, this research suggests, and transitions can be stressful and set back their development. If that is the case, our free-market system, by giving rise to high levels of family instability, is particularly harmful for children.

In sum, while some of the differences in outcomes between children raised in fragile families and those raised in stable, dual-parent families are the result of selection effects, others are not. Some of these differences could be ameliorated by good public policies that supported all forms of families, but others probably remain beyond their reach. All told, the very different upbringings US children are receiving today in fragile families versus stable, two-parent families are increasing the already wide gulf in the United States between the children of the haves and the children of the have-nots. As the sociologist Sara McLanahan put it, the divergence of family patterns by class means that "children who were born to the most-educated women are gaining resources, in terms of parents' time and money, and those who were born to the least-educated women are losing resources."[110] This is a break from the past. In the mid-twentieth century, less money was spent on raising low-income kids than on raising rich kids (although the divide wasn't as great as it is today), but poor kids still received much the same amount of parental time and attention as their better-off peers did.[111] The fact that this is no longer true today is just one more way that free-market policy is killing the American Dream.

MARRIAGE VERSUS COHABITING RELATIONSHIPS

So far, I have been discussing the advantages of stable, two-parent families without considering the role that marriage itself plays. But of course a couple can form a stable, two-parent family without being married. Is that still as good for them and their kids? Put another way: if a long-term committed couple decided to marry rather than cohabit, would this improve outcomes for their children? Or is it just the stable relationship that matters, marriage certificate or no marriage certificate?

The answer here is that marriage yields few, if any, benefits beyond what people get from a stable, cohabiting relationship.[112] The key factor that really makes a difference to adults' and children's well-being is the long-term stable nature of the relationship.[113] And long-term stable relationships can occur among both married and cohabiting couples.

With that said, in the United States today, cohabiting relationships tend to last far less long and be far less stable than marriages. Children in the United States born to cohabiting parents are twice as likely to have their parents separate as those of married parents. Almost half of cohabiting mothers without college degrees will no longer live with the father before their child turns twelve, while fewer than one-fifth of married mothers with college degrees will do the same.[114] Much of the difference in relationship stability is the result of selection effects. For starters, couples who marry tend to be wealthier and more highly educated than those who don't, as well as more certain that they are compatible enough with their partners to make a permanent commitment. All these factors increase the likelihood of long-term relationships.[115]

Yet some of the increased stability of marriages compared with cohabitation likely derives from the fact of marriage itself and its meaning in our culture.[116] The association of marriage with a lifetime commitment and the public vows it entails may make married couples more prone to invest in their relationships and to work through the inevitable difficulties that occur.[117] In those countries where nonmarital partnerships are likeliest to be long-lasting, cultural expectations have arisen that stabilize these relationships as well.[118] In addition, many of these countries give legal rights to unmarried cohabitants, which reinforce the stability of these relationships.[119] In the United States, though, no such stabilizing expectations or legal frameworks have developed around nonmarital relationships. (In fact, when laws allowing "civil unions" were passed that gave same-sex couples the same legal rights as married couples, few same-sex couples entered into them. This wasn't only because they saw these unions as conferring status-class status, but also because the term "civil union" didn't connote a lifetime commitment of love the way "marriage" does.) In the United States, so far, it's largely marriage or bust.

In sum, we have good reasons to treat the decrease in marriage rates and the rise of fragile families as concerns to be addressed rather than as variations on family forms that we should celebrate. Although it is stability rather than marriage that is the relevant concern for public policy, the fact of the matter is that marriage currently makes for more stable relationships in the United States. This, and the fact that, for most Americans, marriage is an integral part of their vision of the good life, are important reasons that we should ensure that access to marriage doesn't depend on economic position. Since not all couples wish to marry, though, we also need to ensure that we have the public supports in place to help strengthen and stabilize cohabiting relationships, particularly those involving children. And because every American child deserves access to the American Dream, we also have to ensure support for single-parent families.

ECONOMIC VERSUS CULTURAL EXPLANATIONS

Some critics would take issue with my claim that economic forces have devastated the family structures of poor and working-class Americans. The problem, they'd maintain, is with the dysfunctional culture that has developed in these communities. Unwillingness to commit to and take responsibility for, as well as work hard at, jobs and relationships, these folks would contend, are the real source of America's family ills.

J. D. Vance's 2016 blockbuster memoir, *Hillbilly Elegy*, which focuses on the dysfunction of Appalachian culture, makes this case. Vance's book became a bestseller in the aftermath of the 2016 elections, with readers treating it as a kind of Rosetta Stone for understanding the views of the white working class that elected Donald Trump. Vance tells the story of the descendants of what he calls the "hillbilly highway," meaning the families who left Appalachia for the Rust Belt in the late 1940s and 1950s in search of a better life. As a youth in one of these Rust Belt communities in the 1990s and 2000s, Vance describes the single-parent families, the drug use, and the poor work habits he grew up in and around. He pushes back against the notion that this dysfunction stemmed from the economic woes that had befallen the community, instead attributing it to the community's roots in the culture of Appalachia.[120]

For example, Vance discusses a summer job he held at a tile distributor near his hometown in Ohio. Although well-paid manufacturing jobs in the Rust Belt had plummeted in the preceding decades, this particular employer paid well enough—$13 an hour to start and $16 for employees who'd been there a few years—to put employees' families well above the poverty line. Yet the managers still had a tough time filling warehouse positions with long-term employees. This, for Vance, supports his claim that the problems in his community "run far deeper than macroeconomic trends and policy." In his words, "Too many young men immune to hard work. Good jobs impossible to fill for any length of time. . . . There is a lack of agency here—a feeling that you have little control over your life and a willingness to blame everyone but yourself. This is distinct from the larger economic landscape of modern America."[121]

But as the sociologist William Julius Wilson recognized, when the economy gets tough, the culture of distressed communities changes in ways that are profoundly damaging.[122] When a community becomes economically troubled, its members tend to become isolated from mainstream patterns of work and other behavior. Economic misery can then exacerbate problematic behaviors like the drug and alcohol use that exist in virtually all communities, while dulling industriousness. The fact that better-off families tend to exit communities that become highly distressed, leaving the worst-off behind, and that those remaining are not as capable of policing rising levels of antisocial behavior, makes things worse. As Wilson describes it, this social decline is inextricably tied to the community's blocked economic opportunities; considering the problematic behaviors and norms apart from their economic determinants misses the picture.[123] The funny thing about this is that Vance comes very close to recognizing this himself. In his memoir, he describes reading Wilson's description of ghetto life and is astounded by its resemblance to life in his own community. In Vance's words, "Wilson's book spoke to me. I wanted to write him a letter and tell him that he had described my home perfectly. That it resonated so personally is odd, however, because he wasn't writing about the hillbilly transplants from Appalachia—he was writing about black people in the inner cities."[124] What the two communities have in common, of course, isn't cultural heritage; in that respect, they are worlds apart. What they share is profound economic distress.

In fact, Vance's story makes sense only if we treat economics as a central driver of the problems he identifies. Vance tells us that the families who left Appalachia in search of a better life in the 1950s generally found that better life in the Rust Belt. This was true for his grandparents, who settled in Middletown, Ohio, at about that time. As he points out, within two generations, the families that took the hillbilly highway to the Rust Belt largely caught up with others in their new communities when it came to income. And during that era, most of the transplants, including his grandparents, believed in hard work. His grandmother represented that larger community of transplants when she told him, "You can do anything you want to."[125] That hardly sounds like the lack of agency and willingness to work hard that Vance saw in the young men at the tile warehouse.

What changed between the late 1940s and 1950s, when these families first arrived in the Rust Belt, and around 2010, when Vance worked in the warehouse? Not Appalachian culture, with its quirks and dysfunction. If anything, that cultural legacy would have diminished during those generations as the transplants assimilated into the wider community.

What changed was the economics. In the 1950s, Middletown had a vibrant working-class community and a bustling downtown. Its largest employer was a steel company, Armco, which employed thousands of workers and paid for the town's nicest parks. But beginning in the 1970s, by Vance's own account, manufacturing began to decline, Armco drastically cut back its hiring, and the town's employment plummeted. Poverty rates ballooned. Because townspeople didn't have enough money, shops were shuttered. Both malls closed, and payday lenders and pawn shops replaced them.

It was only after this decline, while Vance was growing up in the 1990s and early 2000s, that he observed the transplanted Appalachians' attitude of helplessness. That was also when the drug addiction, divorce, and single parenthood he attributes to cultural dysfunction mushroomed. And that was also the era he describes in which "[y]ou can walk through a town where 30 percent of the young men work fewer than twenty hours a week and find not a single person aware of his own laziness."[126] The dysfunctional culture in Middletown looks a lot like the dysfunctional culture these families left behind in poverty-stricken Appalachia, Vance points out. But it looks that way only now that it's poor, just as Appalachia was. Meanwhile, Vance's uncle's family out in well-off Napa Valley, California, is far more functional than the folks in Middletown.[127] So the culture of poverty reappears only when economic conditions get a lot tougher. What does that tell you about what factors are driving the situation?

A more difficult question than whether culture or economics led to the rise of fragile families is whether better economic policies alone today would restore family stability. One troubling recent study suggests that once nonmarital childbirth becomes widespread in a community, even infusions of cash and work opportunities don't cause marriage rates to rebound and nonmarital childbearing rates to diminish.[128] Addressing this issue may be key to public policy that truly supports families.

It's been more than fifty years since the Moynihan Report called attention to the important link between the economy and families' health. In those years, the economic instability that Moynihan warned was devastating African American families spread to poor families generally and, more recently, to the working class. Along with it has come family instability. The result of free-market family policy's laissez-faire attitude when it comes to the market's effects on families has been that the United States has the least stable family relationships of any wealthy country. This means that our children don't get the family structures that would give them their best chance to flourish. Meanwhile, adults are less tightly woven into the social fabric of the community through work and family, less happy, and far more vulnerable to the raging opioid crisis and to deaths of despair. The end result is the scene from the photograph described at the beginning of the chapter, which displayed this unraveling in full color. But even if our family structures are unstable, kids are otherwise getting what they need to flourish under free-market family policy—right?

How We Fail Our Children
Part I—The Caretaking Young
Children Need

The true character of a society is revealed in how it treats its children.
—Nelson Mandela (1997)

The birth of a baby involves one of the biggest transitions—probably *the* biggest transition—that a family will ever make. A new baby not only brings wonder but also places great demands, responsibilities, and stress on the family. Pregnancy is often exhausting for women. Birth takes a physical toll on mothers and requires time for recovery, particularly when complications occur or a cesarean section is necessary. Its aftermath is sometimes accompanied by postpartum depression. Establishing a relationship with, and learning how to care for, a newborn is often joyful, but it is also hard work and stressful. If a mother is breastfeeding, that adds another set of responsibilities and potential adjustments. New babies' schedules are usually demanding and disorienting for parents; sleep is interrupted for months, and care is round-the-clock. And even after babies' schedules have normalized somewhat, they will require long hours of caretaking until they reach school age. On top of all that, the commitments of parenting must be made to mesh with the rest of life, including paid work.

How do different countries deal with this critical transition and these first years? Countries with pro-family policies create the scaffolding to support families through this time. Among other things, public programs ensure that new parents receive a generous period of paid leave from work so that they can recuperate and bond with their new children, they guarantee publicly subsidized caretaking and preschool for kids when parents return to work, they help parents moderate their work hours so that they have time and energy to nurture their kids, and they provide families with cash to help subsidize the cost of kids.[1]

Under free-market family policy, though, we expect families to handle this transition and the critical years that follow completely on their own. How does this work out in practice? When you listen to the accounts of American parents of young children, the word that comes to mind most often is "shell-shocked." As one Baltimore, Maryland, mother put it, "I had no idea how hard it would be."[2] Most of these parents aren't particularly fazed by the difficulty of parenting itself. In fact, many, but not all, find the parenting to be delightful, at least a good bit of the time. What they're shell-shocked by, instead, is the difficulty of keeping all the balls in the air at the same time—meeting the demands of their paid jobs, earning enough money to pay their bills, finding good care situations for their kids, and still having enough time and sanity left over to be good parents in children's early years, when parenting is more than a full-time job by itself.

American parents talk about endlessly interviewing daycare providers who don't seem nearly up to snuff. They describe seemingly interminable waitlists for decent daycare providers. They discuss settling for childcare arrangements that they know aren't great, because they can't afford better. They recount losing jobs they love because they couldn't make their schedule work or simply because they couldn't afford the cost of two kids in daycare on their wages. And they talk over and over about how exhausted they are between traveling to and from work, schlepping kids to and from daycare and to family or friends when they need to work extra hours, while still trying to get enough time with their children. Hearing their accounts gives you the sense that every family is trying furiously to put together a support system from scratch, patching together pieces that, with enough effort, manage to just about keep the family afloat.

Many parents talk about how hard it is emotionally to go back to work just weeks after having a baby, a return required by either an employer's demands or the need for a paycheck. Remember Tricia Olson, discussed in chapter 3, who had to return to work at a tow-truck company less than three weeks after she gave birth? She drank a pot of coffee that first morning to keep her exhaustion in check and then filled her pockets with tissues so she could wipe away her tears while she worked. And even the professional mothers who are comparatively fortunate in our system, some of whom get a full three months of maternity leave, still find that going back to work is really tough because of the long hours their jobs require. Kelly Wallace, a journalist, reports that she burst into tears a few days after returning to work from her leave when her boss told her she'd have to travel to cover a story. She describes her return to work as "anything but easy and seamless. Before I gave birth, I thought I'd return to my hard-charging [job] three months after delivery and pick up exactly where I left off. And then I held my baby and couldn't imagine leaving her for an hour to get a haircut, let alone 12 hours, which is the time I typically logged each day at work before I became a mom. . . . Why hadn't anyone told me how hard it was going to be?"[3]

Mike Cruse, of Alexandria, Virginia, took five unpaid days from his job after his first child, a son, was born. He would have taken more because his wife, Stephanie, was struggling with postpartum depression, but his boss told him he'd lose his job if he didn't return to work. It was really hard on both him and his wife to leave her alone with their newborn son during that time, he says. By the time his daughter was born four years later, Mike had a better job as a warehouse manager. This job didn't provide paid paternity leave either, but he was able to use vacation days to take ten paid days off, even though it meant he'd have no vacation that year. Still, two weeks seemed like far too little by the end of his leave. His wife's physical recovery was slower than the first time, and he would have liked to be home helping her out. He couldn't afford more time off, though.

Two months later Mike reaffirmed that a two-week leave had been too short. Returning to work with a newborn and a recovering wife at home turned out to be extremely stressful. In his words, "I just would lose my cool and get really frustrated . . . with [the baby] not sleeping or her being fussy and not eating, and just not knowing how to fix it." Because of this, he says, those first months, which could have been such a happy time, were really hard. If he'd had his druthers, he'd have taken six to twelve weeks off. What he wants, he says, is "to be involved in every aspect of my children growing up. . . . And not just because I think it would be cool, but because I think that's the way it should be. It shouldn't all be on, you know, my partner."[4]

American parents are also shocked by how hard it is to find good, affordable childcare when they return to work. Half of the people in the United States live in childcare "deserts"—areas in which there are no childcare providers or far too few slots for licensed childcare than there are children who need care. In some areas, parents have to put their child's name on daycare waiting lists early in their pregnancy to have a chance of their child getting in. Even then, many young children still don't have daycare by the time their parents need to return to work. When Megan Carpenter of Alexandria, Virginia, first contacted childcare centers beginning a few months into her pregnancy, she had a list of questions to ask. By the time she had called ten places, she was down to one question: "Do you have a spot?" She and her husband spent more than $1,000 on waitlist fees with different providers in hopes of ensuring a spot before she had to return to work four months after the birth. Despite this, no slot opened up in time, and she and her husband had to convince both of their mothers to fly out to tag-team care for their baby until something became available.[5] Narinder Walia, who works in biotechnology in Fremont, California, reported that she made seventy calls after her baby was born to find him care before she returned to work after four months of leave. Only three daycare facilities had the ability to take him. On visiting them, she found that two were messy and disorganized. She was left with the third.[6]

The accounts of American parents contrast starkly with those of parents in Finland, Denmark, and other pro-family policy countries. Anne Jespersen, the Danish mother we heard from in chapter 2, saw her and her husband's role in terms of finding the best fit for themselves and their children in Denmark's existing well-ordered system: Would a private nursery school at which they could use public subsidies suit their family, or would the public municipal nursery school around the corner be a better fit? And would aftercare at their child's school or another arrangement better mesh with their work schedules? Meanwhile, a government child benefit check showed up in their mailbox every quarter, which eased the financial burden of providing for their kids. In contrast, American parents are just trying to hang in there as best they can.

But, hey, we're Americans. We are a tough, resourceful people who make good things happen when we put our minds to it. So even if free-market family policy makes parents' lives overwhelming, our nation's great wealth and our own gumption mean that our system does well by our kids, right? Unfortunately, dead wrong. It turns out that by far the biggest casualties of free-market family policy are our children.

This is the first of three chapters to explore the extent to which free-market family policy gets children what they need to flourish. We know that kids need both excellent caretaking and generous material support to thrive in their first years. The question for any thriving society is, what system best meets these needs? Countries with pro-family policies go out of their way to make it easy for parents to provide both high-quality caretaking and generous levels of material support for their children. Meanwhile, under free-market family policy, the United States expects parents to negotiate these on their own, arranging for time off from work, reasonable work hours, and daycare providers, all the while earning enough cash to support kids . Guess which system kids do better in?

This chapter focuses on free-market family policy's ability, or rather inability, to deliver the kinds of caretaking that help young children flourish. Chapter 6 then considers how the free-market system affects low-income children in particular. Finally, chapter 7 discusses the outcomes for US children under our free-market family policy system.

WHAT CHILDREN NEED TO THRIVE

To consider how well free-market family policy does in enabling families to give kids what they need, we have to know what conditions help children thrive. Fortunately, in recent decades, a large group of researchers—developmental psychologists, neuroscientists, pediatricians, economists, and education experts—have studied this question intensively. What they have learned amounts to a revolution in thinking about children's development. We used to believe that children's surroundings before they reached school age didn't make much difference to their long-term outcomes, so long as they were safe, fed, and not overly distressed. We now know this thinking was completely wrong. Instead, we've come to understand that children's experiences in their first five years critically affect their long-term well-being and development.

The groundbreaking report on this science, *From Neurons to Neighborhoods*, summarized its main conclusion this way: "[V]irtually every aspect of early human development, from the brain's evolving circuitry to the child's capacity for empathy, is affected by the environments and experiences that are encountered in a cumulative fashion, beginning in the prenatal period and extending throughout the early childhood years." Early childhood is therefore not simply a holding period until children reach grade school and are ready to learn, but a crucial developmental stage in and of itself. Children's environment during this time critically affects whether they'll establish a sturdy or fragile foundation for development throughout the rest of their lives. If children don't get what they need to flourish in these first years, this crucial window of opportunity is lost. It's much harder and more expensive to correct problems later on, if they can be corrected at all.[7]

Neuroscientist Charles Nelson's research on Romanian orphanages helps explain why these early years are so critical. Nelson and colleagues from other American universities moved young children from Romania's notorious, poorly staffed, and grim orphanages, in which tens of thousands of children had been warehoused with little interaction with adults, into foster care situations with carefully vetted adults where they received attentive, nurturing care. The researchers then tracked how well these children did compared with children who remained in the orphanages, as well as with children who lived with families since birth. What the scientists found was that young children who spent their early years in an orphanage had a range of major developmental deficits compared with children raised in families, including serious cognitive and behavioral problems, as well as the inability to form emotional attachments with others. Imaging tests showed that these children had dramatic reductions in particular areas of their brains compared with other children. Interestingly, children who were removed from the orphanages and placed in good foster-care situations before they turned two often regained some of their capacities. Those who were removed after they turned two, though, seldom did so. As one journalist summed up this research, "[N]eglect of very young children does not merely stunt their emotional development. It changes the architecture of their brains."[8]

As Nelson's research showed, the quality of a young child's environment and interactions with the world profoundly affect the development of the neural pathways in the brain, pathways that largely develop in a child's first five years. These pathways, in turn, deeply influence children's most important capacities, including the ability to form deep attachments to others and to function cognitively. These pathways also affect children's executive functioning, the important set of processes that enable them to pursue goals, pay attention, and stay on-task.[9] All of this means that, to do their best, children need supportive circumstances from the very start.

What conditions do children need in order to thrive? To simplify a vast array of research, our new understanding shows us that four caretaking circumstances during kids' first years best help them and their families flourish (since kids don't do well if their families aren't doing well): (1) caretaking by a parent for up to the child's first year; (2) after the first year, caretaking either at home or in a high-quality daycare program; (3) in the year or two before kindergarten, attendance at a high-quality prekindergarten; and (4) throughout early childhood, high-quality time with a nurturing parent.

Parental Caretaking for up to the First Year

After their baby is born, mothers need time to recuperate from childbirth and to adjust to nursing if they are breastfeeding. Parents need time for the many caretaking tasks that come with young babies, to settle into their new family roles, to catch up on often-interrupted sleep, and for bonding with their baby.

What length of time is enough for parents to spend at home with their brand new kids? Far beyond the twelve weeks protected by the FMLA, that's for sure. One important study examined the effect of sixteen European countries' extending partially paid parental leave programs between 1969 and 1994 and found that the extra leave significantly reduced infant deaths. The study extrapolated that a fifty-week entitlement to paid leave would reduce deaths of children who were between four weeks and a year old by about 20 percent, as well as reduce deaths of children between one and five years by about 15 percent.[10] Exactly how does more leave reduce infant mortality? This study couldn't say for sure. But we know that when parents return to work within twelve weeks, their babies are less likely to be taken to the doctor, to get vaccinated, and to be breastfed, all of which increase kids' health risks.[11] In addition, parents are less attuned to kids' safety when they are exhausted from combining the round-the-clock caretaking that babies require and paid work.[12] All of these factors may play a role.

A generous leave period also improves mothers' mental health, which leads to better parenting and sounder kids. Leaves of fewer than twelve weeks are associated with an increase in mothers' depression, decreased concern about their children, and negative impacts on marriage compared to longer leaves.[13]

Similarly, longer leaves of up to six months postpartum have been shown to be associated with a decrease in depressive symptoms and better mental health compared to shorter leaves.[14] Besides the clear benefits that longer leaves provide for children's health and mothers' mental health (which, in turn, benefits children through better parenting), an accumulating body of research suggests that having a parent stay home with a baby during most or all of the first year also has developmental advantages for the child. One of the biggest discoveries in the science of early childhood development is how important the relationship between the baby and a responsive caregiver, usually a parent, is for establishing sound development. One group of scientists stated that this recognition is "likely to be one of the most important discoveries in all of science." When babies form high-quality, reliable relationships with their parents or another responsive caregiver in their first months of life, their brains' wiring develops very differently than when they don't.[15]

When babies form a secure bond with a parent in those first months of life, much of the learning that they do early on happens in this relationship.[16] Those "serve and return" exchanges between parent and baby—in which a baby babbles, coos, and makes faces at a parent to interact with them, and the parent does the same back—are more than just entertaining for the child and parent: they're the first building blocks of the child's learning. The wiring these exchanges develop sets the stage for many of the attributes kids need to become sound adults, including self-confidence, solid mental health, and motivation to learn. In contrast, when a child doesn't have these interactions, his or her brain's wiring sets up patterns that can lead to learning problems, aggressive behavior, and mental health issues.[17]

How much time is optimal for a parent to stay home with the child for developmental reasons? That's a contested question. A sizable number of studies suggest that a mother's (there's little research on fathers yet) full-time return to work before the end of the child's first year can have small but persistent negative cognitive effects on the child; the earlier the mother returns to work, the greater the negative effects.[18] Many of these studies find few or no similar negative effects when a mother returns to work on a part-time basis that first year.[19] But the studies finding harm are contradicted by others that find no relationship between mothers' work during that first year and children's cognitive development.[20] Because of the difficulty of controlling for all the factors that may influence children's development in these situations, including the quality of the care they received in daycare, this controversy still remains unresolved.[21]

Some of the US research showing negative effects on children from mothers' early return to work suggests that the harms to children were later offset by the benefits from the mothers' increased income as a result of their early return to work. In particular, in US families where the mother worked the first year, the child was later more likely to be placed in high-quality, center-based daycare (presumably because the mother's higher income made it affordable), which counteracted the earlier, negative cognitive effects of the mother's work.[22] Note that under pro-family policy, parents could stay home with their kids early on and therefore avoid the initial negative cognitive effects, *and* their kids could still later reap the cognitive benefits that excellent daycare yields because it would be publicly subsidized. In fact, ensuring that families can provide young children with the caretaking conditions that best suit them without worrying that the kids will be penalized by their family's reduced income is a fundamental tenet of pro-family policy.

So to sum up all this research, we know that parents taking longer paid leaves of up to a year reduce children's death rates, and that leaves beyond six months improve mothers' mental health, which leads to better parenting. Furthermore, significant albeit not definitive research suggests that children suffer small but significant cognitive setbacks when parents return to work before a child reaches one year. Based on the incomplete knowledge we have today, the least risky course, and the one that gives children their best chance to thrive, is to allow parents to take that first year off on a subsidized basis. Note that a parent who takes that leave unsubsidized won't necessarily be serving their child's interests in the same way because the income loss to the family may counteract the developmental benefits to the child from the parent's presence at home.

It's important to keep in mind that all this research tells us is about children on average. But, of course, no child is an average child: every child is a unique individual who is born into a unique family. Whether any particular child will do better at home or in daycare after the first months will depend on a variety of factors. Among them are the parent's temperament, level of education, and desire to stay home with the baby, as well as the family's income and the child's home environment. Some parents simply aren't cut out to be a baby's full-time caretaker for months on end. Others have significant other caretaking responsibilities that make caring for a baby full-time difficult, like another child with significant disabilities. Requiring a parent in these situations to be a baby's full-time caretaker does no service to the child. Similarly, the quality of the child's potential daycare options will affect where a child does best. Many kids will do better in early daycare than at home if the quality of care is high; few will do better if it is poor.[23] Further, whether daycare generally, and a specific daycare setting in particular, will be better than parental care for any given child will also vary with the child's temperament. A child who becomes really stressed when separated from their mother is more likely to have negative effects from daycare than a child who adapts easily.[24] In these circumstances, parents are usually the best judges of whether home care or a daycare situation will serve their children best.

After the First Year, Care Either at Home
or in a High-Quality Daycare Program

After the first year, young children can do very well when cared for either by a parent or in high-quality daycare.[25] However, there is strong evidence that top-quality daycare, which is usually provided by a formal daycare center, promotes the development of children from disadvantaged families.[26] In the 1970s, two studies randomly assigned North Carolina children from low-income families either to high-quality, full-time center-based daycare or to a control group in which they were cared for at home or in lower-quality programs. The children were then followed for the next thirty-five years. James H. Heckman, a Nobel laureate in economics, later crunched the numbers and showed that the children who got high-quality daycare did much better over time than those who stayed at home or who got low-quality care: they were more highly educated and earned higher wages, and the men were less likely to use drugs and had lower blood pressure. Children cared for at home came in far behind them. The kids who attended low-quality daycare did worst of all.[27] Heckman ultimately determined that every dollar spent on excellent early childhood programs for low-income children yields a return to society of between $7 and $12, taking into account the increased taxes these kids will pay given their higher incomes, as well as reduced prison costs, unemployment benefits, and other government spending.

The evidence is less robust regarding whether, when their families are higher on the economic ladder, parental care or high-quality daycare serves children between the ages of one and three better. Some evidence suggests that these kids overall do equally well in daycare and at home, but given that their home circumstances tend to be better than those of kids from low-income families, it's a closer call.[28] Recent research suggests that, at least when daycare programs aren't top-notch, children from middle- and high-income families have developmental scores and behavioral and health outcomes that are somewhat more negative than had they been cared for at home, and that these negative effects can persist into adulthood.[29] This is particularly true when daycare is started early.[30] There is no question, though, that for kids who are in daycare, higher-quality care is far better than lower-quality care.

And it's not just the quality of daycare that makes a difference in children's outcomes: the number of hours they spend there likely also has an effect. Long hours in daycare have been linked to increased behavioral problems, particularly when kids begin daycare early in life.[31] As the child development expert Jane Waldfogel put it, the research on this issue "raises a red flag as to the potential adverse effects of long hours of nonmaternal care in the first three years of life."[32] It may be, though, that these behavioral problems appear particularly or only when the daycare isn't top-notch. Several studies that evaluated children in high-quality daycare settings found the care had either positive or neutral effects on their behavior, even when kids were in daycare full-time.[33]

In the Year or Two Before Kindergarten, Attendance at a High-Quality Prekindergarten

In the year or two before kindergarten, children benefit from high-quality early childhood education, meaning the type of programs offered children this age by center-based daycares, preschools, and prekindergartens (all of which I'll call "prekindergarten"). Prekindergarten improves school readiness for all groups of children, helping make sure that when they reach kindergarten they can hit the ground running.[34] But these programs are particularly important for kids from low-income families, because they significantly reduce the large achievement gap between these kids and their peers from wealthier families when they enter kindergarten.[35] As one researcher put it, "[F]or many children, preschool programs can mean the difference between failing and passing, regular or special education, staying out of trouble or becoming involved in crime and delinquency, dropping out or graduating from high school."[36]

The evidence on the benefits of high-quality prekindergarten for children is so strong that more than 1,200 US researchers who study early education across the fields of education, developmental psychology, neuroscience, medicine, and economics signed a consensus letter calling for greater access to high-quality prekindergarten programs. Such programs, the letter states, "produce better education, health, economic and social outcomes for children, families, and the nation." The letter warns, though, that early learning programs that aren't of high quality might actually leave kids worse off.[37]

Throughout Early Childhood, Quality Time with a Nurturing Parent

Last but not least, to develop well, kids need significant time with a nurturing parent throughout their childhood. High-quality time with a parent matters tremendously even when kids get top-notch daycare. In fact, the quality of parenting that kids receive is a far better predictor of their outcomes than their daycare experience.[38]

When it comes to quantity, parents not only need enough time to perform routine childcare for their kids, they also need significant time for interaction and enrichment through activities like reading books. But more important than the quantity of time parents spend interacting with their kids is the quality of their interactions.[39] How sensitive parents are to their kids, as well as how perceptively and appropriately they interact with them, has a lot to do with children's outcomes.[40] Unsurprisingly, one factor that has a huge impact on sensitivity is parents' own mental state, including whether they are experiencing emotional distress, anxiety, or depression. What determinants negatively affect parents' mental states? For one, being a single parent. For another, significant financial stress and insecurity. For a third, work-related stress, including the extra strain that comes from working evening and night shifts or from unstable work hours. On the other side of the coin, when parents have fewer economic pressures it improves their emotional state, which then improves the quality of their parenting.[41]

WHAT YOUNG CHILDREN GET UNDER
FREE-MARKET FAMILY POLICY VERSUS
PRO-FAMILY POLICY

Now that we know the caretaking conditions that serve children best, let's consider how likely they are to get them under free-market family policy versus pro-family policy. As I show, under free-market family policy, few US kids today get all four conditions, no matter how hard their parents try to deliver them.
In large part this is because of free-market family policy's expectation that parents will privately provide what their kids need without help from government. Because of that, not only do parents have to orchestrate children's caretaking, they also need to generate the necessary cash to support their children. These two expectations—providing both caretaking *and* income—work at cross purposes in most families with young kids, since children in their early years have such high caretaking needs. Few parents will be able to earn sufficient cash at the same time as they either provide the caretaking themselves or arrange for it. Ultimately, most parents feel compelled by the need to put food on the table and ensure a roof over their kids' heads, which means sacrificing the caretaking arrangement that would suit their kids best. To provide financial support for their families, they compromise on the caretaking their kids receive—returning to work earlier than they'd like, sacrificing high-quality daycare and prekindergarten, and being less attentive to their children when the family is at home because they're so fried by their busy lives.

Meanwhile, countries with pro-family policies, including Finland, Denmark, and even Estonia, by design make it easy for parents to provide young kids with the conditions that serve them best. Canada, too, offers many of these programs at the federal level, and its provinces often fill in the remaining gaps. Recognizing that early childhood is such a critical time for both children and their families, these governments relax parents' work obligations and subsidize their staying home after children are born or adopted. And when parents return to work, these countries make high-quality caretaking available at no or low cost. These policies mean that parents don't have to trade off financially supporting their family with getting their kids the care they need. The result is that most kids in these systems get the conditions that will help them do best.

Parental Caretaking for up to the First Year

The first condition that supports children thriving is parental caretaking for up to the first year. Let's start with Finland as our model of pro-family policy. The law in Finland makes it easy for parents to stay home with children during that time. When all publicly paid parental leave is combined, most families receive ten-and-a-half months off between the parents upon the birth of a new child, paid at a rate of about 70 percent of the parents' wages.[42] Almost all Finnish families take most or all of this leave (the exception is that only about half of fathers take the entire two months of paternity leave allotted exclusively to them; almost all fathers, though, take at least three weeks of leave).[43] Nine in ten families have a parent take even more time than the allotted months of parental leave, and are compensated by the state for this extra time (until children reach age three) at a fixed, lower monthly rate.[44]

Canada has adopted a similar parental-leave plan. Mothers get fifteen weeks of maternity leave at about 55 percent of their salary. After that, parents have a choice: They can take thirty-five additional weeks of leave at the same 55 percent of their salary, giving them just shy of a year at home in total. Or, under a recent expansion of the parental leave law, they can take that same amount of money (actually, roughly $1,000 more) paid out over eighteen months of parental leave with their child. The first year the extended leave was offered, tens of thousands of Canadian parents chose to take it. The program allows parents to split the weeks between them as they choose. Partners can take leave time simultaneously if they want, which is particularly crucial when a mother is having a hard time recuperating after birth and needs help with childcare.[45]

The province of Quebec has opted to substitute its own parental leave plan for the Canadian plan with still higher subsidies, as well as a design intended to give fathers incentive to take more leave. Under Quebec's leave law, on the birth or adoption of a child, parents get replacement rates of 70 to 75 percent of their work salaries over a maximum of fifty-two weeks. On top of that, fathers (and nonbiological mothers in lesbian couples) get five weeks of "use-it-or-lose-it" benefits to encourage them to take at least some parental leave in order to promote shared caregiving.[46] The result is that more than 80 percent of fathers in Quebec take paternity leave.[47]

Under free-market family policy, how many US kids have a parent stay at home with them for most or all of that first year? Not many. Census data on employment among first-time mothers show that more than half who work during pregnancy are back to work within three months of giving birth. The median length of maternity leave that US women who work report taking is less than eleven *weeks*, as opposed to the almost eleven *months* taken in Finland. One in four US working mothers takes just two weeks or less off after having a child; half of these mothers take a week or less.[48] Fathers, meanwhile, report taking an average of only a week of leave, despite the fact that most research shows that fathers who take more parental leave will be more involved with childcare as their children grow.[49]

Some US mothers quit work altogether, at least for a time, because of the problems of combining work and family in the free-market system. (This means their families will lose the income they would have received if the mother had continued working. Under free-market policy, the family will then have less money to spend on their children, which can itself hinder their development.) But by nine months after the child's birth, almost 60 percent of all mothers have returned to the workforce, the majority of them full-time.[50] While some parents manage to tag-team their child's care overall, almost half of children under one year old wind up in a regular nonparental childcare arrangement. Twenty-seven percent are cared for by a relative, 14 percent are cared for by a nonrelative, and only 11 percent are cared for in childcare centers.[51] These different arrangements have very different outcomes for children, as we'll see later in the chapter.

In sum, about nine in ten kids in Finland have a parent stay home with them for their first year while far fewer than half of American kids get this care. And most of the American children who don't have a parent home that full first year will receive full-time care from their parents for only a few weeks or, at most, a few months—nowhere close to a year. Why is there such a stunning difference between the number of parents who take the amount of time off that likely serves kids best in Finland and the United States? Could it be that US parents love their kids less than Finnish parents, or their jobs more? Of course not. Finland's system just makes it a lot easier for parents to stay home with their kids. Not only does Finland pay parents for the time they take off to care for a new child, it guarantees that they can return to their same job for three years after the child is born. In contrast, most US parents need to go back to work sooner than they would like because they need to keep a roof over their family's heads and therefore can't risk losing their jobs.

Leigh Benrahou, a registrar at a small college, is one of the many parents whose lives were made far more difficult by our free-market system. Leigh planned everything right so that she could get as much time off with her second child as possible without losing her job. She waited to get pregnant until she was sure the baby would be born more than a year after she started work, so she could be assured of getting the twelve weeks of unpaid leave provided by the Family and Medical Leave Act (FMLA). Because she knew that living on just her husband's salary would put her soon-to-be four-person family close to the edge, she also signed on with her employer's disability insurance plan, paying monthly premiums so that she'd receive disability payments during the leave. On top of that, she carefully saved up her two weeks of paid vacation time.

But Leigh's plans went awry when her water broke in late December, more than three months before her April 1 due date. Despite her careful planning, she gave birth too soon to be covered under either the FMLA or her disability policy. Although her son was born a struggling preemie at twenty-six weeks and just over two pounds, Leigh had to go back to work less than two weeks after the birth to avoid losing her job. That meant leaving her tiny newborn in the hospital each morning, not sure he'd make it until she could get back at the end of the day. At work, still suffering from the effects of a C-section, she did her job, occasionally interrupted by emergency calls from the hospital, and used her breaks to pump breastmilk behind the closed door of her office, crying.[52] She spent those first months in a haze, traveling between her work, the neonatal intensive care unit at the hospital where her son spent his first four months and endured two surgeries, her three-year-old daughter's daycare center, and her home.

As Leigh found out, US protections for parental leave are not just weak, they're also full of holes. To begin with, four in ten US workers aren't even covered by the FMLA at all because of loopholes in the law.[53] Uncovered workers aren't guaranteed any time whatsoever away from their jobs, so those who take more leave than their bosses permit can be fired. And even those employees covered by the FMLA have their jobs protected for only twelve weeks. It's no wonder, then, that six in ten parents who take parental leave say they needed or wanted more time off than they were able to take. Almost half of these workers report that they were afraid they'd lose their job—a particular concern of lower-income workers.[54]

What's more, the FMLA guarantees workers only *unpaid* leave, and most workers simply can't afford to take leave without pay for long. Of Americans with savings accounts, the median amount that people under thirty-five have saved is $1,580.[55] But the average out-of-pocket healthcare costs that a family *with* health insurance will incur for the birth of a baby today is $3,400.[56] That means that, with the added expenses of a baby, many families won't have any savings whatsoever to pay for time off. Employers rarely fill this gap. Only one in seven workers receives paid parental leave from an employer. Most of the remaining workers cobble together some pay using vacation days or sick leave, but this comes to weeks rather than months of pay. And almost all low-wage workers receive no pay at all for the time they take off after a child's birth. Most of them will take on debt just to make it through their short leave, adding to their financial challenges.[57]

A few US states have recently pushed back against free-market family policy and put in place paid leave programs for new parents, funded by a payroll tax on employees and, sometimes, employers.[58] These programs don't come close to covering the year that many nations with pro-family policy cover, but they still make a difference to the families who have access to them. California's leave program, for example, allows most employees to receive about two-thirds of their weekly wage (to a maximum of about $1,200) for up to six weeks (rising to eight weeks in July 2020).[59] The program has increased the average length of leave for new mothers by between 2.5 and 5 weeks. The increase in fathers' leave time is less—two to three more days on average. And states that have more recently passed leave laws are providing longer leave lengths and more generous wage reimbursement, so they are likely to lengthen the actual leaves that parents take.[60]

To summarize: Finland makes it easy and relatively affordable for parents to stay home to care for their children during the first year. The result is that almost all infants are cared for by a stay-at-home parent for their first year of life. The United States has done almost nothing to help parents stay home with their children, and most parents therefore return to work far too soon. Because of this, the Finnish system wins hands down when it comes to delivering care that is better for babies that first year.

The score: pro-family policy 1; free-market family policy 0.

After the First Year, Care Either at Home or in a High-Quality Daycare Program

Turning to the second caretaking condition that fosters optimal development—after the child's first year, either having a parent stay home or enrolling the child in a high-quality daycare program—how do our two different policy approaches compare? Let's start with pro-family policy first. Once again, Finland makes this condition easy for parents to provide by supporting both of these options. After the parental-leave period ends, Finland provides that a parent can stay at home with a child full- or part-time while receiving a state subsidy (albeit at a reduced rate than the parental leave subsidy), and later return to work.[61] Alternatively, the child is guaranteed a place in daycare. Parents can choose between a municipally run daycare center or a publicly subsidized family daycare program, usually run in a provider's home.[62] Both are highly regulated for quality; Finland's system is considered among the best in the world.[63]

High-quality daycare costs money, and Finland is willing to pay for it. The country spends an average of more than $19,000 a year for every child under three in daycare, almost all from public funds.[64] Parents' contribution is based on a sliding scale. Low-income parents pay nothing; the highest-earning parents pay about $4,000 a year for their first child, but less for each subsequent child.[65] The upshot is that no children are shut out of good-quality daycare because their parents can't afford to pay.[66]

All this means that, in the Finnish system, almost every child between one and three years old winds up getting some type of caretaking—either at home with a parent or in high-quality daycare—that serves children that age best.[67] Only a small number of children—2 percent of kids aged zero to two and less than 1 percent of three-year-olds—end up in informal childcare with a grandparent, a family friend, or other untrained caregiver, a type of arrangement that generally does not serve kids well.[68] When kids in Finland do wind up in informal care, though, it's generally because a particular informal daycare arrangement is an especially good fit for the child, not because the parents couldn't afford better care.[69]

Countries with pro-family policy fall into one of two camps. Some, like Finland, subsidize parents who choose to stay home with young children after parental leave ends, in addition to subsidizing daycare for children. Other countries nudge parents back into the workforce at the close of parental leave by ending wage-replacement subsidies and simply providing high-quality daycare for kids after that. Denmark falls into this latter camp. After their fifty weeks of parental leave end, Danish parents aren't subsidized to stay home, but can choose from a range of high-quality public and private daycare options that are heavily subsidized by the state.[70] The result is that more than 60 percent of one- to two-year-olds and 96 percent of three- to five-year-olds are enrolled in daycare. Of those children, more than 75 percent are enrolled in fully public daycare, while another 18 percent are enrolled in heavily subsidized and regulated private daycare.[71] Meanwhile, fewer than 1 percent are enrolled in informal daycare.[72]

Under US free-market policy, our system for caretaking after children's first year could hardly be more different from countries with pro-family policy. Although American public policy, like Denmark's, is geared to the expectation that parents will work in paid jobs, the complexities of arranging and paying for childcare are here left almost exclusively to parents. The only assistance most families receive are minimal tax advantages.[73] Poor and low-income families are technically eligible for childcare subsidies, but these subsidies are so underfunded and waitlists so long that only one in ten eligible kids from low-income families actually receives one.[74] Fewer than that—four in a hundred eligible kids—are able to participate in our perpetually underfunded needs-tested daycare program for young children, Early Head Start.[75] All this is despite the fact that providing excellent childcare is the most cost-effective way to help poor and low-income children close the achievement gap.[76]

Also in contrast to the Finnish and Danish systems, most daycare providers in the United States are lightly regulated, if they are regulated at all. There are no federal daycare standards for staffing, curriculum, or safety. This leaves regulation to the states. Most states, though, exempt a sizable proportion of daycare providers from any oversight whatsoever by excusing family daycare providers (caregivers who watch kids in their home for pay) from licensing requirements unless they care for five or more unrelated kids.[77] State regulations then generally set a low bar for the providers who are required to have licenses, simply establishing baseline standards for the facility's health and safety, maximum ratios of caregivers to kids, and minimal qualifications for caregivers.[78] These standards are usually aimed at ensuring children's basic safety rather than their sound development. For example, in North Carolina, the required ratio of caregivers to children is one adult to ten two-year-olds.[79] That ratio may keep kids safe, but it's not close to small enough to support their best development. By contrast, Finland's and Denmark's caregiver–child ratio is set at one adult to three two-year-olds. And US states don't generally regulate curricula for quality at all.[80] One former district director of licensing for Texas described the experience of inspecting hundreds of Texas daycares that met the low bar set by Texas law: "You know, when we walk into some of these places, they're meeting the letter of the standards. . . . But it's like a warehouse for children. You know it when, as the inspector, you are the most interesting thing the kids have seen all day. They attach themselves to you and are trying to engage because there's nothing else going on for them."[81]

How does our lightly regulated system actually work out for our kids? Does our nation's wealth, in combination with the free-market mechanism, act to protect children's well-being, as market advocates suggest? This is a critical question for our next generation since, by the time kids are in their second year, 54 percent wind up in a regular caretaking situation of some sort with an adult besides their parent.[82] These children tend to spend relatively long hours in such care—an average of thirty-six hours a week.[83] By comparison, Finnish kids this age who are enrolled in daycare spend an average of thirty hours a week.[84]

The big difference between our system and that of countries with pro-family policy, though, isn't the number of hours children spend in care; it's the quality of caretaking that kids receive. Market competition, unfortunately, has failed miserably in ensuring quality daycare for our kids. The *New Republic* aptly described the situation when it titled its exposé on American daycare "The Hell of American Daycare." As its author, Jonathan Cohn, summed it up, "[W]e lack anything resembling an actual child care system. Excellent day cares are available, of course, if you have the money to pay for them and the luck to secure a spot. But the overall quality is wildly uneven and barely monitored, and at the lower end, it's Dickensian."[85] Experts agree with the magazine's assessment, rating the majority of daycare arrangements for US children as "fair" or "poor." Less than 10 percent of care is rated "very high quality."[86] In the words of Marcy Whitebook, the director of the Center for the Study of Child Care Employment at the University of California, Berkeley, "We've got decades of research, and it suggests most child care and early childhood education in this country is mediocre at best."[87]

Our nation's problem relates in large part to the type of daycare settings that US children wind up in. Of the one- to two-year-olds whose mothers work, fewer than a third are put in "formal" daycares, meaning a daycare center, a nursery school, or an Early Head Start program. The remainder receive "informal" daycare from grandparents, siblings, friends, or a family daycare provider.[88] But most of the kids in these informal situations get mediocre to lousy care.[89] One study that reviewed 226 of these care situations found these providers have less education, less training, and are much less likely to read books to kids every day than formal providers. On top of that, it found that children in informal care watch more hours of television every day than kids in formal daycare centers.[90] In all, it rated 35 percent of the informal caregiving situations "inadequate," 56 percent "adequate," and just 9 percent "good."[91] Another study concluded that every year a child spent in informal daycare instead of in a parent's care or center-based daycare was associated with a 2.6 percent reduction in later test scores for cognitive achievement.[92] Not developing well isn't even the worst risk of informal daycare settings: kids are seven times more likely to die in informal care than at daycare centers.[93]

Kenya Mire, a mother profiled in the *New Republic* article on daycare, tragically learned this lesson. Her daughter, Kendyll, had been enrolled in a daycare center until Kenya lost her job in the Great Recession. When she started a new job as a receptionist at a Houston oil company, she couldn't afford the few daycare centers that had space for Kendyll. So she enrolled her daughter in a family daycare with an operator who seemed open and honest, and who promised to teach the children Christian values. Although the daycare was licensed by the state of Texas, all that meant was that the owner had a high-school degree or its equivalent and that she'd shown up at a state-sanctioned class. Kendyll died in a fire on her second day at the daycare. The daycare operator, Kenya later found out, had left the kids napping alone while she went shopping at a nearby Target, at the same time as she had left something cooking on the stove. Four children died that day.[94]

And remember Narinder Walia, the Fremont, California mother described at the beginning of this chapter who made *seventy* calls to daycares after her baby was born? She got only three positive responses, but two of those daycares turned out to be messy and disorganized. She enrolled her child in the third, a home daycare. But on her son's first day there, the provider put him face down in his crib to settle him—a violation of accepted safety practices. He died that day of Sudden Infant Death Syndrome, one of the known risks of putting babies to sleep on their stomach.[95]

But even the third of kids put in center-based daycare in the United States—the type of daycare that is generally considered the best—don't usually get good care. One study that followed more than a thousand US children in different daycare arrangements for more than a decade found that the great majority of centers failed to comply with expert recommendations that are critical to children's development.[96] Only one in five classes observed met the expert-recommended caregiver–child ratio of one to three for one-year-olds, and just one in four met the recommended ratio of one to four for two-year-olds (a ratio already higher than Finland's allowed ratios). Only seven in ten met the standards for caregiver education.[97] Even more troubling, the study found that only about one in sixteen three-year-olds received a lot of positive caregiving in the form of sensitive and encouraging interactions with their caregivers. Yet, the study warned, one of the strongest predictors of children's development is their exposure to positive caregiving.[98]

Given the critical importance of sound caretaking in kids' first years to their development, this report card on American daycare is exceedingly bad news. What about the American Dream's promise that every person will "be able to attain to the fullest stature of which they are innately capable . . . regardless of the fortuitous circumstances of birth or position"? Our daycare system is undermining that promise every single day. And good daycare is important not only for kids' futures, but also for their present. Children are, unsurprisingly, a lot happier and more engaged when their quality of care is high.[99]

Why do most American children end up in mediocre daycare, in stark contrast to Finnish children? Because Finland makes it easy for parents to secure the caretaking their kids need to thrive. Under free-market family policy, in contrast, the United States makes it well-nigh impossible.

Young families in the United States today simply can't afford the cost of good daycare. According to the US government, for childcare to be affordable, it should cost 7 percent or less of parents' income. At the 2016 median household income of $59,000, that means a family should spend about $4,100 a year.[100] Yet center-based daycare for toddlers in the United States costs on average $8,900 a year—about the same as in-state college tuition.[101] That puts center-based daycare for one child, let alone more, out of reach of most American parents. Even then, the average daycare here charges less than half of what Finland spends per child. This is largely because US daycare workers are paid much less than Finnish workers and our child–caregiver ratios are higher, both of which lower the quality of care. Most US daycare workers make little more than minimum wage and far less than workers in unskilled jobs like pest control.[102] Daycare workers make so little that most qualify for some form of safety-net benefits.[103] The consequence of these low wages is that few people who would be excellent in this role will seek caregiving jobs if they have other possible career paths open to them.

In one recent study that tallied daycare costs in forty-one states, only two states, Louisiana and Maryland, made it under the 7 percent benchmark for affordability for even the median married-couple household. Eight more states at least made it in under 10 percent—bruising, but potentially manageable if these families scrimped and saved. In the remaining thirty-one states, for couples at the median income and below, putting their kid in center-based daycare would blow up their budget. Massachusetts topped the list, with an average cost of $18,500—16 percent of married couples' median income.[104] And that's for one child; childcare fees for both an infant and a preschooler exceed housing costs for home owners with a mortgage in thirty-five states, as well as annual median rent payments in every state.[105] The situation is even worse for single parents. In almost every state, the cost of care for a single toddler exceeds *21 percent* of the median income for single mothers—three times the benchmark of affordability.[106]

Mike and Shannon Buchmann, of Mishawaka, Indiana, have experienced how hard it is for young families to pay for daycare. Mike is a high school art teacher and football coach. Shannon is an assistant controller at a small private college. They have two school-aged kids and a fourteen-month-old enrolled in a daycare center. The baby's daycare bill runs $660 a month, making it the family's second-biggest expense behind their mortgage. Between these, the family's other basic expenses, and the necessary payments for the family car and Mike's student loans, the family has nothing left over and no savings. To keep the family afloat, on top of the Buchmanns' full-time jobs, his football coaching, and raising three kids, Mike has started driving with Uber. He drives for a few hours once afterschool football practice is over and the kids have eaten, bathed, and been tucked into bed. "It's a little hectic and the hours are insane. But you can sleep when you're dead," he says.[107] The Buchmanns are firmly middle-class, with college degrees and two incomes. They've done everything right, yet they still can't afford daycare for even one child. And while Mike has a great attitude, driving with Uber in the evenings on top of work and parenting is no way to live a sane life. That stress and schedule would be tough on most people's mental health.

In the face of these costs, most parents bypass high-quality center-based care for other, less expensive forms of care. Mothers like Carly Fox, a single parent who earns $42,000 in her job as an educator and organizer at a legal services organization, would love to send her child to center-based daycare. But on her wages, she needs to patch together care for her three-year-old by relying on her parents, other relatives, a neighborhood babysitter, and exchanging babysitting with nearby parents in similar situations.[108] Families with incomes below $59,200, like Carly's, who had kids enrolled in caretaking in 2015 spent an average of $2,080 on care per child. Families with incomes between $59,200 and $107,400 spent an average of $2,870.[109] Neither comes close to the cost of center-based daycare in any state.[110]

The fact that families can't afford the high cost of quality daycare isn't the only reason that most US daycare isn't top-quality. The absence of serious government oversight is also a problem. Decades of research have helped to determine what caregiver–child ratios, education, and experience serve children best. Finland and Denmark use that research to set quality standards. The United States doesn't, expecting the market to sort out quality. But it turns out that the market doesn't perform this task well. One reason is that parents tend to be pretty poor judges of the quality of their children's daycare, giving providers better marks for care than they actually deserve.[111] Another is that parents often get only limited glimpses of a daycare's operations when they drop off and pick up their kids.

Jane Dimyan-Ehrenfeld, a government lawyer in Washington, DC, found out how much a parent can fail to notice about a daycare setting after her daughter had been enrolled in a family daycare for three years. Before her daughter started there, Jane carefully checked the center's references. Three years later, after an aide at the center was fired, the aide revealed to parents that the owner spent her days upstairs selling supplements. This left Jane's daughter and seven other kids with a single aide to care for them, along with two large snakes and attack dogs that were supposed to have been kept in another area of the house. Careful oversight and regular inspections could have caught what Jane missed. But neither of these exist in the United States. Even those daycares that require licenses are, in most states, inspected only once every year or two, if at all.[112]

To sum all this up, Finland's pro-family policy makes it easy for parents by ensuring that they have excellent options for their young children's caretaking. For those parents who want to stay home, public policy makes this choice financially and practically possible by providing subsidies and guaranteeing their jobs until they return. For those who want to go back to work, the country makes it almost cost-free for most families to put their kids in excellent childcare programs. The result is that almost all Finnish kids get the care that helps them thrive either at home or in daycare.

In contrast, the United States' free-market family policy does next to nothing to make it easy for parents to do right by their kids. In this system, most parents simply can't afford to stay home, and yet most of those who work can't afford to pay for high-quality daycare. Further, even the few who can afford such daycare can't ensure their kids will get it given the lack of government oversight and the unpredictable quality of US daycare. All this is despite the fact that excellent caretaking provides outsized and lifelong benefits to kids, and the impacts of bad care are harmful and often permanent.

The score: pro-family policy 2; free-market family policy 0.

In the Year or Two before Kindergarten, Attendance at a High-Quality Prekindergarten

Does free-market policy do better than pro-family policy in ensuring that children attend high-quality prekindergarten? By now, you won't be surprised to read that the answer is no. The large gains that kids can make in prekindergarten have motivated most highly developed countries to make free, universal prekindergarten available for the year or two before kindergarten.[113] Thirteen countries— Belgium, Denmark, France, Germany, Hungary, Iceland, Israel, Italy, Japan, the Netherlands, Norway, Spain, and the United Kingdom—enroll 95 percent and up of four-year-olds in their preschools. France and the United Kingdom enroll a full 100 percent of four-year-olds. Finnish children start kindergarten later than in most countries, at age six rather than five. The year before, when they are five, 84 percent of Finnish children attend prekindergarten—a relatively low number among wealthy countries, in part because Finland is subsidizing many of these parents to stay home with their younger kids. The United States still comes in well below Finland, though, enrolling just 67 percent of four-year-olds in the year before kindergarten; this puts us thirty-third among thirty-five wealthy countries in enrollment numbers.

The gap between us and other countries is even larger for three-year-olds. Twelve countries—Belgium, Denmark, France, Germany, Iceland, Israel, Italy, Korea, Norway, Spain, Sweden, and the United Kingdom—enroll at least 90 percent of all three-year-olds in preschool. Finland, which enrolls just 73 percent of three-year olds and 79 percent of four-year-olds, trails these other countries, likely because many parents who receive subsidies to stay home with children under three also allow their three- and four-year-old siblings to stay home. But the United States lags much further behind: only 38 percent of our three-year-olds are enrolled.[114] This is hardly the kind of American exceptionalism that gives our country bragging rights.

The main reason for our low enrollment is the high cost of prekindergarten. Unless parents live in one of the few states that offer universal prekindergarten, they have to pay for it. It isn't cheap: the average cost of prekindergarten for four-year-olds is $8,700 a year.[115] Few young families can afford that. Low income children are eligible for the public Head Start program. Because the program is so underfunded, though, only four in ten eligible kids make it from the waitlist into the program.[116] So if you're lucky enough to be well off in the United States, you can swing prekindergarten. If you're poor, you have some—but not an even—chance of getting your kid into prekindergarten. And everyone else stands little chance at all.

Finland beats us not only in prekindergarten enrollment numbers but also in the quality of prekindergarten.[117] That's because Finland's prekindergarten program, like their daycare, is heavily regulated and subsidized to ensure that it's top-notch. Finnish teachers have to have three or four years of college education or its equivalent, and its teacher–child ratio is set at a maximum of one teacher for every ten children. The government spends an average of $10,600 on every child annually for prekindergarten; well-to-do parents must contribute as well.[118]

In contrast, except in the few states implementing prekindergarten programs, prekindergarten in the United States is only lightly regulated. Many states, including North Carolina, don't require that teachers have taken more than a single college class in early childhood education.[119] Only three states require that even directors of these programs have a bachelor's degree, which Finland requires of all teachers.[120] And the average teacher–student ratio is one to thirteen compared with one to ten in Finland.[121] All this contributes to experts' assessment of the general quality of US preschool programs as exceedingly mediocre. A few are good, a few are bad, the rest are just middling.[122] In the wealthiest country in the world.

Six states—Florida, Georgia, Oklahoma, Vermont, West Virginia, and Wisconsin—as well as Washington, DC, have bucked free-market policy and committed to some version of universal prekindergarten, most of them recently. Four of these programs have significant limitations. Florida, which put its program in place in response to a citizen-driven amendment to the state constitution, hasn't come close to developing high standards, in large part because the legislature has refused to fund it properly. Georgia's longstanding prekindergarten program is limited by its lottery funding, and therefore has long waitlists. Vermont is only beginning to scale up its program, and local prekindergartens must currently offer just ten hours of prekindergarten a week. And Wisconsin hasn't adopted some important quality standards like low student-teacher ratios. But Oklahoma's and West Virginia's programs look more promising. Three-quarters of Oklahoma's four-year-olds attend prekindergarten. So do 65 percent of West Virginia's. Both have established ratios of one teacher to ten kids and require teachers to have bachelor's degrees. Spending in both states is relatively high: Oklahoma spends $7,500 on every child, while West Virginia spends $9,500. Meanwhile, Washington, DC, spends more than $16,000 on every child in its universal prekindergarten program—topping every state in the nation.[123] These two states and Washington, DC, are funding the curriculum development and regulation that are needed to ensure high-quality daycare.

We know that excellent prekindergarten programs make a lasting difference in kids' lives. But it will be a while before the effects of these statewide programs become clear.[124] That said, Oklahoma's fourth-grade reading scores have increased significantly since its program has been in place.[125] And in contrast to the Texas daycare facilities that the state inspector described as warehouses for children, consider the following account from the *Hechinger Report* of the public prekindergarten classrooms in Muskogee, Oklahoma, which serve 285 children, the great majority of whom come from low-income families:

> In Nerissa Whitaker's classroom, Kash McDaniel, 4, practiced writing his name at a well-stocked writing and art station. So far, he was only particularly clear on how to make a "K," but he was assiduously making dozens of them. Down the hall, in Elizabeth Salas' classroom, Dante Larson, 5, served coffee and bacon from a play stove to Natalie Hernandez, also 5, who snuggled a baby doll while chatting on a play cell phone. In yet another classroom, this one lit softly and featuring nature-oriented toys and decorations, Grace Marder, age 4, tried to find the right words to describe the leaf she found during an earlier nature walk with her class. The leaf was now glued to a piece of white printer paper.
>
> "It's red," she told her teacher, Jana Dunlap. But then she struggled to find another adjective. Dunlap prompted her with a list of possibilities: smooth, bumpy, rough? "Bumpy," Grace said finally and watched as Dunlap carefully wrote, "It's red and bumpy," below the leaf.[126]

Every four-year-old should have the chance to spend their days like this. Few US four-year-olds do.

These universal prekindergartens are among the few places in which significant inroads against US free-market policy have been made in our era.[127] Thus far, though, these advances have not significantly moved the dial nationally on the proportion of children who attend prekindergarten.[128] In stark contrast, in countries with pro-family policy, all kids get access to a high-quality prekindergarten experience, which helps ensure their readiness for kindergarten and beyond.[129]

The updated score: pro-family policy 3; free-market family policy 0.

Throughout Early Childhood, Quality Time with a Nurturing Parent

Last but by no means least, we turn to the fourth caretaking condition that supports children's optimal development: high-quality time with a nurturing parent. The potentially good news here is that, despite all the pressure to work hard in our free-market system, US parents generally make time for their kids—in fact, *more* time than Finnish parents. On average, US mothers spend just shy of two hours each day focusing primarily on childcare (which excludes, for example, cooking or doing laundry while the kids play) compared with Finnish mothers, who spend about one-and-a-half hours. United States fathers spend a little more than an hour a day compared with Finnish fathers, who spend roughly three-quarters of an hour.[130]

That American parents invest more time in their kids than Finish parents do in theirs, as chapter 3 explained, is likely a product of our country's greater economic inequality and insecurity. Finnish parents simply aren't as focused on coaching and monitoring their kids to improve their chances of success. That's because, in Finland's economy, the chances are much better that their kids will be able to lead good, economically stable lives once they reach adulthood, even if they don't excel as children.[131]

Is the fact that US parents spend more time with their young kids than Finnish parents better for our kids? The short answer is that we don't know for sure. Although regular parental interaction is crucial for kids, and significant time playing with and reading to kids improves cognitive development, we don't know whether more is better. At least one recent study suggests it isn't, at least until kids reach adolescence. But, as chapter 1 showed, we do know that if the extra time is helping US kids, it's still not putting them on a par academically with their Finnish peers.[132]

We also know that the quality of parenting is far more important than the quantity in raising sound children. And here, our free-market family system gives cause for alarm. When parents are highly stressed, abundant research shows that the quality of their parenting declines. This, in turn, has a significant negative impact on kids' outcomes.[133] And if there's one thing our free-market system does in spades, it's imposing stress on parents.

As chapter 3 showed, a large proportion of US parents are stressed as a result of time pressures. That's because they've expanded the time they spend with kids considerably in recent decades, at the same time that families have upped their total hours in the workforce. Parents toward the top of the income ladder are among those most stressed by work–family conflict because of the longer hours they work.[134] But single mothers, too, are time-stressed. They work more hours to support their children than married mothers, while still spending close to the same amount of time with their kids, mostly by cutting the rest of their lives close to the bone.[135] On top of that, many parents from the middle of the income ladder on down, including many single mothers, also deal with the constant stress of economic insecurity; those toward the bottom of the income ladder also contend with the stress of poverty.

Early development experts are only now beginning to understand the pathways through which stress on parents affects their children's development. Some of the most revealing work comes from studies of development in young rats. Rat mothers with low stress levels lick and groom their pups significantly more often than rat mothers with high stress levels do.[136] Because of changes that this grooming induces in pups' brain wiring, pups that are frequently groomed are calmer and do more exploring than other pups. These differences in rat pups last through adulthood, when adult rats that had received more grooming as young rats also tend to lick their pups more often.[137]

Interestingly, when pups of high-stress rat mothers are moved to low-stress mothers, who spend more time licking them, they end up behaving like rat pups born to low-stress mothers. The switched rats' behavior shows that the differences between the rats aren't "hard-wired," meaning caused by unalterable genetic code. Instead, they are "soft-wired," in the sense that the mothers' behavior changes the expression of their children's genes by changing the wiring in their brains.[138] Neuroscientists believe that brain development works in similar ways in humans.[139] That's bad news for American kids given the high stress the free-market system imposes on their parents.

The situation of Natasha Long, a mother of three in Booneville, Mississippi, shows how much pressure our system puts on parents. Natasha returned to working lengthy shifts at a factory three weeks after her third child was born because she was her family's breadwinner. Once she worked her twelve-hour shift, on top of an hour's drive to and from work, Natasha had only ten hours a day to sleep, mother her children, and pump breast milk, in addition to doing all the other chores she needed to accomplish, before she had to return to work. At work, the factory had no lactation room, so she had to pump milk in the cab of her truck in the factory parking lot, crying from stress, as well as worry about being seen pumping. After just a few days of this schedule, Natasha developed an ongoing headache, a sense that she couldn't breathe, and she couldn't stop crying. A doctor determined that the stress of her schedule was causing depression and put her on antidepressants (which carry some risk for breastfeeding infants) to help her get by. Natasha is doing the best she can in our free-market system to do right by her kids, but what we've learned about children's development tells us that this stress won't serve her kids well.

The score: Which system better ensures that kids receive nurturing parenting is at least a more open question than those related to any of our other caregiving conditions, given that American parents spend more time with their kids though they are under considerably more stress. Let's call this one a tie and give each a point.

So the final score: pro-family policy 4; free-market family policy 1.

In sum, how pro-family and free-market family countries approach the caretaking needs of young children could hardly be more different. Under pro-family policy, government partners with parents to support the conditions that children need. In contrast, under our free-market family policy, parents must provide for their kids on their own. This means that parents need to subsidize their own time off to stay home with babies and young children, they have to pay for daycare and prekindergarten themselves, and they have to work out their own balance between home and work, all without government support. If the choice between these systems is dictated by which delivers to young children the conditions that will best help them flourish, this is an easy call: pro-family policy wins hands down. As the next chapter shows, this is especially true when it comes to meeting the needs of children from low-income families.

How We Fail Our Children
Part II—Young Children from Poor and Low-Income Families

> Because children have only one opportunity to develop normally in mind and body, the commitment to protection from poverty must be upheld in good times and in bad. A society that fails to maintain that commitment, even in difficult economic times, is a society that is failing its most vulnerable citizens and storing up intractable social and economic problems for the years immediately ahead.
>
> —UNICEF (2012)[1]

There's no question that poor and low-income families bear the harshest burdens of free-market family policy. And although these policies degrade the lives of adults in these families in both large and small ways, there's also no denying that it's the children of these families who are harmed the most. Critics of state support for families argue that if children from low-income families don't get what they need, it's their parents' fault. Even if we disregard the clear moral precept that children shouldn't be punished for their parents' actions, these critics are woefully misinformed in their assignment of blame. It is simply not possible for low-income parents, even making their best efforts, to provide their kids with what they need to flourish. The unsurprising result is that few US kids from low-income families get what they need to do their best. And that undermines the promise of the American Dream.

Consider the situation of Raven Osborne, a twenty-two-year-old single mother from Tupelo, Mississippi. Because Raven didn't get paid parental leave at her waitressing job, she returned to work just a week after her son, Kylan, was born. Her base pay of $2.13 an hour plus tips, though, wasn't enough to cover her rent, car payments, and the cost of daycare. Consequently, four weeks after the birth, Raven began to leave Kylan with her mother a few nights a week to work overnight shifts at a Texaco. Her sixty-hours-plus of work a week, on top of the college classes she was taking, left her little time to spend with her son except when she got home from work. At those times, she often fell asleep holding him.

After Raven's second child, Anthony, was born, she took four weeks off before returning to work, now at a debt collection agency. To make ends meet, she also worked several shifts a week at a supermarket. Given Raven's long hours, her mother, who held two jobs herself, took the children when she could to supplement their regular daycare. Raven explained her busy work schedule by saying, "I don't like asking for help," an attitude that perfectly reflects our nation's free-market philosophy. Through her own hard work and grit, she carries her family's financial weight at the same time that she orchestrates her children's care.[2]

But despite Raven's herculean efforts, her boys aren't getting the conditions most likely to help them develop their best. Her fleeting maternity leaves means that they had just a small fraction of their first year at home with her. Her meager income means that her children's regular daycare isn't of the highest quality, and her long hours at work mean that her kids spend long hours at daycare and with her mother rather than with Raven. And even when her kids do get time with her, because of her long hours at work, Raven is unlikely to have the time, energy, and emotional reserves to parent as well as she might. Under pro-family policy, Raven wouldn't be facing this situation. Under free-market family policy, she has no choice but to.

The Impossible Trade-off Between Income and Caretaking for Low-Income Families

The preceding chapter described the caretaking arrangements that are best for young children. Caretaking, though, isn't all that kids require—they also need adequate and secure material provision, which in market societies like our own takes cold, hard cash. An adequate family income benefits kids not just directly, through putting food in their bellies and a roof over their heads, but also indirectly.[3] For one thing, parents use this income to buy books and toys that keep kids engaged and help them develop cognitively.[4] And when parents buy more of these things, they spend more time on activities that are good for kids, like reading with them.[5] With more money to spare, parents also spend more fixing up their home. Because they're happier there as a result, they're more nurturing parents, which also improves kids' outcomes. And they also use money in other ways that improve children's lots. They move to safer neighborhoods with less violence and better schools, they involve their kids in activities like music lessons, and they take more trips that enrich their kids' lives, like going to the zoo.[6]

More income, unsurprisingly, turns out to be far better than less income for kids. One study of US families found that coming from a middle-income family increased children's test scores on the Bracken School Readiness Assessment, a test of knowledge for three-year-olds, by eleven points. Coming from a high-income family added ten more points to that score.[7] The reverse is also true: lower incomes and economic insecurity negatively affect kids. These negative effects don't just stem from parents having less money to spend on their kids. They also come from the fact that it's tremendously stressful when you aren't sure you can keep the lights on in your house for yourself and your kids. These economic circumstances increase parents' anxiety, distress, and depression, all of which make them less responsive to their kids' needs and their behavior more punitive than serves kids well.[8] The result of all of this is that children from both low-income and economically unstable families have lower achievement scores than middle- or upper-class kids; they're also less engaged and have more disciplinary problems in school. There has long been an achievement gap in the United States between low- and high-income children, but since about 1980 (just about the time our nation moved decidedly in the direction of free-market family policy) it has mushroomed.[9]

Free-market policy puts most families in a difficult position when it comes to the trade-off between earning income to support a family and caretaking for their kids. But it puts low-income families in an impossible position. Let's consider the choices available to families toward the bottom of the income distribution in our free-market system versus Finland's pro-family system in their children's first years. The last chapter set out four caretaking conditions that best support young children's development: (1) parental caretaking for up to the first year; (2) after the first year, high-quality caretaking either at home or in daycare; (3) in the year or two before kindergarten, attendance at a high-quality prekindergarten; and (4) throughout early childhood, significant time with a nurturing parent. How hard is it for low-income families in Finland and the United States to provide these circumstances for their kids, while still providing them adequate material support? Put another way, which social order—Finland's under pro-family policy or the United States' under free-market family policy—is more likely to produce sound children with the chance to live up to their full potential?

Let's start with a single-parent family, since, with just one possible breadwinner, a disproportionate number of these families are low-income.[10] Imagine a single mother who earns the median income of single mothers in her country and her new baby. In Finland, before the baby was born, this mother, by virtue of her receiving the median income for single mothers, would have an annual after-tax income of roughly $20,200 (in US dollars).[11] The first condition, staying home with her child for up to the first year, should be relatively easy for her to manage. That's because, under Finland's public policy, she gets roughly nine months' paid leave following the birth of her child, at about 70 percent of her usual pay.[12] After that, she can take another three months of leave subsidized by the state at a somewhat lesser rate. On top of this, for the entire first year (and until the child reaches age seventeen), she'll receive roughly $4,300 annually in child benefits from the state, a sum that includes a supplement for single parents and another for custodial parents receiving no support from the other parent.[13] All told, this gives her small family an income of $16,400 for that first year while she stays home. That's not a lot of cash, but it's certainly adequate for a year, particularly given that her and her baby's healthcare costs will be covered, and, at this income, roughly 80 percent of the family's housing costs will be publicly subsidized by the government.[14]

By the same token, our Finnish mother should also have little difficulty providing the second and third caretaking conditions. She can return to work and put her child in Finland's excellent daycare program for the child's second and third years, and in prekindergarten after that, all at no cost given her income.[15] Alternatively, if she wants to stay home with her child, she can do so by receiving Finland's wage substitute, which is supplemented for low-income families, as well as Finland's safety-net assistance (about $10,000 per year).[16]

Finally, this mother should have significant time and energy for bonding with her child without outsized efforts on her part, and therefore can meet our fourth caretaking condition. She would, of course, easily have adequate parenting time during the first year when she is paid to stay home with her child. But even after she returns to work, Finland's laws limiting maximum required working hours, in addition to its laws requiring paid vacation and national holidays, and its publicly paid family leave to care for sick children, will mean that she has the time she needs with her child and the energy it takes to parent well. The relative lack of stress this system imposes on her in terms of time and finances would also bolster her capacity to be a nurturing parent.

By design, the Finnish mother can arrange all the caretaking circumstances her child needs to have an excellent start without putting her family in difficult financial straits. Her family's income will vary between about $16,400 and $25,500 in her child's first years. As described before, she'll pay little to nothing for medical expenses or childcare under the Finnish system. On top of that, her housing will largely be subsidized. That's because, in Finland, housing assistance is considered an entitlement—anyone who is eligible by virtue of their income receives benefits. Applying for this assistance is easy, and applications usually take just three weeks to process. Overall, 11 percent of the Finnish population receives this housing allowance, including more than half of those in the bottom fifth of earners; an additional 6 percent of the population receive the housing allowance Finland provides to pensioners.[17] With her major expenses of health-care, childcare, and housing covered, this mother should have sufficient money left over after she pays the remaining basics for items like books and toys for her child, as well as some money for outings. Finland's set of interlocking public supports are why, when UNICEF's Innocenti Center compared children's economic deprivation across wealthy countries, it found that only 2 percent of Finnish children lived under deprived circumstances, defined in terms of their household not being able to afford two or more of fourteen items considered "normal and necessary" for a child in an economically advanced country, like children's books, bikes and roller skates, and indoor toys.[18]

Now consider the choices available to a new mother in the United States who earns the median income for a single mother, about $31,000 a year.[19] To flesh her situation out still more, let's assume she's a high school graduate and lives in Denver, Colorado. This mother earns significantly more than her Finnish counterpart—in fact, half again as much. At first blush, we might therefore expect her to have an easier time raising a child. However, it turns out that she will have far more difficulty getting her child the conditions needed to flourish under free-market family policy.

To begin with, this mother doesn't stand a prayer of spending her first year at home with her child without losing her job and falling far below the poverty line. If she were lucky enough to be one of the slightly more than half of private-sector workers to be covered by the Family and Medical Leave Act (FMLA), she would have the right to take twelve weeks off without losing her job.[20] But she wouldn't get any publicly paid leave, and her employer would be unlikely to kick in a dime for it; only about one in twenty workers in the bottom quarter of wages gets paid family leave.[21]

Could she rely on savings to take that leave? It's hard to see how, even if she'd saved roughly the median amount for people under age thirty-five of $1,580.[22] Our mother is lucky to find herself in Colorado, where the government covers the healthcare costs of birth for low-income mothers.[23] In other states, medical costs for the child's delivery would have wiped out her savings and put her in debt, even if she received medical insurance from her employer. Still, even in Colorado, she'd need to spend a big chunk of that savings to buy the basic baby equipment and clothing her child needs. With no income and little to no savings left, our American mother is likely to be one of the quarter of US women, most of them low-income, who have to take two weeks' leave or less before returning to work.[24]

On her return to work, the American mother also won't be able to provide her child the second and third caretaking conditions—high-quality daycare and, in a few years, prekindergarten. Even counting in the roughly $3,000 of tax benefits she'll receive, her total annual income will be about $34,000.

The roughly $16,000 average cost of center-based daycare in Colorado would amount to almost half of her income—far too much for her to manage.[25] And although her income may make her technically eligible for a government childcare subsidy, the chronic underfunding of subsidy funds means that she has virtually no chance of actually receiving one.[26] Because of this, our mother, like three-quarters of single mothers in the United States, will likely have little choice but to put her child in informal daycare with a family member, a friend, or a family provider, and to skip prekindergarten.[27] This is a particularly devastating blow to the potential of children from low-income families.[28] As described in the last chapter, high-quality early childhood education is one of the best and most cost-effective tools we have to reduce the income achievement gap and to give low-income kids better futures.[29]

Will our American mother be able to provide the fourth caretaking circumstance—regular time and opportunity for bonding with and nurturing her child? Here, too, she'll be far less well positioned than her Finnish counterpart. Unlike her peer from Finland, most likely she won't be given any paid holidays or vacation, and she'll likely have to work more hours per week. When she does get some time with her child, like Raven Osborne, the mother from this chapter's introduction, the relentless financial and time pressures our system imposes on her by insisting she combine breadwinning with meeting the caretaking needs of a young child will likely impair her ability to parent her best.[30]

One program that will make a tremendous difference between the lives of our American and Finnish single-parent families is housing assistance. As I mentioned, our Finnish mother will have most of her housing costs covered as a matter of right. Not our American mother. Basic rent and utilities for a mother and child in Denver cost roughly $14,000 a year—almost half of this family's income.[31] Although the United States has housing assistance programs, the largest of which is the Section 8 Housing Choice Voucher Program, only about one in twenty-five Americans receive any assistance because of underfunding (compared with the one in six Finns who receive housing assistance in Finland). Continual budget shortfalls have caused many localities to stop taking new applications at all. And in many localities that take applications, being eligible to get benefits just means getting put on a waitlist. The median voucher waitlist has a waiting time of 1.5 years. In many areas, the waitlist is far longer. One Minneapolis grandmother who lives with her daughter and granddaughter was elated when, after being waitlisted for six years, she was told her family would finally receive a Section 8 voucher. A month later, she was notified that, due to public budget cuts, voucher numbers had to be reduced and her family was back on the waitlist.[32]

The situation of a twenty-nine-year-old mother, Kristie Branson, from Milwaukee, Wisconsin, typifies that of many low-income single mothers. Kristie makes $41,000 a year in her day job working with youth on probation—more than our hypothetical US mother. Yet even though her salary puts her right at the top of the income threshold for a low-income family, she has two young boys, and her earnings aren't enough to pay all the bills. To stay within her budget, she had to pull her older son out of an established daycare center. Instead, her eighty-year-old grandmother watched him until he entered kindergarten, and now watches her younger child. Still, to make ends meet, Kristie goes straight from her day job to waitressing three evenings a week. Fortunately, her parents are able to take care of the kids those evenings and put them to bed. But the schedule leaves her constantly exhausted and leaves her older son, a five-year-old, emotionally needy. He asks her every morning, "Mom, do you have to work tonight? Do you have to work tonight?" Over and over again. She says that it's heartrending to tell him that, yes, she does. She wakes up routinely in the middle of the night from the stress of it all. "You just can't be the parent you want to be when you're constantly that tired and stressed," she says. She's been slowly working on an advanced education degree online late in the evening, hoping that someday she'll only have to work one job and can spend more time with her boys.[33]

Although Kristie, like most American single mothers, earns more than her counterparts in Finland, she is in a much tougher spot when it comes to providing her kids with the conditions that will help them do their best. She'd do anything for her boys, but she simply can't afford high-quality daycare or pre-kindergarten. And, although it breaks her heart not to be home with her boys every evening, she couldn't pay the bills if she were. The United States, under free-market family policy, requires that mothers trade off between meeting their children's caretaking needs and putting food on the table. As a matter of basic math, Kristie simply can't do both.

Would a low-income couple in the United States fare any better on the birth of a child than our single mother? Let's consider the situation of a couple of high school graduates who live in Denver and earn 75 percent of the household median income, or about $41,800—significantly higher than the household income of our single mother.[34] To make the situation comparable to what many American couples face, let's also say that they have a three-year-old child, along with a new baby. Although this family would be better positioned than our US single mother to get their children what they need, they, too, would likely have real difficulty providing them the circumstances for optimal development.

When it comes to the first caretaking condition—having a parent stay home after the baby's birth—the family will probably be able to manage one parent taking several weeks of parental leave. This will likely be the mother since she'll need some recovery time and may be breastfeeding. Yet given the likelihood that neither parent will receive paid parental leave from work, this time off will come at the cost of a significant reduction in the couple's income during this period. Assuming the father's wages are slightly higher than the wife's, or $26,000, this would put the family just above the poverty threshold for a family of four during this time.[35] This heavy economic hit gives the mother a strong incentive to return to paid work in short order. Working mothers with moderate household incomes, like our hypothetical mother here, take just ten weeks off on average after the birth of a child. This is roughly one-fifth of the time that considerable research suggests is best for kids, as well as (not coincidentally) one-fifth of the time that is taken by almost all their Finnish counterparts.[36]

But in considering when the parent should return to work, these parents would confront a difficult dilemma. Returning to paid work would considerably ease the family's financial situation. But it would also require them to find childcare. Given this family's low education and income levels, statistically their children would be among those who would benefit most from high-quality center-based daycare. Yet tuition for two children in center-based daycare in Denver is roughly $30,000 a year—likely far more than the mother's entire salary.[37] This cost, even with the tax benefits for kids that the family would receive, would clearly be prohibitive.[38] Assuming both parents work, they'll therefore have to put their children in cheaper, informal daycare, just as our hypothetical single mother did.[39] So if the mother returns to her job, not only will her baby not get the first caretaking condition—having a parent home up to that first year—her kids will also not get the second and third conditions of having high-quality daycare and prekindergarten. If these parents lived in Finland, by contrast, roughly $30,000 would be spent on daycare per year between both children, almost all paid for by the state.[40]

The other option for our American family is to have one parent leave paid work to take care of the children. About one-third of US two-parent families take this option, and it is usually the mother who leaves the workforce.[41] Despite periodic headlines in the national press suggesting that well-to-do mothers are opting out of the work world en masse to raise children, most of the women who leave paid work come from families near the bottom of the economic pyramid. Many of them leave paid work because their wages won't support the cost of high-quality daycare.[42] But while our hypothetical mother's leaving work would mean that she might be able to provide the first and second conditions of giving her kids high-quality caretaking at home for the child's first years, it very likely means that the family can't give them access to our third condition, enrollment in prekindergarten, when they reach that age.

That's the situation that Ashley Schmidtbauer's family is in. With a baby and a preschooler, she decided to stay home with her kids, with the family making do on her husband's $35,000 salary. But as her older child neared kindergarten age, she wanted to send him to prekindergarten to ready him for kindergarten. No way, though, could the family afford a tuition of nearly $9,000 a year. Yet when she tried to enroll her son in the Head Start program, she was told that her family made too much money. The result is that her son will have to stay home with her until he goes to kindergarten.[43]

Our hypothetical family's choice to have one parent leave work also puts the family in a financially precarious position. Assuming the father earned $26,000 a year, even including the family's hefty tax breaks under the Earned Income Tax Credit (EITC) and the Child Tax Credit (CTC), their income would still be roughly $34,000. That puts the family's income at only a couple of thousand dollars above the level needed to pay for just basic expenses in Denver. That would leave the family almost no budget to pay for anything else—no movies, no vacation, no daytrips, and no way to pay for any games, books, or toys for their kids—a deficit that will put these children at a developmental disadvantage.[44] In the event of an emergency, the family likely would have no way to cover it. Even medical bills for a child's broken arm today can cost a family with insurance $8,000 if the break is complex enough. If that happened to one of their kids, this family couldn't pay the bills. And the economic costs to the family from the mother leaving paid work go well beyond the wages lost during the eight or so years she stays out of work before both kids reach kindergarten. Assuming the mother earned $15,000 in wages before she left work, including her lost wages, her reduced wage growth in the future as a result of her being out of the workplace for that time, and her lost retirement benefits, the family's total income loss over the long term will be $350,000.[45] That's money this family could really have used and which would likely have improved the children's outcomes as they grew.

The loss of the wife's income would also increase the family's economic insecurity. With only one wage earner, a layoff, an illness, or a plant closing would likely send the family into financial free fall given the weakness of the US safety net. This is partly why roughly a quarter of "poverty spells"—periods of two months or more spent in poverty—experienced by US families begin with the birth of a child.[46] The mother's leaving work also poses a different set of financial risks for her and her kids: if her marriage is one of the six in ten of couples with high-school degrees or less to fail, she and her children are far likelier to fall into poverty as a result of her having left her job.[47]

Finally, the fact that our system makes it so difficult for both parents to remain in the workforce reinforces gender inequality. Childcare assistance is the public policy most closely tied to women's employment rates. When families can't get good childcare outside the home, many mothers leave the workforce to care for their kids themselves.[48] Our lack of public subsidies for good daycare is a prime reason that US women's work-participation rates are significantly lower than in other wealthy countries.[49] (At last count, of thirty-five wealthy countries, we ranked twenty-second.)[50]

Whichever option this family chooses—having both parents work or having one parent stay home—whether they can provide the fourth caretaking condition of giving their kids quality time with a nurturing parent is also up for grabs. Spending adequate time with their kids will probably not be a problem. Even if they put their children in paid daycare and continue to work full-time jobs, between the two of them they'll probably be able to find enough time to spend with their children. The bigger question is whether the time stress of both parents working, or the financial stress of just one parent working a paid job, will hurt their parenting quality. In our free-market system, few families escape one or the other stressors.

To sum all this up, free-market family policy forces both single- and two-parent families with incomes below the median to make significant trade-offs between providing the caretaking conditions in which kids do their best and providing the cash their families need. These families simply can't do both. On top of that, even if a family chooses to sacrifice the cash, our system still makes it virtually impossible for low-income parents to satisfy all four of the caretaking conditions that would serve their kids best. In contrast, pro-family policy deliberately makes it easy for parents, including low-income parents, to do exactly that.

Poor Children in the Free-Market System

If the situation of low-income children is bad, it's even worse for the children of poor families. Our free-market system is designed to pressure poor mothers into the workplace. It does a pretty good job of meeting this goal (though it would do even better if it ensured that all these mothers had childcare so they could work).[51] When it comes to getting poor kids what they need to flourish, though, our system is a total disaster. The damage goes far beyond parents being unable to provide good caretaking. Our free-market system doesn't even permit poor parents to provide kids with the very basics of a decent life.

Free-market family policy requires virtually all low-income parents to make a trade-off between adequate material support for their kids and meeting the caretaking conditions that will serve them best. But when it comes to poor families, the low wages paid at the bottom of our economy mean that, no matter how hard parents work, most can provide *neither* the material support *nor* the caretaking conditions that enable children to flourish. All in all, our system has created the perfect storm preventing poor parents from getting their children what they need to thrive.

The Need for Adequate Income Support for Poor Kids

Let's start by considering the cash support that children of poor US families receive under free-market family policy. One thing we know for certain is that young kids need consistent, adequate material support to do well.[52] Remember how kids in Romanian orphanages showed less brain matter in brain scans from their lack of contact with a nurturing parent? Neuroscientists have found that something similar happens when kids are raised in poverty. One recent study of US grade schoolers showed that children exposed to poverty in early childhood had less brain matter in areas that affect academic achievement, stress regulation, and emotional processing.[53] This helps explain not only why poor kids miss more school and do worse in school in the short term than other children, but also why they have poorer health, lower educational achievement, lower earnings, and higher mortality when they grow up.[54]

Given the permanent harm that poverty causes children, countries with pro-family policy go to considerable lengths to ensure that kids from low-income families get the material support they need. They do so through a mix of policies, many of which will be familiar to readers by now, including universal programs, like parental leave subsidies and child benefits, as well as programs targeting at-risk families, like child benefit supplements for the kids of single parents, and housing subsidies for low-income families. The goal of these policies is to make sure that kids don't slip into poverty in the first place. That's why Finland's absolute and relative poverty rates, already low, are even lower for families with children, including families with young children, than they are for the population at large.[55] The United States has always had weaker programs of these sorts than other countries, trusting markets to provide for families more than other countries have. The safety valve our nation long relied on when markets failed to enable parents to get their kids what they needed was the Aid to Families with Dependent Children (AFDC) program, often known simply as "welfare." AFDC, though, was repealed during welfare reform in the 1990s. It was replaced by Temporary Assistance for Needy Families (TANF), whose goal, emblematized in the program's name "Work First," was to get poor mothers into paid work and off government support. To do that, TANF scrapped the guarantee of cash for all children who needed it, allowed states to reduce benefit levels, imposed work requirements on adult recipients, and introduced time limits on benefits. In place of guaranteed welfare benefits, Congress increased tax benefits for families through both the EITC and the CTC.

Making sure that poor kids have sufficient resources should have been the top goal of welfare policy, but welfare reform's focus on getting poor mothers into the workplace eclipsed that critical government responsibility from view. How well do our current public policies ensure that all kids get the material resources they need? The answer to this question is certainly "poorly" (no pun intended). Exactly how many children don't get what they need depends on how high we set the bar for the level of resources that we believe kids should get. Under any reasonable measure of what kids should be getting, though, whether that's basic subsistence or the more generous level of support associated with having an adequate life in an advanced country, a large proportion of US children fall below it—and a far larger proportion than in wealthy countries with pro-family policies.

One reasonable place to set the bar is at the level of the basic budget for US families developed by Columbia University's National Center for Children in Poverty (NCCP). That budget calculates basic necessary expenses for families with children in different areas across the United States. The budget includes items like food, rent, utilities, childcare, medical care, and transportation. The NCCP's basic budget isn't set high enough to truly give children the resources that support optimal development, because it includes no line items for games, toys, or computers and no enrichment trips to, say, a museum or the zoo.[56] With that said, it's a useful starting point for determining what constitutes adequate resources to raise kids. Yet even at this low bar, and with government benefits and tax credits taken into account, four of every ten American children don't clear it.[57]

How we compare with other countries with a bar set at this level is difficult to pin down because few good cross-national studies apply a similar standard of basic necessary expenses. The UNICEF Innocenti Center study described earlier in the chapter, though, compared several wealthy countries based on a similar standard, although it excluded the United States. That study set a somewhat higher bar than the NCCP basic budget, in that it included not only basic necessary expenses but also items thought necessary for a decent childhood, like children's books, bicycles, and roller skates. Despite the higher standard, this study found that only 2 percent of Finnish children were raised in households that couldn't provide these items. In Sweden, that figure was 1 percent. In Denmark, it was under 3 percent.[58] So in the United States, the wealthiest country in the world, forty in a hundred kids don't get the basics they need. In Finland, Denmark, and Sweden, fewer than three in a hundred don't.

We can make a still more accurate comparison across countries if we set the bar at the lower rung of avoiding poverty. Most experts rely on a relative measure of poverty, meaning that poverty is measured relative to the living standards in a child's own society, so that the standard of living at the poverty line rises in wealthy countries and falls in poor ones. That's because abundant research shows that once a nation becomes as wealthy as our own, it is relative poverty rather than absolute poverty that matters most. As Richard Wilkinson and Kate Pickett have demonstrated, the social problems associated with poverty in industrialized societies, like drug use, obesity, teenage pregnancy, and violence, don't subside as nations get wealthier, as you'd expect if absolute deprivation caused them. To the contrary, some of the wealthiest nations, including our own, experience these problems at the highest rates. But the severity of these problems declines when the degree of inequality in a country decreases, and it grows when inequality increases.[59]

Stories from Wanda Johnson, the Charlotte, North Carolina mother we met in the book's introduction, about her son's childhood demonstrate why relative poverty matters so much. Throughout her son Deonte's childhood, Wanda says, she simply couldn't afford to give him anything but the basics (and sometimes not even that). So on every birthday, Wanda treated Deonte to some cupcakes and a thrifty dinner at a restaurant to celebrate. But no way could she afford a birthday party with a cake and balloons. When her son reached school age, though, he noticed that other kids were having birthday parties. He started to ask anyone he saw, "When is my birthday?," not understanding why he didn't have parties and receive presents like other kids. That year, his grandmother helped Wanda throw a party for him at her house, but it was the only birthday party he ever had as a kid.

When Deonte reached school age, he also badly wanted to play football and basketball at the local recreation center. Wanda had to tell him no: The programs cost between $65 and $80 dollars a season, and besides that, he'd need an extra pair of shoes. Wanda simply didn't have the money to spend on a non-necessity like this. So Deonte had to sit sports out, except for the one season when Wanda's friend coached the team and waived Deonte's fee. That feeling of standing on the sidelines and watching the other kids play stayed with Deonte.

There is one more story about Deonte's childhood that demonstrates the impact of relative poverty. Remember your first day back at school in the fall, when the teacher would ask all the kids what they did that summer, and they'd describe some great trip they'd taken or the other adventures they'd had? Wanda couldn't afford to take Deonte on vacation, except once, when she managed a trip to the beach. So every year but that one, he, unlike the rest of the kids, had nothing to report on that first day of school. That's the kind of thing that leaves a lasting impression on a kid.

How does the relative poverty rate here in the United States compare with other countries? It turns out that we rank at the rock bottom. A 2017 study compared children across sixteen wealthy countries, calculating relative poverty as the percentage of children living in families whose incomes fell below half the level of the median disposable household income after taxes and government benefits. Of those countries, the United States had by far the highest rate of young children living in relative poverty, at 24 percent. Italy had the next highest, well below us at 18 percent. In comparison, Denmark's and Finland's rates were 6 and 4 percent respectively.[60]

But even if we switch from a relative to an absolute standard of poverty, meaning a standard that defines deprivation without taking the wealth of the country into account, the United States fares almost as badly. The 2017 study on relative poverty just mentioned also compared countries on an absolute poverty measure. That measure was set based on families' ability after government benefits and taxes to pay for a subsistence budget that was set based on the US poverty line, adjusted for local purchasing power across countries. The United States did better here than on the relative poverty measure, dropping from a 24 percent to a 14 percent poverty rate for families with young children. But we still had the fourth-highest rate of the sixteen wealthy countries compared, below only Greece, Italy, and Spain. These countries' higher poverty rates shouldn't be all that surprising, given that those nations are far less wealthy than our own. What is surprising, though, is that our absolute poverty rate for young children is so much higher than that of other countries less wealthy than we are, like Germany and France at 9 percent, Canada at 8 percent, Australia at 7 percent, and Denmark and Finland at 2 percent. These countries manage to do a much better job of using their wealth to ensure that children have the material support they need.[61]

The fact that our poverty rates are higher than those of our peers largely isn't a product of the lower market earnings of poor Americans compared to their counterparts in other countries. Based on market earnings alone, before government programs and taxes, the US relative poverty rate is 31 percent. That makes our market-income poverty rate higher than most, but not all, other wealthy countries. Ireland's market-income poverty rate tops the list of countries at a whopping 42 percent—far higher than the United States. Our country ultimately has so much more poverty than other countries, including Ireland, because our public policies do far less to address the condition than other countries' public policies do. Once government benefits and taxes are factored in, Ireland's relative poverty rate falls to 10 percent—a 32-percentage-point drop as a result of government programs. In contrast, US programs ultimately leave us with a poverty rate of 21 percent—a reduction of only 10 percentage points.[62] So, at the end of the day, Ireland's child poverty rate is less than half of ours because its pro-family policies do a much better job of ensuring that poor kids get the resources they need.

What went wrong with welfare reform's plan to lift poor families out of poverty by pushing mothers into paid work? As I mentioned earlier, the plan did move poor mothers into the workforce: single mothers' labor force participation rose by 10 percentage points, and that of never-married mothers rose by more than 15 percentage points.[63] But these women overwhelmingly moved into low-wage service jobs, and these jobs simply don't pay a living wage today. In fact, one in four jobs in our economy presently don't pay enough to pull a family of four above the poverty line.[64] This means that, despite working as many hours as they can, when just market earnings are taken into account, most poor mothers are still as poor as they were before welfare reform.[65] A number are even poorer.[66] It's just that now many spend long days working away from their kids.

Most poor, single mothers today, 62 percent, work for pay.[67] A number of the single mothers I spoke to while writing this book not only worked full-time, they also worked second and third jobs, which meant less time with their kids. Most were also constantly exhausted between the demands of all that paid work and single parenting. Yet their paychecks still weren't enough to give their kids even a basic, decent life. This meant they lived lives of quiet desperation, always focused on how to get through the month. Many routinely needed to ask relatives for help—for diapers or rent money—and many also relied on food banks to fill out meals. Their kids' lives, meanwhile, were constricted by their family's constant efforts to make do with as little as possible. There were no sleepovers for their kids (the apartments were too depressing and sparsely furnished, and the families couldn't afford to feed another mouth at dinner); no visits to the museum or the zoo (no money for non-necessary bus fares or admission tickets); no toddler music classes or soccer recreational leagues; no nights out even at a fast-food restaurant; no trips to the movie theater. The parents tried to shield their kids from the grimness of a life lived in grinding poverty, but all spoke of moments when that just wasn't possible.

In seeking to force mothers into paid work by removing access to government aid, welfare reform also didn't take account of the many parents who simply can't find steady work, no matter how hard they try. This is increasingly true in an economy in which businesses use flexible scheduling to keep down labor costs. One single mother of four, Teresa Branham, of Tacoma, Washington, told me that although she always worked, many of her employers didn't offer steady hours. After she reached the five-year lifetime limit on TANF, there were periods during which she couldn't afford to put enough food on the table. During those times, she told me with her voice breaking, she'd serve the kids food and hope they'd leave some scraps behind that she herself could eat once they were in bed. At one point, she grew desperate enough that she turned tricks to make a little cash. Today she has three jobs, but there are still times when she can't make ends meet, and her family has been intermittently homeless as a result. When I last spoke to her, she was living on the streets, renting a motel room when she could afford to.[68] Kathryn Edin and Luke Shaefer spent years investigating how poor families survive in the aftermath of welfare reform. Some parents sold their food stamps for a discounted rate and went hungry because they needed cash to buy things their kids needed, like underwear or a school uniform. Other parents sold plasma a couple of times a week at about $30 a session, even though this left them physically depleted.[69]

Despite the misery caused by our inadequate safety net, the US child poverty rate has actually dropped significantly in recent years, according to the US
Supplemental Poverty Measure (SPM), a quasi-absolute measure, when annual
income after government benefits is considered.[70] Poor parents' increased hours
of paid work has very little to do with this. Neither do TANF benefits, which
play an even smaller role in reducing poverty than they did when the program
was first passed.[71] So where did the reduction in our poverty rate come from?
Mostly from government programs other than TANF, like the Supplemental
Nutrition Assistance Program (otherwise known as food stamps) and the two
big tax credit programs directed at families, the EITC and the CTC, which are
giving poor families more help.[72]

Just to be clear, there's nothing about tax expenditure programs like the EITC
and the CTC that makes them inherently better for reducing child poverty than
the periodic welfare checks sent to parents under the AFDC/TANF programs.
The reason our tax programs have moved more US families above the poverty
line in recent years is simply that US policymakers were more willing to increase
funding for these programs than to increase benefits under AFDC/TANF.[73] And
that's largely because they just don't like AFDC/TANF payments given their
view, underpinned by free-market thinking, that they make poor families "dependent" on government instead of the market. Does a family's reliance on tax
expenditure programs make them any less dependent on government than their
reliance on welfare programs? Not in any way that should make a difference.
Of course, recognizing that tax expenditure programs constitute dependence on
government also helps make it clear that it's not just poor families who depend
on government—almost all families rely on the benefits of the CTC (and it's the
well-to-do who disproportionately take the mortgage interest deduction). We
just tend to see this as a problem when it comes to poor families.[74]

While providing income to poor families through tax expenditure programs
is certainly better for the kids in these families than their not getting the income at all, the monthly cash payments families would get through programs
like AFDC/TANF (or, in pro-family policy countries, through the child benefits
that all families with kids receive) would be far more helpful to the children in
poor families. Kids need consistent income provision. Receiving a check at the
beginning of the month is far more likely to deliver this than giving families a
tax break they can only claim at the end of the year. It's the monthly payments
that so many senior citizens receive from Social Security that have drastically
reduced the poverty rates among the elderly. Without Social Security, four in ten
seniors would be poor.[75] With it, fewer than one in ten is. Yet we have no comparable public program for the many children who are equally in need, and for
whom the effects of poverty will last a lifetime.

Recognize this and you'll also recognize why all the US poverty-rate calculations I've discussed so far in this chapter radically *underestimate* the proportion of kids who aren't receiving the material support they need. All these poverty calculations are based on total *annual* income, counting in the tax breaks that families get once a year. But if a family's income is uneven during the course of the year—and we know that most low- and many middle-income families' incomes are—it can drop below the poverty line for months at a time without the family registering as poor in poverty tallies. As I noted in chapter 2, the families of four in ten children fall below the poverty threshold for at least two months of the year, meaning that even their basic subsistence needs won't be met consistently.[76] This, in the richest country this world has ever known.

The Caretaking That Kids Need

So kids from poor families won't get the material support they need, but what are the chances that they will get the caretaking that would serve them best? Quite small. When it comes to having a parent home for the first year of a child's life, the first caretaking condition in our list of four, most poor mothers will have little financial choice but to return to work soon after they give birth.[77] To be sure, some parents will be eligible to receive TANF benefits without having to meet its work requirements because they live in the roughly half of states that waive work requirements during the child's first year.[78] Yet in most states they could stay home only at the cost of living in extreme poverty, at or below one-third of the federal poverty line. The result is that, even in states that waive the work requirements, if they have the opportunity to work, many of these parents will have no choice but to do so.

On top of that, few children from poor families will be placed in excellent daycare, which is the second caretaking circumstance children require. Poor children are technically eligible for the Early Head Start program, which serves children from infancy through age three. But the program's underfunding means that fewer than one in twenty-five eligible kids are actually served.[79] Again because of underfunding, poor families have only a slightly better shot at getting a government childcare subsidy: only about one in five. Those children who don't receive subsidies will generally have to have their children cared for by untrained friends and relatives—a form of daycare that experts find to be generally inadequate. And even those few children who do receive a subsidy generally have little chance of getting high-quality care. This is partly because the level of subsidies that most states provide are inadequate. Only one state pays daycare providers at the federally recommended level; thirty states pay at least 20 percent below the recommended level for one-year-olds. But children from families receiving

TANF also don't receive high-quality care because most states require parents to accept the first job offered to them, which is often a job with unpredictable and unstable hours. Few daycare centers can meet such a schedule. This forces families to accept whatever care is available, without regard to quality. (The "Work First" program could equally have been called "Children Last.")[80]

When it comes to the third caretaking condition, attendance at a high-quality prekindergarten, the picture is slightly more mixed. Between the rise of public prekindergartens and Head Start, there is a reasonable possibility that children from poor families will be able to attend a formal prekindergarten program: one study found that six in ten children from families at the tenth percentile of income attended such a program in 2010. There is far less of a chance, though, that the prekindergarten program they attend will be high-quality. The public prekindergarten program that serves the most poor children in the United States is Head Start, which enrolls four in ten poor children.[81] But, even assuming a family manages to get their child a spot, Head Start doesn't usually provide the quality of care kids need to do their best, in part because of the program's underfunding. One national panel of experts recently found that although few Head Start programs were of poor quality, most were well below average for prekindergarten programs overall in the United States.[82]

Last but not least is the fourth caretaking condition—children spending significant time with a nurturing parent. Free-market family policy's demand that every family support itself financially means that single mothers work longer hours of paid work than coupled mothers (married or cohabiting), who have assistance with breadwinning from their partner. Because of this, single mothers tend to be significantly more "time-poor," which translates into less time with their children. The result is that, even though single mothers cut their free time to the bone to get time with their kids, they still spend between three and five hours a week less on childcare than married or cohabiting mothers. This includes less time for both basic caretaking activities like bathing and feeding their kids and for enrichment activities like playing with and reading to them.[83] There's some dispute about whether greater time with kids improves their outcomes. But we do know that the time parents spend with children in enrichment activities tends to increase kids' cognitive capacities.[84]

Even more important than the quantity is the quality of parenting that children receive. And here free-market family policy raises huge red flags for poor children. As the neuroscientist Michael Meaney, one of the key researchers on the rat development experiments discussed in chapter 5, put it when discussing its implications for children's development, "The single most important factor determining the quality of mother-offspring interactions is the mental and physical health of the mother."[85] Yet the chronic stress that free-market family policy imposes on poor families leads to the deterioration of both. The stress that poverty creates causes or exacerbates a broad array of serious health conditions. One 2016 study calculated that premature deaths in New York City between 2008 and 2012 would have dropped by between 2,800 and 5,500 people—or about one in twelve—if the city's minimum wage had been $15 an hour during that period instead of just over $7 an hour.[86]

Likewise, we know that the chronic stress that poverty imposes on adults drives up mental illness rates.[87] Canada's experiment with guaranteed basic income in the 1970s demonstrated the tight causal connection between poverty and mental illness. When the government told the town of Dauphin's residents that they would receive a moderate basic income of about $17,000 a year if they couldn't otherwise provide for themselves, mental health hospitalizations plummeted.[88] An expert in the Manitoba experiment, Evelyn Forget, explained the drop this way: "It just removed the stress . . . that people dealt with in their everyday lives."[89] Finland's recent experiment with a guaranteed basic income showed the same.[90] We know, as well, that stress on parents diminishes the quality of their parenting in ways that impede their children's development.[91] Recent research helps explain this by showing that, when people are under significant daily stress, it narrows their attention to their daily existence and immediate struggles, and curtails their capacity to invest in the future.[92] But being able to invest in the future is exactly what parents need to do for their children.

To sum all this up, our free-market family policy deliberately uses poverty and insecurity as a stick to drive parents into the workplace and to force them to work for long hours. In doing so, it puts the great majority of poor parents in just the kind of difficult and stressful circumstances that we know undermine good parenting. On top of this, it requires that these parents arrange caretaking for their children largely on their own, with insufficient money to pay for good care. And the few public benefits that poor parents receive often come with arbitrary requirements that make their receipt uncertain and through a process that leaves parents feeling belittled and dehumanized.[93]

Given what we know about how important children's early circumstances are to their sound development, the results of free-market family policy on poor children should be unsurprising. United States infants show no significant differences based on family income. By eighteen months, though, toddlers from poor families are already several months behind their better-off peers. By age four, children from disadvantaged families score at about the 33rd percentile in math and literacy; their advantaged peers score at the 69th percentile.[94] By the start of kindergarten, poor kids are nearly a year behind their wealthier peers, and the gap persists through grade school.[95]

Free-market family policy has shifted the basic fault lines in American society. In the 1970s, the academic achievement gap between white and black students was large, and by far the most potent predictor of a child's achievement in school. This is unsurprising given our nation's long history of racism and segregation. In the half century since then under free-market family policy, though, the racial gap has been dwarfed by the achievement gap between lower- and higher-income students. The gap between a child from a family at the 90th percentile of the family income distribution and a child from a family at the 10th percentile is now more than twice as large as the racial achievement gap.[96] And family income is now far and away the best predictor of school success.[97]

Adverse Childhood Experiences

If all this isn't bad enough, it turns out that free-market policy greatly increases the likelihood that poor kids will be traumatized as a result of their circumstances, and that this trauma will scar them for life. This may sound like hyperbole, but it's actually science. Doctors and scientists have in the last two decades begun to understand the profound impact of what they call "adverse childhood experiences," or ACEs, on children's development. The basic idea is that when children experience significant trauma, like family chaos, bullying, living with someone with mental illness or substance abuse, domestic violence or neglect, parents breaking up, or living in foster care, the stress creates a significant physiological response. If the stress response is severe and prolonged enough, which experts call "toxic stress," it disrupts the development of the wiring in children's brains.[98] Increased ACE exposures, it turns out, drastically and cumulatively affect children's lifetime outcomes. Adults who experience more of them as children have much higher odds of developing alcoholism, substance abuse, or depression; of attempting suicide; of engaging in criminal behavior; and of having an early death.[99]

Our free-market family policy, though, practically guarantees that poor children will be exposed to ACEs. The driving purpose of welfare reform in 1996 was to use poverty as a stick to ensure that single mothers got out of the house and entered paid work.[100] Poverty is usually considered an independent negative factor that reduces children's outcomes, rather than an ACE itself, but it also greatly increases the chances that children will experience ACEs. Parental neglect, domestic violence, substance abuse, homelessness, and a child's being removed to foster care, all of which are ACEs, are driven up by poverty.[101] Furthermore, poverty greatly limits parents' ability to remove kids from many of these situations by drastically curtailing their available living and caretaking options. Finally, our system makes it unlikely that kids will be provided two key circumstances that help to mitigate the negative impact of ACEs—a stable home and strong early childhood education.[102]

Not only does free-market family policy make it likely that poor kids will be exposed to ACEs, it also makes it more likely that they'll process these experiences as toxic stress. Whether a child does so depends not only on how severe the stressor is and the length of time it persists, but also on whether they have access to a supportive adult, usually a parent.[103] A nurturing parent, it turns out, can greatly reduce the child's stress response from trauma. Our free-market family policy, though, requires that parents work, for long hours each day, which means they often won't be there to provide the emotional support that might safeguard their children. To make matters worse, the stress from grinding poverty and insecurity that our free-market system inflicts on poor parents decreases the chances that, even when they are physically present, they'll have the emotional resources to provide the nurturing their kids need.

To understand the importance of parents' role in helping kids process stress, think back to the experiments on rat mothers and their pups described in the last chapter. In these experiments, the calm rat mothers were far more nurturing to their pups than were the stressed mothers. That nurturing, in turn, helped their pups deal with stress, which eventually produced better outcomes for the pups. Meanwhile, the stressed rat mothers were much less nurturing to their pups, which produced worse outcomes. Neuroscientists believe that brain development in human children works similarly.

If the neuroscientists are right, free-market family policy represents a profound danger to poor children. It ensures that children will be trapped in poverty and the stressful circumstances related to it. At the same time, it removes the children from their parents for long hours, which limits parents' ability to help the child process this stress. Finally, it subjects the parents themselves to tremendous stress, which hampers their ability to nurture their kids even when they are together.[104]

In sum, pro-family policy seeks to ensure that all children are raised under conditions that give them the best chance to flourish. To do this, it goes to considerable lengths to ensure that no child is raised in poverty, and that all children get the caretaking that would serve them best. Free-market family policy, by contrast, intentionally puts stress on poor parents in a misbegotten quest to spur them on to market independence. In doing so, this system virtually ensures that children won't get the childhood they need to flourish as adults.

Let me close this section by returning to the account of Wanda Johnson, the Charlotte mother doing her best to raise her son, Deonte, despite the family's poverty. During Deonte's first years, despite Wanda's best efforts, her son dealt not only with constant economic deprivation and the awareness that he had far less than most other kids, but also with a full stable of ACEs—household chaos, bullying, and subpar childcare situations. Because Wanda couldn't afford to rent her own place or pay for decent daycare for Deonte, she had no choice but to keep him in these miserable situations. And when Wanda finally moved out with Deonte after their living situation became intolerable, the pair wound up homeless. The consequence was that Deonte was removed to foster care for a year—another ACE. Wanda admits that the stress of her situation—living in overcrowded homes, constantly worrying about how to put food on the table, having to deal with inconsistent work hours and pay—took a toll on her parenting ability. She was constantly focused on her family's basic survival, which made it hard for her to be the parent she'd hoped to be in her son's first years.

Wanda will tell you that she never wanted a handout. She was always willing to work hard, both at paid work and raising Deonte and, several years later, his younger brother, Trevor. In fact, although her family is still borderline poor, she's been working full-time for the past fifteen years. She just couldn't get all the pieces to fit into place for her family by herself, despite her long hours of paid work and her family's very frugal way of life. And that meant Deonte had a much tougher start than he could have had.[105]

Childhoods like the one Deonte experienced give children long odds. Deonte, unfortunately, didn't beat them. When he reached his teen years, he started to have disciplinary problems at school and small run-ins with the law. None of the counselors Wanda took him to helped. Now twenty, Deonte was recently given a nine-year prison sentence for armed robbery. We can't know for sure how he would have done if he'd had better circumstances in his early years. But we know that his odds of winding up in prison would have been far lower.

The conditions in which Wanda has raised her younger son, Trevor, who is now ten, have been far better. Although her wages still put their family close to the poverty line when he was born, by that time they had their own apartment in a quiet area (temporarily subsidized by Section 8 vouchers), and Wanda had a stable, full-time job with stable pay. Since she was no longer living in someone else's overcrowded place, she could child-proof their apartment and allow Trevor the space to be a kid at home. And because he was grandfathered into his brother's daycare subsidy when he was born, he had pretty good daycare from early on. Because Wanda was under so much less stress by that time, she says she was—and is—a much better parent. She certainly has rules—Trevor has to do his homework right after she picks him up from afterschool care, and he has a set bedtime. But she's more flexible with him about other things. How is Trevor doing these days? Just great.[106]

In countries with pro-family policy, with the help of government, young children from poor and low-income families get both the income and the caretaking that gives them their best chance to develop into sound adults. They have their basic material needs predictably met with the help of regular government checks, have a parent subsidized to stay home with them most or all of their first year, attend quality daycare in the next year or two or have a parent subsidized to stay home with them, and then enroll in high-quality prekindergarten. During these years, public policy also enables their parents to work moderate hours and to return home with relatively low stress so that they can parent their children well.

In the United States under free-market family policy, in stark contrast, poor and low-income children are likely to remain that way as a result of a safety net that is purposely full of holes. By insisting that parents negotiate and pay for their own time off, our free-market system ensures that few kids will get parental caretaking during their first year. By failing to provide high-quality daycare and prekindergarten after that, free-market family policy deprives these children of the best means we know of to close the income achievement gap. Finally, by requiring parents at the low end of the income spectrum to provide for their families on wages too low and insecure to do so properly, this system imposes such significant, grinding stress on parents that it undermines their ability to give their kids the nurturing attention they need to thrive.[105] In fact, it's tough to imagine a system less likely to produce thriving children than our own when it comes to poor and low-income families. So what does this do to kids' outcomes?

Outcomes for Children in the Free-Market Family System

Many of us still see the United States as the world's leader when it comes to children's well-being and development. That is what the American Dream promises us—that all our kids will reach their full potential no matter which family they were born into. Unfortunately, our perception that American children are thriving is starkly opposed to today's reality. Kids in the United States are doing far worse than in the past on a range of important measures. And their outcomes are middling to poor compared with those of kids from other wealthy countries, depending on the measure.

This chapter revisits the indicators on children discussed in chapter 1 and adds a few more to the picture to show how US free-market family policy drags children's outcomes down on happiness, academic achievement, mental health, child maltreatment, and economic mobility. Free-market policy, it makes the case, undercuts the well-being not just of kids from less-advantaged families, but of kids up and down the economic ladder. In this system, few children get what they need to do their best in those first years. After that, almost all must contend with the difficult recognition that, in our unequal economy, other kids' families have more—and as we grow more unequal, far more—than their own. And as they mature, all have to prepare themselves for adulthood in our increasingly insecure economy. In doing so, youths from families toward the bottom of the dirt pile are discouraged by the steep slope they are ill-prepared to climb. Meanwhile, those from families toward the top of the dirt pile are exhausted by the effort it takes to prepare themselves to maintain their place on that slope. So no matter where their families stand economically, children in the United States wind up doing considerably worse than in the past, as well as worse than kids do in countries with pro-family policy.

HAPPINESS

As chapter 1 showed, the United States falls toward the bottom of wealthy countries when it comes to kids' reports of their own life satisfaction. Out of twenty-seven OECD countries, we tie for fifteenth place with seven other countries, among them the Slovak Republic and the Czech Republic. Our children are not only less happy than children in other wealthy countries like Sweden, the Netherlands, and Iceland, but also less happy than children in Slovenia, whose GDP per capita is less than half of ours.[1] These countries are doing a much better job of converting their wealth into kids' happiness than we are.

Why aren't our kids as satisfied with their lives as kids from so many other countries? Happiness researchers have long puzzled over the fact that, once a society becomes moderately wealthy, added wealth doesn't increase overall levels of happiness. In their international bestseller, *The Spirit Level*, Richard Wilkinson and Kate Pickett showed that once a country moves above that threshold level of moderate wealth, the overall level of happiness of its people is far more closely associated with the level of economic equality in the society than with the average wealth of its people. People in wealthy countries that are relatively equal economically tend to be the happiest; as inequality widens within a country, people get progressively less happy. (With that said, within a particular society, rich people tend to be happier than poor people. It's the overall, average levels of happiness in a country that increase as equality increases.)[2] Rising inequality is associated with other indicators of well-being dropping as well, including those relating to mental health, drug use, teen pregnancy, prison rates, and educational performance.[3]

Wilkinson and Pickett's research focused on cross-national comparison, showing that as the association between economic inequality in a country rose, the aggregate indicators of well-being of people in the country dropped. The researchers didn't try to trace exactly how inequality, in their words, "gets under the skin," meaning the causal process through which it negatively affects the lives of individual people. But it may be that what drives the poorer outcomes in unequal countries isn't just economic inequality itself, but also a range of other negative effects of free-market policy. In other words, free-market family policy may be negatively affecting people's outcomes in a number of ways, not just by increasing inequality.

How might free-market family policy drag down kids' satisfaction with their lives?[4] There are several pathways through which this may occur. For one thing, we know that kids from low- and middle-income families are often impacted by the economic instability that their families are subjected to and that this decreases their happiness.[5] For another, economic deprivation itself takes a harsh toll on happiness for those at the bottom.[6] And, as the last chapter discussed, far more

American children experience this kind of deprivation than kids in most other OECD countries.[7]

The economic travails that low- and middle-income families face in our free-market system today also reduces children's happiness in less direct ways. When families are in economic distress, parenting quality drops and child abuse rates rise.[8] Unsurprisingly, both reduce children's reported sense of satisfaction with their lives.[9] Further, poverty confines many families to violent neighborhoods and poor public schools, both of which reduce kids' level of happiness.[10] Moreover, we know from happiness researchers that when people assess life satisfaction, they factor in how well they are doing economically by comparing themselves with others around them, and particularly those who have more wealth.[11] In conditions of stark inequality, as in the United States, this means that children often compare themselves with children from far wealthier families, which lowers their assessment of their own life satisfaction.[12]

Given that wealth tends to make those at the top of the economic ladder happier than those below them, you might expect US kids from highly affluent families to be the happiest in the world. Yet US kids from the top third of families economically, despite their families having far more wealth than the top third of families in other wealthy countries, are no happier than their (somewhat less) well-off peers in other countries.[13] Why might this be the case? There are several likely reasons. First, most of these kids, too, compare themselves with far wealthier peers. Further, increasing economic inequality and uncertainty ratchet up the pressure on kids across the economic spectrum to achieve. If they want to be economically stable when they reach adulthood, these kids learn, they need to excel. While kids from all economic backgrounds in the United States feel more pressure to do well than kids in most other wealthy countries, that pressure is felt most acutely by kids from middle- and upper-middle-class families—the kids who are most commonly the focus of "intensive parenting."[14] That's the reverse of the situation in most other wealthy countries, where low-income kids feel the most pressure to do well, and high-income kids feel the least.[15] And the significant pressure to excel that our system places on teens likely cancels out some of the positive effects of their greater affluence when it comes to their happiness.[16]

The pressure to maintain their place on the dirt pile when they become adults also likely reduces US kids' happiness in another way: it pushes them away from focusing on what researchers call "intrinsic" goals and toward "extrinsic" goals. Goals are intrinsic when the people who hold them determine whether they've been met. So goals like exercising a certain number of times a week, making close friends, and reading a given number of good books are all intrinsic. In contrast, extrinsic goals require validation by others and are sought for instrumental purposes rather than for the simple satisfaction of meeting them. Prominent on the list of extrinsic goals are earning lots of money and getting into a prestigious college.

Although everyone pursues some combination of intrinsic and extrinsic goals, people who are more focused on intrinsic goals tend to be happier, as well as less likely to develop certain psychiatric disorders.[17] Why exactly this is the case isn't completely clear. Some researchers think it's because satisfying intrinsic goals meets our basic needs for autonomy, competence, and relatedness, whereas satisfying extrinsic goals does not meet these needs.[18] Whatever the cause, focusing on external validators, like getting top SAT scores or being accepted into an elite college, is associated with lower levels of life satisfaction.[19] As societies become less equal, though, people tend to focus comparatively more on extrinsic goals than on intrinsic goals. For example, during periods in which economic inequality is higher, college students are more likely to respond with extrinsic reasons for why they went to college, such as "to make more money," than with intrinsic reasons such as "I wanted to get a good education."[20]

Given the association between inequality and extrinsic goals, it's unsurprising that, in the past half-century, our youth have begun to focus more on extrinsic goals than in the past, and particularly on economic success. The shift has been linear, increasing between Baby Boomers and Gen-Xers, and then between Gen-Xers and Millennials.[21] During the 1970s, high school students cumulatively ranked finding meaning and purpose in life third most important on a list of goals; by the mid-2000s, this goal had dropped to sixth place. In 1971, when college students considered which of a number of goals they considered essential or very important, being very well off financially wound up in eighth place; by 1989, it had moved to first place, where it has since stayed consistently.[22] This shift from intrinsic to extrinsic goals among college students in particular shouldn't be a surprise: one of the purposes of intensive parenting is to make certain that kids focus on external indicators of success—winning awards in extracurricular activities, doing well at school and on the SATs, and getting into an elite college—rather than spend their childhood on more playful pursuits like sleepovers and watching movies. And that contributes to American kids overall being less happy as a group than they used to be, as well as less happy than their peers in other countries.

On a related note, although more speculatively, happiness may also be in comparatively short supply for American youths today because, in the competitive system engendered by free-market policy, "productive" activities edge out merely enjoyable ones for these kids.[23] That's why high school baseball coaches report that, after years of private coaching and specialized baseball clinics, promising baseball players can easily hit a line drive but they don't know how to play a game of catch. As one baseball expert observed, there are a lot of features of baseball "that can more inherently be learned in backyard play. But when have you driven around lately and seen kids playing catch for fun?"[24]

In sum, free-market family policy likely reduces the happiness of children from the bottom to the top of the economic ladder through several different pathways. The real economic deprivation that kids at the bottom experience, as well as the decreased quality of parenting they suffer from stressed parents, detracts from their happiness. And the relative deprivation that kids on all rungs of the ladder feel as they compare themselves with kids from wealthier families does the same. Meanwhile, all children, and particularly those at the top, feel increasingly pressured to focus on achieving a place on an ever-steeper economic slope.

ACADEMIC ACHIEVEMENT

Our system does a poor job not only of translating our wealth into happiness but also of translating it into academic achievement. Our kids' mediocre performance on the PISA, the test fifteen-year-olds take worldwide, shows this in spades. Children in the United States scored fortieth on mathematics, putting us well below the average of OECD countries. And they scored twenty-fourth on reading, just above the OECD average. Finland cleaned our clock on the test, scoring twenty places above us in reading and twenty-seven places above us in math. But far poorer countries like Vietnam, Russia, the Czech Republic, Portugal, Spain, Latvia, Malta, and Lithuania also scored above our kids on math.[25]

Our middling academic achievement outcomes have nothing to do with a lack of spending on kids' education. While the United States comes the closest of any country to pure free-market family policy, we have long made an exception for public spending on kids' kindergarten through twelfth grade education. In fact, we spend significantly *more* public dollars per child in those grades than most other countries do, including many pro-family policy countries that spend heavily on education: we rank fifth from highest of wealthy countries in terms of dollars spent per grade school student.[26] (Until a few years back, we were consistently ranked as one of the top two countries in education spending per student.[27] Our country's recent appetite for tax cuts, though, has meant that we've had to cut back on education spending relative to other countries.[28]) Yet the kids of countries with pro-family policies that spend significantly less than we do still leave our kids in the dust when it comes to academic achievement. Slovenia spends one-sixth less than we do to educate kids in grade school, but its students still outmatch ours academically.[29] On top of that, more of our students study for long hours than Slovenian children do.[30] But our poor results shouldn't be a surprise. As experts in early childhood education have been warning for quite some time, when kids don't get what they need in their first years, it's tough to impossible for them to make up for it later.[31] And our free-market policy means few young children will get what they need to thrive.

ACADEMIC ACHIEVEMENT VERSUS HAPPINESS

But it's only when you take account of our children's mediocre marks on *both* happiness and academic achievement that the depth of the failure of free-market family policy to support our kids comes into full focus. Take a look at Figure 7.1. This isn't the easiest chart to understand, but it's worth your while to decipher it. Each point on the chart plots both the average science performance on the 2015 PISA of kids in a country (average PISA scores increase as you move toward the right of the chart) and that country's average of students' reports of life satisfaction (life satisfaction increases as you move toward the top). As the diagonal line from the left-top to the right-bottom makes clear, the graph generally shows a modest negative association between a country's average student science performance and students' average life satisfaction, meaning that kids in countries with higher science performance tend to report lower life satisfaction. This is likely because kids in many higher-performance countries, including Japan and Korea, tend to feel more pressure to perform well academically (rather than, say, to hang out with their friends), which reduces their happiness levels.[32]

Now check out the United States' position on this graph. We're part of the circled cluster of countries close to the center, which puts us close to average compared to other countries on both children's science achievement and life satisfaction, together with Ireland, Latvia, Portugal, and Spain. Except for Ireland, the other countries have a far lower GDP per capita than the United States, making their children's mediocre scores on both measures more justifiable than our own.[33] We, meanwhile, manage to attain mediocre results on two of the most important indicators of kids' well-being in spite of our great wealth and the large amount we spend on kids' educations.[34]

Note that one country appears in the very top-right quadrant of the graph—the sweet spot for countries that score high on both children's achievement and their life satisfaction. That country is Finland. Because Finland's policies give children the best start they can get developmentally in their first years, kids do better academically than in the United States even though fewer of them study for long hours than US kids.[35] By the same token, Finnish kids do well despite reporting feeling far less pressured by schoolwork than US kids or other standouts on the PISA, like kids from Japan and Korea, and so report greater happiness.[36] When it comes to systems that produce children with strong academic achievement and happiness, countries with strong pro-family policies stand out.

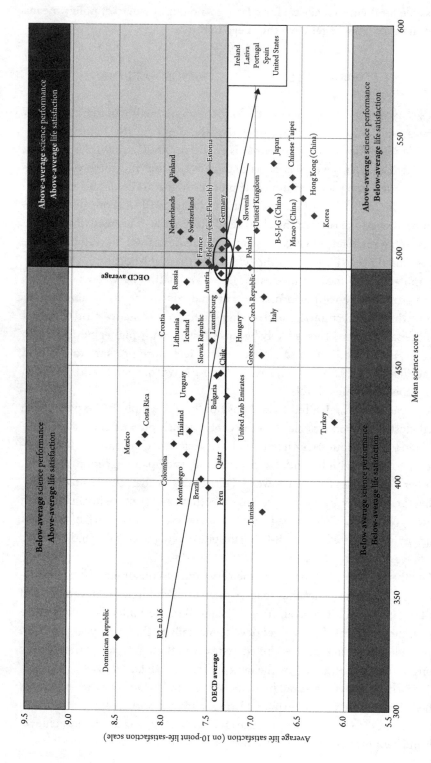

Figure 7.1. Life Satisfaction versus Science Achievement across Countries. Source: OECD (2017a), 74, fig. III.3.3.

MENTAL HEALTH

Free-market family policy also plays a role in our children's snowballing rates of mental health disorders. Up to one in five American children aged two to seventeen has a diagnosable mental, emotional, or behavioral disorder in a given year, and the rates are still rising.[37] So are the rates of mental illness for young adults.[38] One major study found that diagnosable rates of mental health disorders in college students had increased five to eight times between the 1930s and today, holding diagnostic standards constant.[39] Although we don't have good comparative measures for the rates of kids' mental illness across countries, US adults' rates are the top among wealthy countries, and there's little reason to believe that the same pattern doesn't apply to kids.[40]

Why are our children's mental illness rates so high? Across wealthy countries, mental illness rates are strongly associated with levels of income inequality; greater income inequality in a country corresponds to higher rates of mental illness.[41] Scientists haven't yet nailed down exactly how the association between income inequality and mental illness works at the level of individual people, but available research suggests that free-market family policy may increase mental illness through several pathways. For one thing, we know that high-quality parenting reduces rates of mental illness, while low-quality parenting does the reverse.[42] So free-market policy likely increase kids' mental illness rates by subjecting parents to undue stress and thereby diminishing the quality of their parenting.[43] In addition, the harsher caretaking circumstances to which we subject our youngest children may play a role. The neuroscientist Allan Schore recently suggested that the result of the chronically induced stress that young children, particularly boys, experience from being placed in daycare at too early an age may have negative effects on brain wiring that lead to psychopathology.[44]

Another large piece of this puzzle likely has to do with the effects of free-market family policy on adolescents as they prepare themselves for adulthood. As I mentioned earlier, our system makes it more likely that youth will give greater attention to extrinsic goals, like getting into a good college, than intrinsic goals, like doing the best they can. Yet focusing on extrinsic goals makes it more likely that kids will develop mental illness. Youths at the bottom of the income ladder who lean toward extrinsic goals are particularly vulnerable, probably because their prospects for economic success are so grim.[45]

On top of that, the stress that our system puts on young people also increases mental illness rates up and down the economic ladder. Poor adolescents experience higher rates of anxiety and depression than other kids, in part because their futures are significantly bleaker than those of their better-off peers.[46] But the incidence of these conditions in teens from well-to-do families is also high and rising.[47] These kids get the message that intensive parenting impresses upon them: that it's critically important for them to excel so that they can get into a good college and later find a good job. Yet excelling, for many if not most young people, requires spending long hours studying, a grinding schedule of extracurricular activities, and relentless focus. As an Arizona State psychology professor, Suniya Luthar, put it, "There's always one more activity, one more A.P. class, one more thing to do in order to get into a top college."[48]

The increased pace, pressure, and competition are just too much for increasing numbers of kids. When UCLA's Higher Education Research Institute asked first-year college students whether they "felt overwhelmed by all [they] had to do" the previous year, the number of students who answered yes increased from fewer than two in ten to more than four in ten in the years between 1985 and 2016.[49] The science is clear that chronic stress is a significant driver of anxiety and depression.[50] Yet we've created a social order that inflicts increasingly greater stress on our youth.

The growing pressure our system puts on teens means they are sleeping less than they did even a few decades ago.[51] More than half of American teenagers report getting fewer than seven hours of sleep a night—well shy of the eight to ten hours that experts say they need.[52] One education expert reports that teens tell her they routinely sleep five or fewer hours a night so that they can get things done.[53] Yet inadequate sleep is strongly linked to mental-health problems.[54] The sleep deficit is significant enough among the college-bound that schools are sounding alarms. One Silicon Valley high school where the pressure to succeed is intense trained students to be "sleep ambassadors," asking them to come up with slogans to encourage sleep. The winning slogan: "Life is lousy when you're drowsy."[55]

A recent New York Times Magazine story broached the subject of kids' plummeting mental health in an article whose title asked the important question "Why Are More American Teenagers Than Ever Suffering from Severe Anxiety?" The story profiled Jake, a teen from North Carolina. Until partway through his junior year of high school, Jake's schedule looked similar to that of many US kids on the success track. He was taking three Advanced Placement classes that required long hours of study, running with his school's cross-country team, and traveling to Model United Nations conferences. That schedule left him little time for friends, but Jake had decided that time with friends didn't matter; the only thing that did was how well he performed in school. Until his breakdown, Jack worried constantly about failure, and was particularly concerned about failing to get into a good college. But he considered his fear of failure to be one of his strengths, propelling him to work ceaselessly, which kept him doing well at school. One day, though, the pressure on Jack caused him to crumble. In his words: "You know how a normal person might have their stomach lurch if they walk into a classroom and there's a pop quiz? . . . Well, I basically started having that feeling all the time." He refused to go to school, instead curling up on the floor screaming, "I just can't take it."[56]

The *Times* story centered on Jake's path back from severe anxiety to healthy functioning, accomplished with antidepressants and therapy. The story's focus on these treatments accords with the now-dominant view that anxiety and the depression that often accompanies it are caused by neurotransmitter imbalances in the brain and, to a lesser extent, by maladaptive ways of thinking, which modern medicine and therapy can fix.[57] In approaching the issue this way, though, the *Times* missed the real culprit: not Jake's neurotransmitters or his thought patterns, but the social circumstances that cause so many young people to feel anxious and depressed.[58] Jake's story, as well as the stories of the growing number of his peers experiencing anxiety and depression, should be taken as signals that the pressure we're putting on adolescents isn't healthy for them.

The pressure to achieve that our free-market family policy imposes on our youth contributes to their rising rates of suicide. It's no coincidence that hospitalization rates for suicidal teenagers spike every fall when they return to school. More than double the number of suicidal teenagers are hospitalized today than a decade ago.[59] These suicides are often concentrated in well-to-do areas, as in the cluster of five suicides in nine months at a Silicon Valley high school. In fact, one of the towns in Silicon Valley, Palo Alto, leads the country in youth suicides.[60] Elite colleges have been the sites of other suicide clusters: six University of Pennsylvania students killed themselves in thirteen months, and six Cornell students did the same within a single school year. These events have left experts struggling to figure out how to reduce academic pressure in these schools.[61]

A growing array of literature pushes back against the pressure we put on kids, including the long hours of schoolwork and homework we demand of them in order to succeed and the high-stakes college testing.[62] This literature rightly argues for a return to sanity. But sanity will be hard to come by unless we reform our high-stakes economic system, which is driving the craziness in the first place.

In summary, the sharp decrease in mental health among American youth is a strong sign that our free-market family system is unhealthy for them. This isn't the case just for the poor kids whom our policymakers seem quite willing to ignore. It's also the case for kids from families at the middle and top of the economic ladder. Once again we can see that the free-market system isn't a zero-sum game as it is often described, with families at the bottom losing and families at the top winning. Instead, it's a negative-sum game in which all our kids increasingly bear heavy costs.

CHILD ABUSE AND NEGLECT

When it comes to families being able to keep their children safe from physical harm, the numbers are also trending in a tragic direction. Between 2012 and 2016, the number of children in foster care because of abuse or neglect rose by 10 percent, from 397,600 to 437,500 children. In six states, the foster care population rose by a whopping 50 percent during this four-year period. Experts attribute the increase to the mushrooming rates of substance abuse in the United States, particularly those involving opioids. The opioid epidemic has hit children harder than previous drug crises because in past epidemics extended family members would often take in children when their parents abused drugs. Today, though, family members across multiple generations are abusing drugs, leaving no other option for kids besides foster care.[63]

When it comes to children's deaths from abuse and neglect, as Figure 7.2 shows, our rates are almost off the charts compared with those of our wealthy peers. Almost all other wealthy countries have annual rates well below 0.5 deaths per 100,000 children. Our rates are seven or more times higher than that.[64]

Why are US rates of fatal child maltreatment so high compared to other countries? Many features associated with free-market family policy—high rates of poverty, low socioeconomic status, mental illness, financial and job insecurity, and family instability—are recognized risk factors for abuse and neglect.[65] Because the study of child maltreatment is complex, and because these risk factors often occur together, researchers haven't teased out exactly which of them actually cause maltreatment and which are simply associated with it.[66] Nevertheless, it doesn't take a giant leap of imagination to see pathways through which poverty, economic insecurity, and other features of free-market family policy could increase abuse and neglect. We know that poverty and stress make people far more focused on their own daily existence and struggles and less capable of focusing on others and on the future, both of which would increase neglect.[67] We also know that economic stress increases parents' irritability, as well as arbitrary and punitive parenting, which would seem a ready pathway to abuse.[68] Similarly, economic stress causes a deterioration of parents' mental health, which is known to increase rates of abuse and neglect.[69] So even if we don't know exactly which element of the complex of features associated with free-market family policy drive child abuse and neglect, and through which pathways, we have good reason to believe that free-market family policy is an important cause of our high child maltreatment rates.

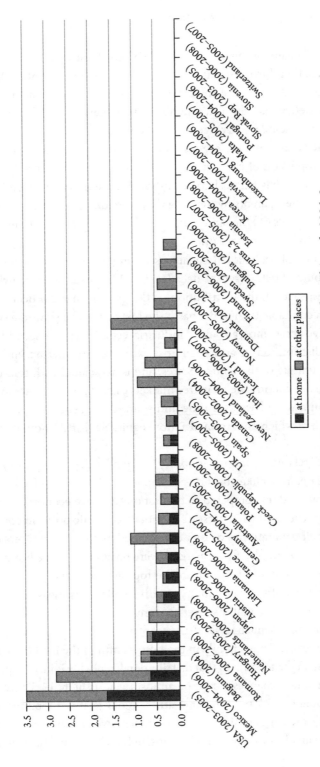

Figure 7.2. Children's Family Violence Death Rates Due to Negligence, Maltreatment, or Physical Assault, 2006–8.

Source: OECD (2013), 5, chart SF3.4.C.

ECONOMIC MOBILITY

The American Dream promises that children won't be constrained by the circumstances of their birth when it comes to achieving their potential. And our common understanding of what the Dream represents promises that each generation will do better than the last. Our ability to achieve both these promises, though, has been squandered by free-market family policy.

As Raj Chetty and his colleagues found, "absolute economic mobility," meaning the proportion of children in a generation who earn more than their parents at age thirty, has fallen sharply. Although nine in ten children born in 1940 out-earned their parents by the time they were thirty, only five in ten children born in the 1980s did the same.[70] Put simply, no longer can our next generation expect to do better than we did.

Chetty and his cohort believe two factors account for the sharp reduction in economic mobility. First, in recent decades, GDP has risen more slowly than in past decades; second, the distribution of the growth that did occur in this period was less equitable than in the past. The first factor, the slow rate of GDP growth, occurred across most advanced industrial economies. The second factor, though—the distribution of growth almost exclusively to the top end of the spectrum— is unique to the United States, and is associated with free-market family policy in our country. Belief in free markets caused policymakers to refuse to raise minimum wage laws over time and spurred weakening of protections for unions, both of which undermined a more equitable distribution of the proceeds of growth.[71]

Measures of "relative economic mobility" also tell a depressing story about the American Dream. Unlike absolute economic mobility, which looks at how an entire generation does compared to the last one, relative economic mobility considers the extent to which a person's eventual economic position compared to the rest of their generation is or isn't constrained by their parents' economic circumstances. For example, if your parents were positioned in the bottom fifth of their generation and you wind up in the top fifth of yours, you've accomplished relative mobility. When Chetty and his colleagues measured relative mobility, they found our country's level has remained roughly level for the past half-century, but that it's much lower than that of other developed countries. The chance that a US child from a family in the bottom fifth of the income distribution will wind up in the top fifth of that distribution later in life is just 7.5 percent. In Canada, that child's chances would be almost twice as high, 13.5 percent. In Denmark, it would be 11.7 percent. And although our relative mobility rate has remained steady, the rungs of the economic ladder have grown further apart as economic inequality has widened. That means, in Raj Chetty and his colleagues' words, "the consequences of the 'birth lottery'—the parents to whom a child is born—are larger today than in the past."[72]

The cold, hard truth is that free-market family policy plays a big part in ensuring that, no matter the herculean efforts of individual US parents or their children, the "birth lottery" largely dictates a child's life chances. Countries with pro-family policy make sure that all families have the resources they need to invest in their children, not just those who have the market power to do so on their own, so that all kids have the chance to succeed. Free-market family policy in the United States ensures that just the opposite happens.

The American Dream promises that all our kids will reach their full potential. In our free-market system, though, that dream actually comes true for very few kids. Although our country possesses fabulous amounts of wealth, free-market family policy prevents that wealth from being used where it matters most— investing in children's well-being and potential. The result is that children are not as happy as kids were in the past, achieve less in school, suffer from higher rates of mental illness, experience more child abuse and neglect, and have lower rates of economic mobility. How did we come to adopt public policy so wrong-headed when it comes to the well-being of American children and their families? As the next chapter shows, free-market family policy was not always a feature of the American system. In fact, the common thread through most of America's history wasn't embracing the free market—it was the willingness to do what it takes to support strong families.

THE ROAD TO FREE-MARKET FAMILY POLICY

Insulating Families from Market Forces—The Rise of the Welfare State

> Modern industry affords, in more generous measure than the human race has before known them, all of those goods which form the material basis of family life—food, clothing, shelter, and the materials and opportunities for subsistence for husband, wife, and children. But modern industry tends to disintegrate the family, so threatens it that the civilized nations are, and for at least one generation have been, actively building a code intended to save the family from this destructive pressure.
>
> —Florence Kelley (1914)[1]

Public policy in the United States did not always rest on the view that families needed to fend for themselves in the market. In fact, for much of the twentieth century, the role of the government in safeguarding the well-being of families against harmful market forces was a fundamental part of our nation's social contract. The story of how that provision of the social contract emerged shows us that the constant in America's relationship with markets hasn't been the acceptance of free-market doctrine, but rather the belief that the economy should serve the interests of families. Eminent historians have already thoroughly documented most of the elements of this story. My role here is mainly to link together the transformations they described in order to show how they led to the nation's commitment to regulating the market economy in order to support families.[2]

THE RISE OF THE MARKET AND ITS PROMISE
FOR FAMILIES

The United States wasn't always a nation that prized free markets, and its people weren't always focused on accumulating wealth. Markets and market

forces played only a bit part in most Americans' lives until the nineteenth century. Before then, except in the nation's seaboard towns, the great majority of
American families lived on landlocked farmsteads. Given that our system of
roads and highways wasn't built until later, these Americans had little access to
trade and little contact with the cash economy or the distribution web that we
today call "the market."[3]

Unlike present-day farms, as historian Charles Sellers has observed, most
early American farms weren't geared to selling crops or livestock to others.
Instead, they simply met the needs of those living on the farmstead. Almost all
these citizens' material goods came from their farms, sometimes supplemented
by goods bartered with their neighbors. Economists call this system for people
to obtain the resources they need a "household economy," in contrast to the
"market economy" we live in today, in which we buy most of the things we need.
The goal of producing resources in the household economy wasn't to accumu-
late as much as possible, as it often is in a market economy. After all, surpluses
couldn't be sold easily, and most of the produce of the farm wouldn't keep that
long, anyway. Instead, the goal of resource production in this economy was
subsistence—meaning freedom from want. The goods produced on the farmstead sheltered, clothed, and filled the bellies of those who lived in the household. After these needs were met, the purpose of work had been accomplished
and production stopped (at least when it came to men; for women, tasked with
reproduction and domestic labor, work was often ceaseless). A family's long-
term economic goal was not to amass savings for retirement or to pass on to
their children, as it is for many of us today, but instead simply to pass their land
on to their children and to maintain their way of life.[4]

This agrarian way of life was central to early Americans' economic ambitions,
which prized self-sufficiency (rather than, say, wealth) above all else. America's
founders had explicitly rejected the model of feudal societies, in which serfs
were beholden to the aristocracy on whose land they resided. A functioning democracy, early Americans believed, required that men own their own land. The
economic independence that came with it would then allow men the ability to
vote in accord with their conscience. (Women, of course, were more than a century away from getting the vote.) John Smith had barely landed at Jamestown
after the turn of the seventeenth century when he observed that in America,
"every man may be master and owner of his owne labour and land." The abun-
dance and fertility of the nation's lands (seized from Native Americans) during
the next two centuries reinforced the notion that economic autonomy was both
possible and valuable for every man.[5] (In truth, these ideals were largely confined to free white men, since women were subject to men's authority, as were
African American slaves.)

Wage work was seen as directly at odds with the economic independence that early Americans esteemed. Work for pay was viewed as vaguely dishonorable, as well as unmanly, because it put the worker in a state of dependence to another. Early Americans associated the wage relationship with the master–servant relationship in the home; like the husband–wife relationship, this affiliation was seen as a "domestic relationship" that was hierarchical and paternalistic.[6] The legal term often still used for the law governing the wage relationship—"master–servant doctrine"—reflects these preindustrial conceptual origins.[7] To the extent that wage work was considered justifiable and honorable at all, it was as a means to a man's buying his own farm and therefore attaining self-sufficiency. As one commentator put it in 1793, "[A] prudent man in a few years may lay up enough to purchase a farm in one of the newly settled towns [and] maintain a family with ease."[8]

The household economy produced far more economic equality among free Americans than existed in European countries of the time, as well as far more than would come to exist in the market economy, although it was equality at the level of a bare-bones material existence. Most families lived in two-room cabins with perhaps a sleeping loft, wore homespun clothes, and owned only a minimal amount of furniture and few personal belongings.[9] Despite that, America's vast and fertile lands meant that most families could eke out a relatively secure, even if very basic, existence. The result was that free Americans' well-being before the rise of the market economy, as measured by physical height and life expectancy, was the highest in the developed world—surpassing even that of the British aristocracy.[10]

Americans' way of life changed radically over the course of the nineteenth century. During this era, the country constructed roads, canals, and then railroads, which increasingly carried Americans away from agrarian life. The nation's population ballooned from 5 million in 1800 to 76 million in 1900—more than a fifteenfold increase.[11] Much of that increase came from the huge influx of immigrants from Europe beginning in the middle of the century.[12] When the century began, there were only a few major towns in America, and only one in twenty Americans lived in a town at all. A century later, there were thirty-eight good-sized cities, and almost half of Americans—eight in twenty—lived in a town or city.[13] As this urbanization occurred, most American families shifted from a household economy to a market economy.

These great transformations couldn't have happened without great changes in the way Americans thought about themselves and their economic goals. The American ideals of agrarianism and economic self-sufficiency were far less suitable for a population that was increasingly abandoning farming for market life in towns. These ideals were also incompatible with the vast increase in wage labor that occurred, particularly toward the end of the century. In the earlier decades of the nineteenth century, many men who moved from agrarianism to market life became independent artisans who owned their own tools and sold their own wares; other men traveled west to seek their fortune and become self-made men; still others were proprietors of small businesses. As industrialization took off, though, and as businesses were consolidated to capture economies of scale, increasingly more people were drawn into wage work. By 1860, almost 60 percent of the labor force was employed by others.[14] Black men and women joined this wage work once slavery was ended. By 1873, the Massachusetts Bureau of Statistics of Labor could proclaim that wage labor had become "a system more widely diffused than any form of religion, or of government, or indeed, of any language."[15]

For Americans to make the shift from the agrarian household economy to the urban market economy, both the market economy and wage work had to be recast as worthwhile. Put bluntly, the market economy needed a sales job. It turns out that the sales pitch came to be based on what the market economy could do for families. That pitch was founded on a set of ideas that began to take shape in the late eighteenth century but came into full flower only in the nineteenth century. Historians often call this set of ideas the "ideology of separate spheres," or sometimes the "cult of domesticity," or even just "domesticity" for short. This way of seeing the world began in the Northeast, but spread widely across the United States.[16]

Separate spheres ideology was named for the separation this emerging thought drew between the spheres of work and family.[17] In the household economy, work and home on the farmstead had been seen as an undivided realm that functioned, in historian Alice Kessler-Harris's words, "as a business, a school, a training institution, a church, and often as a welfare institution."[18] This realm had been controlled by the man, with the assistance of his wife. In the market economy, though, paid work moved out of the household and into the workplace. In the picture that domesticity painted of the world, work was now something that happened outside of the home, and was performed by men. That realm stood separate from and in contrast to the domestic realm, which was supervised by women, who oversaw the home and the raising of children. (This demarcation between the work and domestic realms of course overlooked the considerable unpaid labor that women of this era performed in the home.)

Separate spheres ideology recast the market world and wage work as honorable, and as fully consistent with American ideals. The bright line that domesticity drew between the realms of home and work helped repackage wage work as a manly endeavor by firmly locating it in the male work world, away from its patriarchal master–servant associations in the household. In keeping with its new masculine image, wage work was depicted as rough and competitive. The Freedmen's Bureau instructions to freed male slaves about their new role after the Civil War demonstrated the new masculine tinge to wage work: "Be a MAN. Earn money and save it."[19]

This reconceptualization of the wage contract borrowed heavily from the newly developing field of modern economics.[20] As Adam Smith explained in *The Wealth of Nations*, first published in 1776, "Every man lives by exchanging, or becomes in some measure a merchant."[21] This thinking was used to support the proposition that the worker who enters into a wage relationship should not be seen as a servant who submits to another's authority, but as an entrepreneur who freely enters into a relationship of equality with his employer when he agrees to sell his labor. The journalist E. L. Godkin in 1872 put the principle this way: "A contract, both in law and in political economy, is an agreement entered into by two perfectly free agents, with full knowledge of its nature, and under no compulsion either to refuse it or accept it."[22]

The idea of the marketplace as a domain where men met one another as equals erased any expectations left over from the premarket master–servant relationship that an employer should behave with benevolent paternalism toward his worker. Instead, the liberty and equality newly associated with the wage contract came to justify the rising economic brutality and inequality that emerged in the labor market in the late 1800s. As one senator in 1857 melodramatically portrayed the competitiveness of the work world, "[L]et him labor in the same sphere, with the same chances for success in promotion—that the contest be exactly equal between him and others—and if, in the conflict of mind with mind, he should sink beneath the billow, let him perish."[23]

Why would American men choose to give up the economic autonomy they had on the farm and submit themselves to the longer hours and growing ruthlessness of the workplace? Separate spheres ideology gave a clear answer: for the sake of their families' well-being. Men's reward for their toil in the workplace was a warm hearth and home to return to, as well as a happy wife and well-raised children to greet them at the door.[24] One New Hampshire pastor put it this way in 1827:

> It is at home, where man . . . seeks a refuge from the vexations and embarrassments of business, an enchanting repose from exertion, a relaxation from care by the interchange of affection: where some of his finest sympathies, tastes, and moral and religious feelings are formed and nourished;—where is the treasury of pure disinterested love, such as is seldom found in the busy walks of a selfish and calculating world.

Nothing can be more desirable, than to make one's domestic abode the
highest object of his attachment and satisfaction.[25]

The farmstead had been depicted unsentimentally in the era of the household
economy. Not so the home in the market world. Under separate spheres ideology, the domestic realm became a place of warmth and happiness. Phrases like
"home is sweet" and "there is no place like home" proliferated.[26] Mothers' childrearing responsibilities were emphasized as particularly critical to society.[27] And
the price of the warmth and happiness of this realm was men's wage work. As
Senator Henry Wilson declared decades later to men newly freed from slavery
in Charleston, South Carolina, at the end of the Civil War: "Freedom does not
mean that you are not to work. It means that when you do work you shall have
pay for it, to carry home to your wives and the children of your love."[28]

While the ideology of domesticity certainly offered material rewards, the central lure was the thriving families it promised. The idea that family life was the reward for the drudgery of wage labor was clearly distilled in this poem, published
in the *National Labor Tribune* in 1874:

> Though coarse his fare, and scant his means of life,
> Thought of his children and loving wife
> Makes rich amend for all his toil and strife.
> As fades the last ray of setting sun,
> His home is reached, his daily task is done;
> His young ones watching at the open door
> He sees with joy, and hastens on the more.
> Within the housewife, partner of his weal,
> Prepares with busy hand the evening meal. . . .
> Arrived within, she greets him with a smile
> And sweet caress—the welcome home.[29]

The market economy wasn't seen as an inevitable feature of the world, like a
long-standing mountain, as it is so often seen today. Nor was it seen as virtuous
in itself, regardless of its effects. Instead, it was considered valuable as a means to
an important end: flourishing families.

Separate spheres ideology said little to nothing about the role of government;
it assumed that the market itself would support thriving families without any
action on the part of the state. As the market economy expanded to encompass
most Americans, however, and particularly as industrialization progressed, it became increasingly clear that the market on its own couldn't sustain the family life
promised by separate spheres ideology. To the contrary, market forces gradually

came to encroach on the domestic sphere. When that happened, it was the damage caused to families that prompted calls for government action.

THE GILDED AGE AND THE MISERY OF
WORKING-CLASS FAMILIES

By the late nineteenth century, the market economy and industrial capitalism had both come into their own in the United States. These shifts made the country as a whole far wealthier, but also created huge economic disparities. As in our own era, the concentration of wealth held by the rich increased radically.[30] By 1890, the top 12 percent of families held 86 percent of America's wealth.[31] And not only did the rich pull away from the rest, the middle class pulled away from the poor. Before the market revolution, because most Americans lived relatively hardscrabble lives, the "middling sorts" were usually lumped together with the poor, and distinguished from the rich. The market economy, though, required a growing number of nonmanual workers, including clerks, salespersons, bookkeepers, merchants, and attorneys. As the nineteenth century wore on, these workers lived increasingly comfortable family lives; by midcentury, they came to be distinguished from both the poor and the rich as "the great middle class."[32]

As the middle class improved their lot, manual laborers fell far behind. The rise of manufacturing meant that unskilled workers could be easily replaced by other willing workers. The result was that they had little market power, and came to be paid much less than they needed to support a family.[33] The seasonal nature of most wage work, combined with employers' common practice of laying off workers during slack periods, increased workers' travails. A laborer who worked four days a week during three seasons of the year was doing comparatively well.[34] Workers' woes were made still worse by the emergence of boom-and-bust business cycles as the market economy expanded in the last several decades of the century; in the bust years, cities were overwhelmed by the poor and unemployed.[35]

Although poverty had certainly existed earlier in America, the ranks of the poor had largely consisted of women with young children, or of those too young, too old, or too sick to work. As industrial capitalism progressed, however, grinding poverty became an established fact of working-class life.[36] When a man was employed, his wages weren't enough to support his family. The situation was worse during work interruptions, because families had few, if any, savings to turn to. In the household economy, these families would have had home production to fall back on during lean times, giving them shelter and a garden plot or farm animals. When wages stopped coming in to an urban family, though, it was reduced to abject poverty.[37]

As a result, family life for the working class began to diverge sharply from that of the middle class. The broad middle of society had become focused on raising children to assume their place in market society, and on tending to an increasingly comfortable home. Working-class families, though, struggled simply to survive. They moved often—sometimes to find work, sometimes because they could not afford rent.[38] This cut them off from the extended families they had relied on in agrarian America. Their material conditions went from the bare-bones level of the household economy to downright poor and miserable. In contrast to the middle class, whose living spaces expanded during the nineteenth century, working-class families' living spaces shrank as the population grew. This hindered their ability to take in kin who needed lodging, even if they could afford to give them food.[39] Squalid tenement rentals sprang up in industrial cities to house these families, including much of the nation's burgeoning immigrant population.[40] In these rentals, it was common for three or more people to sleep in the same bed. Lucky tenants shared sinks and toilets located in a hallway with tenants living in other units; less fortunate tenants had to use a privy and communal tap in the backyard. In these crowded and difficult conditions, cleanliness was almost impossible, and sickness was a constant presence.[41]

For these working-class families, life was not the neat split between the spheres of work and home promised by the ideology of domesticity. Early manufacturing workers labored for exceedingly long hours—eleven to thirteen hours a day, six days a week, regardless of the weather or the season.[42] And given the insecurity and irregularity of wage labor, when men were not working, they spent much of their time searching for work.

The situation was no better for their wives. Poverty led them on an endless quest to meet basic family needs. Because they lacked the money to buy most goods and services, wives were left to fill the gap through home production and management. The great majority of working-class women spent their days ceaselessly laundering, sewing, and mending their family's few clothes, cleaning, shopping, cooking, fetching water, tending to children, and hawking and scavenging in the street. Few had enough money to shop for more than a day's supply of food, and no refrigerator or icebox to store it in even if they had.[43]

More income than what men's wages could provide was necessary for the family's survival. Despite this, few white wives worked outside the home, partly because of their already-long list of home production and childcare obligations, partly because of prevailing social norms, and partly because most jobs available to white women were restricted to single women.[44] A significant portion of African American women worked outside the home, though—more than one-third, by one count—generally as maids or in commercial laundries.[45] Wives without outside work generally needed to make extra money in their home, taking in boarders, laundry, or piecework. These extra hours of labor, on top of the long ones necessary for maintaining their own household, meant constant exhaustion.[46]

Children's situations in these families were grim. Given the endless quest to make ends meet, working-class mothers had little time or energy for the nurturing or supervision of children. What's more, economic need made children's labor necessary for the family's survival. In large cities, children as young as six or seven were sent to scavenge for wood, ashes, spilled food, and anything that could be sold to junk dealers. Meanwhile, older children were sent out to work for wages.[47] One study of Philadelphia industrial workers in 1860 found that three-quarters of those in the lowest-paid group relied on the wages of their children.[48] Across American families from all classes, the 1890 US Census showed that almost one of every five children between the ages of ten and fifteen worked for pay.[49] Child labor was particularly common among black and foreign-born children, whose fathers had the lowest-paying jobs.[50]

Children living under the rough conditions of colonial America had been expected to help with work, including clearing land and building settlements. Yet these children were being socialized and taught skills they would need in their adult lives. In contrast, the many children who worked in factories and mills at the end of the nineteenth century were being denied the schooling they needed to gain decent-paying positions when they became adults. They also worked long hours in filthy, extremely loud, and dangerous conditions. The great number of children who worked in cotton mills in the South, for example, generally began at age twelve and labored eleven to twelve hours a day, five-and-a-half days a week, including many night shifts.[51] Because heat and moisture prevented the cotton from breaking, windows were kept closed and the air moist—even in extreme heat. As a result, the air was filled with dust and lint, which seeped into workers' lungs, causing chronic bronchitis and other respiratory diseases. Boys who worked in the mills had half the chance as other boys of living until age twenty; girls had even less.[52]

The tens of thousands of children who worked in coal mining, some as young as ten or eleven, had it still worse.[53] They worked underground for ten to eleven hours per shift, performing repetitive work in air laden with coal dust, often with only the light from their work helmets. Conditions were hazardous, and children were injured at roughly three times the rate of adult mineworkers. Those who avoided accidents often still became anemic, disabled, or underdeveloped, and possessed extremely limited vocabularies and cognitive skills. Describing this situation, an 1869 editorial in the *New York Times* warned readers that "a great multitude of the youth . . . are thus growing up, stunted in body, and with not even the rudiments of school training, a prey to the insatiable requirements of industry and capital."[54]

In these harsh circumstances, well-being declined sharply. Infant mortality rates in New York City began to match those of the worst English factory districts.[55] The life expectancy of free citizens, which had topped out at fifty-six years in 1800, had fallen to forty-eight years in 1900. The mean physical height of native-born, white American males plummeted. By the 1880s, Americans were shorter than both the English and the Swedes, even though previous generations of Americans had been considerably taller.[56] And unlike those of earlier Americans, their heights diverged on the basis of economic class; children of the working class were much shorter than their peers.[57] This decline in well-being wasn't all due to the extreme privation of working-class families. Other factors, like the increasing density of cities, growing immigration, and improved transportation, created conditions ripe for disease.[58] But the poverty of the working class played a big role in this diminished well-being.

Separate spheres ideology had sold Americans on the market economy by touting the benefits it would bring their families. By the close of the nineteenth century, though, it was clear that, for an increasingly wide cross-section of Americans, the market was failing to deliver. In response, Americans began to call on the government to safeguard the market's promise. It was the insistence that the market be regulated to support families that eventually produced the twentieth-century welfare state.[59]

THE MARKET'S PROMISE FOR FAMILIES AS A CALL TO GOVERNMENT ACTION

In the last decades of the nineteenth century, the notion that government had the responsibility to regulate the market to protect families was controversial. It would have been less so more than a century before: colonial Americans had a broad view of government's role in furthering citizens' happiness and the public well-being.[60] During the market's rise in the first half of the nineteenth century, though, that view had been increasingly challenged. Much as they do today, many people began to see government's proper sphere as limited by citizens' market liberty.[61] This appraisal was sounded most loudly by lawyers and judges, who increasingly gave weight to private property rights as against the government's "police power."[62] The more limited notion of government's role that emerged, largely geared toward keeping the peace and ensuring citizens' security, existed in uneasy tension with the older, broader view of government's role. While each side of the debate won some skirmishes in the ongoing battle between them, the narrower view of government had increasingly gained the upper hand by the middle of the nineteenth century.[63]

The push toward small government was furthered by the fact that Americans associated bigger government with the interests of the wealthy. Thomas Jefferson's victory over Alexander Hamilton, who had favored a strong federal government run by elites, helped establish in American minds the link between small government and the common people.[64] Jefferson stated in 1801 that the best government was "a wise and frugal government, which shall restrain men from injuring one another, which shall leave them otherwise free to regulate their own pursuits of industry and improvement, and shall not take from the mouth of labor the bread that it has earned."[65] That vision of the role of government worked well in an agrarian America in which there was sufficient land for all comers to provide for themselves and their families. It worked much less well in an interdependent market economy, particularly one in which, hard as some tried, they couldn't earn enough to sustain their families.

As the market economy developed in the United States, Americans at first had difficulty understanding the deteriorating situation of working-class families. In the agrarian economy, Americans had learned the lesson that, with hard work, self-sufficiency was possible for every family. Acknowledging that hard work wouldn't necessarily bring self-sufficiency in the market economy didn't come easily. The spread of poverty among the working class was at first either ignored or attributed to the fault of the poor themselves, due to laziness or drunkenness. Beginning in the 1830s, this disregard for the growing misery was fed by free-market economic principles that began to circulate broadly in American thought.[66] The views of Herbert Spencer, an English social theorist, were particularly influential. Spencer drew on Charles Darwin's work to argue that working-class suffering was a painful but necessary part of weeding out the weak in order to foster the "survival of the fittest" (a term that Spencer, not Darwin, coined).[67] By the late nineteenth century, however, working-class poverty had become so deep and widespread, as well as so obviously tied to broader business cycles, that it became harder to blame it on the poor themselves.[68]

In the century's last decades, critics increasingly turned to separate spheres ideology to call for government action to address the situation of working-class families. This ideology hadn't said anything about government at all; the market was supposed to support the domestic realm on its own. But as people became aware of the wide gap between the promised benefits of market society for families and the market's actual effects on working-class families, they began to call for government action to enforce these promises.[69]

In 1869, the Massachusetts Bureau of Statistics of Labor became the first government agency to conduct a serious investigation of wage labor's effects on working-class families.[70] In the process, the Bureau compared the actual lives of Boston working-class families against the promise of domesticity: "[U]nder a proper organization of society," the Bureau asserted, the working man "would accrue such recompense of his daily toil, as would secure the family comfort from his earnings alone."[71] The reality, however, demonstrated the radical shortcomings of the current system. The historian Amy Dru Stanley summarized the investigation's findings:

> "No cheerful smile greets a returning father whose six days' earnings pay for but five days' meat." Rather, poverty destroyed domesticity. It "kills love and all affection, all pride of home . . . nay, emasculates home of all its quickening powers." On returning home, the "hapless father, seeking rest and comfort after toil, and finding neither, takes to the loafing spots of the streets . . . and the high road of ruin is opened before him." The bureau's most striking tenement images were of wives "toiling at wash-tub and iron board" for other families and of men whose wages left them destitute of home life.[72]

Not only did the Bureau discover that workers' wages weren't supporting their families adequately, it found the reverse to be true: the market system had absorbed entire families, changing "homes into houses."[73] Accordingly, in 1870, the Bureau called for legislation to ensure workingmen a decent wage.[74] State labor bureaus in other states soon followed suit.[75] They called for government to close the gap between the market's promise for families and its actual delivery.

About the same time, an emerging group of political economists joined the call for government regulation. In response to laissez-faire thinkers like Herbert Spencer, they argued that unregulated market competition rewarded not the fittest, but simply those willing to fight the dirtiest—employers who refused to pay workers a wage that could support their families and who required workers to labor exceptionally long hours.[76] Regulation, they argued, was needed to restore the moral basis of competition.[77] While markets had an important role to play, they contended, that role was limited and should be determined collectively rather than by the market's invisible hand.[78] The economist Richard Ely put it this way: "While we recognize the necessity of individual initiative in industrial life, we hold that the doctrine of laissez-faire is unsafe in politics and unsound in morals; and that it suggests an inadequate explanation of the relations between the state and the citizens."[79]

By the first decade of the twentieth century, it had become clear that some action was needed to counter the market's devastation to families. What exactly should be done and whether it was the government that should do it, though, were still contested. The White House Conference on Dependent Children, convened by President Theodore Roosevelt in 1909, had a pivotal role in focusing the drive for action. Called to deal with the problem of children put in almshouses or orphanages because of their parents' poverty, delegates unani-mously supported aid for families with children rather than removing the chil-dren, resolving:

> Children of parents of worthy character, suffering from temporary mis-fortune and children of reasonably efficient and deserving mothers who are without the support of the normal breadwinner, should, as a rule, be kept with their parents, such aid being given as may be neces-sary to maintain suitable homes for the rearing of the children.

The delegates didn't resolve whether it was government's role to provide this aid; this issue was still too contentious. They resolved instead that "aid should be given by such methods and from such sources as may be determined by the general relief policy of each community, preferably in the form of private charity, rather than public relief."[80]

Within two years, however, the situation was seen as unfixable without gov-ernment action. States stepped in first. As sociologist and political scientist Theda Skocpol has elegantly documented, state legislatures began to pass laws called "mothers' pensions," which laid the first bricks in the foundation of US social welfare policy supporting families. These pensions provided cash benefits to widows with children, and potentially to other mothers without husbands at home.[81] Significantly, the pensions were considered to be honorable subsi-dies that supported the valuable labor rendered by mothers. In the words of one pension activist, "We cannot afford to let a mother . . . be classed as a pauper, a dependent. She must be given value received by her nation, and stand as one honored. . . . If our public mind is maternal, loving and generous, wanting to save and develop all, our Government will express this sentiment."[82] Forty states passed such pension laws between 1911 and 1920.[83] By the early 1930s, six more states had been added to the list.[84]

These pension programs had significant flaws when it came to getting benefits to those families who most needed them. No benefits were allowed to poor families with men at home, even when the family was in dire need. Moreover, whether to award pensions, and how much to award, was left to the discretion of local authorities, who often exercised it in an arbitrary or discriminatory manner. Minority families were particularly left in the cold. Furthermore, the "morality" of recipients was scrutinized by caseworkers to determine whether their home was suitable.[85]

Despite their flaws, the pensions constituted a tremendously important advance. They represented the recognition that government had an impor-tant role to play in cushioning the domestic realm from the harmful effects of market forces. Importantly, families who received pensions weren't treated as dishonorable or as failures simply by virtue of their needing government help.[86] In fact, the payments were called "pensions" precisely to recognize both the dignity of the care work that mothers performed and the public responsibility for supporting this work.[87]

As states were passing these pensions, the federal government began to consider other legislation to restrain the effects of the market on families. The first such legislation came in the form of limits on child labor.[88] In 1914, the reformer Florence Kelley, also quoted in the epigraph to this chapter, summed up the wave of regulation that occurred during this era:

> Originally, the typical home was a farm which furnished subsistence, and the children received within the family group industrial, religious and moral training. Our departure from this early ideal under the pressure of modern industry is conspicuous. The paradoxical tendency of the family to disintegrate under the pressure of the same industry which affords it infinite material enrichment offers the key to a complex, varied legislative movement going forward in all the civilized nations. Seemingly incoherent, this movement is a ramified effort to safeguard the family.[89]

Put simply, government in the United States, and indeed in industrialized countries across the world, were committing themselves to the principle that it was government's responsibility to ensure that the market economy functioned in a manner that supported families' well-being, as separate spheres ideology had promised it would.

THE NEW DEAL

In 1933, reeling from the Great Depression, America entered the New Deal era. At this point, the principle that the federal government had the responsibility to ensure that families were safeguarded from the risks of the market economy became a cornerstone of the social contract.[90] The most far-reaching of the legislation built on this view was the Social Security Act of 1935. Among other programs, this act created the program we today call "Social Security" to provide resources to a family after the retirement of its breadwinner, and Unemployment Insurance to support a family if the breadwinner became unemployed. It also created Aid to Dependent Children (ADC) (later Aid to Families with Dependent Children, or AFDC), a successor to state-level mothers' pension programs, which provided support to mothers and their children on the death of, or the mother's divorce or separation from, the breadwinner.[91] The goal of the reforms was to smooth the rough edges of the market system when it came to families, ensuring that costs of predictable risks associated with the market economy weren't borne by particular families, but instead were broadly shared across the citizenry—a principle known as "social insurance."[92]

Other New Deal legislation introduced market regulation to ensure that the economy supported thriving families. The Fair Labor Standards Act of 1938 installed a statutory minimum wage to make sure that workers at the low end of the income ladder earned wages that could support their families. That wage, set at 25 cents an hour, was the equivalent of 27 percent of the average output of a worker at that time. (Today's minimum wage is less than half that percentage.) Congress also bolstered workers' ability to bring a fair share of pay home by empowering them to bargain collectively. The National Labor Relations Act of 1935 set out a legal structure that guaranteed workers the right to unionize and created the National Labor Relations Board to oversee the collective bargaining process.[93] In doing so, the act helped ensure that a significant portion of the benefits of increasing productivity in the next decades would go to workers, a stark departure from past (and present) decades.[94]

New Deal legislation also buffered the boundaries between family and market in other ways. For example, Congress prohibited children from accepting certain dangerous jobs, such as those in manufacturing and mining, as well as from working during periods that would interfere with their schooling.[95] An early version of the Fair Labor Standards Act also proposed restricting workers' maximum weekly work hours to ensure that they had adequate family time, although the version ultimately passed simply mandated that workers be paid time-and-a-half overtime after working forty hours in a given week.

To pay for the new programs, the federal government needed to raise far more in tax proceeds than it had previously. For starters, the Social Security payroll tax was added in 1935. During World War II, Congress introduced payroll withholding and quarterly tax payments. The proportion of Americans who paid federal income taxes rose from fewer than one in ten before the New Deal to more than six in ten by the end of World War II.[96] Much of the new tax burden was structured progressively to increase the relative burden on the wealthiest Americans. After Congress passed the Revenue Act of 1942, marginal tax rates on income peaked at 94 percent in the highest tax bracket.[97] This meant that taxpayers whose income exceeded a very high threshold—$200,000 ($2.5 million in today's dollars)— were permitted to keep only 6 percent of their earnings above that threshold.

When America entered the post–World War II era, the New Deal reforms helped families up and down the economic ladder thrive for the next three decades. Families' rising gains wouldn't have happened without the market economy, but neither would they have happened without government action to ensure that families were protected in this economy.[98]

It would be easy to overstate the government's commitment to supporting families during this era. Our nation's social insurance programs, even at their prime, were relatively weak compared with those of other countries.[99] And we long offered far more support to middle-class families than we did to poor and working-class families, particularly as we moved further from the New Deal era.[100]

The New Deal protections were marred by other flaws as well. The 1935 social insurance programs were modeled on separate spheres ideology's gender stereotypes. They assumed a male breadwinner who earned a family wage and a female caregiver who stayed home to tend to the household and raise the children.[101] What's more, they privileged the benefits associated with men's paid work over those associated with women's unpaid work. Social Security retirement benefits, which attached solely to market earnings, were treated as an entitlement and were paid according to a set schedule. In contrast, Aid to Dependent Children benefits, which were paid to single mothers with children at home, were left to the discretion of local officials rather than paid according to a set schedule, and, like the earlier mothers' pensions, recipients' sexual conduct was scrutinized to ensure that it was "moral." These program features suggested that benefits paid for women's unpaid work were a matter of charity, whereas benefits paid for men's paid work were a matter of right. This left women, particularly those without husbands, far more economically vulnerable than men. Structuring government benefits on these gender roles also failed to protect the many American families who didn't comport with this picture of family life. These included the many families in which women worked for pay, who were disproportionately African American and immigrant, as well as unmarried and same-sex couples.[102]

The New Deal was stained by racism as well.[103] Agricultural and domestic workers were deliberately excluded from Social Security at the insistence of southern senators in order to force African American and Latino workers to accept low-wage jobs. In addition, strong federal standards for ADC eligibility were omitted to ensure that black and Latina women, along with the relatives who might support them, could be compelled to rely on market earnings. The requirement that ADC stipends be high enough to create a "reasonable subsistence" was removed for the same reason.[104] As Charles Houston put it when the NAACP refused to support New Deal legislation, "[F]rom a Negro's point of view it looks like a sieve with the holes just big enough for the majority of Negroes to fall through."[105]

Despite these flaws, the New Deal installed a critically important principle in our nation's social contract with its citizens: government is obligated to ensure that the market economy benefits families generally, at the same time that individual families are buffered from the harms that market forces can cause them. The programs put in place based on this social contract functioned relatively well in allowing most American families to engage in market work and raise a family for the next four decades, so long as they ordered their family lives according to the traditional male-female gender contract.

In sum, principles of free-market family policy haven't been a permanent feature of our nation's history. To the contrary, in America's earliest years, it was the household economy rather than the market economy that was prized for supporting American ideals. The transition to the market economy was accompanied by the promise that markets would support thriving families. Beginning early in the twentieth century, after it had become clear that markets alone wouldn't allow America's families to flourish, the government stepped in to secure that promise.

Ultimately, a broad social understanding emerged that it was government's role to ensure that both the market's benefits and its risks were fairly shared across families. The laws our nation adopted to secure this commitment were far from perfect. Yet their basic goal—ensuring that the market supported the well-being of American families throughout society—was right on target. The legislation passed to further this end helped usher in an era in which a wide range of families across American society flourished in the decades after World War II. It was only toward the end of the twentieth century that the public commitment to making the market safe for families began to be undermined. Even then, as the next chapter shows, the removal of government protections was, according to its proponents, intended to serve the well-being of American families.

The Death of the Welfare State and the Rise of Free-Market Family Policy

The United States' adoption of free-market family policy was hardly a given. Until the last few decades of the twentieth century, the nation considered safeguarding families from the full brunt of market forces to be a basic function of government. In fact, in the early 1970s, it looked like the government would move still further in this direction. President Lyndon B. Johnson's War on Poverty in the 1960s called for using government to create a society "where no child will go unfed, and no youngster will go unschooled."[1] The anti-poverty programs adopted in that era included Medicare, Medicaid, and food stamps, all of which significantly eased the distress of poor families. After that, toward the beginning of President Richard M. Nixon's administration, it seemed likely that the United States would pass both a guaranteed income plan and a universal childcare program as well. Nevertheless, by the turn of the twenty-first century, the United States had decisively adopted free-market family policy, closing its eyes to its increasingly struggling families.

As this chapter shows, America's veering off the pro-family policy path occurred during an era in which policymakers across industrialized Western countries were considering how to deal with their increasingly outmoded welfare models. Those models, including our own, had assumed that women would stay home to care for children and the household while men worked. Women in these countries, however, were increasingly working for pay outside the home. In response, other countries besides our own updated their welfare states to adapt to the realities of two-income families. They transformed old programs built on outmoded expectations, as well as introduced new programs to help working families, including paid parental leave and universal daycare. The United States alone simply scrapped its welfare protections as outmoded in an era in which women worked, and refused to replace them with updated programs.[2] In tossing out these protections without installing the new ones that families badly needed, our nation threw out the baby with the bathwater.

THE RISE OF FREE-MARKET FAMILY IDEOLOGY

Beginning in the late 1960s, the relationship between the spheres of work and family experienced a sea change almost as momentous as the one that had taken place the century before with the rise of the market economy and industrialization. In the late twentieth century, though, it was not men leaving home for paid work, but rather women. Sometimes because of economic necessity and sometimes because of choice, women began to enter the paid workforce in increasingly larger numbers and to stay there even after having children. In 1960, only 18 percent of women with children under six worked paid jobs. By 1979, that figure was 43 percent, and rapidly rising.[3] (By 2017, the percentage of working mothers with young children grew to 65 percent.[4])

The New Deal welfare model, which assumed that women would stay home to perform unpaid work, had always ignored the true diversity of American families. This model looked past the fact that many women—including a disproportionate number of African Americans—had long worked outside the home. It also ignored families that didn't fit the heterosexual marital family model, including the families of same-sex and unmarried couples. With women's increased entry into the paid workforce in the last third of the twentieth century, though, the contradictions between this model and the lived reality of American families could no longer be ignored.

During this same era, the rolls of America's cash welfare program, Aid to Families with Dependent Children (AFDC)—often known simply as "welfare"—began to expand significantly. Between 1960 and 1974 alone, the number of families served by AFDC more than tripled to almost eleven million.[5] A combination of factors contributed to the rising rolls, including Supreme Court decisions that expanded the number of families eligible for benefits; growing unemployment due to changes in the economy; and the rise of single-mother families, itself spurred by economic shifts.[6] Because AFDC was a combined federal/state benefit program, this expansion placed an increasing burden on state budgets. Local and state politicians began to politicize the issue, complaining that the added burden was breaking state budgets and arguing that something needed to be done.[7]

Tangled up with the growing anti-AFDC sentiment was racism—the great stain on our country's history. Until the 1960s, neither the AFDC program nor poverty had been particularly associated with race in the public's mind. Certainly many blacks were poor, but Americans had seen many images of white poverty in Appalachia during the War on Poverty. A perceived link between race and government benefits, though, began to develop in the last third of the century. This was partly because the expansion of the welfare rolls in the

1960s considerably increased the proportion of African American families receiving AFDC benefits. This increase was due in part to the courts having recently struck down racist rules denying benefits to black families. It was also
partly due to the fact that the economic restructuring beginning to take place hit
black men first and hardest, leading to a growing number of African American
single-parent families. Black families never comprised the majority of recipients
of AFDC, but because of their poor economic situations, they received a disproportionate share of benefits compared to their numbers in the population.
Increasingly, the public began to associate welfare recipients with black mothers.
As they did, they were more likely to see welfare recipients as undeserving, as
well as to see mothers who received subsidies as taking generous government
handouts because they preferred to do nothing rather than work. This negative
perception of welfare recipients stood in stark contrast to the way the mothers
who had collected mothers' pensions in the early twentieth century (envisioned
as white) had been viewed; these mothers had been seen as virtuous for staying
home with their children.[8]

Politicians began to feed the racialized stereotype of the "welfare queen," a
woman who supposedly had babies simply to milk the government for benefits.
Barry Goldwater, the Republican presidential nominee in 1964, stated, "I don't
like to see my taxes paid for children born out of wedlock. I'm tired of professional chiselers walking up and down the streets who don't work and have no
intention of working."[9] A decade later, Ronald Reagan invoked the stereotype in
his run for president when he described a woman who used multiple names to
collect welfare, drove around in a Cadillac, and scammed the government out of
benefits in order to buy luxury goods.[10]

By the end of the 1960s, the combination of mothers' increased entry into
the workforce, the rising cost of welfare programs, and growing public anti-
welfare sentiment made clear that the US welfare state needed updating.[11] Two
major pieces of legislation to accomplish this began to make their way through
Congress: the Family Assistance Plan (FAP), a proposal to ensure a guaranteed
minimum income to every family; and the Comprehensive Child Development
Act (CCDA), a plan to set up a national network of government-funded childcare centers available to families of all incomes. Passing even one of these laws
would have put the country on the path to pro-family policy. And, in fact, both
came very close to passage. The failure of each was more the product of happenstance than of any deep-seated resistance to pro-family policy at the time. The
failure of both, though, decisively shifted the country onto the road that led to
free-market family policy.

The FAP was newly elected President Nixon's own proposal to correct the
problems of the existing welfare system. The plan guaranteed a minimum income
to every family with at least one child, including two-parent families. A family of

four was guaranteed at least $1,600 a year—roughly $10,700 in today's dollars. To the extent that families fell below that line, the government would subsidize them. The plan would have greatly expanded the federal government's role in public assistance, increasing the number of Americans who received government subsidies by 10 million. In doing so, it would have cut the nation's poverty rate by 60 percent.[12]

Nixon announced the plan in August 1969, calling it, probably correctly, the most significant piece of legislation since the Social Security Act of 1935. The plan, he said, would place "a floor under the income of every family with children in America."[13] Interestingly, the FAP wasn't considered particularly controversial at the time. The accepted wisdom had it that some form of a guaranteed income program was inevitable in the United States; the only question was which one it would be. At the time, different versions of guaranteed income plans had support across the US political spectrum.[14]

The FAP almost made it into law. It passed the House of Representatives in both 1970 and 1971 by large majorities. Both George H. W. Bush, a Texas congressional representative at the time, and Donald Rumsfeld, then the director of the Office of Economic Opportunity, supported the plan.[15] Commentators expected it to pass the more liberal Senate as well. However, due to discontent on both the right and the left, the guaranteed income measure never came to a vote in the Senate. Conservatives were concerned that it might deter the poor from accepting low-paying jobs. The racism lurking beneath these views was often barely disguised. Arthur Burns, a Nixon policy adviser, argued that white working-class voters would punish Republicans if they passed the FAP because it would be seen to benefit blacks.[16] Liberals, meanwhile, wanted to pass a guaranteed basic income plan that would benefit more than just poor families.[17]

During this same time, another important piece of legislation directed at updating the welfare state was also making its way through Congress. The CCDA sought to acknowledge the reality of the growing number of working mothers by setting up a network of federally funded childcare centers across the country. The preamble to the CCDA stated its bold and farsighted mission:

> It is the purpose of this Act to provide every child with a fair and full opportunity to reach his full potential by establishing and expanding comprehensive child development programs and services designed to assure the sound and coordinated development of these programs, to recognize and build upon the experience and success gained through Head Start and similar efforts, to furnish child development services for those children who need them most, with special emphasis on preschool programs for economically disadvantaged children, and for children of working mothers and single parent families.[18]

Daycare under this plan would be made available to families of all incomes for a sliding-scale fee. Furthermore, the centers would provide nutritious meals and medical care in addition to daycare.[19] The CCDA was budgeted at $2 billion for the first year—about $11.5 billion in today's dollars.

The CCDA made its way through both houses of Congress in 1971. It passed the Senate with broad public support, with a bipartisan vote of 63 to 17. The House vote was considerably closer at 211 to 187, with 180 Democrats and 31 Republicans supporting it.[20] Passing this bill sent the message that, although the American family was changing and more mothers were working, government still had its back. The bill then went to President Nixon for his signature. Nixon hadn't been involved in the bill's construction or passage. But he had on several occasions affirmed his "commitment to providing all American children an opportunity for a healthful and stimulating development during the first five years of life." Further, several members of his administration had given their support during negotiations over the bill.[21] Despite this, the president ultimately vetoed the act.

The reasons for Nixon's veto of the bill are still debated. Some speculate that the move was an attempt to mollify conservatives angry at him for scheduling a diplomatic trip to China.[22] Others suggest he feared that passage of the CCDA would weaken support for his FAP, which contained its own childcare proposal.[23] Still others link the veto to specific provisions of the legislation, or to an internecine battle between two Nixon aides fighting for power.[24] Whatever the reason, Nixon's veto statement, drafted by his aide, the conservative Patrick Buchanan, established the ideological foundation of the free-market family policy to come. It decried the "family-weakening implications of the system" that the CCDA created.[25] The statement specifically recognized "the needs . . . for day care, to enable mothers, particularly those at the lowest income levels, to take full-time jobs." But the government's provision of this day care would, the statement said, make the CCDA "the most radical piece of legislation to emerge from the Ninety-second Congress." The federal government's role "wherever possible should be one of assisting parents to purchase needed day care services in the private, open market." For the government itself to provide such day care risked diminishing rather than enhancing "both parental authority and parental involvement with children." So the right way for the government to meet the need for daycare was to "support increased tax deductions" for parents with children enrolled in these programs.[26]

You already know what happened next: after Nixon vetoed the CCDA and Congress failed to overturn the veto, the FAP failed as well.[27] The defeat of these pieces of legislation wasn't inevitable. Both could easily have gone the other way.[28] But their failure put our nation on a different path than we had been on before, one that has made us an outlier among wealthy democracies.

Scholars have often described the political shift during this era in terms of disputes over women's proper role. In their accounts, conservatives began to claim the mantle of family protection against the liberals and feminists who were seeking to upend public policy predicated on women's proper place being in the home.[29] Certainly these scholars are right that some of the massive political realignment in the next decades turned on disagreements over women's proper role in the family. But enough attention hasn't been paid to the emerging disagreements over the *government's* role.[30] As Nixon's veto statement made clear, the problem with the CCDA in the emerging conservative view wasn't that it prompted women to leave home for paid work: conservatives accepted the reality that many women worked for pay, and were particularly approving of mothers working when it came to poor women. The problem with the CCDA was the role it envisioned for government: The statement cast government action—even action intended to support families—as harmful to families' well-being. Government support, in this view (apart from tax deductions), didn't shore up families—it took them over. Collective action to help families was deemed un-American, favoring "communal approaches to child rearing over against the family-centered approach." Never mind that the CCDA didn't require any families to put their children in government daycare centers, that providing daycare for poor families was considered fine despite being "communal," or the fact that the country had been providing public education for school-aged children for more than a century. A decade later, Ronald Reagan gave voice to a similar sentiment: "[G]overnment is not the solution to our problem; government *is* the problem."[31]

Moving government action from the helpful to the harmful column for families was not the only major development apparent in Nixon's veto statement that would set the stage for things to come. The statement also shone a new, rosy spotlight on the market. Getting mothers off the welfare rolls and into full-time jobs was the way things *should* work, the statement posited, because families should get what they needed through market transactions. The historian Daniel T. Rodgers described the rising esteem in which the market was held during this era: "In an age when words took on magical properties, no word flew higher or assumed a great aura of enchantment than 'market.'"[32] President Reagan put it similarly in 1982: "You know, there really is something magic about the marketplace when it's free to operate."[33]

The widespread recognition at the beginning of the twentieth century that market pressures could be destructive to families, and that it was the government's role to buffer families from these forces, was being turned on its head. Government action was increasingly associated with damage to families. Meanwhile, government leaving families to fend for themselves against market forces was now seen as healthy and normal. In this new world of distrust of government action but respect for the market, free-market advocates argued, not fully coherently, that tax breaks for market work were a more pro-market, less interventionist means to support families than either a guaranteed income plan like Nixon's FAP or a public system of daycare like the CCDA. Accordingly, in the wake of the FAP's and CCDA's defeats, Congress in 1975 passed the Earned Income Tax Credit (EITC), which provides a tax credit to low-income working families. In subsequent years, that break was expanded, becoming one of the major ways that the federal government supports families today.[34]

In the next decade, particularly during Reagan's first term, the country moved still further down the road to free-market family policy by shrinking the existing safety net. Working with Congress, the Reagan administration made sharp cuts to AFDC eligibility and benefits and drastically cut spending on other programs like Medicaid and housing support.[35] The number of states that subsidized a working mother with three children whose wages put her 50 percent below the US poverty line decreased by almost half, from forty-seven states to twenty-four. The number of states that supplemented the wages of that same working mother if her earnings equaled the poverty line decreased from thirty-three to one. Meanwhile, because of the drop in AFDC benefit amounts, the total, after-benefits income of a mother whose market earnings put her at 50 percent of the poverty threshold dropped by an average of almost $2,000.[36] The nation was pulling away from its commitment to ensuring that all families with children had the basics, even when their parents couldn't provide them through the market. In response, the percentage of poor children in the country spiked 5 percentage points by 1983.[37]

Charles Murray's tremendously influential 1984 book, Losing Ground, delivered the death blow to the view that government has a responsibility to protect families from harsh market forces.[38] Two decades before, the Moynihan Report had recognized that broken families were caused by market forces and had called for a government jobs program to address this. Murray now asserted that the causation was actually the reverse: broken families were caused by government action, and the solution was to subject families entirely to market forces. Losing Ground made the case that government benefits wound up hurting poor families through promoting "dependency" on government and undercutting incentives for adults to support themselves and their families.

Murray marshaled large amounts of data to make his argument that government was the source of families' problems. Almost all of it fell into two broad categories. The first showed that government spending on social welfare programs rose rapidly in the late 1960s and 1970s in the aftermath of the War on Poverty. Most of this increase entailed spending on Social Security, Medicare, and Medicaid, rather than AFDC and food stamps, but Murray didn't break these numbers out separately. The second showed that at the same time as government spending was increasing, poverty from market earnings was also increasing, as were a range of social problems. These included rising rates of nonmarital children, single-mother families, unemployment among young black men, and both property crimes and violent crimes .

As any social-science student learns, correlation doesn't prove causation. The fact that government spending on the poor had increased during the same era in which social problems increased didn't show that the government spending *caused* these problems. The rise of the market-income poverty rate could equally (or, in fact, more likely) have been the result of other factors. In particular, the increasing unemployment rates of the era, as well as the drop in wages at the lower end of the wage spectrum for men, would account for the growing market-income poverty rate and therefore explain the greater need for government benefits in these years. And these economic shifts, we now know, spurred the rise of many, if not most, of the social problems that Murray identified.[39]

The rest of Murray's evidence that government benefits were the cause of rising poverty and fragile families rested on the thought experiment he constructed about the choices that a hypothetical couple—Phyllis and Harold—would supposedly confront. The couple was pregnant and unmarried, with low education, and deciding how to deal with their situation under two different policy regimes: the more generous AFDC benefit rates of 1970 or the less generous AFDC benefit rates of 1960, before the War on Poverty. Murray asserted that under the earlier benefit rates, the couple's best alternative would be for them to marry and for both to work for pay. In the presence of 1970 benefit amounts, though, Murray contended, the couple's incentives would change drastically. Phyllis would reject marriage to Harold, since it would deprive her of AFDC benefits. Meanwhile, Harold would have no incentive to assume full-time work when he could live with Phyllis and rely on her AFDC benefits. Instead, he would work only periodically, which meant he would never advance at work. The result was that the couple would become "dependent" on government benefits, ultimately becoming even poorer than if they'd never had access to these benefits in the first place. Decisions by millions of adults just like Phyllis and Harold, Murray claimed, were how increased government benefits led to more rather than less poverty and to rising rates of social problems.

In the aftermath of *Losing Ground*, critics using a far larger evidence base and much sounder methodology than Murray largely decimated his claims that government benefits caused the social problems that he'd identified. They showed that, contrary to Murray's assertions, minimum-wage work was far more profitable than AFDC benefits (in many states, twice as profitable) in most areas of the country in 1970. Further, the number of households headed by women and the rate of black unemployment increased across the country in that era—not just in the states with high AFDC benefits, as would be expected if Murray's argument were correct.[40] Academics constructed precise tables comparing AFDC rates at various points in time with rates of market-earning poverty and unemployment rates to reveal that the decline of real median income beginning in 1973 accounted for the rise of market-earning poverty and fragile-family structures far better than did rising government benefits. And they showed that if Murray had considered Harold and Phyllis's situation under the declining benefit levels in 1980, his thesis would predict declining amounts of poverty, as well as fewer single-parent families and less black unemployment beginning at that time. Yet no such changes had occurred.[41]

Researchers also discredited Murray's claims that poor families developed welfare "dependency." It turned out that most recipients turned to AFDC after a divorce or separation or on the birth of a child, and stayed on it for fewer than two years, although many returned to it after another crisis.[42] A 1988 *Science* review summarized the studies of individual families' use patterns as follows: "[T]his evidence suggests that the welfare system does not foster reliance on welfare so much as it acts as insurance against temporary misfortune."[43] And those who did stay on ADFC long-term did so not because welfare made them dependent, but because of persistently low earnings as well as other characteristics not attributable to government benefits, like disabilities.[44]

Furthermore, top scholars debunked claims that AFDC benefit levels led to the rise of fragile-family structures. Harvard Professors David Ellwood and Mary Jo Bane released a landmark comparative study of state AFDC programs showing that nonmarital birth rates shot up and divorce rates increased even during periods in which state benefits declined.[45] They concluded that "welfare simply does not appear to be the underlying cause of the dramatic changes in family structure of the past few decades."[46] In fact, as Moynihan had surmised and William Julius Wilson later helped document, it was market forces—through the increase in male joblessness in the economy—that drove the decline of marriage and the growth of fragile-family structures.[47]

More recently, Johns Hopkins sociologist Andrew Cherlin used historical means to undercut Murray's claim that government benefits had led to the drop in marriage among the poor. He showed that disparaties in marriage rates among the classes have varied with the rate of economic inequality in the United States for at least 130 years.[48] In fact, today's marriage gap between wealthy families and other families is the second time such a large gap has occurred in US history. Presumably, any explanation of today's gap should also explain the earlier gap. But the first gap occurred in the late nineteenth century—before the birth of the welfare state. What the two eras had in common was not big government, but high and rising economic inequality.[49] Murray had gotten it backward: the market, not government, was the source of the problem.

The one place where Murray turned out to be somewhat right was his claim that AFDC benefits reduced recipients' work hours. As AFDC was structured, it had a high, often 100 percent, phaseout rate, meaning that for every dollar in wages a recipient earned, she lost a dollar in benefits. That meant, as Murray had argued, that the program reduced participants' incentives to work, at least on the books. (Because benefits didn't pay enough for families to live on, recipients often sought off-the-books work or even illegal work that wouldn't reduce their benefits.)[50] Programs structured differently, however, wouldn't have the same effects on work hours. A group of four MIT and Harvard economists recently reanalyzed data from seven randomized experiments on universal basic income programs in developing countries. They concluded that cash transfers in these programs caused women to work just a half hour less per week, and men to slightly *increase* their hours worked.[51] Of course, the fact that poor mothers are able to spend a little more time at home with their kids and a little less time at paid work isn't necessarily a bad thing anyway.

In sum, Murray's critics demonstrated that *Losing Ground* was wrong about— well, almost everything. More than that, they showed he had ignored the real good that government spending on the safety net had accomplished. A large part of the money used to fight the War on Poverty that Murray decried was spent on Medicaid, which cut infant mortality in half between 1965 and 1980. Another large chunk of these funds went to Medicare, which reversed the growing mortality of men over sixty-five and increased life expectancy at birth by more than four years. The introduction of food stamps significantly reduced the nutrition gap between low-income Americans and the rest of the country.[52] Although poverty rates hadn't declined, as Murray asserted they should have if the rising government spending was doing any good, the fact that poverty rates hadn't climbed during a period in which the unemployment rate had doubled meant they had actually done a lot of good.[53] In fact, AFDC benefits had done precisely what they were supposed to do: helped relieve the poverty of the families who received them.[54]

Yet despite Murray's unsound evidence, as well as the fundamental errors of his central conclusions, his message immediately began to have a profound influence on public policy.[55] In his 1986 State of the Union Address, President Reagan showed that it had hit home. Reagan asserted that welfare programs had created "a spider web of dependency" that fostered a dysfunctional culture in which the "breakdown of the family . . . reached crisis proportions." And he committed himself to "revis[ing] or replac[ing] programs enacted in the name of compassion that degrade the moral worth of work, encourage family breakups, and drive entire communities into a bleak and heartless dependency."[56]

The 1986 report issued by President Reagan's White House Working Group on the Family, headed by Gary Bauer, adopted Murray's arguments wholesale and solidified the new anti-government, free-market family policy ideology. Government action, no matter how well intended, it asserted, undermined families' interests. Federal spending to address poverty among children in the 1960s and 1970s, it claimed, caused children's "delinquency rates [to] double. Their Standardized Aptitude Test (SAT) scores plummeted. Drug and alcohol abuse skyrocketed."[57] Never mind that crime and drug use were increasing in the prosperous white suburbs of New York and Los Angeles as well as in Harlem and Watts and that the overall drop in SAT scores had little to do with the scores of poor children.[58]

Further, the report maintained, government involvement with families was fundamentally at odds with how families properly functioned:

> For most Americans, life is not a matter of legislative battles, judicial decrees, and executive decisions. It is a fabric of helping hands and good neighbors, bedtime stories and shared prayers, lovingly packed lunchboxes and household budget-balancing, tears wiped away, a precious heritage passed along. It is hard work and a little put away for the future.[59]

Strengthening families required, not help from government, but instead "turning back to the households of this land the autonomy that once was theirs, in a society stable and secure, where the family can generate and nurture what no government can ever produce—Americans who will responsibly exercise their freedom and, if necessary, defend its families." According to Bauer's report, once liberated from an overweening government, American families could once again engage with the institution that truly nurtured it: the market. "[D]emocratic capitalism through 'its devotion to human freedom, its creation of wealth, and its demand for personal responsibility—made the modern family possible.'" Meanwhile, "the family which is tied together with love is the source of all productivity and growth."[60]

In this vision of the proper order of things, families and the unregulated market created a virtuous cycle in which one improves the health of the other. Free-market ideology had arrived in government.[61] And it was based on the claim—as false as it was—that government support hurt rather than helped families, who truly need only the market to flourish.

THE ROLLBACK OF THE WELFARE STATE

The victory of free-market family policy culminated in the welfare overhaul of 1996 under President Bill Clinton.[62] The Personal Responsibility and Work

Opportunity Reconciliation Act (PRWORA) was so named because it was supposed to promote personal responsibility and paid work over government dependence. As Pennsylvania Senator Rick Santorum, an enthusiastic PRWORA sponsor, later put it, we needed to recognize that "[w]hen government steps in and imposes a bureaucratic solution," it weakens rather than strengthens families.[63] To roll back government involvement, the legislation repealed more than three dozen federal anti-poverty programs that had entitled poor families to benefits, replacing them with just five fixed-amount block grants to states. PRWORA therefore effectively ended the long-standing promise that government would have the backs of the poorest American families.[64] In the words of New York Senator Daniel Patrick Moynihan, a reform opponent, the bill was "the first step in dismantling the social contract that has been in place in the United States since at least the 1930's."[65] Or as President Clinton succinctly put it in his 1996 State of the Union Address, "[T]he era of big government is over."[66]

One of PRWORA's block grants replaced AFDC with a new cash relief program for poor families, Temporary Assistance for Needy Families (TANF). Under the AFDC program, some eligibility requirements had been federally set, which limited states' ability to exclude applicants from receiving benefits. TANF, though, gave states far greater discretion over eligibility. Furthermore, when recipients were entitled to benefits, AFDC had mandated that federal and state matching funds be paid. The result was that, under AFDC, both state and federal spending had increased in times of economic distress and decreased at other times. In contrast, under TANF, the amount of the federal block grant is basically fixed regardless of the economic circumstances. That block-grant structure means that, in tough economic times when more families are in poverty, the federal block grant doesn't increase, and states aren't required to expand TANF rolls. In fact, because the block-grant structure permits states to divert funding from poor families to a broad array of programs, during the Great Recession, some states actually *cut* their TANF programs to help make up for their budget loss from reduced tax payments.[67] Over time, states have redirected a large portion of funds from core welfare services like cash relief and childcare assistance to other programs. About a third of TANF block-grant funds now go for items that have little relationship to basic support programs. Michigan has used some of the money for college scholarships. Louisiana has spent some on anti-abortion crisis pregnancy centers.[68] This means that even less cash goes to needy families.

PRWORA also put a federal sixty-month lifetime limit on TANF benefits to ensure that poor families didn't become "dependent" on government handouts.[69] And it allowed states to shorten the lifetime limit still more if they chose. Yet PRWORA passed during a period in which wages at the low end of the economic spectrum were falling, economic insecurity was rising, and increasing numbers of low-wage workers were working full-time without earning enough to pull their family out of poverty. With the five-year or less limit on benefits, as well as the inadequate benefit rates PRWORA allowed states to set, many parents with children would have little hope of earning enough income to keep their kids out of poverty. In that economy, how did Congress expect poor mothers to provide for their families?

The preface to PRWORA provides a clue to policymakers' thinking. Rather than beginning with praise for single mothers achieving financial independence through market work, as one might expect if that were the legislation's driving purpose, it opens with a paean to the traditional marital family: "Marriage is the foundation of a successful society. Marriage is an essential institution of a successful society which promotes the interests of children. Promotion of responsible fatherhood and motherhood is integral to successful child rearing and the well-being of children."[70] The act's preface then lays out four goals:

1) provide assistance to needy families so that children can be cared for in their own homes or in the homes of relatives;
2) end the dependence of needy parents on government benefits by promoting job preparation, work, and marriage;
3) prevent and reduce the incidence of out-of-wedlock pregnancies and establish annual numerical goals for preventing and reducing the incidence of these pregnancies; and
4) encourage the formation and maintenance of two-parent families.[71]

Little in PRWORA assisted with the fleetingly mentioned goal of "job preparation," insofar as that term meant anything other than compelling adult recipients to work.[72] So how were poor, single-parent families in which the breadwinner didn't earn a living wage supposed to get by over the long haul without government benefits? The preface's focus on marriage and two-parent families suggests the ultimate goal of the legislation: by compelling poor mothers to work low-wage jobs, and making benefits meager and short-lived, PRWORA sought to compel them to marry.[73] If their family's miserable predicament didn't convince them to find a husband, it would at least serve as a warning for other women contemplating going it alone.[74] As Senator Santorum revealingly described it, "Traditional liberal welfare policy is all about transferring income to individuals in such a way that their dependence on government is increased and their dependence on family decreased. We need[ed] to change these safety net programs so that they lead not only to independence from the government but also create [economic] incentives for the formation and maintenance of families."[75] Or as Senator Moynihan bluntly put it: PRWORA was based on the premise that "the behavior of certain adults can be changed by making the lives of their children as wretched as possible."[76]

The welfare reform package exhibited notably little concern for the children it relegated to poverty. Aside from the fantasy that subjecting poor families to poverty would result in poor mothers marrying their partners, which would magically stabilize the family economically, there was virtually no attention paid to getting these kids the material support they needed to do well. The PRWORA preface, which cited findings that children in two-parent families do better than children in single-parent families, was therefore an unintentionally ironic self-fulfilling prophecy: Children raised in two-parent families do better than those in single-parent families largely because these families tend to be wealthier and can invest more resources in their children. By consigning poor children from single-parent families to the significant harms that poverty inflicts, as well as ensuring that their parents were subjected to economic stress and insecurity that were bound to have a negative impact on their parenting, PRWORA guaranteed that children from poor single-parent families would indeed do far worse than children from two-parent families.

As in earlier decades, racism played a corrosive role in the development of this welfare policy. Political scientists have found that voter stereotypes of black laziness and sexual irresponsibility were the most powerful predictors of support for welfare reform.[77] After the bill became law, states with higher percentages of African Americans receiving benefits adopted tougher work requirements, lower time limits, and stiffer sanctions for program violations.[78]

PRWORA's misbegotten strategy of ending government support in order to increase marriage rates, of course, got it completely backward. It was the rise of inequality and poverty—not the presence of government benefits—that was driving the decrease in marriage rates. Because of this, after passage of PRWORA, marriage rates continued to drop. In 1996, when welfare reform was passed, the annual marriage rate was roughly fifty marriages per thousand unmarried women. By 2017, that figure dropped to thirty-two marriages per thousand unmarried women.[79]

Could it be that even though US welfare benefits are low, they're still somehow high enough to deter poor, pregnant women from marrying, as Charles Murray might argue? One easy way to test this theory is to look at what has happened in Mississippi. As chapter 2 described, Mississippi is so opposed to TANF benefits that recently it basically has stopped awarding them. Between 2003 and 2010, about half of the applicants for TANF benefits were granted them, but starting in 2011 that rate fell to 10 percent and has been decreasing ever since. In 2016, the state granted under 2 percent of TANF applications. And even those poor families who managed to get benefits received a maximum of just $170 a month for a family of three.[80] If access to welfare benefits causes nonmarital births to rise, Mississippi is the place where nonmarital births should have plummeted. Exactly the opposite happened, though. In 2004, Mississippi's nonmarital birth ratio (meaning the ratio of nonmarital births to all births) was about 48 percent. By 2016, not only had this rate not fallen, it had climbed to over 53 percent.[81]

What welfare reform accomplished, instead of shoring up two-parent families, was to greatly increase the misery of America's poorest families. The year it passed, sixty-eight of one hundred poor families with children received AFDC benefits. By 2017, only twenty-three of one hundred poor families with children received TANF benefits. Given their discretion to determine eligibility, this number varies widely among states.[82] Furthermore, because TANF benefit rates are so low, it does much less to relieve the misery of the nation's poorest children than AFDC used to. AFDC had lifted more than 2.7 million children out of deep poverty in 1995, the year before PRWORA passed. TANF lifted only 349,000 children out of deep poverty in 2015.[83]

In the aftermath of reform, Professors Kathryn Edin and Luke Schaefer interviewed some of the country's poorest families to figure out how they were getting by. These included many families where parents couldn't find steady work—and not for lack of trying, since they applied for job after job. Before welfare reform, most of these families would have had access to AFDC and other government supports when they needed them. Now they fell between the cracks. Edin and Schaefer discovered that few of these families even considered TANF a possibility anymore, instead making do under conditions of extreme poverty. As mentioned in chapter 6, some parents who had access to food stamps sold them and went hungry in order to pay for things their kids needed. Other parents sold plasma as often as they could, despite the resulting physical depletion. Some families collected and sold scrap metal, which paid poorly but at least brought in some cash. Edin and Schaefer discovered that the absence of government support meant kids were being raised in wretched circumstances that didn't come close to providing them with what they needed, and which led to horrifying outcomes: attempts at suicide, serious mental health issues, and multiple sexually transmitted diseases (which kids contracted by selling their bodies to pay for food).[84] The poverty and misery that welfare benefits had long sought to relieve, and which had been thought to have been eliminated in the United States, is back.

The one significant piece of legislation passed by Congress since PRWORA that did not fit neatly into the category of free-market family policy was the Family and Medical Leave Act of 1993 (FMLA). But even this law was far from taking a significant step toward pro-family policy. Despite the great need for caretaking leave guarantees in an era in which most women with young children had joined the workforce, the twelve weeks of unpaid leave that the FMLA put in place for about half the workforce not only represented just a shadow of the ambitious supports passed the generation before, but was much weaker than that put in place in every other industrialized country. Yet even this minimal set of protections triggered significant opposition. The proposed legislation lingered in Congress for nine years before it was enacted. After Congress finally passed it in 1991 and 1992, it was vetoed both times by George H. W. Bush. In a letter to Capitol Hill, Bush stated, "I want to emphasize my belief that time off for a child's birth or adoption or for family illness is an important benefit for employers to offer employees. . . . I strongly object, however, to the federal government mandating leave policies for America's employers and work force." Instead, he asserted, the issue should be left to private negotiation between employees and employers.[85] The legislation was finally signed into law by Bill Clinton in 1993.

Other ways the New Deal had safeguarded families from the market besides safety-net protections were also undermined in the last three decades of the twentieth century. A combination of state legislators' assaults, weakened federal protections, and hostile court decisions have left workers' collective bargaining rights in a severely weakened condition. Almost four decades of anti-tax activism led to a far less progressive tax structure and tax revenues so low as to make new social programs (and, indeed, existing programs) unsupportable without major adjustments in government spending.[86] Furthermore, the current federal minimum wage of $7.25 an hour hasn't been updated since 2009. If the minimum wage had been adjusted from its original rate to keep up with increases in US productivity, it would be $19.33 today.[87] These three shifts—weakened unions, the undermining of the progressive tax structure, and the reduced real value of the federal minimum wage—have contributed to the massive rise of inequality in the United States since the 1970s that has substantially eroded American families' well-being.[88]

The United States' shift from the goal of ensuring that all families with children get the resources they need to the current free-market family policy, where the government lets the market do what it will, wasn't preordained. Our nation could have easily traveled down the road to pro-family policy that most other wealthy democracies have. Yet once we veered onto the road to free-market family policy, we rarely looked back, despite the great harm this has caused American families. Ironically, with each further effort to undermine family supports, lawmakers have never retreated from touting the importance of families. In fact, just the opposite: those most set on eviscerating family protections continue to stress the critical importance of families to children and the nation. But they wrongly assert that government support undermines families' well-being.

Family policy in the United States bet its future on the losing proposition that the free market alone, without government regulation or assistance, would create flourishing families. The result is the decimated state of American families today. The question that remains is how to go about reversing this harmful agenda and to structure an economy that truly supports families.

PART III

REVIVING
THE AMERICAN DREAM

What's an Economy For?

The past half-century's push to privatize families has been based on the claim that families are best supported simply by ensuring healthy markets. In the decades since, our nation's gross domestic product (GDP) has increased three times over. Meanwhile, the well-being of our families—the top item on Americans' list of priorities—has gone rapidly downhill. Market forces are squeezing the life out of them. And instead of helping families get the resources they and their members need to thrive, policymakers keep cheering the market on while telling families they just have to work harder to achieve their dreams.

It's time that we lay to rest the misguided view that families can do it all by themselves if we just let the market work its supposed magic. Few ideas have caused as much harm as this one has. Markets serve a valuable function in putting many goods and services into the hands of people who want them, but they alone can't ensure that families have the conditions they need to thrive. The current state of US families demonstrates this in spades.

Markets, Families, and Government

We need an economy that supports, rather than undercuts, the well-being of families. To build that supportive economy, we need to put markets in their proper place. This may surprise some readers, since today we often treat markets as if they *are* the economy. That's because we wrongly view the ultimate goal of the economy as an ever-increasing GDP. As the economist Kate Raworth has observed, though, those who equate economic success with rising GDP don't ask hard enough questions about the purposes the economy should serve. Raworth likens the way that GDP growth has taken over as our economic goal to the egg of a cuckoo bird that has been laid in the nest of another variety of bird. Just as the unsuspecting feathered foster parents nurture the young cuckoo in their nest in the belief that it is their own, Raworth argues, policymakers have mistakenly nurtured GDP growth, considering it the be-all, end-all of economic success. As a result, markets eclipse everything else in the economic picture.[1] But the question that we should really b e asking about the economy is this: How can we ensure that all Americans have the resources—material, caretaking, educational, and leisure—they need to flourish? In other words, How can we make the American Dream a reality for every adult and child?

When it comes to getting people the needed resources, markets do very well at a limited range of tasks: producing and distributing goods and services that can be monetized to people with the ability to pay for them. But many things that people need to flourish, like the nurturing that parents provide, aren't distributed through markets. And some important things that are distributed through markets, like high-quality daycare, aren't affordable to many of the families whose children would benefit from them. These gaps reveal the importance of two other players in the economy that are every bit as important as markets: the family and the government.

Mainstream economic theory's obsessive focus on the market has caused it to ignore the tremendously important functions performed by families. Instead, conventional economists have tended to view families simply in their role as consumers of goods and services. But as feminist economists like Nancy Folbre and Heather Boushey have pointed out, even the shortsighted goal of increasing GDP couldn't be attained without families' (mainly women's) unpaid caretaking and human development work to produce future workers—services that aren't tallied up in the GDP.[2] And once we move to the more farsighted goal of supporting human flourishing, families move even closer to the center of the economic picture. The many tasks they accomplish—including raising children, grocery shopping, cooking, straightening the house, and caring for aging parents—all ensure that children and adults of all ages get the resources they need to thrive. Yet it is these tasks that are getting squeezed out by the increasing demands of the market. To support Americans flourishing, we need to structure the economy to ensure that families have both the conditions and the resources they require to do their job well. We also need to ensure that the important caretaking and human development work traditionally performed by women (and still disproportionately done by them) is being done well in our era in which most women work for pay, as well as being done in a manner that fulfills our nation's commitment to sex equality.

That brings us to the role of government. Free-market advocates are openly derisive of the government's role in the economy. Government, they claim, improperly distorts market incentives when it acts in the economic sphere. And to the extent that they concede the government has any role in regulating markets, it is only to correct supposed market failures, like parents not having enough information to make good decisions about daycare. Once we focus on ensuring that families get the resources they need to flourish, though, a far broader role for government emerges, and it's one that goes well beyond correcting market failures.

The state has five critical functions to serve in supporting the economic well-being of families. First, the government must partner with parents in providing the conditions our youngest children need at home. Second, it should invest in excellent daycare and prekindergarten programs. Third, it must reduce the economic inequality and instability to which markets are prone. Fourth, it must backstop families who can't afford important market goods by establishing a strong social safety net. Fifth, it needs to play "traffic cop" in order to keep the market within its proper bounds, making sure that workers have the time they need for fulfilling family lives and leisure. The next section describes each of the five functions of government in pro-family policy. The section after that lays out the public policies that support each of these functions.

PRO-FAMILY GOVERNMENT FUNCTIONS

Partnering with Families to Provide the Conditions Our Youngest Children Need at Home

Good public policy can be summed up by the credo that it should "make it easy for people to do the right thing." For parents of young children, doing the right thing means investing significant time, attention, and nurturing in their kids. Yet our free-market family policy sets up the vast majority of parents to fail at this fundamental parental responsibility by insisting that, during their child's early years, they must also provide all the material support their families need. Doing so requires that young families work paid jobs for long hours at the same time that their children's caretaking needs are likely the highest they'll ever be. The usual result is that parents wind up sacrificing the time with their kids that would be best for them in order to put food on the table. This system also ensures that little of the great wealth that markets generate in this country will be used to support our kids.

Pro-family policy corrects these flaws through the government partnering with parents to make it easy for them to get their kids what they need. This means publicly subsidizing parents to stay home with their child during the first year or years, so that they don't have to make a choice between keeping the lights on and caring for their child. It also means that government subsidizes families' budgets to ensure that every child gets a consistent floor of material support, even when parents' market earnings are inadequate or erratic. Using public funds to support children is a way of paying it forward. Later, when children require less parental caretaking and their parents' salaries increase, the state will generally recoup these funds through the taxes parents pay during the remainder of their careers.

Generous Public Investment in Daycare and Prekindergarten Programs for Young Children

Today, most US children don't get the daycare and prekindergarten they need to develop best, largely because most young families can't afford to purchase high-quality early childhood education at market prices. Pro-family policy would change this by heavily subsidizing programs that support children's early development so that every child would have access to them. It would also set compulsory, high-quality standards for daycare and preschool that would offer kids the best start possible.

Limiting Economic Inequality and Insecurity

Families today must obtain the resources their members need in an economy that is increasingly unequal and insecure. Their struggles to do so harm family members in multiple ways. At the bottom of our steep economic slope, low incomes and inconsistent employment prevents adults from entering into stable, long-term relationships and from providing their children conditions that would help them thrive. Up and down the slope, inequality and insecurity create fierce competition that sap vital time and energy from the family sphere and impose heavy pressure on youth. The government has an important role to play in limiting economic inequality and insecurity. Regulation of the market to limit wage inequality would reduce the incline of our economic slope. This, in turn, would provide the conditions that facilitate stable relationships and would decrease market competition to a more humane level. Public programs that decrease economic insecurity would also reduce competition on that slope, ensuring that all families can consistently get the resources, as well as the peace of mind, they need to function well no matter where they wind up on the slope.

Establishing a Strong Social Safety Net

Generous subsidies to all families with children combined with measures that decrease economic inequality would significantly reduce the number of families unable to make ends meet, and who therefore need to rely on the social safety net. That's a very good thing. Still, there will inevitably be situations in which the combination of market income and routine public subsidies won't be adequate to meet particular families' needs over the short or long term. For families in these situations, the state needs to construct a generous social safety net. Put simply, our public policy should guarantee that no family with kids should be poor in a country as rich as our own.

Playing Traffic Cop: Ensuring That Workers Can Combine Work and Family

As we've seen in the past five decades, market pressures can compel workers to concentrate increasing time and energy on paid work to the detriment of their families. Accordingly, last but not least, the government has an important role to play in regulating the labor market to ensure that workers can combine their paid work with meaningful family lives. Basically, the state should act like a traffic cop to ensure that the market stays in its lane when it comes to the role of paid work. In this capacity, government can limit the hours employees can be made to work so they can balance work with family responsibilities. After work hours, it can set buffers that help ensure that work interruptions don't interfere with family life. Unlike free-market policy, pro-family policy would not tell workers just to get a job; it would help citizens get a life.

Provisions that help workers balance work and family won't stop all adults from choosing to spend long hours at work. Their neighbors, though, won't be compelled to do the same. Instead, they could choose to devote more time to their young children (or to catch up on sleep or to spend more time alone or with their partners). They might not make as much money as their ambitious neighbors, and because of this, they might not be able to afford the Restoration Hardware sofa, the marble countertops, or a custom-built house. But their decision to work moderate hours wouldn't risk their losing their jobs or not being able to afford getting their kids what they need.

PRO-FAMILY POLICIES

What public policies would carry out the five government functions laid out in the preceding section? We don't need to be particularly creative here: countries that have embraced pro-family policy have already done a lot of work to figure this out. It turns out that there are a number of tried and tested programs that effectively serve these purposes.[3] This section organizes these programs according to the five pro-family functions laid out in the preceding discussion.

Partnering with Families to Provide the Conditions Our Youngest Children Need at Home

Parents have a lot on their plates in their children's first years. Yet the conditions they provide their children in those years will critically affect the rest of their lives. The government can help ensure that parents have four important resources during that time that will help children do their best—personal maturity, time, cash, and community support. Four government programs—(1) family planning, (2) paid parental leave, (3) child benefits, and (4) home visitation—will accomplish this.

Access to Effective Family Planning

Kids do better when their parents are mature and actively plan to become parents. Today, though, roughly 45 percent of US pregnancies aren't planned.[4] That was true for Wanda Johnson, the single mother from Charlotte we met in the introduction, who became pregnant at eighteen when she was a junior in high school. Government can and should provide women like Wanda easy access to birth control, including long-acting reversible contraceptives (LARCs). LARCs, which include intrauterine devices and contraceptive implants, are safe and far more effective at reducing unintended pregnancies than contraceptives like birth control pills, which must be taken daily, or condoms, which require users to take affirmative steps to avoid pregnancy each time they engage in sex. Nevertheless, LARC use is relatively uncommon in the United States compared to other wealthy countries because their up-front cost to US users is comparatively high.[5] The Affordable Care Act of 2010 improved this situation by mandating that LARCs be free for those with health insurance and for most women covered by Medicaid.[6] That still leaves many women unsubsidized, though. Further, because state Medicaid budgets are generally underfunded, many women covered by Medicaid still can't get LARCs.

Pro-family policy would fill these gaps by ensuring that all women who seek LARCs could get them for free. It would also ensure that American teens and adults have access to high-quality family planning through making certain that family planning providers have the capacity to serve everyone in the state. Colorado recently engaged in a concerted push to make sure all women had access to high-quality clinics that provided LARCs. The effort reduced unintended pregnancy and abortion rates in the state dramatically. It also raised the average age of first-time mothers by almost two years, reduced the births of second children to teen mothers by 85 percent, and lowered the number of births to women without a high school degree by more than a third between 2009 and 2017. The decreased number of unplanned pregnancies saved almost $70 million in public funds when Medicaid, TANF, SNAP, and other programs were taken into account.[7]

Pro-family policy would also encourage general healthcare providers who see women for routine care to ask them whether they want to get pregnant and, for those women who do not, to make LARCs and other forms of birth control available to them at the same appointment. A few years ago, Delaware took this course in partnership with a nonprofit organization, and the project significantly increased the rates of LARC use. Two more states—Washington and Massachusetts—are beginning to take similar measures.[8]

Publicly Paid Parental Leave for the Child's First Year
(and up to the First Few Years)

Remember Maya Hall, the lawyer in Durham who was hospitalized for post-partum depression after she had to return to work too soon (chapter 3)? And Raven Osborne, the Tupelo mother who returned to work a week after her baby's birth because she couldn't afford to stay home any longer (chapter 6)? In a country as wealthy as our own, both parents and their children deserve better. Publicly paid parental leave, subsidized at all or most of the parent's wage rate, would allow parents to stay home for up to their child's first year. This would help ease the major transition families undergo on the birth or adoption of a new child, as well as improve children's well-being.

The optimal length of time for babies to be cared for by a parent at home, as discussed in chapter 3, is complicated and contested. The accumulating weight of the evidence suggests that most kids do better with up to a year at home, but this will vary with a number of factors, including parents' temperament, education, and income as well as the baby's personality.[9] Given this complexity, the state should leave the choice to parents, since they are generally in the best position to judge what will serve their children's interests, as well as the most motivated to make the right choice. Staying home with older babies should be a readily available option for parents who choose it. But parents who choose to return to work well before the end of their child's first year should also have access to optimal-quality daycare.

Paid parental leave should include a combination of maternity leave to allow the mother to recuperate, a fixed amount of parental leave that can be split among parents as they choose, and some period of "use-it-or-lose-it" leave that the father (or the partner of the birth mother) can take. This last type of leave is now in place in all Nordic countries because mothers had taken almost all the leave when all parental leave could be split between the parents.[10] The introduction of leave that can be used only by the other parent has increased the time that fathers take with their infants. After these leaves, most research suggests that fathers are more involved in their children's lives.[11] This greater involvement, in turn, is linked to a broad range of benefits for family well-being, including improved outcomes for children and increased gender equality both at home and in the labor market, which in turn reduces the parents' chances of divorcing.[12]

As mentioned in chapters 2 and 5, several US states have already started to provide short-term paid parental leave to help fill the gap currently left by federal law, funded by payroll taxes on employees and, in some cases, employers. These programs are a very important start but, in some of these states, benefit levels need to be increased; in all states, leave lengths need to be extended; and, of course, coverage needs to be extended to all US families.[13] When the government rather than employees pay for the leave, the total cost is quite modest when spread across the taxpaying population.[14] In fact, most countries with leave programs find almost all the costs of the leave are repaid through the added tax dollars collected on mothers' salaries over time. This is because mothers are significantly more likely to return to work if they are given a paid leave of up to a year than if they receive a leave of six months or less.[15]

In the child's second and third years, the research is more equivocal on whether children do better at home or in high-quality daycare, although studies suggest children from low-income families do better in daycare. In these years, the state would do well to subsidize both options, as Finland does. This would allow parents who choose to do so to stay home with their young children, although potentially at a lower rate of wage replacement than during the child's first year. Meanwhile, parents who choose to return to work would be able to access high-quality daycare.[16]

Child Benefits

In the course of this book, we've heard from many families who live from paycheck to paycheck, constantly worried about whether they'll be able to give their kids the basics. It takes a significant amount of cash for kids to do their best, particularly during their early years. Yet the earning trajectory of Americans today means that few families will have ample cash coming in or saved up until far later in their lives than when they have young kids.

By providing a monthly child-benefit check to every family with children, government can play a critical role in ensuring that all children get the steady support they need. Most wealthy countries besides the United States already provide these benefits.[17] In Belgium, the basic child allowance ranges from $1,300 annually for the first child up to $3,600 for the third child (an incentive for Belgians to have multiple children).[18] Canada pays about $5,000 per year for each child under six, and $4,200 for older children, with some variation by province and family income.[19]

These benefits are particularly important for poor families. A $4,000 child benefit per year by itself would cut US child poverty by almost one-half, bringing our poverty rates down to roughly the norm among wealthy democracies.[20] Further, unlike the EITC, child benefits would help those children in the most dire economic circumstances of all, cutting the rate of children in *deep* poverty by more than half.[21] On top of that, child benefits would make a start in narrowing the large gap between the cash that lower-income families have to spend on their kids and what higher-income families spend.

Child benefits would also help the roughly half of American families— middle-class as well as working-class—who experience big shifts in household income from month to month.[22] These parents would have the assurance of knowing they could put food on the table and pay for a bus ride to the library, even in months that are tough financially. The peace of mind that this knowledge would give parents would make it easier for them to focus on their kids rather than worrying about how to make ends meet.[23]

Critics of welfare-state spending in the United States sometimes argue that poor parents would spend the benefits on themselves. Yet research from other countries shows the opposite to be true. Parents who received benefits routinely didn't spend more on items like tobacco or alcohol. Instead, they passed them on to their kids, spending more on things like schooling, medicine, and housing.[24] Children's psychological outcomes, health, and academic achievement all improved as a result.[25] Likewise, when US researchers gave cash to low-income families in four different experiments between 1967 and 1980, the money was associated with higher school attendance, better grades on standardized tests, and improved child nutrition and health.[26]

A child benefit program would do a far better job of meeting US children's need for consistent income than the Child Tax Credit (CTC) does today. Because that credit comes only at the end of the year, it doesn't perform the same income-smoothing function as a monthly child allowance. And the poor families who need income most don't even receive the full amount since the CTC is only partially refundable.[27]

Our country's failure to provide child benefits is particularly ill advised given policymakers' focus on expanding GDP. Experts have repeatedly concluded that these benefits yield high economic returns, particularly when they go to poor families. Child poverty costs the United States roughly $500 billion a year, or 4 percent of GDP, in lost productivity, increased crime rates, and increased healthcare costs.[28] On this basis, the economist Steven Pressman calculates that a $4,000 child allowance per year would *save* the US economy $250 billion a year.[29]

Home Visitation Services

Government should also make home visitation services available to parents with young children in order to help them make a smooth transition into parenthood. In home visitation programs, a nurse or other professional trained in child development visits a family beginning shortly before or after the child's birth. In the baby's first weeks, visitors educate parents about their baby's health, well-being, and developmental stages, and can provide help with breastfeeding. After that, they help parents develop effective parenting strategies and encourage talking and reading to young children. Visitors serve other functions as well. They help identify postpartum depression early and can help mothers get appropriate care. They can also spot parents who are becoming socially isolated and develop parenting groups that offer support and companionship. And they provide contacts, advice, and services that help prevent child abuse and neglect.[30]

Research on existing home visitation programs shows that they significantly improve parenting practices over the long term.[31] And improved parenting translates into lifelong gains for children in verbal ability, general school performance, and social and emotional competence.[32] These programs have also been associated with reduced child abuse and neglect, as well as reduced substance abuse and crime as these children grow up.[33]

Home visitation programs are particularly valuable for children from low-income families.[34] Researchers have found that some differences in parenting associated with class can have an impact on children's achievement. Studies suggest that children in low-income homes hear far fewer words than do children in high-income homes.[35] Researchers have also found that parents with lower incomes read to their children less than higher-income parents do and take them to fewer new places.[36] Supporting parents in changing these practices is an important way to ensure that poor children have as many opportunities as other children.[37]

Most countries operate home visitation programs through their national health system. The United States doesn't need to follow such a model, but we already have the foundations of such a program in place on a limited scale: the legislation that created the Affordable Care Act funded home visitation programs across the country.[38] These programs now serve more than 150,000 participants in over 76,000, mostly low-income, families in upward of one-quarter of the counties in the United States.[39] Including the home visitation programs supported by state funds as well, raises the total number of US families served today to 301,000.[40] Still, as law professor Clare Huntington points out, "[H]ome-visiting programs still reach only a tiny fraction of the families who would benefit."[41] We can and should do better.

Generous Public Investment in Daycare and Prekindergarten Programs for Young Children

In this book, we've heard from plenty of parents who couldn't afford to enroll their children in high-quality daycare and prekindergarten while they worked. The strong relationship between children's early caretaking and their ultimate outcomes makes it imperative for government to ensure that kids have access to top-notch daycare and prekindergarten programs. To achieve this, the state could either publicly provide this early education or subsidize high-quality private programs and regulate them for quality. Access to families could be either free or on a sliding-scale basis, with subsidies sufficiently generous to allow access to children from all families. The strong relationship between attending prekindergarten and subsequent school readiness for children from all income levels means that the state should encourage the maximum possible prekindergarten enrollment.

Limiting Economic Inequality and Insecurity

Government can help families up and down the economic spectrum by limiting economic inequality and insecurity. All families lose in an economy characterized by these conditions. Regrading the economic slope so that it isn't as steep and ensuring that those who wind up at the bottom can still support their children are critical measures that make the economy work for all families.

Limiting Inequality

The government's commitment to broadly distributing market gains in the New Deal era spurred the increase in economic equality that occurred during the middle of the twentieth century.[42] Its retreat from this commitment has since caused inequality to mushroom.[43] Reversing this inequality requires reinvigorating three measures central to the New Deal: a high minimum wage, progressive taxation, and support for collective bargaining.

Raising the minimum wage and then indexing it to inflation to prevent the increase from being eroded in future years are two of the most important steps we can take to help families at the bottom of the income ladder.[44] These measures would greatly improve the well-being of our most vulnerable kids. Nineteen million children would benefit from increasing the minimum wage to $15—nearly a quarter of all US children. Not only would raising the minimum wage increase the material support parents pass along to their kids, it would also allow many parents to spend more time at home with their kids rather than work a second job. And when they were home, it would let them focus on their kids instead of worrying about paying the bills. One 2017 study concluded that raising the minimum hourly wage by just $1 would cause child-neglect reports to drop by almost 10 percent.[45]

We also need a tax system that puts a greater share of the burden on the wealthy than it does today. Increasing marginal tax rates on the very rich not only reduces the tax burden on low- and middle-income workers, it also helps reduce economic inequality, both by constraining accumulation by the wealthiest households and by reducing incentives for CEOs and hedge fund managers to draw the highest salaries they can.[46] High marginal tax rates at the upper end of the income ladder also reduce workers' incentive to spend long hours in the workplace in order to compete for disproportionate rewards. These tax rates therefore discourage the kind of race to the bottom we see today, where high-powered professionals work exhaustingly long hours to make it up the next rung of the economic ladder. During the 1950s and early 1960s, the top income tax bracket was taxed at a marginal rate of higher than 90 percent of earnings. (The income that the taxpayer made before he or she hit that top tax threshold was, of course, taxed at a lower rate.) Today, at a rate of 37 percent, it is far less than half of that.[47] It's time to raise tax rates for the wealthy.

Further, we need to strengthen the hand of unions to bargain collectively. A significant part of the increase in economic inequality in the United States has come from unions' diminished power in recent decades.[48] Union membership has dropped from 28 percent in 1954 to 11 percent today.[49] Most of this decline is due to two factors: employers' heightened efforts to restrain unions and the weakening of laws protecting collective action by employees (including so-called right to work laws).[50] We can turn this situation around by empowering workers to organize and unions to negotiate with employers at the firm level and even beyond it, so that collective bargaining covers all employers in a particular sector of the economy, in order to secure higher wages and improved terms of work.[51]

A number of wealthy European democracies have already put all these programs in place, including high minimum wages,[52] tax rates that are far more progressive than our own,[53] and generous protections and support for unions.[54] We should put in place these measures here as well.

Limiting Insecurity

To put goods and services into the hands of the families who want them, employers need to have sufficient flexibility to respond to market signals. But this means that some workers will inevitably be laid off as market demands decrease for particular things. Pro-family policy gives employers the flexibility to respond to these signals even as it meets the material needs of workers and their families. To serve both ends, rather than guaranteeing workers their jobs, pro-family policy seeks to build economic stability for families into the broader economic system. As the Swedish minister for employment and technology put it, "The jobs disappear, and then we train people for new jobs. We won't protect jobs. But we will protect workers."[55]

Denmark, Finland, and Sweden have all adopted a model premised on these tenets, sometimes called "flexicurity," reflecting its joint goals of employer flexibility and worker security.[56] This model makes it easy for employers to hire and fire workers on the basis of market demand.[57] At the same time, laid-off employees receive unemployment benefits to tide them over until they find new jobs. In Denmark, benefits are available for two years. (In contrast, most US states provide a half-year's benefits; North Carolina and Florida are the stingiest states, allowing only twelve weeks of benefits.)[58] Danish workers get high levels of benefits, as well—about 90 percent of their wage rate for workers at the low end of the wage scale (in contrast to US workers' receipt of about 55 percent of their usual wage).[59] Denmark also actively seeks to help displaced workers find new job opportunities.[60] To accomplish this, it spends far more public funds than we do on active labor market programs, including those that provide incentives to private employers to hire.[61] We should adopt similar measures in the United States.

Not only would building more security into the larger economic system ease families' burdens when market dislocations occur, they would make life easier and less stressful in the normal course of affairs. Reducing economic insecurity would lessen the incentives for anxious employees to work excessively long hours in order to keep their jobs. It would allow people to move more freely between work and caretaking at the end of the day, as well as give them more time for leisure and other pursuits.[62] And when workers were home with their families, they'd be able to focus on their partners and children rather than worry about the security of their job.

Establishing a Strong Social Safety Net for Families

The reduced economic inequality and insecurity that result from pro-family policy would mean that far fewer families would need safety-net programs. But there will inevitably still be situations in which some families need these last-ditch measures. Dealing adequately with the situations of families in crisis requires a far stronger social safety net than the one we currently have.

Recall Teresa Branham, the single mother of four kids from Tacoma, Washington (chapter 6). After her family was cut off TANF benefits when she reached the program's five-year cap, they had so little food that she'd serve her kids their dinner and eat scraps from their plates once they were in bed, and her family was intermittently homeless for years. Pro-family policy would not allow any families with children in a country as rich as our own to go hungry or to sleep without a roof over their heads. Instead, the combination of cash assistance and other public programs would raise every needy family out of poverty.

Would safety-net programs reduce parents' incentive to work? If the question is whether these benefits would cause poor mothers to quit their day jobs or to cut back their full-time hours significantly, no evidence bears this out. Research makes clear that cash benefits have somewhere between no effect and a very minimal one on parents' work hours.[63] With that said, we should still hope that benefits would reduce the need of parents to work second and third jobs just to put food on the table. Many of the low-income parents I spoke to while writing this book were working these extra jobs, barely able to get time with their kids, and pushed to the limit. To the extent that benefits help stressed single parents like these spend more time with their children, this would be a very positive outcome. And these benefits would have a large effect on the well-being of their kids.

Although we have grown accustomed to considering child poverty in the United States as a problem too large to solve, this view is patently untrue. The cost of raising all 5.7 million poor families with children and the 105,000 poor children not living with their families above the poverty line in 2017 was about $64 billion per year in 2017 dollars.[64] That is just one-third of 1 percent of the nation's GDP.[65] This is approximately $17 billion less than the increase in defense spending (not defense spending itself—just the *increase*) passed by Congress in 2017—an increase considered so insignificant that it sailed through with minimal notice by the mainstream press.[66] What's more, the annual amount needed to eliminate child poverty is roughly 11 percent of what we spend on defense annually—despite the fact that our defense spending amounts to more than that of the next seven highest-spending countries combined.[67] And the cost to lift these children out of poverty for the next *ten years* is little more than a third of what Congress spent on the 2017 tax cuts.[68] As the Center for American Progress observed, if we hadn't made those tax cuts, "[t]here would be so much money left over after we boosted these kids out of poverty that the United States could also pay tuition and fees for all of them to get an in-state education at a four-year public university, and it still wouldn't cost as much as the tax plan."[69]

Playing Traffic Cop: Ensuring That Workers Can Combine Work and Family

Finally, pro-family policy would give the many Americans who work long hours the ability to combine sane work schedules with healthy family lives. Workers would no longer have to rely on their individual bargaining power with their employers to secure reasonable work schedules; instead, public policy would ensure employees time for their lives away from work. Six pro-family policies together would enable workers to reconcile work with family responsibilities: (1) reasonable limits on work hours; (2) paid vacation requirements; (3) advance notice of work hours; (4) right to part-time work; (5) policies requiring work-time flexibility; and (6) paid caretaking leave.

Reasonable Limits on Work Hours

Today, the overtime provisions of our Fair Labor Standards Act don't provide adequate protection even to the increasingly few workers covered by the act, since it just requires paid overtime without giving employees who want it the option to refuse that overtime. Pro-family policy would make it easier for workers to leave at the end of the workday so they could tend to their families and have rich, full lives beyond paid work.

To do so, pro-family policy would set a reasonable standard workday of eight hours and a workweek of forty hours, the same baseline used in many European countries.[70] Work beyond that up to a maximum number of hours (now forty-eight hours a week in European Union countries) should be allowed only under certain conditions, normally including an employee's willingness to work over-time and their option to choose between overtime pay and compensatory time for those extra hours (along with protections to ensure that workers could make these choices freely, and are able to use any comp time they acquired). To ac-commodate intermittent periods of high demand, employers would be able to average the maximum hours over a period of weeks, so that they could ex-ceed the maximum weekly hours for short periods of time. This system would allow for individual variation based on both employers' needs and employees' preferences, yet it would also give employees more clout in limiting their work hours if they choose to.

Paid Vacation

It's also time for the United States to put in place a statutory minimum period of annual leave, paid by the employer. The minimum of twenty paid vacation days set in most European Union member states is a reasonable place to start.[71]

Advance Notice of Work Hours

Pro-family policy would help employees like Jannette Navarro, the San Diego Starbucks barista whose constantly fluctuating work schedule threw her family into constant crisis (chapter 3). We need legislation throughout the United States like the "fair workweek" law that Oregon passed in 2017 to ensure that workers' time is respected and appropriately valued. That law requires employers to give service employees two weeks of advance notice of their work schedules so that they can plan their lives and their childcare.[72] Employers should also be required to give good-faith estimates of the number of hours that employees will likely work at the time they are hired, as well as whether employees will have to work on-call shifts. And employees should be entitled to at least ten hours off between shifts, as both New York City and Seattle now mandate.[73]

Rights to Part-Time Work

Parents and others with caretaking responsibilities need to be able to work part-time without being disproportionately penalized. For that to be possible, workers need the right to request and to work part-time schedules in certain situations and the right to receive parity in pay and benefits when they do work part-time.

Many countries, including Germany, Spain, and Australia, have parental leave policies that allow parents to work part-time in the first few years after a child's birth.[74] Other countries allow all parents, or even all employees, to request part-time work. The United Kingdom has one law of the latter type. Under it, employees have the right to request reduced working hours. Employers don't have to grant the request, but they can refuse it only for specified business reasons.[75] The United Kingdom enacted this policy in 2002 to protect parents with either a child under six or a child with disabilities. A million parents—one-quarter of the number of parents eligible—made requests in the first year alone.[76] The law worked so well that, in the years that followed, it was gradually expanded to cover relatives of aging parents and parents of older children. In 2014, the United Kingdom extended the right to request part-time work to all employees. Roughly eight in ten requests for temporarily reduced work hours are approved by employers under the system, as are nine in ten requests for permanently reduced work hours.[77] The Netherlands recently introduced a law that provides even stronger protections, requiring that employers show a compelling business interest in order to reject a request for part-time scheduling.[78]

Those employees who do work part-time also need to be assured that they will receive pay and benefits comparable to those of full-time employees for the hours they work. United Kingdom law requires that part-time workers be paid the same hourly rate as full-time workers, receive benefits on a pro rata basis, and be treated no less favorably than comparable full-time workers when it comes to layoffs.[79] Adopting comparable rights here would give much-needed help to American families.

Work-Time Flexibility

Pro-family policy would also support employees' ability to adjust their work schedules to accommodate family responsibilities. Where it is practicable for the employer, employees should be able to negotiate any of several types of adjustments: shifting their daily work hours for all or particular days (often called "flextime"), adjusting breaks in their normal working hours, or working from home for a certain amount of time each week ("telework").

Even in the United States, policies exist that support these kinds of scheduling adjustments. Since 2014, Vermont employees have had the right to request a flexible work arrangement for any reason without retaliation by the employer. Employers must grant the request unless it is "inconsistent with business operations," although the circumstances that fall within this category are broad.[80] The federal government has made inroads on these issues as an employer as well. In 2010, President Barack Obama signed into law the Telework Enhancement Act, which requires that all federal agencies establish telework policies for federal employees.[81]

Federal flextime legislation has been introduced, but hasn't gotten far. The Schedules That Work Act would require that an employer grant certain employee requests for flexibility when the requests are made for priority circumstances—health conditions, child or elder care, a second job, or continued education or job training—unless a bona fide business reason exists for not doing so. If a request is made for other reasons, the employer still must consider it and could not retaliate against the employee. Any legislation would need to ensure adequate protections for workers.[82]

Paid Caretaking Leave

Finally, the unpaid leave currently provided under the Family and Medical Leave Act to workers who need time off to care for a family member should be transformed into publicly paid leave and extended to loved ones who aren't biologically or legally related. Here, too, models for such paid leave are already in place in the great majority of wealthy democracies. The bulk of these countries pay for these leaves wholly from public funds, while a minority combine public funds with a contribution from the employer. Most of these programs provide a wage replacement rate of at least 80 percent. Roughly half of these countries provide at least three months of paid leave for children's health needs, while a minority of them also provide three months paid leave for adult family members' health needs. It's time we joined these countries.

The American Dream promises every American the resources that will let them thrive. The only way to accomplish this is by putting the market back in its proper place, as one important part of the economy—but only a part—alongside families and the government. Without the functions performed by families, neither children nor adults can achieve their full promise. And without government, the dynamics of the market can easily undermine families. This means that the government has a critical role to play in structuring the economy to support families. But how much will these changes cost, and will government's restructuring of the market interfere with the freedom that Americans value so dearly?

Toward Thriving Families

We've examined many American families whose lives, in ways large and small, are made more difficult by our expectation that they must provide the resources their members need entirely privately through the market, and without assistance from the government. Pro-family policies could make a world of difference for these families. They would particularly help the nation's children. Our own happiness and well-being and that of our fellow citizens also hang in the balance. And given the political waves that isolated and disillusioned Americans are beginning to make, the future of our democracy depends on it as well. At this critical juncture, it's time to make the correct turn in our nation's path.

We need to put markets in their proper place. To do that, we need to treat them as a part of the larger economy, the overall goal of which is to ensure that all Americans have the resources they need to thrive. Doing so aligns our nation with the story we have been telling about ourselves all along: the American Dream. And that means supporting flourishing families through government regulation of the market.

An economy that supports thriving families may seem like a pipe dream in the United States today. We have become so accustomed to political gridlock on so many issues that it's difficult to imagine our government serving a constructive role in supporting its citizens. Believing a supportive state is politically unachievable, though, would be a self-fulfilling prophecy. Remember that in the decades before the 1970s, the rollback of the welfare state would have been considered equally unthinkable, and the political consequences untenable. And in the early 1970s, the received wisdom had it that the country would soon adopt a guaranteed income plan and federally funded high-quality daycare for families of all incomes. In fact, both plans almost became a reality.

Many goals seem like pipe dreams until a tipping point is reached. The push for same-sex marriage began with a paper by a Harvard Law School student on a subject so legally improbable that he couldn't find a professor to supervise it.[1] And yet a couple of decades after the push began, same-sex marriage is now broadly accepted, not just legally, but politically, and in the court of public opinion.

And for a long time passage of comprehensive healthcare legislation seemed politically impossible until the Affordable Care Act passed in 2010. Even then it remained politically controversial until Americans recognized the effect it had on their daily lives. Between 2013 and 2017, as the future of the Affordable Care Act was being debated, the percentage of Americans who thought that government had an obligation to ensure healthcare coverage for all citizens rose a remarkable 14 points—from 42 percent to 56 percent.[2]

If movement is possible on same-sex marriage and healthcare, it is also possible on government support for families. The huge toll that the free-market system takes on the daily lives of the vast majority of us, as well as on the well-being and capacity of our children, give us strong motivation to unite on this issue. We need to stop accepting free-market family policy as inevitable. And we need to start pointing out that in today's free-market economy everyone loses, while pro-family policy creates an economy in which everyone—kids and adults—have their best chance to flourish because their families will have the support they need to flourish. Then we need to start electing politicians committed to enacting these programs.

Some of the blocks for building this coalition are already in place. Eight in ten Americans already believe that women should receive paid maternity leave.[3] Given the harsh anti-government rhetoric of the past several decades, it's not surprising that most of those who support paid maternity leave feel that individual employers should pay for it rather than the government.[4] But the case for why government is better positioned to spread the benefits and risks of the market economy through enacting paid-leave programs hasn't been widely disseminated to the public. Once it has been, the argument in favor of government responsibility is compelling.

Three primary concerns arise in response to pro-family proposals. The first is that pro-family policies will make our economy less competitive. The second is that pro-family policies will cost too much. The third is that moving away from free-market policy will stifle Americans' freedom. Let's consider each in turn.

PRO-FAMILY POLICIES, PRODUCTIVITY, AND EMPLOYMENT RATES

Would adopting pro-family policies make our economy less competitive or our country less wealthy? It's important to recognize that countries with pro-family policies have deliberately chosen to allow citizens to lead sane lives with more leisure over long hours of work. To account for this, the correct measure for comparing our system with theirs isn't GDP per capita (since it doesn't account for the trade-off they've made between paid work and other activities that don't pay a wage and so aren't reflected in GDP), but instead GDP *per hour worked*. In the abstract, it's unclear whether people would be more productive on an hourly basis under a free-market or pro-family system. On the one hand, workers under free-market family policy might seem more likely to work harder during an average hour, given that the penalty of losing their job is high and the potential benefits of a promotion are substantial in a highly unequal system. On the other hand, workers under pro-family policy would likely have higher human capital as a result of better conditions to develop in their first years, reduced levels of poverty, reduced rates of mental illness and drug abuse, and higher academic achievement (a product of the hospitable conditions of their first years and higher college attendance because of the subsidized tuition). They would also be likely to have more energy for work in any given hour since they would generally work fewer hours overall.

So which system over time actually winds up producing more productive workers? Looked at in the light most favorable to the United States, at best it's a draw between the two systems. More likely, pro-family policy is the system that produces higher productivity over the long term. Figure 11.1 compares trends in worker productivity per hour in Finland and Denmark, countries with pro-family policy, and in the United States. In 1970, we were the clear leader in productivity. But that changed in the following decades, as we moved to free-market family policy and the Nordic countries moved further along their

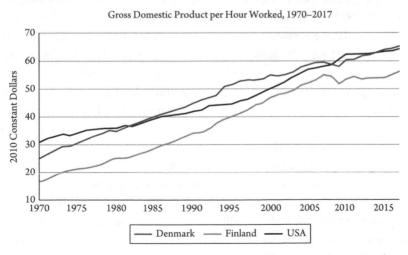

Figure 11.1. Gross Domestic Product per Hour Worked (2010 Constant Dollars). Source: Data from OECD (2019b).

pro-family policy tracks. At the beginning of this time frame, Finland's workers were only about half as productive per hour worked as workers in the United States. By 2006, that gap had closed to 8 percent. The gap has increased to just under 12 percent in the past few years, but that's mostly a result of somewhat idiosyncratic factors—the decline in the production and sales of Nokia phones, which had been a key engine of growth in Finland, as well as weak demand for paper, a key Finnish export.[5] In those same decades, Denmark caught up to and has since moved beyond us. The higher rate of growth under pro-family policy comports with Richard Wilkinson and Kate Pickett's demonstration that the rate of patents issued per capita across countries varies with their level of economic equality—the more equal economically a country is, the more patents per person it tends to have. Which country tops the list of nations in terms of patents per head? Finland.[6] All this suggests that pro-family policy is a better bet to increase productivity over the long haul.

Our country's own economic history also suggests that many of the features of pro-family policy—a relatively robust welfare state, support for unions, market regulation to support families, and high marginal tax rates on the wealthy—improve rather than impede productivity. All these policies were in place for the three decades after World War II, when our nation's GDP growth was stronger than it has been since then.[7] So, no, adopting pro-family policies likely wouldn't make the United States less competitive. To the contrary, by investing in our human capital, we would be able both to increase our productivity and to work fewer hours. And we could do so in an economy that helped all families and all their members thrive.

Not only would growth not be stifled under pro-family policy, increases in productivity would be far more likely to be widely distributed among American families. The fact of the matter is that although the average US GDP per household has risen considerably in the past five decades under free-market policy, almost none of these gains have been passed along to middle-class families with children, as Figure 11.2 shows.[8] Instead, that money has overwhelmingly gone to the wealthiest households through increasingly high executive salaries and shareholder dividends. Pro-family policy, both through building in measures to decrease inequality and through its emphasis on universal spending programs, would help ensure that gains are more equally distributed among families, as they were in the decades following the New Deal.

If we don't need to worry that our workers will be less productive under pro-family policy, should we be concerned that fewer people will work under this system and that the "takers" will overwhelm the "makers"? We've all heard many times from American politicians and pundits that generous welfare benefits cause many people to leave the workforce in order to, as some put it, "suck on the public teat." But in fact, pro-family policies actually do better at keeping more adults engaged in paid work. Take a look at Figure 11.3, which

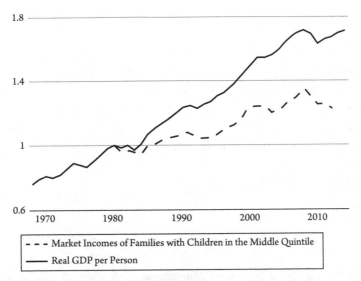

Figure 11.2. Growth of Middle Class Market Incomes and GDP Per Person Over Time (1979 = 1). Source: Duke and Schwartz (2015) (based on analysis of data from Sarah Flood and others, "Integrated Public Use Microdata Series, Current Population Survey: Version 4.0.)

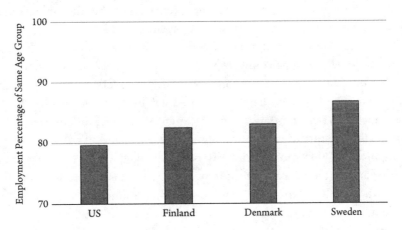

Figure 11.3. Employment Rates of 25–54 Year Olds by Country, 2018. Source: Data from OECD (2019d).

compares workplace participation in workers' prime years in the United States and in several countries that have implemented pro-family policy. Fewer adults in the United States work during their prime years than adults do in these other countries. This is partly because pro-family policies make it easy for mothers of young children to return to paid work, due to both paid leave and universal daycare.[9] And it is partly because education and flexicurity policies help workers who don't have jobs acquire skills, training, and income support while they're looking for work so that they don't get discouraged and drop out of the work-force altogether.[10]

Increasing GDP and employment rates shouldn't be the ultimate measure of the economy, though; increasing well-being and the quality of our lives, individually and collectively, should. Pro-family policy would bring us closer to meeting these goals up and down the income ladder. Families of all backgrounds and income levels would have a better work–life balance, their members would be happier and have better mental health, and children would get the resources that would best help them achieve their potential. That's the kind of use of our economic resources that we should be aiming for.

THE COST OF A FAMILY-FRIENDLY ECONOMY

Can we afford all these programs? The answer is a clear yes, for two simple reasons. First, we could take the same amount of money our country spends both publicly and privately on social well-being today and simply spend it better. That way we could pay for every one of these programs without needing to spend a penny more. Second, in a country as wealthy as our own, we could raise taxes to pay for these programs, and do it in ways that eased rather than increased the burden on the middle class and those with low incomes.

As discussed in chapter 2, we're *already* spending every bit as much money on people's well-being as countries with far more robust welfare states do, a fact that becomes apparent only once you add up different countries' public *and* private spending over the course of people's lives across areas like health-care, education, pensions, and unemployment.[11] The real difference between us and other countries isn't the total amount we spend, it's that Americans spend most of this money directly, out-of-pocket, on daycare programs, doctors, and so on.[12] Meanwhile, Finns, Danes, and people from other countries with robust welfare states pay more of their money in taxes to the government, which then spends it on programs like daycare and healthcare.[13] In fact, once we factor in both government spending and private spending, we spend *more* on people's well-being than almost every other country. In 2014, the United States spent more on social welfare as a percentage of GDP than any other country besides France.[14]

The real reason the United States trails other countries so badly on overall well-being isn't because of how many total dollars we spend. It's because of who we spend our money on and when we spend it.[15] Because we spend most of our money on social well-being privately, we spend it only when families have the money to pay. And that means US spending is skewed toward later in life, after families have accumulated more earnings, rather than when they have young children and need it most.[16] Skewing US spending even more in this direction, our biggest public social programs, Social Security and Medicare, make huge public investments in senior citizens. These programs were built on the recognition that markets are an inadequate means of meeting people's needs toward the end of life. In today's economy, it's clear that markets work even less effectively to meet people's needs at the beginning of life. But so far we've failed to develop similar social programs that invest in our children. Our social welfare outcomes would be significantly higher, though, if we shifted some of this money to children early on because of the returns this investment would yield throughout their lives.

Furthermore, the too-little money we do spend on young kids today, because most of it is spent privately, is distributed massively unequally among them. The relatively few families at the top of the economic ladder who can afford to spend generously on their kids—basically only the high end of professional families—do so, whereas parents at the middle and bottom of the economic ladder can't afford to pay close to what their children need to do their best. But the many dollars that well-to-do parents spend on their children have diminishing marginal returns. The hundredth book in a toddler's library has a much smaller impact on that child's development than the first five books would have had on the development of a child from a poor family. Because of that, we would get far higher social welfare payoffs if we shifted to a social welfare system that spent more money publicly and therefore distributed that spending more equally. Shifting spending from private to public would also allow us to shift more money from the end of life to the beginning, when most families have few private funds to spend. That's what countries with pro-family policy do. And if we shifted more money for seniors from private to public spending, we could still achieve the same or better outcomes towards the end of life (since money on senior citizens would be spent more equally, and more focused on actual need), as many other wealthy countries that spend publicly have done.[17] In this way, we could implement the full range of pro-family policies in the United States called for in the preceding chapter without spending a penny more than we spend today on social welfare.

Even if we didn't reform our entire social welfare system, we could simply and with relative ease (speaking in terms of policy rather than politics) increase taxes to pay for these programs. We can get a rough sense of how much these policies would cost by looking at what other wealthy countries spend on them. When it comes to the core programs often referred to as "family programs," including parental leave, child benefits, other cash transfers to parents (including safety-net benefits like TANF), and early childhood education, most of the countries at the top of the spending list—Finland, Denmark, France, Sweden, Iceland, and Luxembourg—spend between 3.2 percent (Finland) and 3.5 percent (Iceland) of their annual GDP.[18] The United States spends less than 1.5 percent of its GDP on family programs.[19] To our spending shortfall on these core family programs of between 1.7 to 2.0 percent of GDP, we also need to add the cost of a home visitation program and paid leave to care for sick family members, which amount to about 0.13 percent of GDP combined. That means that we could, overall, expect to spend roughly 1.8 to 2.1 percent of GDP more in public spending on these family programs than we do today.[20] One lesson to draw from this is that, despite the enormous benefits family programs yield and the many ways they improve people's lives, they are simply not that expensive compared with other large government programs like pensions and healthcare. Adopting Denmark's flexicurity system to give workers more economic security would bump that number up by another 3 percent of GDP.[21]

Can we afford this? Of course we can. Far less wealthy countries have adopted these programs, including Estonia, whose per capita GDP is roughly a third of ours. We would, though, need to raise taxes. Our country raised the equivalent of 27 percent of our GDP in taxes in 2017 (and that was before the massive 2017 tax cuts went into effect), compared with 43 percent for Finland and 46 percent for Denmark.[22] Adopting the tax increase needed to pay for pro-family policies would still put our tax rate far below the rates of these other countries. Furthermore, if this tax increase were progressive (meaning that the wealthier paid proportionally more), as it should be, far more of these costs would be borne by those at the top end of the income ladder. Meanwhile, families at the bottom and the middle would benefit from the relatively equal distribution of public spending, which would allow all kids to receive the resources that only upper-middle-class and wealthy children receive today.

Recognize that the public money spent on these programs is not at all like public funding for the military or NASA, where few tax-paying families see direct returns. When it comes to family programs, the money paid out by taxpayers goes right back to help families, and at the time they need it most. So while most Americans would pay somewhat more in taxes throughout their lives, most of them would get it back in spades during their years with young kids (and, in future years, all would have received the benefits of these programs when they were young kids). Further, in this system, parents would no longer have to shell out money for many of the things they pay for today, like daycare and prekindergarten.[23] Today, middle-class parents spend an average of $10,865 a year on each child.[24] Not only would that amount drop significantly, for the items they still had to spend on, parents would be able to use the public money they receive as child benefits first, before dipping into their own pockets.

Although this book has made the case against considering the ultimate goal of the economy to be increased GDP, the fact of the matter is that pro-family policy would still pay for itself, even in narrow economic terms. The Urban

Institute estimated that child poverty alone creates social costs today, including reduced productivity, increased crime, and increased healthcare costs, equal to about 4 percent of GDP. The entire array of family programs would pay for itself by avoiding just those costs. But there would be considerably more economic benefits besides. For starters, some economists calculate a net benefit of more than $7 for every dollar spent on disadvantaged children on early childhood education.[25]

Furthermore, much of the public spending on these programs would be recouped over time by both increased tax proceeds as a result of increased earnings spurred by these programs, as well as by the reduced needs for spending they cause. Over the short to medium term, a substantial amount of the public money spent would be returned through the greater income taxes paid by mothers, since more of them would return to work under pro-family policy and therefore earn more over time. The comparative welfare state expert, Gøsta Esping-Andersen, used very conservative assumptions to calculate how much of Denmark's generous public spending on early childhood education was repaid by mothers' increased income tax payments. The answer, it turned out, was all of it—and with interest![26] Over the long term, we would also reap the added taxes on children's increased earning as a result of them having far better conditions in which to develop their human capital.[27] Factor in the reduced costs across the population of mental health care, teen pregnancy, and imprisonment as a result of pro-family policy, and you can see how hugely irrational *not* implementing pro-family policy is.

But the more important reasons for adopting pro-family policy, by far, go beyond the narrow range of rationales considered "economic" in US market-obsessed thinking. Above all, pro-family policy would support all US kids in getting the best start we could give them. And that's where we should be putting our nation's great wealth. When it comes to adults, by limiting economic inequality and insecurity, pro-family policy would improve our mental health, increase our life satisfaction, restore sanity to our work and family lives, and help reknit our social fabric. These, too, are the ways we should be using the many benefits that the market has provided us. In truth, all these aims should be the central goals of the economy.

FREEDOM AND THE MARKET

Market advocates may interpret this call for pro-family policy as a call for government overreach. If Americans wanted the kinds of conditions for their families suggested here, these advocates would argue, they'd negotiate these terms for themselves on the market. Milton Friedman, one of the loudest cheerleaders of free-market capitalism in the twentieth century, famously put the point this way: "What most people really object to when they object to a free market is that it is so hard for them to shape it to their own will. The market gives people what the people want instead of what other people think they ought to want. At the bottom of many criticisms of the market economy is really lack of belief in freedom itself."[28] Was Friedman right? Would pro-family policy reduce individual freedom?

The equating of markets with freedom has a long history. Adam Smith, writing in eighteenth-century Scotland, made a similar case for the link between the two. The rise of markets, he maintained, helped mark the break with feudalism. He proclaimed that the most important effect of markets was "the liberty [that they produced] . . . of individuals . . . who had before lived almost in a continual state of . . . servile dependency upon their superiors."[29]

Linking markets with freedom, though, as the philosopher Elizabeth Anderson points out, made far more sense in Smith's time than in our own. Smith wrote before the Industrial Revolution and the rise of wage labor. That's the reason that most of the people increasing their freedom in Smith's examples were butchers, bakers, and other small business owners. These proprietors worked as their own masters, took their goods to market, and went home better off after they sold their wares.[30] The relationship between markets and freedom is far murkier today. In contrast to the independent craftsmen of the days of yore, today's market actors are generally employees who must agree to do their boss's bidding, often for most of their waking lives. Employers set the hours and place of work, choose employees' co-workers, determine the goals employees will pursue, set the pace of work, and then supervise employees' performance. This makes most people, at least for the hours they're working, look a lot more like serfs subject to the bidding of a lord than like the market actors controlling their own destinies described by Adam Smith.[31]

Many of those who aren't directly employed by businesses still work in the gig economy, in which they may be able to choose their own hours, but their activities and work product are still carefully regulated and monitored by the businesses they work for. And in the new economy, the significant levels of control exercised over employees aren't limited simply to those who perform menial jobs. White-collar employees at Amazon, for example, are routinely expected to stay late; emails regularly arrive in the wee hours of the morning, followed by text messages asking why they haven't been responded to; and there's a routine annual cull of employees who don't measure up. One Amazon marketing employee reported that "nearly every person I worked with, I saw cry at their desk."[32] That doesn't sound too far removed from the "continual state of . . . servile dependency" associated with feudalism that Smith decried. Of course there are still big differences between wage labor and feudalism. The big one is that workers get to go home at the end of the day. But even that time off is being encroached on by work demands today. Most workers today feel obligated to check their email repeatedly. A significant number wind up on call. And many perform work tasks on their own time. Another big difference between wage labor and feudalism is that workers today can quit their jobs if they choose. That said, they would still likely have to submit themselves to the bidding of *some* employer to keep themselves and their family afloat financially, and probably for long hours. That means that most adults will have to devote a large chunk of their lives to doing what an employer tells them to do rather than spending their time on their children or other activities that give meaning to their lives.[33]

Framed in this way, market society today looks less like a vehicle carrying us merrily along the road toward freedom, and more like a system imposing its own set of constraints and pressures on how we lead our lives. These constraints and pressures make ways of life ordered around long hours of market work systematically easier, and other ways of life systematically harder. Despite this, the constraints and pressures imposed by the market system are often difficult for Americans to recognize. Much of this is likely the product of our political tradition, which emerged out of our rejection of government tyranny. Because of that, we are far more attuned to recognizing threats to freedom from the government than we are to seeing the ways that the market can limit freedom and constrain our lives. Americans can certainly exercise the freedom of choice that exists within these market constraints, but we shouldn't ignore the fact that many would prefer a different range of choices about how to live our lives than the market makes available to us today.

The idea that citizens' market decisions represent pure, uncomplicated "free choice" also ignores the way that government action affects our choices. The state has hardly been neutral when it comes to families' relationship with market forces. As we have seen, in the past fifty years, government has shifted laws deliberately to make families more beholden to the market. During this same era, policymakers have actively undermined the balance of power that had been struck earlier between unions and employers, tilting it decidedly in favor of the latter. Policymakers have also passed corporate laws that favor shareholders over employees, and tax laws that favor the rich over the poor. So equating free-market policy with true freedom or even the absence of regulation is nonsense. In this light, pro-family policy shouldn't be thought of as regulating the genuinely "free" market, but instead as *re*-regulating the market, this time for the benefit of families rather than corporations and the wealthiest citizens.

Even beyond these external constraints, the argument that Americans' endless grind is an exercise of simple free choice ignores what we know about how people make decisions. The choices that Americans make to work long hours don't come from preferences that are fixed at birth. Instead, these preferences were developed in a culture in which pro-work messages are loudly sounded. These messages didn't arise spontaneously. They were first disseminated by early capitalists, who recognized that it would be far easier to maximize the output of their employees if the workers themselves internalized the virtues of hard work. They were right: once the public absorbed this work ethic, productivity increased, and family and leisure time declined in order to make more time for work and for consumption.[34]

Furthermore, our current views of what constitutes an adequate standard of living, as we saw in chapter 3, are influenced not just by our current living standards but also by our neighbors' standards. All this has been bolstered by the mushrooming economic inequality in the United States, as citizens take notice that the Joneses have far more consumer goods (flat-screen plasma televisions, iPads, big houses, luxury cars) than they do and feel the need to try to keep up with them. Whatever we have now, we want at least that much into the future, and if our neighbors have something, we want that too. The same is true when it comes to our notion of how many work hours are acceptable. These views are reinforced by the strong consumerist culture in the United States. This culture, too, hasn't developed organically. It has been driven by the ceaseless barrage of advertisements and obsessive media focus on the wealthy to which American citizens, including young children, are subjected from early in the morning to late in the evening.[35]

None of this is to suggest that Americans are completely powerless when it comes to negotiating their relationship with the market. It is, however, to recognize that any simple equation between the market and freedom no longer holds today, if it ever did. Market advocates might argue that few of us would forgo the benefits markets bring us if we had the choice. And they would likely be right. Even if rejecting the benefits of market society were truly possible—so that, for example, plots of land were freely available and those who withdrew from market society could work the land without having to pay taxes—probably few would choose this option. But why are the available choices only between accepting the benefits of market society as it is currently structured or accepting none? Why can't we regulate the market in ways that we collectively agree to in order to temper its negative effects on families and to improve all our lives?

How can government regulation of the market increase our freedom rather than limit it? It all comes back to the kinds of collective-action problems the market creates. In chapter 3, we saw how the expanding number of hours that families work results from the competition created by rising economic inequality and insecurity. And we saw, as well, that individual families couldn't retreat from the competition without jeopardizing the well-being of their members. The thing about collective-action problems, though, is that they can be solved—through collective action. That's where the government, with its unique ability to change the rules governing the market, comes in.

Once we pay attention to the way that our lives are restricted by market forces today, we can see how adopting government programs that support families would be liberating rather than a drag on our freedom. In the presence of publicly paid family leave policies, for example, parents with a new baby could take time off from work that they can't take today. And with a child benefit program and a functioning safety net, parents wouldn't live in constant fear that the next unexpected expense would prevent them from feeding their child. That might mean that they could decide to spend evenings at home rather than driving for Uber. In this way, pro-family policy would give Americans more choices about how to structure their lives in ways that were not so strictly ordered around the market's demands, and therefore provide them more freedom.

Countries with pro-family policy have long had a better understanding of the ways that markets and market society can limit citizens' lives and cut off many valuable ways of living. They have more clearly recognized the ways in which workers' continual need to secure income to meet their families basic expenses is itself a significant form of *un*freedom. Because of this recognition, they have embraced public policies that "decommodify" the basic goods that citizens need, freeing people up to pursue lives rich with family time, as well as other ways of life that escape the endless grind. These countries have rightly recognized that seeing freedom solely in terms of market choices, and allowing citizens only this limited version of freedom, too tightly constrains the kinds of lives that citizens can lead. Real freedom is enhanced rather than curtailed when citizens can access the resources they need without devoting their entire lives to the market.

Free-market policy's insistence that American families privately negotiate what they need on the market without the help of government is crushing them. It's time to replace this system with one that actively partners with families to support their well-being, along with the well-being and promise of all our citizens. We have more than enough economic wherewithal to make this shift. In fact, we wouldn't need to spend a penny more than we do today, so long as we radically reconfigure how we spend that money. All we need is to muster the political will. Our own freedom and happiness, the well-being of our families, the future of our children, and even perhaps the fate of our democracy, depend on it.

NOTES

Introduction

1. Adams (1931), 214–15.
2. Two insightful books, June Carbone and Naomi Cahn's *Marriage Markets* (2014) and Robert Putnam's *Our Kids* (2015), already make this connection.
3. I use the term "low-income families" to describe families whose earnings are less than twice the poverty level, or about $42,000 in 2018 for a family of three. (The 2018 poverty level for a family of three was $20,780.) By "poor families," I mean those at the federal poverty level or below.
4. To put a more human face on the broad array of national and comparative data relied on in the book, in the course of writing, I spoke to thirty-nine parents from a wide variety of US families. I reached these parents through a broad network of contacts. Most of the low-income parents I interviewed responded to a call for interviews from organizations affiliated with the Closing the Women's Wealth Gap Initiative, including the national nonprofit EARN and the Tacoma Community House. Because a number of the parents I spoke to requested anonymity, I decided to use pseudonyms in recounting their stories. Their stories are meant to be illustrative only; I make no claim that they represent the situations of all US parents. I also spoke to four parents of families in other countries. In my conversations with parents, I discussed their finances before they had kids through the present; their work, living situations, and schedules as they raised kids; how their finances influenced the circumstances their children received; which, if any, government programs the family relied on; and how these programs affected the families' circumstances.
5. I use the term "middle-income families" to describe families with earnings that fall between 2 and 6.5 times the federal poverty level, or about $42,000 to $135,000 for a family of three in 2018.
6. Interview with the author.
7. I use the term "high-income families" for those with incomes more than 6.5 times the federal poverty level, which in 2018 was roughly $135,000 or more for a family of three.
8. Interview with the author.
9. Harter (2018).
10. Patten and Parker (2012), 4; Pew Research Center (2008); Harrington, Van Deusen, and Humberd (2011), 10, chart 3.
11. Jacobs and Gerson (2004), 64–9, 72–3. See also Golden and Tesfayi (2007); Rose (2016).
12. See *infra* chapter 3.
13. See *infra* chapter 11, n. 6 and accompanying text; Krugman (2017).
14. Santorum (2005). Numerous other statements from Republican politicians and conservative economists express similar views. In the words of former Arizona Republican Representative Trent Franks, "If we employ free market principles, we can help everyone." Wright (2011). Or, as President George W. Bush put it, "Free-market capitalism is far more than an economic

theory. It is the engine of social mobility, the highway to the American dream." Stolberg and Pear (2008).

Conservative economist Thomas Sowell explained this view this way: "It was Thomas Edison who brought us electricity, not the Sierra Club. It was the Wright brothers who got us off the ground, not the Federal Aviation Administration. It was Henry Ford who ended the isolation of millions of Americans by making the automobile affordable, not Ralph Nader. Those who have helped the poor the most have not been those who have gone around loudly expressing 'compassion' for the poor, but those who found ways to make industry more productive and distribution more efficient, so that the poor of today can afford things that the affluent of yesterday could only dream about." Sowell (2010).

15. Clinton (1996); Davis and Lemieux (2000).
16. Economist Robert H. Frank's insightful book, *The Darwin Economy* (2011), lays out a number of similar examples in which unbridled market competition leads to "arms races" that reduce benefits to individuals and the group.
17. I owe this term to my son, Eli.
18. Glass, Simon, and Andersson (2016), 891, 906–7.
19. Schultz (2013).
20. Brooks (2014).
21. Esposito et al. (1998), 40–1.
22. For one intelligent discussion of the ways that government could but doesn't support families headed by unmarried parents, see Huntington (2015).
23. Texas Senator Ted Cruz expressed the point this way in 2015: "America is in crisis now. I believe in America. And if we get back to the free market principles and constitutional liberties that built this country, we can turn this country around." Team Fix (2015).

Chapter 1

1. The term "infrastructure" is used by Heather Boushey in her book, *Finding Time* (2016).
2. Bowlby (1951), 158.
3. National Scientific Council on the Developing Child (2009), 1. See also World Health Organization (2004); Howard et al. (2011).
4. Hildyard and Wolfe (2002), 690. See also National Scientific Council on the Developing Child (2012).
5. National Scientific Council on the Developing Child (2009); World Health Organization (2004); Howard et al. (2011); Harvard Center on the Developing Child (2013); Waldfogel (2006).
6. Dowd (2018), 42–9.
7. OECD (2015a), 174, fig. 4.32, analyzes data from the World Health Organization, *Health Behaviour in School-Aged Children (HBSC, 2009/2010 Survey)*. See also UNICEF (2013), 39, fig. 6.0; OECD (2017a), 39, fig. III.1.1, which rates the US average life satisfaction score of fifteen-year-olds twenty-eighth out of forty-eight countries and economies.
8. OECD (2015a), 169, fig. 4.25; (2017a), 76, fig. III.3.5.
9. OECD (2016a), 177, fig. 1.5.1.
10. Ibid., 191–2, fig. 1.5.8.
11. OECD (2016a), 67, fig. 1.2.13, 149, fig. 1.4.1.
12. OECD (2016b), 183, fig. B1.3, 196, table B1.5a, 192, table B1.1.
13. Perou et al. (2013), 2, citing Merikangas et al. (2010) and Angold et al. (2002); see also Bitsko et al. (2016), 222.
14. Wilkinson and Pickett [2009] (2010), 68.
15. Twenge et al. (2019). Regarding suicide rates, see Plemmons et al. (2018); Curtin et al. (2018), 3; Centers for Disease Control and Prevention (2017). Regarding the prevalence of anxiety and depression, see Bitsko et al. (2018), 399; Weinberger et al. (2018), 1310; BlueCross BlueShield (2018), 6; Mojtabai, Olfson, and Han (2016), 4. See also Perou et al. (2013); Twenge (2015).
16. Twenge et al. (2010), 152 (1938–2007 data).

17. Account taken from Schrobsdorff (2016).
18. Luthar and D'Avanzo (1999); Luthar and Barkin (2012); Luthar and Becker (2002); Luthar (2003); Kang (2015). See Weinberger et al. (2018).
19. Chetty et al. (2017), 400, fig. 1.
20. Chetty (2016), 37.
21. Truslow Adams [1931] (2012).
22. Waldinger (2015).
23. Smith (2004), 352–3; Kaye, Harrington, and LaPlante (2010), 20; Doty (2010); National Alliance for Caregiving and AARP Public Policy Institute (2015), 6, 17.
24. Swartz (2009), 196–8; Bengston (2001), 12–13; Connidis (1992), 980. See also Hogan, Eggebeen, and Clogg (1993); Riley and Riley (1993).
25. Bengston (2001).
26. OECD (2017b).
27. Stokes (2011), quoting the economist Carol Graham from the Brookings Institution.
28. Hari (2018).
29. Friedli (2009), 38.
30. World Health Organization (2018).
31. Ahrnsbrak et al. (2017).
32. Murphy et al. (2018), 1; Ducharme (2018); Bernstein (2018).
33. Rogers (2016).
34. Hedegaard, Miniño, and Warner (2018).
35. Carey (2018). See Centers for Disease Control and Prevention (2018).
36. Carey (2018).
37. Ibid., quoting Dr. Thomas Insel.
38. Phillips et al. (2010), 685.
39. Case and Deaton (2015), 15079. See also Stein et al. (2017).
40. Case and Deaton (2017), 39.
41. See Cherlin (2009).
42. Bianchi, Robinson, and Milkie (2006), 55, table 3.4, 118, fig. 6.1 (2000 figures).
43. Pew Research Center (2015a), 2, 7–8. See generally Schulte (2014); Bianchi, Robinson, and Milkie (2006); Parker and Wang (2013b), 19.
44. Schulte (2014), 25 (data from 2004 General Social Survey). See also Boushey (2016).
45. Amato et al. (2007), 67; Milkie, Raley, and Bianchi (2009).
46. Bianchi and Wight (2010), 35–6.
47. Bianchi, Robinson, and Milkie (2006), 135; Bianchi and Wight (2010), 40.
48. Glass, Simon, and Andersson (2016), 906–14, esp. 907, table 3.
49. Cherlin (2009), 25.
50. Parker and Stepler (2017).
51. Bramlett and Mosher (2002),17.
52. Ibid., 14; Guzzo (2014), 833–4. See also Cherlin (2009), 16–17; Manning (2015).
53. DeRose et al. (2017), 11, fig. 1. See also Kennedy and Bumpass (2008), 1685.
54. OECD (2018a), 4, indicates that the US crude divorce rate is second-highest among OECD nations.
55. DeRose et al. (2017), 11–12, fig. 1.
56. DeRose et al. (2017), 11–13; Cherlin (2009), 17–18; OECD (2011), 27, fig. 1.6.
57. DeRose et al. (2017), 11–13.
58. Heuveline, Timberlake, and Furstenberg (2003), 57; Cherlin (2009), 3, 18.
59. OECD (2018b), 3 (2016 figures).
60. Reeves, Sawhill, and Krause (2016).
61. Wilcox and Marquardt (2010), 39–40. See Cohen (2018), 1.
62. Wang (2015).
63. Cohen (2018).
64. Wildsmith, Manlove, and Cook (2018). See also Carbone and Cahn (2014).
65. Cherlin (2014), 5, 145, citing Carter et al. (2006) (based on data from the 1979 Cohort of the National Longitudinal Survey of Youth (NLSY79)).

66. Putnam (2015); Pew Research Center (2015b), 15.
67. Wilcox and Marquardt (2010), 25–6 (based on data from the 2006 to 2010 National Survey for Family Growth).
68. Pew Research Center (2015b), 17.
69. Carbone and Cahn (2014), 19.
70. Wilcox and Marquardt (2010), x. See June Carbone and Naomi Cahn's *Marriage Markets* (2014) for an in-depth, intelligent treatment of the marriage divide.

Chapter 2

1. The typology I present here is based on one that the sociologist Gøsta Esping-Andersen laid out in *The Three Worlds of Welfare Capitalism* (1990). The model I call "free-market family policy" is based on Esping-Andersen's "liberal" welfare state model. Meanwhile, my "pro-family policy" model is loosely based on his "social democratic" model. Esping-Andersen (1990), 26–8.
2. I discuss these research findings further in chapter 5.
3. OECD (2000), 4.
4. Kela (2018a). This and all other conversions between euros and dollars in this book are based on the exchange rate of 1 euro to 1.14 dollars on December 21, 2018; see also Kela (2015), 9; (2018b), 2.
5. Kela (2019), 4-5. This includes 17.5 weeks of maternity leave (two of which must be taken before the child's birth), 26 weeks of parental leave that can be divided among parents, and 9 weeks of paternity leave.
6. OECD (2000), 22.
7. Ministry of Education and Culture (2018).
8. With regard to ratio, "there must be at least one trained member of staff to a maximum of seven children in day care, who have reached the age of three. For younger children, there must be at least one person with vocational education to a maximum of four children." Further, care and education staff must have some sort of higher education or qualification, such as a bachelor's degree in early childhood education. OECD (2000), 42–4.
9. Kela (2015), 7; (2018b), 3, 7.
10. Ministry of Economic Affairs and Employment (2011), chap. 3, sec. 6, chap. 4, secs. 17–18.
11. Ministry of Employment and the Economy (2016), 5–6.
12. Ministry of Economic Affairs and Employment (2001), chap. 2, sec. 2.
13. Federal Office for Migration and Refugees (2016).
14. Federal Office for Migration and Refugees (2015c).
15. DPA (2018); Deutsche Welle (2018). See also Expatica (2018).
16. Federal Office for Migration and Refugees (2015b); Federal Office for Migration and Refugees (2015d).
17. This benefit increases with the number of children in the family, up to a maximum of $250 for four or more children. Federal Office for Migration and Refugees (2015a).
18. Germany Trade and Invest (2019).
19. Family and Medical Leave Act of 1993, Pub. L. 103-3, 29 U.S.C. §§ 2601–2654 (2008). At the time of publication, eight states and the District of Columbia had recently begun to fill this gap by passing legislation providing at least partial pay for a period of weeks funded by payroll withholding from employees and/or employers. Several of the earliest states to pass paid leave measures have more recently extended paid leave periods. The states are California (six weeks, extending to eight weeks in mid-2020), Connecticut (twelve weeks), Massachusetts (twelve weeks), New Jersey (six weeks, extending to twelve weeks in mid-2020), New York (eight weeks, extending to twelve weeks in 2021), Oregon (twelve weeks, plus an additional two weeks for pregnancy, childbirth, or a related medical condition), Rhode Island (four weeks), and Washington (twelve weeks). Oregon's law, passed as this book went to press, is the first to provide low-wage workers full pay during those weeks, which means that it will be genuinely accessible to low-wage employees. For a detailed comparison of all these laws, see A Better Balance (2019).
20. Isaacs et al. (2018).
21. Ibid., 24.

22. The Fair Labor Standards Act doesn't cap mandatory hours, but does require that employers pay certain employees (executive and professional employees are excluded, among others) extra for overtime beyond forty hours per week. See Fair Labor Standards Act of 1938, 29 U.S.C. § 201.
23. Ray, Sanes, and Schmitt (2013), 4, table 2; Van Giezen (2013).
24. US Bureau of Labor Statistics (2017). See Horowitz et al. (2017), 58–62, 64.
25. Gornick and Meyers (2003), 195–97. See also Cohn (2013).
26. Farrington (2014). See also Krupnick (2015).
27. Amendment of 1986 Code, H.R. 1 2018 (2017), Sec. 11022.
28. Under the CTC's temporary increase to $2,000 annually, parents who don't owe enough taxes to get the full benefit of the tax credit can only get up to $1,400 per child as a tax refund. Ibid. See Whitehurst (2017), 5–6; Greenstein et al. (2018), 1–2.
29. Earned Income, 26 U.S.C. § 32 (2018); Whitehurst (2017), 5. The US tax code also contains two smaller tax programs that help families with kids. Under the Child and Dependent Care Tax Credit (CDCTC), adults working for pay can get a tax credit for a portion of their child-care expenses. The average credit awarded per family is between $600 and $700. 26 U.S.C. § 21; Crandall-Hollick (2018), 9–10, 14–15. Under the Dependent Care Assistance Plan (DCAP), employees of participating employers can set aside part of their salaries, up to a maximum of $5,000 ($2,500 for married taxpayers who file separately), to cover costs for qualifying dependents. Taxpayers cannot use CDCTC and DCAP to cover the same out-of-pocket care expenses. 26 U.S.C. § 129; Stoltzfus (2015), 2.
30. Earned Income, 26 U.S.C. § 32. See US Department of the Treasury (2019), 229–31.
31. Center on Budget and Policy Priorities (2018b), 4.
32. Earned Income, 26 U.S.C. § 32; (2018); Crandall-Hollick (2018), 9–10, 14–15; Stoltzfus (2015), 2; Whitehurst (2017), 5.
33. Center on Budget and Policy Priorities (2018b), 3.
34. Block Grants to States for Temporary Assistance for Needy Families, 42 U.S.C. §§ 601–619 (1996).
35. Cohen et al. (2016), 238–9, Tbl. L6.
36. The amount that states spent on childcare subsidies for TANF recipients reached a fifteen-year low in 2013. Walker and Schmit (2014). See also Office of Family Assistance (2014b); Lower-Basch and Schmit (2015), 20. While in 2000, $4 billion was spent on childcare for TANF recipients, that number had fallen about 35 percent to $2.6 billion annually as of FY 2015. Walker and Matthews (2016). See also Office of Family Assistance (2017). By one estimate, only roughly 30 percent of low-income families using center-based childcare receive any financial assistance with childcare costs. Williams and Boushey (2010), 16. A few states have sought to universalize early childhood education (ECE) in recent years in recognition of its benefits for children. Yet the demand has exceeded supply. Quinn (2017). Low-income children in 2010 were even less likely than their counterparts in 1998 to attend formal childcare or preschool programs in the year before kindergarten and were more likely to be cared for solely by their parents. In contrast, middle- and high-income parents had shifted from private to public ECE, possibly in response to states' recent efforts to universalize access to public preschool programs. Bassouk et al. (2016), 9, 13.
37. Falk (2014), 4, Fig. 1.
38. Cohen et al. (2016), 158, 183–4. According to the Administration for Children and Families (ACF), the TANF benefits of 58,000 families were reduced in 2012 as a result of family caps. (2012 was the last year that the ACF reported the distribution of families by grant reduction reason.) For obvious reasons, most of these families were likely to have young children. Their TANF benefits were reduced by an average of 20 percent. Lower-Basch and Schmit (2015), 12; Office of Family Assistance (2014a), table 15.
39. Stanley, Floyd, and Hill (2016), 10.
40. Covert and Israel (2017).
41. Lower-Basch and Schmit (2015), 6.
42. Mississippi Department of Human Services (2018); Floyd (2017), 15.
43. The accounts of the Zoladz and Ruohonen families are taken from George Lorenzo's (2015) article in *Fast Company*.

44. This shouldn't blind us to the downsides of these decades, including the fact that families of color had it far tougher than other families because of racism, as well as the fact that many women were expected to stay home to care for children rather than pursue work outside the home. The fact that economic conditions were more favorable for families during this period had a lot to do with the fact that America's free-market philosophy was not as strong at the time. Policymakers therefore regulated the market to a greater degree to support economic security and equality. Carbone and Cahn (forthcoming); Hacker and Pierson (2016).
45. Piketty, Saez, and Zucman (2018), 587, fig. V.
46. Saez (2015), 4; Piketty, Saez, and Zucman (2018), 587, fig. V.
47. Hacker and Pierson (2010b), 4, note, "Since around 1980, we have drifted away from that mixed-economy cluster, and traveled a considerable distance toward another: the capitalist oligarchies, like Brazil, Mexico, and Russia, with their much greater concentration of economic bounty." See also Beaubien (2018).
48. Hacker and Pierson (2010b), 21–5. See also Wolff (2017), 13.
49. The Heritage Foundation, for example, makes this argument using just such a pie analogy. See Azerrad and Hederman (2012), 15: "A free-market economy creates wealth. For one person to make a dollar does not mean that another needs to lose one. There is not just one dwindling pie to be divided up among the population, but rather a proven recipe to grow the pie to serve everyone. All the talk about the rich 'grabbing' too large a share of the national income therefore rests on a flawed understanding of this basic truth of free-market economics."
50. Mishel et al. (2012), 7, 214–15.
51. Cherlin (2014), 7–9; Autor, Katz, and Kerney (2008), 319–20. Another significant reason for this drop is likely workers' decreased ability to join labor unions, a result of both laws less friendly to organizing and employers' increasing hardball union-busting tactics. I discuss unions in greater detail in chapter 10.
52. Cherlin (2014), 123–4; Autor and Dorn (2013), 1584.
53. The proportion of married women in the workforce with children under six years of age rose from 18 percent in 1960 to 43 percent in 1979, more than doubling in less than twenty years. Reich (1984). By 2012, that number had grown to 65 percent, where it remains today. US Bureau of Labor Statistics (2014), 24; (2018b), 2, table 7.
54. This was a key finding of Elizabeth Warren's bestseller, *The Two-Income Trap*. Warren and Tyagi (2003); Mishel et al. (2012), 36–8, 123–6.
55. Mishel et al. (2012), 36–8, 123–6.
56. See Stancyzk (2016), 33–4. See also Laughlin (2011), 10; Warren and Tyagi (2003).
57. Laughlin (2011), 19. See Stancyzk (2016), 27.
58. Traub, Hiltonsmith, and Draut (2016), 10.
59. Economic Policy Institute and Oxfam America (2016), 4–5, 12.
60. Desmond (2018).
61. Wolff (2017), 9. See also Bricker et al. (2017); Congressional Budget Office (2016), 1.
62. See Pfeffer and Schoeni (2016).
63. Fry et al. (2011) (in 2010 dollars), 1. For updated figures, see Emmons, Kent, and Ricketts (2018).
64. Hiltonsmith (2013), 10, found that student loan debt reduces lifetime net assets by $207,690 on average. According to LIMRA (2015), $30,000 in student loan debt could reduce long-term retirement savings by $325,000.
65. Warren and Tyagi (2003).
66. Declercq et al. (2013), 46.
67. Lino et al. (2015).
68. See Daly, Hobijn, and Pedtke (2017), 2–3; Pew Research Center (2016b), 8.
69. Fairlie and Sundstrom (1999), 255; Desilver (2013).
70. Wilson and Rodgers (2016), 3.
71. Daly, Hobijn, and Pedtke (2017), 3; Cajner et al. (2017), 23. See also Wilson (2015); Bertrand and Mullainathan (2004).
72. Bertrand and Mullainathan (2004).
73. Pager (2007).

74. Across all American families, one study found that income instability increased by more than one-third between 1980 and 2012. Hardy (2016), 10. Other researchers have observed an increase as well, though their numbers differ. See Dynan, Elmendorf, and Sichel (2012) (36 percent increase in volatility); Ziliak, Hardy, and Bollinger (2011) (15 percent increase in men's earnings volatility between the 1970s and 1980s). See also Dahl, DeLeire, and Schwabish (2011); Gottschalk and Moffitt (2009); Hardy and Ziliak (2013).
75. See Hacker (2006).
76. Ibid.
77. See US Government Accountability Office (2015), 15–16; NPR and Marist (2018); Morduch and Schneider (2013), 3; Katz and Krueger (2016).
78. Golden (2015), 1.
79. See Morduch and Schneider (2013), 3.
80. Mishel et al. (2012), 200, table 4.10; Schoen, Radley, and Collins (2015), 4, 6; Henry J. Kaiser Family Foundation (2008); Claxton et al. (2017), 8, 106. See also *Patients' Perspectives on Healthcare in the United States: A Look at Seven States and the Nation* (2016), 12; Olen (2017).
81. Hacker (2006), 68–9, 71.
82. The account of Mr. Sanchez is taken from Casselman (2016).
83. Aon (2014). See also Claxton et al. (2018), who found that average out-of-pocket expenditures increased 54 percent between 2006 and 2016.
84. Claxton et al. (2018).
85. Henry J. Kaiser Family Foundation (2018), 1.
86. Jacoby and Holman (2014), 56–60.
87. The account of the Bixler family is taken from Landau (2012).
88. Morduch and Schneider (2017), 159; US Census Bureau (2016b).
89. Board of Governors of the Federal Reserve System (2018), 21.
90. Cohen (2017).
91. Hardy (2017), 323.
92. Jones, Cox, and Navarro-Rivera (2014), 11; See also Hacker, Rehm, and Schlesinger (2010), 21–2; Hacker (2011), 27.
93. Hardy (2016).
94. Edwards (2014), 6.
95. Warren and Tyagi (2003). See also Hacker (2006), 91, 94, 101 (citing data from Elizabeth Warren's 2001 Consumer Bankruptcy Project).
96. See, e.g., Keys (2008); Attanasio and Weber (2010). See also Hill et al. (2013); Gennetian et al. (2015).
97. Hacker (2006), 92.
98. Many thanks to Fernando Filgueira for the points here and in the next paragraphs. See also Blofield and Filgueira (forthcoming); Esping-Andersen (2002), 51; Blofield et al. (2018).
99. See Stancyzk (2016), 32–3; Isaacs et al. (2018).
100. Esping-Andersen (2009), 109.
101. This was a key insight of Gøsta Esping-Andersen's groundbreaking works, *The Three Worlds of Welfare Capitalism* (1990) and *The Incomplete Revolution* (2009).
102. Broken down in terms of all social expenditures, the United States spent a total of 30 percent of its GDP in 2015 when public and private expenditures were added together. That put us second-highest in terms of spending based on percentage of GDP, behind only France, which spent 31.7 percent of GDP. OECD (2019c). See also Esping-Andersen (2009), 105, 108–9.
103. National Transfer Accounts (2016).
104. See Isaacs et al. (2018), 4.
105. Lino et al. (2017), 19 (values adjusted for future inflation).
106. See Bhattarai (2017), who notes that estimating a four-year degree would "add an extra $181,480 at private university and $80,360 at a public one."
107. Aisch, Buchanan, Cox, and Quealy (2017).
108. Winton (2019).
109. Thirteen countries—Belgium, Denmark, France, Germany, Hungary, Iceland, Israel, Italy, Japan, the Netherlands, Norway, Spain, and the United Kingdom—enroll 95 percent and

upward of four-year-olds. France and the United Kingdom enroll a full 100 percent. OECD (2018c), 175. A few US states have established universal prekindergarten. These programs are discussed in more detail in chapter 5.

Chapter 3

1. Keynes (1930).
2. Pew Research Center (2015a), 5. See generally Schulte (2014); Bianchi, Robinson, and Milkie (2006).
3. Parker and Wang (2013b), 19; Schulte (2014), 25.
4. Schulte (2014). See also Boushey (2016).
5. Autor (2015), 8.
6. Maddison (2001), 185, table A1-c, shows that the GDP per capita increased from $5,301 in 1913 to $27,331 in 1998. See also Friedman (2015), 230; Keynes (1930), 364–5.
7. Depending on how the term "wealthy" is defined, the possible exception here is South Korea, whose employees work more hours than US employees. OECD (2019a). Following South Korea's steep increase in wealth since the 1960s, and after a highly publicized suicide due to overwork, the government is putting the issue of overwork on the national agenda. President Moon Jae-in, when he was still a candidate, wrote on Facebook, "We can no longer be a society where overwork and working late is a given." The Ministry of Labor's recorded voice message now states: "Our society is breaking away from overwork." Lee and May (2018).
8. Jacobs and Gerson (2004); Mishel, Bernstein, and Shierholz (2009).
9. Reich (1984); US Bureau of Labor Statistics (2014), 24; (2018b), 2, table 7; Thompson (2013).
10. U.S. Bureau of Labor Statistics (2014).
11. Medalia and Jacobs (2008), 149, table 6.3.
12. Jacobs and Gerson (2004), 31–40; Kuhn and Lozano (2008); Frase and Gornick (2013), 709–10.
13. Kuhn and Lozano(2008), 319.
14. Veblen (1899).
15. In 2014, fully 37 percent of fathers with a high level of education compared with 17 percent of fathers with a low level of education worked forty-five or more hours a week. OECD (2016c), 19–20, table LMF2.2.G. The same was true of 14 percent of highly educated mothers compared with 5 percent of mothers with a low level of education. OECD (2016c), 21–2, table LMF2.2.H.
16. Perlow and Porter (2009), 102. See also Suroweicki (2014); Williams and Boushey (2010); Jacobs and Gerson (2004).
17. Jacobs and Gerson (2004), 35.
18. Schwartz (2010), 1527–8; Schwartz and Mare (2005), 21–3.
19. Medalia and Jacobs (2008), 16, table 3.
20. For all nonelderly adults in the United States, couples in the lowest quintile worked an average of 1,645 hours per year; couples in the highest quintile worked 3,605 hours. Smeeding (2005), 57, table 8 (data from the 2000 Luxembourg Income Study).
21. OECD (2016c), 15–9, tables LMF2.2.E and LMF2.2.F.
22. Livingston (2018b). See also Pew Research Center (2015a), 2.
23. Miller (2015).
24. Stone (2007). Stone's analysis comports with a 2009 Center for Work-Life Policy survey of "high-value" women employees, defined as women with advanced degrees or with high-honors undergraduate degrees, and who left paid work. That survey found that 69 percent of respondents said they would not have done so if their workplace had offered more flexible work arrangements. See also Forster et al. (2010).
25. See Blau and Kahn (2013); OECD (2016d), 4, chart LMF1.2.C.
26. Collins (2019).
27. Jacobs and Gerson (2004), 32–3; Kuhn and Lozano (2008), 318.
28. See Wight, Raley, and Bianchi (2008), 266–7.

29. Kantor (2014).
30. Ibid. Starbucks changed its scheduling policies after this article was published. The scheduling software it was based on, though, remains in place in many other service establishments.
31. Kantor (2014). See also Presser (2003).
32. See Rippeyoung and Noonan (2012), 260.
33. Golden (2015), 1.
34. Jacobs and Gerson (2004), 64–9, 72–3; Golden and Tesfayi (2007), 24–6. See also Rose (2016).
35. Kan et al. (2018).
36. Harter (2018).
37. Patten and Parker (2012), 4 (based on eighteen- to sixty-four-year-old women and men).
38. Pew Research Center (2008).
39. See Harrington, Van Deusen, and Humberd (2011), 10.
40. This quotation is generally attributed to Ben Franklin, although its source is unclear.
41. Prescott (2004), 3. See also Mishel (2013).
42. See Orloff (2006), 231–2.
43. Mishel, Bernstein, and Shierholz (2009), 363–9.
44. See Personal Responsibility and Work Opportunity Reconciliation Act of 1996, Section 114(b)(3).
45. Eurofound (2003). In many countries, but not Finland, the maximum hours are set by the European Union's Working Time Directive of 1993, which establishes a forty-eight-hour weekly maximum including overtime.
46. The earnings of roughly 92 percent of salaried employees were above that pay threshold in 2015. Ross-Brown and Teuscher (2015). The Department of Labor under President Obama issued a revised regulation that would have doubled the threshold, but that rule was put on hold by a court. *Nevada v. United States Department of Labor* (2016), Civil Action No. 4:16-CV-00731.
47. Jacobs and Gerson (2004), 36–7, 183.
48. According to Golden and Jorgensen (2002), "[A]bout 44 percent of 'exempt' workers work longer than 40 hours per week, compared to only about 20 percent of non-exempt workers." See also Golden and Wiens-Tuers (2005); Rohwedder and Wenger (2015); Kuhn and Lozano (2008).
49. Maye (2019), 5, fig. 1.
50. International Labour Office (2014), 16.
51. Klerman, Daley, and Pozniak (2014), 21; US Department of Labor (2017).
52. Horowitz et al. (2017), 4, 14–15. They are less likely, though, to believe that the government should pay for this leave rather than employers. Horowitz et al. (2017), 4.
53. The account of Ms. Olson is taken from Deahl and Ludden (2016).
54. Interview with author.
55. Email to author.
56. American Psychological Association (2019), 1.
57. Wilkinson and Pickett [2009] (2010), 229–30, esp. fig. 15.4. See also Bowles and Parke (2005), who show that differences in working hours changed in association with shifting levels of inequality from 1963 to 1998.
58. See Bell and Freeman (2001), 200. See also Frank (2011), esp. chap. 4.
59. Bell and Freeman (2001); Kuhn and Lozano (2008), 341.
60. Cohan (2015).
61. Boswell, Olson-Buchanan, and Harris (2013).
62. Farber, Haltiwanger, and Abraham (1997), 85–8; Schmidt (1999), S136–40.
63. Yahoo-ABC News Network (2017), reporting on Rep. Tom MacArthur's town hall, May 20, 2017.
64. Freeman (2007), 59. See also Boswell, Olson-Buchanan, and Harris (2013); Sverke, Hellgren, and Näswall (2002).
65. Ray, Sanes, and Schmitt (2013), 4, table 2 (data from the 2012 National Compensation Survey). Both the chances of getting paid vacation at all and the number of vacation days paid are far lower for low-wage workers.

66. Goldsmith (2010).
67. Maume (2006), 184. See also Schulte (2014), 7.
68. See Harrington et al. (2015), 7. See also Weber (2013); Deloitte (2016).
69. Schelling [1978] (2006), chap. 7. The economist Robert H. Frank's work on the limits of markets and the benefits of government pointed me to Schelling's example. See Frank (2011), 8.
70. See Bell and Freeman (2001), 181, who conclude that "hours worked is positively related to earnings inequality in cross-section occupational contrasts and that hours worked raises future wages and promotion prospects in longitudinal data."
71. Frank, Levine, and Dijk (2014), 71–2; Schor (1998).
72. See Schor (1998); Frank (1999).
73. Conley (2008). See also Bowles and Park (2005), F410.
74. Neumark and Postlewaite (1998), 179–80.
75. Frank, Levine, and Djik (2014) discuss "expenditure cascades," in which increased expenditures by some lead others just below them on the income scale to spend more as well, in turn leading others just below the second group to spend more, etc.
76. U.S. Department of Commerce (2015), 345; Perry (2016).
77. Pew Research Center (2017).
78. Schor (1998).
79. Warren and Tyagi (2003), 24–5; Thompson (2012).
80. Kaplan, Violante, and Weidner (2014), 80–1 (data from 2010 and surrounding years).
81. Schor (1992), 128–9. See also Jacobs and Gerson (2004), 74–5.
82. Weeks (2011), 37–8.
83. Bianchi (2011), 27, table 1, shows that in 1965, mothers spent 10.2 hours a week in active childcare; in 2003–8 they spent 13.9 hours. Mothers' hours in active childcare declined at the beginning of this era as mothers increased their hours of paid work. Between 1965 and 1975, their hours spent in active childcare per week decreased from 10.2 to 8.5. These hours began to rise again after 1985, and reached almost 14 hours per week during the 2003–8 period. This doesn't mean that employed and nonemployed mothers spend the same hours in active childcare—employed mothers spend about 8 hours less per week. Ibid., 35. But both employed and nonemployed mothers have significantly increased their childcare time since the mid-1980s. In fact, employed mothers now spend as much time in active childcare as nonemployed mothers did in the past. Ibid., 28.
84. Ibid., 29, table 2, shows that in 1965, fathers spent 2.5 hours a week in active childcare; in 2003–8, they spent 7.0 hours a week.
85. Abel, Dietz, and Su (2014), 4–5.
86. Peralta (2014).
87. Mishel et al. (2012), 198–206.
88. See Hays (2003), 129; Lareau (2011).
89. Reardon (2013a). In the words of the sociologist Melissa Milkie: "[T]here are a lot of cultural pressures for intensive parenting—the competition for jobs, what we think makes for a successful child, teenager and young adult, and what we think in a competitive society with few social supports is going to help them succeed." Schulte (2015).
90. Tavernise (2012); Reardon (2013a).
91. Reardon (2013a).
92. Interview with author.
93. Doepke and Zilibotti (2017), 1333; (2018). Miller (2018) quotes the University of Maryland sociologist Philip Cohen saying, "As the gap between the rich and poor increases, the cost of [kids] screwing up increases. . . . The fear is [kids will] end up on the other side of the divide." See also Ramey and Ramey (2010).
94. Reardon (2013a).
95. Esping-Andersen (2009), 100.
96. Bassok et al. (2016).
97. Chua (2011), 4.
98. Zernike (2011).

99. Lareau (2011), 39, notes: "Ironically, the greater the number of activities children are involved in, the fewer opportunities they have for face-to-face interaction with members of their own family."
100. Bianchi, Robinson, and Milkie (2006), 118, fig. 6.1 (2000 figures).
101. Ibid., 55, table 3.4.
102. Slaughter (2012).
103. Hochschild and Machung (1989), 262.
104. Ibid., 3.
105. Miller (2015).
106. Bianchi, Robinson, and Milkie (2006).
107. GFI Software (2015). See also Kelleher (2013); Schawbel (2014).
108. Parker and Patten (2013), 1.
109. Ibid., 7.
110. Feinberg and Choula (2012), 1.
111. Parker et al. (2015), 40.
112. Bianchi, Robinson, and Milkie (2006), 91–3. Women cut their housework time from about twenty-eight hours per week to fifteen hours per week during this period. Men, meanwhile, increased their housework time from four hours in 1965 to about nine hours in 2011. Parker and Wang (2013a), 32. See also Esping-Andersen (2009), 30–1; Bianchi (2011).
113. Offer and Schneider (2011), 821, 824. See also Nelson (2010).
114. Amato et al. (2007), 67.
115. Bianchi (2011), 35–6.
116. Ibid.
117. Bianchi, Robinson, and Milkie (2006), 135.
118. Graham (2017), 103–5.
119. Almost four in ten parents who say balancing home and work responsibilities is hard find being a parent tiring at least most of the time. Pew Research Center (2015a), 6.
120. Glass, Simon, and Andersson (2016), 906–14, esp. 907, table 3. "In those countries with the strongest policy packages, the parental deficit in happiness was completely eliminated." Ibid., 914. In his ninety-four-country analysis, Luca Stanca (2012), 742, reports that the level of negative parenthood well-being worldwide corresponds most to the level of financial strain experienced by parents. "[T]he negative effect of parenthood on well-being is explained by a large adverse impact on financial satisfaction that dominates the positive impact on non-financial satisfaction."
121. I owe this insight to Hochschild (2003), esp. chap. 15.
122. Putnam (2000).
123. See National Center for Health Statistics (2017).
124. See Office of Adolescent Health (2016); Stone (2018).

Chapter 4

1. City of East Liverpool, Ohio (2016).
2. Ingraham and Johnson (2016); Siemaszko (2016); Millsap (2017).
3. Steinbuch (2016).
4. Many of the insights in this chapter were spurred by June Carbone and Naomi Cahn's book, *Marriage Markets* (2014), which called attention to how rising US inequality was creating unstable families among the poor and working class.
5. Murray (1994); Murray (2012).
6. Cherlin (2014), citing Andersson (2002), 358, and Heuveline, Timberlake, and Furstenberg (2004), 56.
7. Moynihan (1965).
8. Ibid., 6–7. The Bureau of Labor Statistics, which helped compile the data, noted it was likely that white middle-class families hid illegitimate births, making these figures disputable. See Geary (2015).
9. Moynihan (1965), 22.

10. Ibid., 23.

11. Ibid., 47–8.

12. See ibid., 29–30. See also Carbone and Cahn (2014), 22–7.

13. Moynihan (1965), 30.

14. Ryan (1965), 383.

15. Wilson (1987).

16. Ibid., 84–9, figs. 3.1–3.6.

17. See Carson (2015), 15; Schmitt, Reedt, and Blackwell (2017).

18. Wilson (1987), 86, fig. 3.3.

19. Ibid., 66–71.

20. Furstenberg (2009).

21. Trustees of Princeton University (2019).

22. McLanahan (2009), 118–20.

23. Ibid., 120.

24. Ibid. See also Harknett and McLanahan (2004), 803; Gibson-Davis, Edin, and McLanahan (2005), 1307.

25. Edin and Kefalas (2005), 201.

26. Ibid., 202.

27. Harknett and McLanahan (2004), 808. In a 2014 Pew Research Center survey, 78 percent of never-married women reported that whether a man had a steady job would be a very important factor for them in choosing a spouse or partner; 46 percent of never-married men said the same about their spouse or partner having a steady job. Wang and Parker (2014).

28. Wang, Parker, and Taylor (2013). For calculations on the distribution of income within opposite-sex married couples from 1970 to 2014, see Cohen (2014), and for an updated trend through 2017, see Cohen (2018b).

29. Cherlin (2009), 139–43, 174–5. See also Cherlin (2014), 15.

30. Cherlin (2009), 139–43.

31. Ibid., 178–80.

32. Cherlin (2014), 15.

33. Harknett and McLanahan (2004), 803, 806.

34. Ibid., 802–3.

35. Tierney (2013), quoting Professor Carl Hart. See Hart (2013, 2014). See also Bickel et al. (2014).

36. Carlson, McLanahan, and England (2004), 254.

37. Cherlin, Ribar, and Yasutake (2016), 752; Cherlin (2014), 15.

38. Wilson (1996), 97–8. See Taylor, Funk, and Clark (2007), 8–9.

39. Edin and Kefalas (2005), 31–2.

40. Ibid., 37, 43. Studies have shown that women and men vary in their use of contraception according to their level of education. Copen (2017), 3–4; Mosher and Jones (2010).

41. Edin and Kefalas (2005), 97.

42. Hotz, McElroy, and Sanders (2005), 712–13, report, "Our results suggest that much of the 'concern' that has been registered concerning teenage childbearing is misplaced, at least based on its consequences for the subsequent educational and economic attainment of teen mothers. . . . Rather, it appears that these ["poor"] outcomes are more the result of social and economic circumstances than they are the result of the early childbearing of these women. . . . Moreover, we find that teen mothers may actually achieve higher levels of earnings over their adult lives than if they had postponed motherhood."

43. Edin and Kefalas (2005), 206.

44. Ibid., 174–5.

45. Ibid., 208–10.

46. Kearney, Hershbein, and Jácome (2015), 2.

47. Edin and Nelson (2013), 64–5.

48. Ibid., 51, 55, 58.

49. Ibid., 78.

50. See ibid., 73; McLanahan (2011), 116; Wilson (1996), xviii, 72; Edin and Kefalas (2005), 75–9, 100.

51. Edin and Kefalas (2005), 203–4. See also Wilson (1996), 105; Carbone and Cahn (2014).

52. Edin and Nelson (2013), 75, 83, 91; Edin and Kefalas (2005), 75–9, 100. In the words of the sociologist Frank Furstenberg (1995), 144: "Fatherhood occurs to men who often have a personal biography that poorly equips them to act on their intentions, even when their intentions to do for their children are strongly felt. And fatherhood [in the inner city] takes place in a culture where the gap between good intentions and good performance is large and widely recognized."

53. Edin and Nelson (2013), 186–9, 209–10, 214–16.

54. World Bank (2019) (2016 births).

55. Child Trends (2018).

56. Furstenberg (2009), 108. See also Wilcox and Marquardt, 44 (2010); McLanahan (2009).

57. See Andersson (2002), 358.

58. Wilcox and Marquardt (2010), 18–24. See also generally Cherlin (2014).

59. Wilcox and Marquardt (2010), ix, 15. See also Carbone and Cahn (2014).

60. Wilcox and Marquardt (2010), 27.

61. Cherlin (2014), 4–10, 126. One important recent study evaluated twenty-four years of downturns in men's employment in manufacturing jobs and showed that these downturns preceded decreases in marriage rates and increases in nonmarital birth rates. This study was a lot more methodologically sophisticated than the Moynihan Report half a century before, but it showed the same thing: harsh economic forces undermine family stability. The study suggested that one way these forces destabilize relationships is by increasing men's opiate and alcohol use, thereby making them less desirable partners. Autor, Dorn, and Hanson (2017). Another recent study showed that both marriage rates and nonmarital birth rates vary significantly with local labor market conditions, and particularly with the availability of middle-skill jobs that pay a living wage. Cherlin, Ribar, and Yasutake (2016), 762.

62. Cherlin (2009).

63. Carbone and Cahn (2014), 100–1. See also Wilcox and Marquardt (2010), 19–20; Amato et al. (2007), 123–4, 138; Cherlin (2014), 141. It should be noted that college-educated families can afford these last services only because of the huge wage inequality between the wife's professional salary and the pay of the household workers. Thus, what used to be the wife's responsibility has been privately offloaded onto women below her on the economic ladder.

64. Carbone and Cahn (2014).

65. OECD (2018a), 2; Cherlin (2009).

66. See Cohen (2018a).

67. OECD (2018a), 4, chart SF3.1.C.

68. Andersson and Philipov (2002), app. 2, 230, table 27; Cherlin (2009), 17; DeRose et al. (2017).

69. Bramlett and Mosher (2002), 14; Guzzo (2014), 833–4. See also Cherlin (2009), 16–17; Manning (2015).

70. DeRose et al. (2017), 11–12, fig. 1.

71. Ibid., 11, 13 (figures for mothers with moderate education). See also Kennedy and Bumpass (2008), 1685; Cherlin (2009), 16–17; Guzzo (2014).

72. OECD (2018b), 3 (2016 figures).

73. Brown, Stykes, and Manning (2016).

74. Reeves, Sawhill, and Krause (2016).

75. Carbone and Cahn (2014).

76. Wang (2015).

77. Cohen (2018a); Guzzo (2014), 835, table 2. See also Wilcox and Marquardt (2010), 23–4, 73.

78. Wildsmith, Manlove, and Cook (2018). See also Carbone and Cahn (2014), 17, fig. 1.2 (1982 figures).

79. See June Carbone and Naomi Cahn's *Marriage Markets* (2014) for an intelligent treatment of this issue.

80. Wilcox and Marquardt (2010), 25 (statistics drawn from the 2006–2010 National Survey for Family Growth for girls).

81. Edin and Kefalas (2005), ix.

82. Ibid. (2005), 9–10.

83. Wilcox and Marquardt (2010), 27.

84. Cherlin (2014), 172.

85. "Overall, then, many less-educated men and women experience little that is lasting in their lives—not intimate relationships, not jobs, not religious beliefs. The lack of permanence is so broad that is has come to be seen as normal to young adults who cannot imagine anything lasting for life. . . . The hollowing-out of the labor market—the loss of industrial jobs to offshoring and computerization—has removed the economic foundation of the kind of working-class lives that their mothers and fathers led." Ibid., 174–5.

86. Stokes (2011), quoting economist Carol Graham from the Brookings Institution.

87. OECD (2017b). See also Layard (2005); Wilkinson and Pickett [2009] (2010), 6–10.

88. Layard (2005), 63.

89. Friedli (2009). See also World Health Organization (2018). Johann Hari (2018) concurs, arguing that we need to stop seeing depression and anxiety as individual biological or social malfunction and recognize them as "a necessary signal that our needs are not being met."

90. Wilkinson and Pickett [2009] (2010).

91. Hari (2018).

92. Zoorob and Salemi (2017); Wilkinson and Pickett [2009] (2010), 70–2.

93. Case and Deaton (2017).

94. Ibid., 39.

95. Carey (2018).

96. Phillips et al. (2010), 685.

97. Case and Deaton (2017), 38–43.

98. McLanahan and Sandefur (1994), 41–5; Garfinkel and McLanahan (1986), 28–30. Recent evidence suggests that the disadvantages associated with single-parent families may be more significant for boys. Autor et al. (2016).

99. One study found that once the background factors of socioeconomic differences, the immigration status of the parents, and whether the national language was spoken at home were taken into account, the achievement disparity between children in single-parent versus dual-parent families in the United States was reduced by over 60 percent. Woessman (2015), 10.

100. McLanahan and Sandefur (1994), 80, 89–91; Carlson and Berger (2013). Studies show that the drop in income associated with single parenthood is the "single most important factor" in accounting for worse outcomes of children being raised in single-parent families. Garfinkel and McLanahan (1986), 134. See also Guo and Harris (2000), 439–40, who note that "living in poverty has a consistent and significant negative effect on all four measures of intellectual development."

101. Garfinkel and McLanahan (1986), 134. See also Guo and Harris (2000), 439–40.

102. Gornick and Nell (2017), 23, table 3.

103. Pong, Dronkers, and Hampden-Thompson (2003), 696. See also Woessman (2015), Figure 2 (finding that United States had the sixth-largest achievement gap of 28 OECD nations compared).

104. I owe this point to June Carbone.

105. Carlson and Berger (2013), 216. See also Dornbusch et al. (1985); Astone and McLanahan (1991); Thomson, Hanson, and McLanahan (1994).

106. Sara McLanahan (2009), 127–8, concluded that half of the negative association between children's family context and behavioral problems can be accounted for by the greater stress and therefore poorer parenting exhibited by single mothers and mothers in unstable partnerships, and where multi-partner fertility is a factor.

107. Graham (2017), chap. 4. See also Mistry et al. (2002), 947; Paxson and Waldfogel (2003), 102, table 4; Jackson et al. (2000).

108. See Carlson and Berger (2013), 217, 232, 243; Amato and Gilbreth (1999), 565. See also Manning and Smock (1999, 2000); Manning, Stewart, and Smock (2003); Tach, Mincy, and Edin (2010).

109. Fomby and Cherlin (2007); Hadfield et al. (2018).

110. McLanahan (2004), 614.

111. See Carbone and Cahn (2014), 85.

112. Brown (2011), 1070; McLanahan (2009), 127; Manning (2015), 58.
113. See Fomby and Cherlin (2007), 198–9.
114. Wilcox and DeRose (2017). See also Guzzo (2014).
115. McLanahan (2009), 127–8.
116. Garrison (2014), 8–9, 10.
117. Ibid., 10.
118. See Andersson and Philipov (2002), app. 2, 224, table 24, 230, table 27; Cherlin (2009), 16–18.
119. Ellman et al. (2010), 962–4.
120. Vance (2016), 5, 7.
121. Ibid., 7.
122. According to Wilson (1996), 72, one can "avoid the extreme notion of a 'culture of poverty'" while still recognizing "a more subtle kind of cultural analysis of life in poverty."
123. Ibid., 6–12, 61–2.
124. Vance (2016), 144.
125. Ibid., 36.
126. Ibid., 57.
127. Ibid., 79–80.
128. Kearney and Levine (2018).

Chapter 5

1. See generally Boushey (2016).
2. Interview with the author.
3. Wallace (2017).
4. The account of Mr. Cruse is taken from NPR Staff (2016).
5. The account of Ms. Carpenter is taken from Deahl (2017).
6. The account of Ms. Walia is taken from ibid.
7. Shonkoff and Phillips (2000), 4, 6; Harvard Center on the Developing Child (2007a), 1; Fiscella and Kitzman (2009), 1075.
8. Nelson, Fox, and Zeanah (2014), esp. chap. 7; Cohn (2011).
9. Nelson, Fox, and Zeanah (2014), chaps. 7 and 10; Cohn (2011).
10. Ruhm (2000), 951–2.
11. Berger, Hill, and Waldfogel (2005), F44.
12. See Skinner and Oschorn (2012), 5–6; Berger, Hill, and Waldfogel (2005), F45.
13. Feldman, Sussman, and Zigler (2004); Chatterji and Markowitz (2012).
14. Gjerdingen and Chaloner (1994); Dagher, McGovern, and Dowd (2014); Chatterji and Markowitz (2005).
15. Leckman and March (2011), 334.
16. National Scientific Council on the Developing Child (2009), 1. See also World Health Organization (2004); Howard et al. (2011).
17. National Scientific Council on the Developing Child (2009), 1. See also Harvard Center on the Developing Child (2013), 1.
18. For a review of the research on the effects of mothers' early return to work, see Waldfogel (2006), 49–57. For studies that show negative effects of maternal employment, see, e.g., Baydar and Brooks-Gunn (1991); Belsky and Eggebeen (1991); Blau and Grossberg (1992); Brooks-Gunn, Han, and Waldfogel (2010); Ruhm (2008); Baum (2003); Berger, Hill, and Waldfogel (2005); Conway et al. (2017); Herbst (2017), 329.

     According to some but not all of this research, these negative effects apply equally to black, white, and Hispanic children, although they may be greater for white children and for boys than girls. Herbst (2017); Han, Waldfogel, and Brooks-Gunn (2001); Waldfogel (2006), 57. See also Loeb et al. (2007). But see Brooks-Gunn, Han, and Waldfogel (2010), who find no negative effect for African American children.
19. Conway et al. (2017), 2246; Berger, Hill, and Waldfogel (2005), F43, n. 24; Brooks-Gunn, Han, and Waldfogel (2010), 52.

20. Parcel and Menegan (1994); Greenstein (1993).

21. Most studies showing negative effects of early employment have not controlled for the quality of the care the child has received. See, e.g., Baydar and Brooks-Gunn (1991), 935; Belsky and Eggebeen (1991), 1095; Han, Waldfogel, and Brooks-Gunn (2001), 352; Ruhm (2000); Waldfogel, Han, and Brooks-Gunn (2002), 375; Herbst (2017), 350–1. Some studies that controlled for care quality found that center-based daycare has no negative effects. Bernal and Keane (2011), 498. But see Conway et al. (2017), 2249.

22. Brooks-Gunn, Han, and Waldfogel (2010), 79–80, 85–6.

23. Gregg et al. (2005), F74–5; García et al. (2016); 25–6. See also Waldfogel (2006).

24. Waldfogel (2006), 59; Coplan, Findlay, and Schneider, 185 (2010).

25. Waldfogel (2006), 54. Gupta and Simonsen (2010), 40–1, write, "We find that, on average, participating in non-parental care is neutral compared to home care.... Preschool, where children are met with highly qualified staff in environments that allow for specialization of labor, is found to be as good as home care." See also Votruba-Drzal et al. (2013), 829. For evidence based on experimental studies of high-quality interventions, see Barnett (1995); Currie (2001); Haskins (2004); Karoly et al. (1998); Waldfogel (2002). For evidence from observational studies of center-based childcare programs, see Smolensky and Gootman (2003); Clarke-Stewart and Allhusen (2005).

26. Waldfogel (2006), 54–5, 94.

27. See Heckman (2016), 2; García et al. (2016), esp. 23–4, tables 3–4. See also Vandell and Wolfe (2000); Magnuson and Duncan (2016), 123; Council of Economic Advisers (2014), 30; Deming (2009), 126; Reynolds, Ou, and Temple (2018).

28. See Votruba-Drzal et al. (2013), 829, who found center-based daycare to be less advantageous to children's cognitive outcomes as family income increases. See also Gupta and Simonsen (2010) on Danish home care vs. high-quality daycare.

29. Kottelenberg and Lehrer (2013, 2014); Baker, Gruber, and Milligan (forthcoming).

30. Kottelenberg and Lehrer (2014).

31. NICHD Early Child Care Research Network (2003), 976. See also Brooks-Gunn, Han, and Waldfogel (2010).

32. Waldfogel (2006), 59.

33. E.g., Karoly et al. (1998), 107–8; Yoshikawa (1995), 66. See also Waldfogel (2006), 61.

34. See the research summary by Yoshikawa et al. (2013). Evidence is weaker for the positive effects of two years of preschool rather than one, but preliminary results suggest significant albeit smaller benefits for the second year. Ibid., 5.

35. Ruhm and Waldfogel (2011); Campbell and Ramey (1994); Schweinhart, Weikart, and Larner (1986).

36. Barnett (1995), 43. See also Haskins (2004); Karoly et al. (2008); Waldfogel (2002); Deming (2009); Yoshikawa et al. (2013); European Commission et al. (2014), 17.

37. See "ECE Consensus Letter" (2019).

38. Belsky et al. (2007), 693–5.

39. See Milkie, Nomaguchi, and Denny (2015), 367–8.

40. See Mills-Koonce et al. (2015); Mesman, van Ijzendoorn, and Bakermans-Kranenburg (2012); Belsky and Fearon (2002).

41. Regarding single parenthood, see Meier et al. (2016). Regarding financial stress and insecurity, see Dooley and Prause (2002), 799–800; Yeung, Linver, and Brooks-Gunn (2002), 1875; Mistry et al. (2002), 947; Jackson et al. (2000). Regarding nonstandard work schedules, see Perry-Jenkins et al. (2007); Han and Waldfogel (2007); Strazdins et al. (2004); Grzywacz et al. (2011). Regarding the relation between home environment and parenting stress, see Yeung, Linver, and Brooks-Gunn (2002), 1875.

42. Kela (2015), 5. Among lesbian couples, the spouse or partner of the mother is allowed to take "paternity" leave. Kela (2017).

43. Topping (2017).

44. Duvander, Mussino, and Tervola (2016), 6–7; Kela (2015), 7 (child home care allowance). See also Repo (2010), 47.

45. Department of Finance (2019).

46. Éducaloi (2019).

47. Lero (2015), 3.
48. Lerner (2015).
49. Horowitz et al. (2017), 52. See also Harrington et al. (2015), 7. See, e.g., Nepomnyaschy and Waldfogel (2007), who found that fathers taking more parental leave are more involved with child caretaking activities nine months later.
50. Washbrook et al. (2008).
51. Redford, Desrochers, and Mulvaney (2017), 9, report that 46 percent of children under one are placed in a nonparental caretaking arrangement. Children with multiple care arrangements are counted in each arrangement.
52. Account taken from Lerner (2015).
53. Klerman, Daley, and Pozniak (2014). To be covered, an employee must (1) work for a firm with fifty employees within seventy-five miles of the employee's worksite; (2) have twelve months of tenure with this firm; and (3) have performed 1,250 hours of service in the past year (about twenty-four hours per week). "Eligible Employee [under the Family and Medical Leave Act]" 29 CFR § 825.110.
54. Horowitz et al. (2017), 15.
55. Smith (2018), drawing on data from the Federal Reserve's Survey of Consumer Finances.
56. Declercq et al. (2013), 46.
57. See US Bureau of Labor Statistics (2017); Horowitz et al. (2017), 58–62, 64.
58. At the time of publication, eight states had passed such leave programs, along with the District of Columbia. In New Jersey, paid leave provides up to two-thirds of wages up to $637 a week for six weeks, rising to twelve weeks in July 2020. State of New Jersey Department of Labor and Workforce Development (2018). In Rhode Island, four weeks of paid leave are provided at a rate between $89 and $831 per week, based on earnings. Rhode Island Department of Labor and Training (2018); National Conference of State Legislatures (2016). New York's paid family leave program, which began in 2018, started with a maximum benefit amount of 50 percent of an employee's average weekly wage for up to ten weeks, capped at $652.96 per week, increasing to twlve weeks in 2021, and gradually to 67 percent in 2022. New York State (2018). California's paid family leave law provides for up to six weeks of benefits (rising to eight weeks in July 2020), paid at approximately 60 to 70 percent of a worker's average weekly earnings up to a cap of $1,252 per week. Employment Development Department (2018). Additionally, there are several states whose paid family leave laws are scheduled to take effect in the next few years. Washington State passed a paid parental leave program that will take effect in 2020. This program will offer wage replacement of up to 90 percent of an individual's average weekly earnings for up to twelve weeks, capped at $1,000 per week. Employment Security Department (2018). Connecticut's paid family law is scheduled to take effect in 2022 and will provide wage replacement of 95 percent of weekly earnings, capped at $900 weekly, for up to twelve weeks. Connecticut (2019). In Massachusetts, twelve weeks of paid leave with a replacement rate of 80 percent, capped at $850 per week, will be provided starting in 2021. Massachusetts (2019). DC's paid family law, set to begin providing benefits in 2020, will provide up to eight weeks of paid parental leave at a 90 percent replacement rate, capped at $1,000 per week. Bates et al. (2019). And Oregon is set to provide the nation's most generous paid leave, allowing workers to receive 100 percent of their average weekly earnings for twelve weeks, up to a weekly limit of $1,215, plus an additional two weeks relating to pregnancy, childbirth, or a related medical condition including lactation. Bradbury (2019). For a detailed comparison of all these laws, see A Better Balance (2019).
59. Employment Development Department (2018a); National Conference of State Legislatures (2016); Bartel et al. (2014), 3; A Better Balance (2019).
60. Bartel et al. (2014), 4–5, suggest increased maternity leave by 2.4 weeks on average; Rossin-Slater, Ruhm, and Waldfogel (2013) found increased maternity leave by three weeks; and Baum and Ruhm (2016) reported increased maternity leave by five weeks and average paternity leave by two to three days. For a comparison of these state laws, see A Better Balance (2019).
61. See Kela (2015), 5, 7–8; (2018b), 2–4.

62. Parents can also choose to put their children in private daycare and receive a state subsidy. Kela (2015), 8. Because the state-supported options are of such high quality, few parents—about 3 percent—choose this option. Ministry of Social Affairs and Health (2013), 25.

63. See Taguma, Litjens, and Makowiecki (2012), 9–10; Hujala, Fonsén, and Elo (2012), 310. By law, the staff–child ratio is set at 1:3 for children under three years and at 1:8 for children three years and older for both public and private service providers. At least one-third of the staffers must have a bachelor's degree or its equivalent; the remainder must have a high school degree or its equivalent. See OECD (2006), 322; (2016e), 13, n. 6. See also Pascal et al. (2013), 26–7, who associate Finland's strong performance on PISA tests with the country's high staff–child ratio, high levels of childcare regulation, stringent staff training requirements, and regulated national curriculum guidelines. Ripley (2013), 85–6, discusses the selectiveness and rigor of education in Finland; and Pölkki and Vornanen (2016), report that Finland's childcare system has strong benefits for child welfare clients.

64. OECD (2018e) (early childhood educational development spending); OECD (2018d).

65. See Ministry of Education and Culture (2018); Khazan (2013).

66. OECD (2016f), 4, chart PF3.2B, shows little variation in formal daycare participation across incomes.

67. OECD (2006), 320.

68. OECD (2016g), 2, chart PF.3.3.A.

69. OECD (2016g), 3, chart PF.3.3.B.

70. See Juhl (2018).

71. OECD (2016f), 2, chart PF3.2.A, 5, chart PF3.2.E; Schreyer and Oberhuemer (2017), 4, table 3, citing Jensen (2014).

72. OECD (2016g), 2, chart PF.3.3.A.

73. Chapter 2 describes the tax benefits available to those who pay for childcare. The OECD database calculates that these tax benefits save the average US couple with two kids in daycare and average incomes just 2 percent of the cost of daycare. A low-income single mother would save even less—under 1 percent of the cost of daycare as a result of tax advantages. OECD (2017e), 3–4.

74. See US Government Accountability Office (2016), 9–10. Twelve percent of families living in poverty with a preschooler reported receiving help from the government (this includes 29 percent of parents receiving TANF), compared with 3 percent of those living above the poverty line. Five percent of all children under five in daycare received government subsidies for that care. Laughlin (2013), 17, 19.

75. Schmit et al. (2013), 6.

76. Karoly (2017); Friedman-Krauss, Barnett, and Nores (2016); García et al. (2016); Heckman et al. (2010); Magnuson and Waldfogel (2005); Laughlin (2013), 17, 19.

77. Child Care Aware of America (2016a), 29.

78. Gornick and Meyers (2003), 190–1; Schochet (2017), 3. See also Cohn (2013).

79. North Carolina Division of Child Development and Early Education (2016).

80. Gornick and Meyers (2003), 190–91.

81. Quoted in Cohn (2013).

82. Redford, Desrochers, and Mulvaney (2017), 9, fig. 3 (2012 data).

83. Laughlin (2013), 3, 6.

84. OECD (2018p), 4, chart PF3.2.D.

85. Cohn (2013). See also Harbach (2015).

86. National Institute of Child Health and Human Development (NICHD) (2006), 11.

87. Quoted in Cohn (2013).

88. Laughlin (2013), 3, table 2.

89. See Galinsky et al. (1994); Kontos et al. (1995); NICHD Early Child Care Research Network (1997), 127–8. Fuller et al. (2004), 353–4, found that "just over one fifth of all child care providers, working outside centers, have four-year college degrees" and that some state fiscal activism is necessary to increase the quality of daycare options in a community. Hansen and Hawkes (2009) noted a negative effect of grandmother care relative to formal center-based

care. Gregg et al. (2005) found that early maternal employment reduces subsequent child test scores only if children were placed in informal care.

90. See also Bassok et al. (2016), 1635–6.
91. Galinsky et al. (1994), 81; Kontos et al. (1995), 206.
92. Bernal and Keane (2011), 462.
93. Wrigley and Dreby (2005), 737.
94. Cohn (2013).
95. Deahl (2017).
96. "[T]he more standards a child care setting meets, the more positive the caregiving. The more positive the caregiving, the higher the quality of care and the better the children's outcomes." National Institute of Child Health and Human Development (2006), 12.
97. Ibid., 9, table 3. The standards were set by the American Academy of Pediatrics and the American Public Health Association.
98. Ibid., 11, fig. 1.
99. Vandell and Wolfe (2000), 2.
100. See US Department of Health and Human Services (2015), 80515.
101. Child Care Aware of America (2017a), 10–11.
102. Whitebrook et al. (2018), 32–6.
103. Ibid., 41.
104. Child Care Aware of America (2017b), 8.
105. Child Care Aware of America (2017a), 20.
106. Child Care Aware of America (2017b), 8.
107. The Buchmann family's account is taken from Pao (2016).
108. Ms. Fox's account is taken from Quart (2013).
109. Lino et al. (2017), 24, table 1 (2015 figures).
110. Child Care Aware of America (2016b), 6, app. 3. The lowest annual cost of center-based infant care in 2015 was $5,045 (in Mississippi).
111. See Mocan (2007).
112. Ms. Dimyan-Ehrenfeld's account is taken from Quart (2013).
113. OECD (2010), 13.
114. OECD (2018c), 175, table B2.1a.
115. Child Care Aware of America (2017a), 11.
116. Schmit et al. (2013), 6.
117. Economist Intelligence Unit (2012); Pascal et al. (2013), 26.
118. OECD (2016e), 2.
119. North Carolina simply requires that all lead teachers take one four-credit course in early childhood education, without distinguishing between prekindergarten and daycare. See North Carolina Division of Child Development and Early Education (2017).
120. Lieberman (2017), 14.
121. OECD (2018c), 177, table B2.2.
122. See "ECE Consensus Letter" (2019).
123. Friedman-Krauss et al. (2018), 24, 28–9 (for 2016–2017 school year); Johnson (2014).
124. See Farran and Lipsey (2016).
125. Nation's Report Card (2018).
126. Mongeau (2016).
127. Bassok et al. (2016), 1.
128. Ibid., 3; Barnett et al. (2017), 7.
129. Bassok et al. (2016), 9, 13; National Center for Educational Statistics (2018).
130. Huerta et al. (2014), 13, fig. 1.
131. See Schulte (2015), who quotes the sociologist Melissa Milkie saying, "[T]here are a lot of cultural pressures for intensive parenting—the competition for jobs, what we think makes for a successful child, teenager and young adult, and what we think in a competitive society with few social supports is going to help them succeed."
132. Milkie, Nomaguchi, and Denny (2015). But see Waldfogel (2015).
133. On work stress and parenting, see Repetti and Wood (1997); Roeters, Lippe, and Kluwer (2010); Crouter et al. (2004); Crouter and Bumpus (2001). On economic stress and

parenting, see Conger et al. (1992); McLoyd et al. (1994); Jackson et al. (2000); Repetti, and Wood (1997); American Psychological Association (2011).

134. Pew Research Center (2015a), 5.
135. Kendig and Bianchi (2008).
136. After I finished writing this chapter, I discovered (with some regret) that Robert Putnam's excellent book, *Our Kids* (2015), also discussed these same experiments, and did it well.
137. Zhang and Meaney (2010); Zhang et al. (2004, 2005, 2006).
138. Francis et al. (1999).
139. Essex et al. (2001, 2002, 2003, 2013); Goodman and Gotlib (1999); Halligan et al. (2007); Bayer et al. (2008); Mistry et al. (2008); Ellis, Essex, and Boyce (2005).

Chapter 6

1. UNICEF (2012), 1.
2. This account and several others noted were taken from the excellent *In These Times* article by Sharon Lerner (2015), "The Real War on Families: Why the U.S. Needs Paid Leave Now."
3. See Smith et al. (1997), 164–5; Yeung, Linver, and Brooks-Gunn (2002), 1872–3, figs. 2, 3; Duncan and Brooks-Gunn (1997), chaps. 5–17; Duncan et al. (1998), 416–17, table 4.
4. Yeung, Linver, and Brooks-Gunn (2002), 1871–4, figs. 2, 3.
5. Ibid., 1875.
6. Mayer (1997), 46. See Yeung, Linver, and Brooks-Gunn (2002), 1862.
7. Hann, Brooks-Gunn, and Waldfogel (2004); Waldfogel (2006), 54–5.
8. Yeung, Linver, and Brooks-Gunn (2002), 1875, found that "family income was associated with maternal emotional distress and parenting practices not only through the perception of economic pressure . . . but also through family resources" and that "mother's psychological well-being and positive parenting behavior . . . were significantly associated with child's behavior problems." Sampson and Laub (1994), 538, concluded, "[P]overty appears to inhibit the capacity of families to achieve informal social control, which in turn increases the likelihood of adolescent delinquency." Smith and Brooks-Gunn (1997), 781, 783–4 reached the judgment that "[b]eing poor was . . . significantly associated with increased harsh discipline" and that "for girls, those children who experienced high discipline at 12 and 36 months of age had IQ scores that were on average 8 points lower (almost one half of a SD) than those for girls who experienced low discipline at 12 and 36 months of age." Yeung, Linver, and Brooks-Gunn (2002), 1875, found that "income instability was consistently associated with maternal depressive affect, which tended to be associated with more punitive parenting behaviors, which in turn were associated with lower letter-word scores and more externalizing behavior problems." Finally, Gennetian et al. (2015), 468–9, reported that "[h]igher [income] instability [is] negatively associated with adolescent school engagement and positively associated with expulsion/suspension rates."
9. Gennetian et al. (2015), 468–9; Reardon (2013b).
10. Williams and Boushey (2010), 8.
11. "Factor Income" (total income) minus "Current Transfers Paid" (taxes paid) of single-parent households in 2016. Statistics Finland (2018a).
12. This is slightly less leave than two-parent families receive because our single mother won't get the paternity leave to which the partners of mothers are entitled. See Kela (2015), 5.
13. This includes $1,322 a year in child benefits, $743 annually as a single-parent supplement, and $2,179 annually because the mother receives no child support from the child's father. See Kela (2018c, 2018d).
14. Kela (2019b).
15. City of Helsinki (2019); Vantaa (2018).
16. The home care allowance for one child is roughly $400 per month, with an additional $210 per month care supplement (paid to low-income families), for a total of $610 per month. The child benefits she will be paid would raise this to $963. Kela (2018d, 2019c).
17. According to data from Statistics Finland, this single mother's household would have annual expenses amounting to approximately $15,500, which include housing expenses subsidized at the maximum rate. See Statistics Finland (2018b) (average annual consumption

of single-parent families with children, excluding unnecessary expenditure categories); Kela (2019b). For information on Finland's housing subsidies, see Eerola and Saarimaa (2017), 8–9; OECD (2016h), 2; KELA/FPA (2015), 29–33.

18. UNICEF (2012), 2. The entire list included the following items: (1) three meals a day; (2) at least one meal a day with meat, chicken, or fish (or a vegetarian equivalent); (3) fresh fruit and vegetables every day; (4) books suitable for the child's age and knowledge level (not including schoolbooks); (5) outdoor leisure equipment (bicycle, roller skates, etc.); (6) regular leisure activities (swimming, playing an instrument, participating in youth organizations, etc.); (7) indoor toys (at least one per child, including educational baby toys, building blocks, board games, computer games, etc.); (8) money to participate in school trips and events; (9) a quiet place with enough room and light for doing homework; (10) an internet connection; (11) some new clothes (i.e., not all secondhand); (12) two pairs of properly fitting shoes (including at least one pair of all-weather shoes); (13) the opportunity, from time to time, to invite friends home to play and eat; and (14) the opportunity to celebrate special occasions such as birthdays, name days, and religious events.

19. US Census Bureau (2018a) (2017 figures). This analysis presumes that the fathers of these children do not contribute to their support, as is the case with almost three in ten children of parents living apart. Grall (2013), 1. Tax refund based on 2018 tax year.

20. Jorgensen and Appelbaum (2014), 3. See also Klerman, Daley, and Pozniak (2014).

21. US Bureau of Labor Statistics (2017), 1. A few states have closed this gap somewhat by providing short-term paid leave. See *supra* chapter 5, n. 58.

22. Smith (2018) (data from the Federal Reserve's Survey of Consumer Finances).

23. Colorado's Child Health Plan Plus (CHP+) program provides low-cost health insurance to pregnant women over the age of nineteen who earn less than 260 percent of the federal poverty level. Under this program, all pregnancy care, including labor and delivery, is free, with no copays. Colorado Department of Health Care Policy and Financing (2018).

24. Lerner (2015) reports on data collected by Abt Associates (Klerman, Daley, and Pozniak, 2014).

25. Including center-based daycare, the National Center for Children in Poverty calculates the budget for a single mother with a one-year-old living in Denver at $51,494. Without daycare, it calculates the budget at $28,535. National Center for Children in Poverty (2018a). See also Child Care Aware of America (2016a). The Department of Health and Human Services reports that childcare should cost at most 7 percent of a family's income to be affordable. See US Department of Health and Human Services (2015), 80515.

26. Our hypothetical mother earns more than 150 percent above the poverty threshold. See US Census Bureau (2018b). Only 3 percent of federally eligible children with family incomes greater than 150 percent of the poverty threshold received subsidies. Chien (2015), 4, figs. 2a–2b. For Early Head Start and Head Start eligibility, see Benefits.Gov (2018). See also Schulman and Blank (2016), 9, 26.

27. Bernal and Keane (2011), 462. See also Laughlin (2013), 8, 4, table 2; Bassok et al. (2016), 13.

28. See Waldfogel (2006), 54–5.

29. Heckman (2016), 2; García et al. (2016), esp. 23–4, tables 3–4.

30. Yeung, Linver, and Brooks-Gunn (2002), 1875; Mistry et al. (2002), 947; Jackson et al. (2000).

31. Based on National Center for Children in Poverty basic budget calculator for Denver.

32. Center on Budget and Policy Priorities (2017b); National Low Income Housing Coalition (2016); USA.Gov. (2019); Center on Budget and Policy Priorities (2017a); Harris (2013).

33. Interview with the author.

34. Posey (2016), 2, notes that the median household income for the United States was $55,775 in 2015.

35. Based on a poverty threshold of $24,339 for a family of four. US Census Bureau (2016a).

36. Horowitz et al. (2017), 14 (for household incomes between $30,000 and $74,999).

37. National Center for Children in Poverty (2018a) (for the city of Denver).

38. The federally funded, state-subsidized Early Head Start program serves children from birth, and may enroll up to 10 percent of children from families that are income-ineligible for Head Start, as well as 35 percent of children from families who are income-ineligible but remain

below 130 percent of the poverty guideline. 42 U.S.C. § 9840(B)i–iii. In 2015, however, fewer than 5 percent of children under the age of three and living in poverty were served. Barnett and Friedman-Krauss (2016), 4. Overall, government programs to assist low-income families do not come close to satisfying the existing need; many have extensive waiting lists.

39. Families whose incomes are less than $59,200 spend an average of about $2,100 on childcare and education per child when they spend money on these services. Lino et al. (2017), 24, table 1. This is less than one-fifth the average cost of center-based daycare nationally. Child Care Aware of America (2016b), 4.

40. Finland spends roughly $12,332 per year on children in early childhood education, including $19,423 on its youngest children. OECD (2018e).

41. Pew Research Center (2015a), 2.

42. The percentage of mothers who are employed for pay increases from about half of mothers like ours with no college education to three-quarters of those with a college degree, and to still more of those with postgraduate education. In contrast, most men with children are employed regardless of their educational background, including three-quarters of those with no college education and almost all of those with postgraduate education. Saad (2012).

43. Schmidtbauer (2014).

44. The National Center for Children in Poverty (NCCP) calculates a basic budget for a single-income two-parent family with two children ages one and three to be $31,326. And the NCCP's budget includes only expenses for housing, food, transportation, healthcare, payroll and income taxes, and a little more for other necessities such as clothing and school supplies. It includes no durable goods such as furniture or household appliances and, more importantly, no enrichment activities or games, toys, and books, all of which improve children's cognitive and social development. National Center for Children in Poverty (2018); Gould, Mokhiber, and Bryant (2018). If both parents worked and placed their children in center-based care, their required annual budget would balloon to $75,810, as calculated by the NCCP, well beyond their incomes after tax. See National Center for Children in Poverty (2018a) (2015 calculations for Denver: two-parent families with two children, ages one and three, with and without the second parent employed); Center on Budget and Policy Priorities (2018b, 2018c).

45. Using calculations from Center for American Progress (2018) for a twenty-two-year old mother earning $15,000 per year who began work at eighteen and left work for eight years beginning at age twenty-four.

46. Covert (2015).

47. Crittenden (2001), 151; Wang (2015). See also Bane and Ellwood (1994), 54, who found that 40 percent of poverty spells begin with a wife becoming the head of household.

48. Olivetti and Petrongolo (2017), 228.

49. Blau and Kahn (2013).

50. OECD (2018f).

51. Miller and Tedeschi (2019).

52. Dowd (2018), 42–9.

53. Luby et al. (2013); Hair et al. (2015).

54. Chaudry and Wimer (2016); Ratcliffe (2015); Cohen et al. (2010).

55. Gornick and Nell (2017), 18, table 1.

56. Bassok et al. (2016), 3–5.

57. Koball and Jiang (2018a), 1.

58. See UNICEF (2012), 2, 10, fig. 1a, where falling short means that a child lacks two or more categories of items. The UN's Innocenti Report Card has developed an index to assess cross-cultural material deprivation, but thus far has not had the data to assess the United States in this comparison. UNICEF (2013), 9.

59. Wilkinson and Pickett [2009] (2010), 24–5.

60. Gornick and Nell (2017), 18.

61. Ibid.

62. Ibid., 20, table 2.

63. Waldfogel et al. (2001), 5; Mishel et al. (2012), 419.

64. Mishel et al. (2012), 419; Edin and Shaefer (2015), 43.
65. The Center on Budget and Policy Priorities calculates that child poverty from market work (before government benefits are taken into account) declined only from 27 percent in 1967 to 25 percent in 2016. Shapiro and Trisi (2017), 3.
66. See Edin and Shaefer (2015), 9–10.
67. Child Trends Databank (2018) (2016 figure).
68. Interview with the author.
69. Edin and Shaefer (2015). See also Edin and Lein (1997).
70. The Center on Budget and Policy Priorities calculated, based on the federal government's Supplemental Poverty Measure, that child poverty has reached a record low of 16 percent from a high in 1967 of 28 percent. Shapiro and Trisi (2017), 4.
71. Ibid., 4, n. 7.
72. Ibid., 4.
73. The basic TANF block grant has been set at $16.5 billion each year since 1996. As a result of inflation, the real value of this funding has fallen by almost 40 percent. Center on Budget and Policy Priorities (2018d), 2.
74. See Mettler (2011).
75. Romig (2018), 1.
76. Edwards (2014), 64.
77. According to Pew, low-income mothers take an average of six weeks' maternity leave, compared with ten weeks taken by middle-income mothers and twelve weeks by high-income mothers. Horowitz et al. (2017), 14. Some sources, however, have found this number to be even lower. See, e.g., Rossin-Slater, Ruhm, and Waldfogel (2013), 242, who found that disadvantaged mothers took an average of one to two weeks of maternity leave prior to the passage of California's paid family leave law.
78. Cohen et al. (2016), 248.
79. Schmit et al. (2013), 6.
80. Layzer and Burstein (2007), 3; Johnson, Ryan, and Brooks-Gunn (2012); Lower-Basch and Schmit (2015), 7; Isaacs, Greenberg, and Derrick-Mills (2018).
81. Schmit and Walker (2016), 9–10; Bassok (2016), 10, table 3.
82. Yoshikawa (2013), 7.
83. Milkie, Nomaguchi, and Denny (2015); Waldfogel (2016); Kendig and Bianchi (2008), 1237.
84. Del Bono et al. (2016) (UK); Fiorini and Keane (2014) (Australia); Villena-Rodán and Ríos-Aguilar (2011); Price (2010) (mother–child reading).
85. Warwick (2004), 1, quoting Dr. Michael Meany.
86. Tsao et al. (2016); Desmond (2019).
87. Brown and Harris (1978); Khan and Khan (2017); Mah, Szabuniewicz, and Fiocco (2016); Chiba et al. (2012); Praag (2004).
88. Forget (2011); Hari (2018).
89. Quoted in Hari (2018).
90. Raphael, Angell, and Hall (2017).
91. Lower-Basch and Schmit (2015); Meier et al. (2016); Yeung, Linver, and Brooks-Gunn (2002); Mistry et al. (2002); Jackson et al. (2000).
92. Graham (2017), 12, chap. 4, 128; Mullainathan and Shafir (2013).
93. See Graham (2017), 83–6.
94. Waldfogel and Washbrook (2011), 3, fig. 1.
95. Wolf, Magnuson, and Kimbro (2017), 378; Karoly, Kilburn, and Cannon (2005), 2.
96. Reardon (2013b), fig. 1.
97. Reardon (2013a, 2013b). Recent research has shown that this gap narrowed modestly between 1998 and 2010, but would take approximately sixty more years to fully close if it continued to narrow at the same rate. Reardon and Portilla (2016), 12.
98. See Weiss and Wagner (1998); McEwen (2006); Luby (2015).
99. National Scientific Council on the Developing Child (2007), 10; Shonkoff and Garner (2012), 236; Felitti et al. (1998); Edwards et al. (2003); Anda et al. (2006); Brown, Thacker, and Cohen (2013); Kelly-Irving et al. (2013).
100. See Wade et al. (2014); Dowd (2018), 111–12.

101. For examples of the ACEs regularly measured by researchers, see Halfon et al. (2016), S71; Kwong (2014), 10; Wade et al. (2014); Sacks, Murphey, and Moore (2014), 2. To see how these ACEs are aggravated by poverty, see Sedlak et al. (2010), 12 (child neglect and abuse); Renzetti (2009) (domestic violence); Galea and Vlahov (2002) (drug abuse); Zilberstein (2016) (foster care system); McGuinness and Schneider (2007) (child maltreatment and foster care); Wade et al. (2014) (homelessness). See also Wilkinson and Pickett [2009] (2010).
102. Murphey, Bandy, and Moore (2012), 2; OECD (2018g), 6, fig. HC1.2.3. See *supra* chapter 6 notes 79–82 and accompanying text.
103. According to the National Scientific Council on the Developing Child (2007), 10, "The essential feature of toxic stress is the absence of consistent, supportive relationships to help the child cope and thereby bring the physiological response to threat back to baseline." See also Luby et al. (2013), 114.
104. Graham (2017), esp. chap. 4; Quart (2018); Lower-Basch and Schmit (2015), 16.
105. Ekono, Jiang, and Smith (2016), 11.
106. Interview with author.

Chapter 7

1. OECD (2015a), 174, fig. 4.32. See also UNICEF (2013), 39, fig. 6.0; OECD (2017a), 39, fig. III.1.1, which ranks the US average life satisfaction score of fifteen-year-olds twenty-eighth out of forty-eight countries and economies.
2. Wilkinson and Pickett [2009] (2010), 15–30. See also Oishi and Kesebir (2015); Payne (2017).
3. Layard (2005), 32–3; Wilkinson and Pickett [2009] (2010), 3–30. Some researchers disagree with the proposition that increases in the average wealth of a society make no difference above a particular income threshold. They argue that the increased wealth hasn't appeared to increase average happiness in many countries only because inequality has increased at the same time and canceled out the gains from increased affluence. See, e.g., Oishi and Kesebir (2015).
4. The term is Wilkinson and Pickett's [2009] (2010), 31.
5. See OECD (2015b); Ridge (2011), 76–7; Parkes, Sweeting, and Wight (2016), 1425–6; Main (2014), 468–9. See also Wade et al. (2014), e16.
6. Graham (2017), 79–80.
7. Gornick and Nell (2017). See also Edin and Shaefer (2015).
8. See Wood et al. (2012), e360–1, who found that for each 1 percent increase in ninety-day loan delinquency, there is an estimated 3 percent increase in abuse admission rates. Regarding the impact of financial stress on parenting quality, see Yeung, Linver, and Brooks-Gunn (2002), 1875.
9. Greger et al. (2016); Parkes, Sweeting, and Wight (2016), 1425–6; Ben-Zur (2003); Petito and Cummins (2000).
10. Lee and Yoo (2015), 167; Andresen (2016), 30–1; Butler (2005), 8. See also Ridge (2011), 78–9.
11. Layard (2005), 41–9; Luttmer (2005); Solnick and Hemenway (1998).
12. See Layard (2005), 30–1, 41–8; Children's Society (2017), 55, fig. 24; Holder and Coleman (2008); LoBue et al. (2011) (recognition of inequality in three-year-olds).
13. OECD (2015b).
14. OECD (2015c). See also Petre (2016); Kang (2015); Luthar (2003, 2013); Luthar, Barkin, and Crossman (2013); Luthar and Becker (2002); Lareau (2011), 242.
15. OECD (2015c).
16. OECD (2015a), 169, fig. 4.25; Graham (2017), 103–5.
17. Kasser and Ryan (1996); Cohen and Cohen (1996), chap. 7; Sheldon and Kasser (1995), 536–7; (1998), 1328–9. See also Lapierre, Bouffard, and Bastin (1997); Dykman (1998).
18. Niemiec, Ryan, and Deci (2009), 303; Ryan et al. (1996), 17.
19. Kasser and Ryan (1993, 1996); Chan and Joseph (2000); Niemiec, Ryan, and Deci (2009); Cohen and Cohen (1996); Sheldon et al. (1995); Sheldon and Kasser (1995, 1998); Lapierre, Bouffard, and Bastin (1997); Dykman (1998).

20. Twenge and Donnelly (2016).
21. Twenge, Campbell, and Freeman (2012), 1058.
22. Twenge, Campbell, and Freeman (2012); Eagan et al. (2017), 47; Astin et al. (1997), 12–13; Panos, Astin, and Creager (1967), 34.
23. See Twenge and Park (2019), 644–5, T.1 (1976–2016 data).
24. See Pennington (2017), quoting Rick Riccobono, the chief development officer of U.S.A. Baseball.
25. Chapter 1, fig. 1. See also OECD (2016a), 149, fig. 1.4.1, 177, fig. 1.5.1.
26. OECD (2016b), 183, fig. B1.3, 196, table B1.5a, 192, table B1.1.
27. OECD (2012), 216, fig. B1.1.
28. OECD (2017e), 202, fig. B4.1, 210, table B4.2; Cornman (2016), 3.
29. OECD (2016b), 183, fig. B1.3, 192, table B1.1.
30. OECD (2017a), 76, fig. III.3.5.
31. Harvard Center on the Developing Child (2007a), 1. See also Fiscella and Kitzman (2009), 1075.
32. OECD (2015a), 168–9, fig. 4.25.
33. OECD (2017g).
34. OECD (2017a), 39, fig. III.1.1, 74, fig. III.3.3.
35. Ibid., 76, fig. III.3.5. In the area of China charted as "B-S-J-G China" on the graph, for example, 41 percent of the students study more than sixty hours a week both in and out of school. In comparison, this is true for only 4 and 12 percent of students respectively in Finland and Estonia.
36. See OECD (2015a), 168–9, fig. 4.25 (academic pressure known to be high in Japan and Korea). See also Lee and Larson (2000); Bossy (2000) (academic pressure on Japanese students).
37. Angold et al. (2002), 893; Merikangas et al. (2010), 77; Bitsko et al. (2016), 222. See also Perou et al. (2013), 2.
38. Regarding the increased prevalence of anxiety and depression, see Bitsko et al. (2018); Weinburger et al. (2018); BlueCross BlueShield (2018), 6, exhibit 3; Mojtabai, Olfson, and Han (2016). See also Perou et al. (2013); Twenge (2014).
39. Twenge et al. (2010), 152 (1938–2007 data).
40. Wilkinson and Pickett [2009] (2010), 67–8.
41. Ibid., 66–9.
42. See Scott (2012); Stewart-Brown and Schrader-Mcmillan (2011); Sanders (2008); Tracy et al. (2008).
43. Roelofs et al. (2006) found a significant association between negative childrearing practices and children's internalizing behaviors, particularly depression and anxiety. Leve, Kim, and Pears (2005) concluded that harsh discipline increases boys' internalizing behaviors. Muris, Meesters, and Brake (2003), 235, reported a positive relationship between anxious childrearing, parental overprotection, and parental rejection and children's anxiety symptoms. Muris (2002) found that children's anxiety or worry increases based on perceptions of parental childrearing as anxious or overprotective. Muris and Merckelbach (1998), 1204, concluded there is a significant association between paternal warmth and children's anxiety. Rapee (1997) found an association between parental rejection and control over children and children's depression and anxiety. Garber, Robinson, and Valentiner (1997) concluded that maternal acceptance is negatively associated with childhood depressive symptoms, while maternal psychological control is positively associated with such depressive symptoms. Shaw et al. (1997) demonstrated that childhood exposure to parental conflict is associated with greater anxiety and depression. Santiago, Wadsworth, and Stump (2011) discussed the impact of poverty-related stress on the mental health of families. Finally, Ebbert, Infruna, and Luthar (2018) observed that children's perceptions of increased alienation and decreased trust from parents in middle school and high school were associated with higher rates of depression and anxiety in grade twelve.
44. Schore (2017), esp. 35–8.
45. Adkins et al. (2009), 50–1; Schraedley, Gotlib, and Hayward (1999), 105.

46. See Taylor et al. (2014), 250, who discuss the link between adolescent awareness of family financial struggles on their own future prospects and poor outcomes. See also McGee, Williams, and Nada-Raja (2001), 289, who find low socioeconomic status is associated with low self-esteem and feelings of hopelessness, both of which are linked to suicide ideation.
47. Luthar and Becker (2002); Luthar and D'Avanzo (1999); Luthar and Barkin (2012); Luthar (2003); Kang (2015); Weinberger et al. (2018).
48. Denizet-Lewis (2017), quoting Suniya Luthar.
49. Astin et al. (1985), 79; Eagen et al. (2017), 40. See also Denizet-Lewis (2017).
50. Brown and Harris (1978); Khan and Khan (2017); Mah, Szabuniewicz, and Fiocco (2016); Chiba et al. (2012); Praag (2004).
51. Keyes et al. (2015).
52. Ibid., 463; National Sleep Foundation (2018).
53. Bruni (2015), quoting Denise Pope.
54. Short and Louca (2015) (increased depression and anxiety); Tarokh, Saletin, and Carskadon (2016) (cognition, emotion regulation, and problem behaviors in teens); Owens (2014), e926–7 (depression and suicide ideation); Smaldone, Honig, and Byrne (2007) (depressive symptomology).
55. Pope, Brown, and Miles (2015), 32–3; Menlo-Atherton High School (2015), 1. See also Bruni (2015).
56. Denizet-Lewis (2017).
57. Ibid.
58. See Brown and Harris (1978). See also Hari (2018).
59. Plemmons et al. (2018), 4.
60. Lee (2017).
61. Denizet-Lewis (2017).
62. See, e.g., Pope, Brown, and Miles (2015); Lythcott-Haims (2015); Lahey (2015); Tough (2012); Levine (2006).
63. Radel et al. (2018), 1, 4.
64. OECD (2013), 5. See also Friedman, Horwitz, and Resnick (2005), 1578.
65. See Committee on Child Maltreatment Research, Policy, and Practice for the Next Decade: Phase II and Board on Children, Youth, and Families (2014), chap. 3; Berger and Waldfogel (2011).
66. See Berger and Waldfogel (2011).
67. Graham (2017), chap. 4; Mullainathan and Shafir (2013). See also Mistry et al. (2002), 947; Paxson and Waldfogel (2003), 102, table 4; Jackson et al. (2000).
68. See, e.g., McLoyd (1989) (impact of paternal job loss on children); Wood et al. (2012), e360–1 (loan delinquency and increase in abuse admission rates); Yeung, Linver, and Brooks-Gunn (2002), 1875 (relationship between family income and maternal distress and parenting practices).
69. See, e.g., Conger et al. (1992); McLoyd et al. (1994); Jackson et al. (2000); Repetti and Wood (1997); American Psychological Association (2011).
70. Chetty et al. (2017), 400.
71. The issues of minimum wage laws and collective bargaining are discussed in further detail *infra* in chapters 8–10.
72. Chetty et al. (2014), 1.

Chapter 8

1. Kelley (1914), 3.
2. The UC Berkeley economic historian Charles Sellers (1991) described the transition of the United States from an agrarian country characterized by a household economy to a bustling market economy in the first half of the nineteenth century. Three other historians—Nancy Cott (1977) of Harvard University, Mary P. Ryan (1981) of Johns Hopkins University, and Amy Dru Stanley (1996) of the University of Chicago—documented the changes in ideology that marked the shift to a market society. Professor Stanley also explored how this ideology motivated calls for government regulation. Finally, two other eminent academics, Columbia

University historian Alice Kessler-Harris (2001, 2003), and Harvard sociologist and political scientist Theda Skocpol (1992), detailed the relationship between the development of the American welfare state and the unpaid work traditionally done by women in families.

3. Seaboard towns in the Northeast were also already participating in market trade by, for example, exporting surplus grain to Europe. Appleby (1984), 40–2. There were exceptions to the household economy outside seaboard towns. Most prominently, the South contained some large plantations on which a large number of slaves produced goods for export, although family farms were far more numerous even there. Licht (1995), 11; Sellers (1991), 4–5.

4. As Sellers (1991), 15, argues: "From the perspective of economic historians, farm folk who bartered a few hams or a tub of cheese for a frying pan or piece of calico sometimes seem incorporated into the market. But from the perspective of the household devoting its labor overwhelmingly to subsistence, the market remained marginal." See also Boydston (1990), 2, 11. Gutman (1973), 532, notes that "the Protestant work ethic was not deeply ingrained in the nation's social fabric. . . . Even in the land of Benjamin Franklin, Andrew Carnegie, and Henry Ford, nonindustrial cultures and work habits regularly thrived and were nourished by new workers alien to the 'Protestant' work ethic." Sellers (1991), 5, also observes that "rural production of use values stopped once bodies were sheltered and clothed and bellies provided for."

5. Foner (1995), xiii, quoting John Smith (1616). In Eric Foner's words: "It was an axiom of eighteenth-century political thought that dependents lacked a will of their own, and thus did not deserve a role in public affairs. . . . Representative government could rest only on a citizenry that enjoyed the personal autonomy that arose from ownership of productive property and was thus able to subordinate self-interest to the public good." Ibid., xii.

6. Stanley (1998), 9–10; Blumin (1989), 105.

7. See Foner (1995), xii.

8. Appleby (1984), 44. See also Merrill (1995), 322–3.

9. See generally Blumin (1989), epilogue.

10. The mean height for native-born white American males peaked in 1830 at nearly 174 centimeters. Slave children, however, were significantly shorter than white children. They were also 6 to 14 percent more likely than their Caucasian peers to die before the age of five. Fogel (1986), 471–2, fig. 9.3. Furthermore, free Americans' life expectancy topped out at fifty-six years in 1800, the highest in the developed world. The life expectancies of Americans exceeded those of even English aristocracy by more than ten years. Ibid., 445, 511; Fogel (2004), 2.

11. US Census Bureau (1990). See also Gallman (2000), 13.

12. Laurie (1989), 26.

13. US Census Bureau (1990); Blumin (1989), 298.

14. Katz (1986), 4–5; Matthaei (1982), 104.

15. Massachusetts Bureau of Statistics of Labor (1873), 440.

16. See Cott (1977), xx–xxii, 1, 33; Ryan (1981), 230–6. This is not to say, however, that the ideology of domesticity was universally or passively accepted. Both Christine Stansell (1986) and Nancy Cott (1977) describe the many ways that urban working-class women resisted its demarcation between private and public. For a discussion of black families' ambivalent reaction to the ideology, see, e.g., Horton (1979); Sterling (1984); Jones (1985).

17. See generally Cott (1977), 64–8.

18. Kessler-Harris (2003), 4.

19. Stanley (1998), 37, 76–7.

20. Ibid., 12–17.

21. Ibid., 13, quoting Adam Smith, *An Inquiry into the Nature and Causes of the Wealth of Nations*, 22 [1776] (1937).

22. Stanley (1998), 2, quoting E. L. Godkin (1867), 184.

23. Foner (1995), 25, quoting Senator Harlan of Iowa, Cong. Globe, 24 Cong., 1 Sess., Appendix, 276 (1856).

24. Stanley (1998), 148.

25. Burroughs (1827), 18–19.

26. Cott (1977), 63, 70.

27. Ibid., 85, where Abbott [1833] (1972), 165, is quoted as follows: "Mothers have as powerful an influence over the welfare of future generations as all other earthly causes combined."
28. Child (1866), 260.
29. Stanley (1998), 165.
30. Sellers (1991), 238–9; Atack, Bateman, and Margo (2004), 186, table 3, 190; Steckel (1990).
31. Licht (1995), 183.
32. Boydston (1990), 66, quoting Foster (1850), 69; Blumin (1989), 17–18, 73–4, 121.
33. See Atack, Bateman, and Margo (2004), 188-90; Katz (1983), 10–11. See also Licht (1995), 184; Blumin (1989), 272.
34. Licht (1995), 18, 185; Katz (1983), 11; Margo (2000), 242; Boydston (1990), 61–2.
35. See Haines (1981), 244; Gallman (2000), 9–10.
36. Stansell (1986), 3–4.
37. Katz (1983), 10–11.
38. One well-regarded study concluded that fewer than half of the Bostonians counted in the census of 1830 still lived in the city ten years later. A staggering 3,325,000 people moved through Boston at one time or another between 1830 and 1890, although in total this yielded a net population growth for the city of only 387,000 persons. Sellers (1991), 239.
39. Katz (1983), 10.
40. Riis (1890), 5–7. In 1880, 45 percent of San Francisco's population was composed of immigrants, as was 30 percent of St. Louis's, 37 percent of Cleveland's, 40 percent of New York's and Milwaukee's, 39 percent of Detroit's, and 41 percent of Chicago's. Gibson and Lennon (1999), table 19.
41. Riis (1890), 2–3, 11–14; Stansell (1986), 49–50. See also Katz (1983).
42. Margo (2000), 229–31. See also Gutman (1973).
43. Stansell (1986), 49, 217–18; Cott (1977), 9–10; Licht (1995), 184.
44. Cott (1977), 6.
45. Licht (1995), 184.
46. Haines (1981), 260, table 6; Blumin (1989), 188; Blewett (1983), 224–25; Stansell (1986), 12–13, 111; Boydston (1990).
47. Licht (1995), 184; Stansell (1986), 50–3.
48. Haines (1981), 260, table 6; Licht (1995), 184. See also Blumin (1989), 190, table 5.1, 272.
49. Trattner (1970), 36. Child labor in factories was especially widespread in southern states after Reconstruction because of the desperate economic circumstances of many families there. According to Walter Trattner (1970), 40, "A former president of the Cotton Manufacturers' Association declared that the adoption of a minimum working age of fourteen would close every mill in North Carolina—simply because 75 per cent of the spinners in that state were under fourteen."
50. Margo (2000), 212, 216.
51. Child Labor in North Carolina Textile Mills (2019a, 2019b).
52. Squiers (2005), 28.
53. According to the 1900 US Census, 24,000 children under sixteen years of age worked in coal mines. Department of Commerce (1924), 45; Margo (2000).
54. New York Times (1869).
55. Stansell (1986), 199.
56. Fogel (1986), 511; (2004). It was probably only with the cohort born in the last decade of the nineteenth century that the dramatic increase in physical heights that occurred in the twentieth century began. Fogel (2004), 18.
57. Costa and Steckel (1997), 61, fig. 2.5; Komlos (1987), 902–3.
58. Haines (1981), 253–8; Haines, Craig, and Weiss (2003); Fogel (2004), chap. 1; Gallman (2000), 36–8.
59. In the words of the historian Amy Dru Stanley (1996), 91: "At the heart of the ideological shift that ushered in the regulatory state lay a perception that the spheres of home and market were overlapping in a way that endangered what contemporaries called 'the future of the race.' . . . In the name of the family . . . the market in labor began to be regulated by the state."
60. Trattner (1974), 17; Tomlins (1993), esp. chap. 2; Novak (1996), esp. 13–14; Scheiber (1997), esp. 824, n. 6.

61. See Scheiber (1997); Hurst (1964).
62. Charles Sellers (1991), 47, memorably referred to lawyers in the mid-nineteenth century as the early "shock troops of capitalism." As Justice Story articulated this view in 1829, "[G]overnment can scarcely be deemed to be free, where the rights of property are left solely dependent upon the will of a legislative body, without any restraint. The fundamental maxims of a free government seem to require, that the rights of personal liberty and private property, should be held sacred." *Wilkinson v. Leland*, 27 U.S. 627, 657 (1829). See also Horwitz (1977).
63. See Scheiber (1997), 860.
64. Appleby, 53–4 (1984). Christopher Tomlins (1993), 86–8, argues that Jefferson had a more robust vision of government at the state and local levels.
65. Jefferson (1801).
66. Katz (1989), 5–7; Pimpare (2004), 20–36, 194–7.
67. Spencer (1852), 379. Following up on this line of thought, Andrew Carnegie [1889] (2017), 3, wrote that the law of natural selection "is here; we cannot evade it; no substitutes for it have been found; and while the law may sometimes be hard for the individual, it is best for the race, because it insures the survival of the fittest in every department."
68. Pimpare (2004), 21–4; Licht (1995), 181–6.
69. Katz (1983), 2–3; Fine (1956), esp. 20–2. See also Boltanski and Chiapello (2007), xx.
70. Massachusetts Bureau of Statistics of Labor (1870), 71; Stanley (1998), 149.
71. Massachusetts Bureau of Statistics of Labor (1870), 182.
72. Stanley (1998), 151, citing Massachusetts Bureau of Statistics of Labor (1870), 161, 163, 178.
73. Stanley (1998), 151–2.
74. Massachusetts Bureau of Statistics of Labor (1870), 158–64, 197.
75. Stanley (1998), 154.
76. See, e.g., Adams (1887), 38.
77. Ibid., 41–6.
78. Ely (1910), 57.
79. Ely (1886), 6–7. See also Fine (1956), 211–16.
80. *Proceedings of the Conference on the Care of Dependent Children* (1909), 9, 192–3.
81. Their passage is described in Skocpol (1992), 465–6.
82. Ibid., xxi, quoting Mrs. G. Harris Robertson (1911).
83. See Leff (1973), 401, table 1; Skocpol (1992), 10.
84. Skocpol (1992), 10.
85. Gordon (1994), 45–50.
86. Skocpol (1992), 465.
87. Gordon (1994), 38–9.
88. The Supreme Court subsequently struck down the federal Keating-Owen Child Labor Act of 1916, which put modest limits on child labor, on the ground that it exceeded Congress's power under the commerce clause in *Hammer v. Dagenhart* (1918). *Hammer* was eventually overruled in part by *United States v. Darby* (1941). See generally Trattner (1970), 23.
89. Kelley (1914), 4.
90. I owe thanks to June Carbone for discussions with me about the New Deal's regulation of the market to make it safe for families.
91. Kelley (1914), 4–5; Social Security Act, Ch. 531, 49 Stat. 620 (1935). The Aid to Dependent Children Act, Pub. L. No. 74-271, 49 Stat. 620 (1935), was later renamed the Aid to Families with Dependent Children Act, Pub. L. No. 78-257, 58 Stat. 277 (1944).
92. Gordon (1994), 149–50.
93. National Labor Relations Act, Pub. L. 74-198, 49 Stat. 449–57 (1935).
94. Rosenfeld (2014), 2–4.
95. Fair Labor Standards Act, Pub. L. 75-718, 52 Stat. 1060–69 (1938); Forsythe (1939), 466–7.
96. Sparrow (2011), 124, 263, chart A.5.
97. Brownlee (2016), 115, 142.
98. Levy and Temin (2007); Hacker and Pierson (2016).
99. Alesina, Glaeser, and Sacerdote (2001), 195, table 4.
100. Gordon (1994), 6; Mettler (2011), 18–19, 22–3.

101. Kessler-Harris (2001), 4. After World War II, new programs expanded this gendered set of assumptions to include credit access, income tax rates, mortgage rates, and special access to jobs, to name a few. Ibid., 4–5. See also Orloff (2006), 238.
102. Gordon (1994), 5–8, 45–6, 180–81, 303; Kessler-Harris (2001), 130–43.
103. Kessler-Harris (2001), 96, 105–6; Bach (2013), 318–19.
104. Gordon (1994), 5, 275–7.
105. Senate Committee on Finance (1935), 640–1.

Chapter 9

1. Johnson (1964).
2. See O'Connor, Orloff, and Shaver (1999); Gornick and Meyers (2003), chaps. 5–7.
3. Reich (1984).
4. US Bureau of Labor Statistics (2018b), 2.
5. Patterson (2009), 166.
6. Katz (1996), 76, 262, 275–6; Lampman (1969), 3–4; Moffitt (2003), 294–5. For some of the Supreme Court's rulings, see, e.g., King v. Smith, 392 U.S. 309, 333 (1968) (striking down Alabama rule disqualifying children whose mothers lived with a man other than the one required to pay support to the children); Shapiro v. Thompson, 394 U.S. 618, 641–42 (1969) (striking down District of Columbia law limiting benefits based on a one-year residency requirement); Townsend v. Swank, 404 U.S. 282, 286 (1971) (striking down Illinois law denying benefits to dependent children aged eighteen to twenty who attended college or university but granting benefits to children that age who attended vocational or high school).
7. Katz (1996), 290–2, described the 1975 economic crisis in New York as "the first skirmish in the new war on welfare" as New York leaders pointed to the state's rise in welfare payments as one of the causes of its $12.3 billion debt. See also Steensland (2008), 72; Lampman (1969), 5.
8. Katz (1996), 275.
9. Goldwater (1961), 54.
10. Reagan described a Chicago woman who had "80 names, 30 addresses, 12 Social Security cards and is collecting veterans' benefits on four nonexisting deceased husbands." New York Times (1976).
11. Edin and Shaefer (2015), 15–16.
12. Nixon (1969a).
13. Nixon (1971a).
14. Samuelson (1968), 76; New Republic (1968), 4.
15. George Bush for President (1988), 2; Livingston (2016), 14–15; Steensland (2008), ix, 2.
16. Steensland (2008), 104, citing a memo from Burns to Nixon, May 26, 1969.
17. Ibid., ix, 2, chaps. 4–5.
18. The Comprehensive Child Development Act, H.R. 6748, 92 Cong. (1971), was included in the passage of the Economic Opportunity Amendments, S. 2007, 92nd Cong. (1st Sess. 1971).
19. Self (2012), 128–30; The Comprehensive Child Development Act, H.R. 6748, 92 Cong. (1971).
20. The Comprehensive Child Development Act, H.R. 6748, 92 Cong. (1971), was included in the passage of the Economic Opportunity Amendments, S. 2007, 92nd Cong. (1st Sess. 1971), and vetoed by President Nixon on December 9, 1971. See also Rosenthal (1971); Self (2012), 128–30.
21. Nixon (1969b); Mondale (2010), 98.
22. Roth (1976), 29; Karch (2013), 83; Ludden (2016). See also Mondale (2010), 100.
23. Roth (1976), 30–1; Rose (2010), 56–7; Karch (2013), 84.
24. Roth (1976), 27–9; Morgan (2001), 231–32.
25. Nixon (1971b), 46058.
26. Ibid.
27. Steensland (2008), ix, 2, chaps. 4–5.
28. See Phillips and Zigler (1987), 15; Ludden (2016).

29. E.g., Self (2012), 6.
30. The exception here, although not specifically focused on the government-family issue, is Jacob Hacker and Paul Pierson's book, *American Amnesia* (2016), which recounts the war on government that business and leading intellectuals on the right waged at the end of the twentieth century.
31. Reagan (1981) (emphasis added). Robert Self (2012), 337, notes that a broad Gallup survey of American attitudes in the run-up to President Carter's White House Conference on Families, which was active between 1977 and 1980, "revealed a paradox. Eighty percent of Americans reported family to be the 'most' or 'one of the most' important elements of their lives." Most of those surveyed supported changes in tax, welfare, and housing policies to support families. Yet when asked which institutions should be the "main factor" in strengthening families, few mentioned "government laws and policies." In Self's words, "Americans on the whole associated family life with private, not public, concerns. In the coming years, conservatives would take advantage of this important subtlety in public opinion." Ibid.
32. Rodgers (2011), 41.
33. Reagan (1982), quoted in Rodgers (2011), 41.
34. Tax Reduction Act of 1975 (1975), Section 43; 26 U.S.C. § 32 (2015); Isaacs et al. (2015), 14.
35. Omnibus Budget Reconciliation Act of 1981 (OBRA). Pub. L. 97-35, 95 Stat. 357 (1981); 45 FR 5648-50, 1982 WL 129733 (1982). See also Katz (1996), 296-8.
36. Katz (1996), 287.
37. See ibid., 298. The number of children in poverty increased by 3.7 million from 1979 to 1983, totaling almost 14 million children. Congressional Budget Office (1984), 12. See also Drogin (1985); US Department of Health and Human Services (2002), 59.
38. Murray (1984). As Jane Mayer (2016), 135-46, describes, "The backstory to *Losing Ground* . . . was a primer on the growing and interlocking influence of conservative nonprofits." Mayer summarizes Murray's rise from unknown academic to bestselling author and public intellectual with the help of the conservative network of funders.
39. Moynihan (1965), 19.
40. Greenstein (1985), 13.
41. Danziger and Gottschalk (1985), 33-4.
42. Bane and Ellwood (1986), 17 (1994), 29; O'Neill, Bassi, and Wolf (1987), 244; Blank (1989); Fitzgerald (1991), 559-60; Harris (1993), 331.
43. Duncan, Hill, and Hoffman (1988), 470.
44. Duncan and Hoffman (1988), 251.
45. Bane and Ellwood (1994). See also Ellwood and Summers (1985), 18, who note, "It seems difficult to argue that AFDC was a major influence in unmarried births when there was simultaneously a rise in the birth rate to unmarried whites and a fall in the rate for unmarried blacks."
46. Ellwood and Bane (1985), 143.
47. Wilson (1987).
48. Cherlin (2014), 16-20, esp. 17, fig. 1.2.
49. Ibid., 16-19.
50. Edin and Lein (1997).
51. Banerjee et al. (2017), 157-8, 173-4.
52. Greenstein (1985), 17.
53. Ibid., 14; Danziger and Gottschalk (1985), 34.
54. As Sheldon Danziger and Peter Gottschalk (1985), 35, put it, " '[T]hrowing money' at problems can have a dramatic impact."
55. Greenfield (1985), 80.
56. Reagan (1986).
57. White House Working Group on the Family (1986), 21.
58. This point in response to Charles Murray was first made by Christopher Jencks (1985).
59. White House Working Group on the Family (1986), 5.
60. Ibid., 3, 10, citing George Gilder, *Wealth and Poverty* (1981), 27.
61. Self (2012), 368-369.

62. The Personal Responsibility and Work Opportunity Reconciliation Act (PRWORA) of 1996, Pub. L. 104-193, 110 Stat. 2105 (1996) (codified as amended primarily in scattered sections of 7 and 42 U.S.C.).
63. Santorum (2005), 68.
64. Katz (1996), 327–30.
65. Pear (1996).
66. Clinton (1996).
67. Floyd, Burnside, and Schott (2018), 1, 5, 17–19, table 3.
68. Schott, Floyd, and Burnside (2018), 14; Wogan (2016); CLASP (2016); Matthews (2016b).
69. The Personal Responsibility and Work Opportunity Reconciliation Act, Pub. L. No. 104-93, 110 Stat. 2105 (1996) (codified as amended primarily in scattered sections of 7 and 42 U.S.C.). Title I replaced AFDC with TANF.
70. US Congress (1996, Pub. L. 104-93, Title I, Section 101); and noted by Hays (2003), 17.
71. 42 U.S.C. § 601 (1997) (current through Pub. L. 115-72; Title 26 current through 115-73).
72. Hays (2003), 39–40, 65.
73. This point is made in the the thoughtful analysis by Hays (2003), 17–23 .
74. Ibid., 19.
75. Santorum (2005), 126.
76. Quoted in Pear (1996).
77. Soss et al. (2003), 237–9; Gilens (1996). See generally Schram, Soss, and Fording (2003).
78. Soss, Fording, and Schram (2008). See also Soss, Fording, and Schram (2011), 145.
79. Hemez (2016); Schweizer (2018), 1.
80. Williams (2017), 11, 14.
81. Martin et al. (2006), 61, table 20; National Center for Health Statistics (NCHS) (2019).
82. Floyd, Burnside, and Schott (2018), 1.
83. Ibid., 7.
84. Edin and Shaefer (2015), 93, 109, 112 156; and reported by Matthews (2015).
85. Bush (1990).
86. Hacker and Pierson (2016); Levy and Temin (2007).
87. Cooper (2017).
88. Levy and Temin (2007), 36–41.

Chapter 10

1. Raworth (2017), 27–31.
2. See, e.g., Folbre (2001); Boushey (2016).
3. For an insightful and detailed discussion of family-support policies internationally, see Filgueira and Rossel (2017).
4. Guttmacher Institute (2019), 1 (2011 figures).
5. Guttmacher Institute (2018), 3; Joshi, Khadilkar, and Patel (2015), S61–2. Strasser et al. (2016), 26, suggests that cost is the most common barrier to LARC use among US women. A LARC can cost anywhere from $500 to $900, and this amount does not include initial and follow-up visit charges, which increase the total cost to more than $1,000.
6. See Snyder et al. (2018).
7. LARC4CO (2019). Published by LARC4CO, a coalition composed of more than sixty public and private health agencies and organizations. The Colorado Family Initiative (CFPI), launched in 2008 after the Colorado Department of Public Health and Environment received private funding, provided support to clinics for training, operations, and LARCs. Ibid., 1. See also Strasser et al. (2016), 42–3.
8. Upstream USA (2019). Among women ages twenty to thirty-nine participating in Delaware's Title X family planning program who weren't trying to become pregnant, LARC use jumped from 14 percent to 32 percent between 2014 and 2017. Meanwhile, the percentage of women using no birth control fell from 5.4 percent to 2.9 percent. Welti and Manlove (2018).
9. For a review of the research on the effects of mothers' early return to work, see Waldfogel (2006), 49–57. Chapter 5 discusses this issue in more detail. See also Brooks-Gunn, Han, and

Waldfogel (2002), 1066–7; Waldfogel, Han, and Brooks-Gunn (2002); Christian, Morrison, and Bryant (1998), 516.

10. Haas and Rostgaard (2011), 178; Arnarson and Mitra (2010), 678; Cools, Fiva, and Kirkebøen (2015), 805.

11. Arnalds, Eydal, and Gíslason (2013), 341; Nepomnyaschy and Waldfogel (2007), 447; Almqvist and Duvander (2014), 25; Tanaka and Waldfogel (2007), 42; Patnaik (forthcoming); Huerta et al. (2014), 334. See also Eydal and Rostgaard (2016). But see Ekberg, Eriksson, and Friebel (2013); Kluve and Tamm (2013).

12. Sarkadi et al. (2008); Sigle-Rushton (2010), 21; Patnaik (2015), 59; Cools, Fiva, and Kirkebøen (2015); Carbone and Cahn (2014); Blofield et al. (2018). See also Cabrera, Shannon, and Tamis-LeMonda (2007).

13. See supra chapter 2, note 19; chapter 5, notes 58–60 and accompanying text.

14. According to the OECD (2019c), even countries with the most robust paid family leave policies pay less than 1 percent of total GDP to fund these programs. In 2013, Iceland spent 0.4 percent, Norway spent 0.6 percent, and Sweden spent 0.7 percent. Based on OECD demographic and GDP data for 2014, if the United States were to match the programs of other nations, it would spend, at most, 0.7 percent of GDP. See OECD (2018i, 2018j, 2018k).

15. Esping-Anderson (2009), 137–8.

16. Relevant research cited in chapter 5.

17. OECD (2014a).

18. FAMIFED (2018). The rate for the Flanders region is slightly lower, however.

19. Matthews (2016a); Canada (2018a).

20. Pressman (2011), 330.

21. Shaefer et al. (2018), 33 (calculated based on a $3,000 annual child benefit).

22. Morduch and Schneider (2017). See also Currier et al. (2015), 4, fig. 2.

23. See Leinonen, Solantaus, and Punamäki (2002); Parke et al. (2004); Robila and Krishnakumar (2006).

24. Cunha (2014), 229; Raschke (2016); Bailey (2013), 19; Jones, Milligan, and Stabile (2015) .

25. Raschke (2016), 469; Akee et al. (2010); Milligan and Stabile (2011); Fernald, Gertler, and Neufeld (2008); Davala et al. (2015).

26. Institute for Research on Poverty (1976), 76: Kehrer (1977), 12–13. See also Levine et al. (2005), 100; Salkind and Haskins (1982), 172–5; Institute for Research on Poverty (1973); Stanford Research Institute and Mathematica Policy Research (1978).

27. Amendment of 1986 Code, H.R. 1 (2017), Section 11022. See supra chapter 2 for a discussion of the refundability of the CTC.

28. Holzer et al. (2007), 22.

29. Pressman (2011), 330.

30. Kamerman and Kahn (1993), 42–3.

31. See Vogel et al. (2010), B.13; Kirkland and Mitchell-Herzfeld (2012), 4–5; DuMont et al. (2011), 71–5.

32. Kirkland and Mitchell-Herfzeld (2012), 4–5; Kitzman et al. (2010); Olds et al. (2007); Sidora-Arcoleo et al. (2010), 40; Olds et al. (2004); Vogel et al. (2010), 23.

33. DuMont et al. (2010), 71, chap. 6; Olds et al. (1998); Kitzman et al. (2010); Eckenrode et al. (2010), 13.

34. See Kitzman et al. (2010), 414; Olds et al. (2007).

35. Gilkerson et al. (2017), finding that children in low-income families hear four million fewer words by age four than do children in high-income families. This word deficit, while significant, is far lower than that found in the classic study on the word gap, which found that poor children heard thirty million fewer words by age four than did wealthy children. Hart and Risley (1995), 32, 252. The more recent study is likely more accurate, as it relied on a larger sample size and used recordings over continuous twelve-hour periods, rather than relying on the reporting of a researcher in the room during the evening hours, as the earlier study did.

36. Bradley et al. (2001), 1860–1; Lareau (2011), 159; Phillips (2011), 224. See also Putnam, Frederick, and Snellman (2012), 9–11.

37. Huntington (2019).

38. Patient Protection and Affordable Care Act (2010), Section 2951, amending Title V of the Social Security Act by adding Section 511 (allocating annual funds for maternal, infant, and early childhood home visiting programs, from $100,000,000 for 2010 to $400,000,0000 for 2014). Ibid., (j)(1). Those funds have since been renewed by Congress, extending the program through 2022. Bipartisan Budget Act of 2018, Section 50601.
39. US Health Resources and Services Administration (2019), 2–3.
40. National Home Visiting Resource Center (2018), 3 (2016 figures).
41. Huntington (2019), 143.
42. Levy and Temin (2007), 16–21.
43. Ibid. See also Hacker and Pierson (2010b). Reynolds (2007) argued that all of the recent growth in high-end inequality is a result of shifts in tax law.
44. See Maag (2007), 3–4.
45. Raissian and Bullinger (2017).
46. Piketty, Saez, and Stantcheva (2014), 268, argue for higher marginal tax rates on large incomes for just this reason. See also Mishel and Schieder (2017), 21; Saez and Zucman (2019).
47. Tax Policy Center (2018); Saez and Zucman (2019).
48. Farber et al. (2018); VanHeuvelen (2018); Western and Rosenfeld (2011).
49. Mayer (2004), 23. The US Bureau of Labor Statistics (2018a), 1, reported that 10.5 percent of wage and salary workers belonged to unions in 2018, compared with 20.1 percent in 1983, the first year with "comparable" data for union membership, according to the Bureau.
50. Hacker and Pierson (2010b), 57–9.
51. Mishel and Eisenbrey (2015), 10–12; Madland (2018). Labor unions and collective-bargaining strategies have been shown to have a wide range of positive effects in workplaces, even for nonunion members, including raising wages for all workers and helping to close both the gender and racial payment gaps. See Bivens et al. (2017), 7, 11–12. See also Esping-Andersen (2009), 56.
52. OECD (2018l).
53. Alvaredo et al. (2018), 10; Desilver (2017); Economist (2012); Piketty and Saez (2007), 21–2.
54. OECD (2017h), 132–4; Western (1997), 58. See also Scruggs (2002); Holmlund and Lundborg (1999). Rothstein (1992), 42, estimates that union-run unemployment systems make a difference of about 20 percent in union density.
55. Goodman (2017).
56. Carbone and Cahn (2014), 154–6, called my attention to the value of flexicurity.
57. Bekker et al. (2008).
58. Missouri cuts off at thirteen weeks and Georgia at fourteen weeks. See Center on Budget and Policy Priorities (2018a), 2– 3; OECD (2018o), 3–4.
59. OECD (2017i) (figures for 2015, based on a single parent with two children).
60. OECD (2016i), 135–6. See also Stephan (2017) .
61. Denmark spent 3.3 percent of GDP on labor market programs in 2015 with 2.05 percent devoted to active labor market programs, compared with the United States, which spent 0.3 percent of GDP on labor market programs overall and 0.1 percent on active labor market programs. See OECD (2017j), table Q; see also OECD (2016i), 86, 135–6.
62. Beck (2000); Kalleberg (2011).
63. According to the US. Census Bureau, there were 5,417,000 families with children and 139,000 children living without families in poverty in 2017. The mean deficit (number of dollars below the poverty line) for families with children was $11,612 and that for individuals (including children living without families) was $7,394. See US Census Bureau (2018d, 2018e). The cost of providing these families and children with the average monetary assistance needed to rise above the poverty level would be $63,929,970,000.
64. Calculated based on 2018 GDP of $20.494 trillion. See OECD (2018i).
65. Congress authorized approximately $692 billion in defense spending for FY 2018 (National Defense Authorization Act for Fiscal Year 2018 [2017], Title I), compared with $611 billion for FY 2017 (National Defense Authorization Act for Fiscal Year 2017 [2016], Title I), amounting to a difference of about $81 billion. See also Daniels (2017); Cohen (2017); Williams and Towell (2016), 1.

66. The United States had more than $609.5 billion in military spending in 2017, compared with $578 billion of military spending by the next seven countries combined. See Stockholm International Peace Research Institute (2018). The $65.5 billion needed to raise all American children out of poverty would amount to approximately 10.7 percent of these annual military expenditures.

67. It has been estimated that the 2017 Tax Cuts and Jobs Act (Pub. Law 115–97) will increase the projected deficit by $1.854 trillion for the 2018–28 period. Congressional Budget Office (2018), 129, app. table B-3. Conversely, if expenditures to raise children out of poverty remained constant over the next ten years, it would cost $655 billion to keep children out of poverty in the next decade, significantly less than half the cost of the 2017 tax act.

68. West (2017).

69. Eurofound (2016), 35.

70. Ibid., 49.

71. S.B. 828, Sess. of 2017 (Or. 2017), Section 5a. There appears to be a growing momentum for such laws. Several cities and municipalities have recently passed similar predictive scheduling ordinances. See Article 33G § 3300G.4(b) (San Francisco 2014); Emeryville Municipal Code § 5-39.03(d) (City of Emeryville 2017); New York City Administrative Code § 20-1221 (New York City 2017); Seattle Municipal Code § 14.22.040 (City of Seattle 2017). In addition, as this book went to press, Philadelphia and Chicago passed fair scheduling laws. See Spielman (2019); Fair Workweek Initiative (2019).

72. New York City Administrative Code § 20-1231 (New York City 2017) (requiring eleven-hour rest period); Seattle Municipal Code § 14.22.035 (City of Seattle 2017) (requiring ten-hour rest period).

73. Hegewisch (2009), 6; Hegewisch and Gornick (2008), 18; Fair Work Ombudsman (2018).

74. These reasons include the burden of additional costs, an inability to reorganize work among existing staff members or to recruit additional staffers, a detrimental impact on quality/performance/ability to meet customer demand, insufficient work for the periods the employee proposes to work, or a planned structural change to the business. See Acas (2014), 6.

75. Waldfogel (2006), 68.

76. Department for Business, Innovation, and Skills (2014), tables 27, 31. This report also found that 60 percent of requests to shift to part-time work were granted (see table 23), while 79 percent of flexible work requests overall (including reduced hours and part-time work) were approved by employers. Ibid., 44.

77. Bird and Brown (2018), 74.

78. GOV.UK (2018).

79. Vermont General Assembly (2014), 21.005.001 § 309(f). For similar statutes, see New Hampshire State Legislature (2016), § 13.275:37-b; San Francisco Administrative Code, Section 12Z.4 (2013).

80. Telework Enhancement Act (2010), Section 6502.

81. H.R. 2942: Schedules That Work Act (2017), Section 3. This bill was referred to several House Committees in June 2017. As of the time of this writing, no further action had been taken.

82. Raub et al. (2018), 2–4.

Chapter 11

1. Cole (2016), 1.

2. Newport (2017). The Pew Research Center put that number even higher in 2017, at 60 percent. Kiley (2017).

3. Horowitz et al. (2017), 19 (82 percent).

4. Ibid., 9.

5. OECD (2019b). Regarding weak demand for Finnish paper products, see Economic Commission for Europe, Timber Committee (2016), 4.

6. Wilkinson and Pickett [2009] (2010), 226.

7. Saez and Zucman (2019).

8. Kenworthy (2014), ch. 6.

9. Blau and Kahn (2013).
10. See Arndt and Hörisch (2015), 8–9.
11. OECD (2019e), 6, fig. 4.
12. A comparison of private social expenditures among OECD countries shows that the United States spends the most by far, at almost 11 percent of GDP. No other OECD country spends above 8 percent of GDP in private social expenditures, and the OECD average is 2.7 percent. OECD (2016j), 6 (2013 figures).
13. In 2016, the United States ranked twenty-fourth of all OECD countries in gross public social expenditures. OECD (2016j), 1.
14. OECD (2019e), 6 (2015 figures, the last date for which data was available).
15. Esping-Andersen (2009).
16. See National Transfer Accounts (2016). See also Isaacs (2009).
17. Fishback (2010) compares net social spending, distribution of benefits, and outcomes between the United States and Nordic countries. See also Esping-Andersen (1990), 85–6.
18. Based on data from the OECD family database. OECD (2017k), 2.
19. Ibid., 2.
20. A home visitation program resembling the Health Access Nurturing Development Services (HANDS) program (beginning home visitations from trained visitors in the first trimester of pregnancy, continuing to the child's second birthday, with frequency and intensity of visits varying with the needs of each family) would cost approximately $2,500 per family per year and $6,875 per family for the duration of the program. See Home Visiting Evidence of Effectiveness (2015a, 2015b). It would cost approximately $26.5 billion to provide services to all new mothers of a given calendar year, derived from the 2017 birthrate of 3,853,472. Hamilton et al. (2018), 7. Deducting the annual amount currently earmarked by the federal government for nurse visitation programs ($400 million), the cost of this program would require an additional 0.127 percent of GDP to fund, based on the 2018 GDP of $20.494 trillion. See Bipartisan Budget Act of 2018, Section 50601; OECD (2018i). Adding in the estimated cost of a modest paid family leave program that would enable parents to take time off to care for sick family members ($1.4 billion), this funding figure would increase by less than 0.01 percent of GDP (estimating weekly wage replacements of 66 percent up to a cap of $1,000 for approximately four weeks per year). Hayes and Hartmann (2018), 2, table 1.
21. Denmark spends 3.22 percent of GDP total on its unemployment and job retraining system. This is much more than US spending (0.3 percent overall). OECD (2018m) (2016 figures).
22. OECD (2018n) (2017 figures).
23. Based on figures from the Department of Agriculture, for those families with children between ages zero and five who had childcare and early childhood education expenses, families in the lowest third of income groups spend $2,080 per year, families in the middle spend $2,870, and families at the top spend $5,170. Lino et al. (2017), 24. Assuming that America's 24 million children are equally distributed among income groups, private spending by parents on ECEC amounts to approximately 0.48 percent of GDP, based on the 2016 GDP of $18.62 trillion.
24. Cumulatively from ages zero to seventeen. Ibid.
25. Esping-Andersen (2009), 95.
26. Council of Economic Advisers (2014), 30.
27. García et al. (2016), 54.
28. Friedman [2002] (1962), 15.
29. Smith [1902] (1776), 107. See also Anderson (2017), 35–6, 18.
30. Anderson (2017), 4. See Smith [1902] (1776); Dorfman (1940); Appleby (1984), 49–50.
31. See Anderson (2017).
32. Kantor and Streitfeld (2015), quoting Bo Olson.
33. Anderson (2017).
34. Himmelweit (1995), 11; Sellers (1991).
35. Schor (1992, 1998).

REFERENCES

Aaron, Lauren and Dallaire, Danielle H. 2010. "Parental Incarceration and Multiple Risk Experiences: Effects on Family Dynamics and Children's Delinquency." *Journal of Youth and Adolescence* 39(12): 1471–84.

Abbott, John J. C. 1972. *The Mother at Home; or, the Principles of Maternal Duty Familiarly Illustrated*. New York: Arno Press.

Abel, Jason R., Deitz, Richard, and Su, Yaqin. 2014. "Are Recent College Graduates Finding Good Jobs?" *Current Issues in Economics and Finance* 20(1). https://www.newyorkfed.org/medialibrary/media/research/current_issues/ci20-1.pdf

Acas. 2014. *Code of Practice 5: Handling in a Reasonable Manner Requests to Work Flexibly*. http://www.acas.org.uk/media/pdf/f/e/Code-of-Practice-on-handling-in-a-reasonable-manner-requests-to-work-flexibly.pdf.

Adams, Henry Carter. 1887. "Relation of the State to Industrial Action." *Publications of the American Economic Association* 1(6): 471–549.

Adema, Willem, Clarke, Chris, Frey, Valerie, Greulich, Angela, Kim, Hyunsook, Rattenhuber, Pia and Thévenon, Olivier. 2017. "Work/life balance policy in Germany: Promoting equal partnership in families." *International Social Security Review* 70(2): 31–55.

Adkins, Amy. 2015. "Majority of U.S. Employees Not Engaged Despite Gains in 2014." *Gallup Poll*. http://www.gallup.com/poll/181289/majority-employees-not-engaged-despite-gains-2014.aspx.

Adkins, Daniel, Wang, Victor, Dupre, Matthew E., van den Oord, Edwin J. C. G., and Elder, Glenn H. 2009. "Structure and Stress: Trajectories of Depressive Symptoms Across Adolescence and Young Adulthood." *Social Forces* 88(1): 31–60.

Ahrnsbrak, Rebecca, Bose, Jonaki, Hedden, Sarra L., Lipari, Rachel N., and Park-Lee, Eunice. 2017. *Key Substance Use and Mental Health Indicators in the United States: Results from the 2016 National Survey on Drug Use and Health*. HHS Publication No. SMA 17-5044. US Department of Health and Human Services, Substance Abuse and Mental Health Services Administration. https://store.samhsa.gov/system/files/sma17-5044.pdf.

Aisch, Gregor, Buchanan, Larry, Cox, Amanda, and Quealy, Kevin. 2017. "Some Colleges Have More Students from the Top 1 Percent than the Bottom 60." *New York Times*, January 18. https://www.nytimes.com/interactive/2017/01/18/upshot/some-colleges-have-more-students-from-the-top-1-percent-than-the-bottom-60.html?_r=0.

Akee, Randall K. Q., Copeland, William E., Keeler, Gordon, Angold, Adrian, and Costello, E. Jane. 2010. "Parents' Incomes and Children's Outcomes: A Quasi-Experiment Using Transfer Payments from Casino Profit." *American Economic Journal: Applied Economics* 2(1): 86–115.

Alesina, Alberto, Glaeser, Edward L., and Sacerdote, Bruce. 2001. "Why Doesn't the United States Have a European-Style Welfare State?" *Brookings Papers on Economic Activity* 2: 187–277.

Allington, Richard, McGill-Franzen, Anne, Camilli, Gregory, Williams, Lunetta, Graf, Jennifer, Zeig, Jacqueline, Zmach, Courtney, and Nowak, Rhonda. 2010. "Addressing Summer Reading Setback among Economically Disadvantaged Elementary Students." *Reading Psychology* 31(5): 411–27.

Alltucker, Ken. 2018. "Voters Expand Medicaid in Red States: Gridlock in Congress Likely to Protect Obamacare." *USA Today*, November 7. https://www.usatoday.com/story/news/politics/elections/2018/11/07/health-care-politics-medicaid-expansion-affordable-care-act-obamacare/1916657002/.

Almqvist, Anna-Lena and Duvander, Ann-Zofie. 2014. "Changes in Gender Equality? Swedish Fathers' Parental Leave, Division of childcare and Housework." *Journal of Family Studies* 20(1): 19–27.

Alvaredo, Facundo, Chancel, Lucas, Piketty, Thomas, Saez, Emmanuel, and Zucman, Gabriel. 2018. *World Inequality Report 2018.* World Inequality Lab. https://wir2018.wid.world/files/download/wir2018-full-report-english.pdf.

Amato, Paul, Booth, Alan, Johnson, David, and Rogers, Stacy. 2007. *Alone Together: How Marriage in America Is Changing.* Cambridge, MA: Harvard University Press.

Amato, Paul and Gilbreth, Joan G. 1999. "Nonresident Fathers and Children's Well-Being: A Meta-Analysis." *Journal of Marriage and Family* 61(3): 557–73.

Amendment of 1986 Code, H.R. 1. 2017. https://www.congress.gov/115/bills/hr1/BILLS-115hr1enr.pdf.

American College Health Association. 2012. *National College Health Assessment: Reference Group Executive Summary, Fall 2011.* https://www.acha.org/documents/ncha/ACHA-NCHA-II_ReferenceGroup_ExecutiveSummary_Fall2011.pdf.

American College Health Association. 2016. *National College Health Assessment: Spring 2016 Reference Group Executive Summary.* https://www.acha.org/documents/ncha/NCHA-II%20SPRING%202016%20US%20REFERENCE%20GROUP%20EXECUTIVE%20SUMMARY.pdf.

American Psychological Association. 2011. "Stressed in America." *Monitor on Psychology* 42(1). http://www.apa.org/monitor/2011/01/stressed-america.aspx.

American Psychological Association. 2019. *What Is Postpartum Depression and Anxiety?* https://www.apa.org/pi/women/resources/reports/postpartum-depression-brochure-2007.pdf.

Anda, Robert F., Felitti, Vincent J., Bremner, Douglas, Walker, John D., Whitfield, Charles, Perry, Bruce D., Dube, Shanta R., and Giles, Wayne H. 2006. "The Enduring Effects of Abuse and Related Adverse Experiences in Childhood: A Convergence of Evidence from Neurobiology And Epidemiology." *European Archives of Psychiatry and Clinical Neuroscience* 256(3): 174–86.

Anderson, Elizabeth. 2017. *Private Government: How Employers Rule Our Lives (and Why We Don't Talk about It).* Princeton, NJ: Princeton University Press.

Andersson, Gunnar. 2002. "Children's Experience of Family Disruption and Family Formation: Evidence from 16 FFS Countries." *Demographic Research* 7(7): 343–64.

Andersson, Gunnar and Philipov, Dimiter. 2002. "Life-Table Representations of Family Dynamics in Sweden, Hungary, and 14 Other FFS Countries: A Project of Descriptions of Demographic Behavior." *Demographic Research* 7(4): 67–144.

Andresen, Sabine. 2016. "Germany." In *Children's Views on Their Lives and Well-Being in 17 Countries: Key Messages from Each Country.* Children's Worlds, International Survey of Children's Well-Being (ISCWeB). http://isciweb.org/_Uploads/dbsAttachedFiles/KeyMessagesfromeachcountry_final.pdf.

Angold, Adrian, Erkanli, Alaattin, Farmer, Elizabeth M. Z., Fairbank, John A., Burns, Barbara J., Keeler, Gordon, and Costello, Jane. 2002. "Psychiatric Disorder, Impairment, and Service Use in Rural African American and White Youth." *Archives of General Psychiatry* 59(10): 893–901.

Aon. 2014. "Aon Hewitt Analysis Shows Upward Trend in U.S. Health Care Cost Increases." *Investor News*, November 13. https://ir.aon.com/about-aon/investor-relations/investor-news/

news-release-details/2014/Aon-Hewitt-Analysis-Shows-Upward-Trend-in-US-Health-Care-Cost-Increases/default.aspx.

Appleby, Joyce. 1984. *Capitalism and a New Social Order: The Republican Vision of the 1790s.* New York: New York University Press.

Arnalds, Ásdís A., Eydal, Guðný Björk, and Gíslason, Ingólfur V. 2013. "Equal Rights to Paid Parental Leave and Caring Fathers: The Case of Iceland." *Icelandic Review of Politics and Administration* 9(2): 323–44.

Arnarson, Bjorn Thor and Mitra, Aparna. 2010. "The Paternity Leave Act in Iceland: Implications for Gender Equality in the Labour Market." *Applied Economics Letters* 17(7): 677–80.

Arndt, Christoph and Hörisch, Felix. 2015. "Flexicurity Policies in Europe—Diffusion and Effects of Flexicurity Labour Market Policies." *Cupress Working Paper Series.* Working Paper No. 02. http://cupesse.eu/fileadmin/cupesse/downloads/working-papers/CUPESSE_Working-Paper_2.pdf.

Astin, Alexander W., Green, Kenneth C., Korn, William S., and Schalit, Marilynn. 1985. *The American Freshman: National Norms for Fall 1985.* University of California at Los Angeles, American Council on Education. https://www.heri.ucla.edu/PDFs/pubs/TFS/Norms/Monographs/TheAmericanFreshman1985.pdf.

Astin, Alexander W., Parrott, Sarah A., Korn, William S., and Sax, Linda J. 1997. *The American Freshman: Thirty Year Trends, 1966–1996.* Cooperative Institutional Research Institute. https://www.heri.ucla.edu/PDFs/pubs/TFS/Trends/Monographs/The American Freshman30YearTrends.pdf.

Astone, Nan Marie and McLanahan, Sara. 1991. "Family Structure, Parental Practices and High School Completion." *American Sociological Review* 56(3): 309–20.

Atkinson Centre for Society and Child Development. 2017. *Early Childhood Education Report 2017.* http://ecereport.ca/media/uploads/2017-report-pdfs/ece-report2017-en-feb6.pdf.

Attanasio, Orazio and Weber, Guglielmo. 2010. "Consumption and Saving: Models of Intertemporal Allocation and Their Implications for Public Policy." *Journal of Economic Literature* 48(3): 693–751.

Aurand, Andrew, Emmanuel, Dan, Yentel, Diane, Errico, Ellen, Chapin, Zoe, Leong, Gar Meng, and Rodrigues, Kate. 2016. "The Long Wait for a Home." *Housing Spotlight* 6(1). https://nlihc.org/sites/default/files/HousingSpotlight_6-1.pdf

Autor, David. 2015. "Why Are There Still So Many Jobs? The History and Future of Workplace Automation." *Journal of Economic Perspectives* 29(3): 3–30.

Autor, David and Dorn, David. 2013. "The Growth of Low Skill Service Jobs and the Polarization of the U.S. Labor Market." *American Economic Review* 103(5): 1553–97.

Autor, David and Wasserman, Melanie. 2013. *Wayward Sons: The Emerging Gender Gap in Labor Markets and Education.* Third Way. https://thirdway.imgix.net/downloads/wayward-sons-the-emerging-gender-gap-in-labor-markets-and-education/Third_Way_Report_-_NEXT_Wayward_Sons-The_Emerging_Gender_Gap_in_Labor_Markets_and_Education.pdf.

Autor, David, Dorn, David, and Hanson, Gordon. 2017. "When Work Disappears: Manufacturing Decline and the Falling Marriage-Market Value of Men." *National Bureau of Economic Research Working Paper Series.* Working Paper No. 23173. http://www.nber.org/papers/w23173.

Autor, David, Karbownik, Krzysztof, Roth, Jeffrey, and Wasserman, Melanie. 2016. "Family Disadvantage and the Gender Gap in Behavioral and Educational Outcomes." *National Bureau of Economic Research Working Paper Series.* Working Paper No. 22267. http://www.nber.org.libproxy.lib.unc.edu/papers/w22267.

Autor, David, Katz, Lawrence, and Kearney, Melissa. 2008. "Trends in U.S. Wage Inequality: Revisiting the Revisionists." *Review of Economics and Statistics* 90(2): 300–23.

Azerrad, David and Hederman, Rea. 2012. *Defending the Dream: Why Income Inequality Doesn't Threaten Opportunity.* Heritage Foundation, B. Kenneth Simon Center for Principles and Politics. Special Report No. 119. http://thf_media.s3.amazonaws.com/2012/pdf/SR119.pdf.

Bach, Wendy. 2013. "The Hyperregulatory State: Women, Race, Poverty, and Support." *Yale Journal of Law and Feminism* 25(2–3): 318–80.

Bailey, Sarah. 2013. *The Impact of Cash Transfers on Food Consumption in Humanitarian Settings: A Review of Evidence*. https://reliefweb.int/sites/reliefweb.int/files/resources/cfgb---impact-of-cash-transfers-on-food-consumption-may-2013-final-clean.pdf.

Baker, Michael, Gruber, Jonathan, and Milligan, Kevin. Forthcoming. "The Long-Run Impacts of a Universal Child Care Program." *American Economic Journal: Economic Policy*. http://faculty.arts.ubc.ca/kmilligan/research/papers/BGM-Final.pdf.

Bane, Mary Jo and Ellwood, David T. 1986. "Slipping into and out of Poverty: The Dynamics of Spells." *Journal of Human Resources* 21(1): 1–23.

Bane, Mary Jo and Ellwood, David T. 1994. *Welfare Realities: From Rhetoric to Reform*. Cambridge, MA: Harvard University Press.

Banerjee, Abhijit V., Hanna, Rema, Kreindler, Gabriel E., and Olken, Benjamin A. 2017. "Debunking the Stereotype of the Lazy Welfare Recipient: Evidence from Cash Transfer Programs." *World Bank Research Observer* 32(2): 155–84.

Barnett, Steven. 1995. "Long-Term Effects of Early Childhood Programs on Cognitive and School Outcomes." *Future of Children* 5(3): 25–50.

Barnett, Steven. 2011. "Effectiveness of Early Educational Intervention." *Science* 333(6045): 975–8.

Barnett, Steven W. and Friedman-Krauss, Allison H. 2016. *State(s) of Head Start*. Rutgers University, National Institute for Early Education Research. http://nieer.org/wp-content/uploads/2016/12/HS_Full_Reduced.pdf.

Barnett, Steven, Friedman-Krauss, Allison, Weisenfeld, G. G., Horowitz, Michele, Yasmin, Richard, and Squires, James. 2017. *The State of Pre-School, 2016*. Rutgers University, National Institute for Early Education Research. http://nieer.org/wp-content/uploads/2017/05/YB2016_StateofPreschool2.pdf.

Bartel, Ann, Baum, Charles, Rossin-Slater, Maya, Ruhm, Christopher, and Waldfogel, Jane. 2014. *California's Paid Family Leave Law: Lessons from the First Decade*. https://www.dol.gov/wb/resources/california_paid_family_leave_law.pdf.

Bassok, Daphna, Finch, Jenna, Lee, RaeHyuck, Reardon, Sean, and Waldfogel, Jane. 2016. "Socioeconomic Gaps in Early Childhood Experiences: 1998 to 2010." *AERA Open* 2(3):1–22.

Bassok, Daphna, Fitzpatrick, Maria, Greenberg, Maria, and Loeb, Susanna. 2016. "Within- and Between-Sector Quality Differences in Early Childhood Education and Care." *Child Development* 87(5): 1627–45.

Baum, Charles L. 2003. "Does Early Maternal Employment Harm Child Development? An Analysis of the Potential Benefits of Leave Taking." *Journal of Labor Economics* 21(2): 409–48.

Baum, Charles L. and Ruhm, Christopher J. 2016. "The Effects of Paid Family Leave in California on Labor Market Outcomes." *Journal of Policy Analysis and Management* 35(2): 333–56.

Baydar, Nazli and Brooks-Gunn, Jeanne. 1991. "Effects of Maternal Employment and Child-Care Arrangements on Preschoolers' Cognitive and Behavioral Outcomes: Evidence from Children on the National Longitudinal Survey of Youth." *Developmental Psychology* 27(6): 932–45.

Bayer, Jordana K., Hiscock, Harriet, Ukoumunne, Obioha C., Price, Anna, and Wake, Melissa. 2008. "Early Childhood Aetiology of Mental Health Problems: A Longitudinal Population-Based Study." *Journal of Child Psychology and Psychiatry* 49(11): 1166–74.

Beaubien, Jason. 2018. "The Country with the World's Worst Inequality Is . . ." *NPR*, April 2. https://www.npr.org/sections/goatsandsoda/2018/04/02/598864666/the-country-with-the-worlds-worst-inequality-is.

Bechteler, Stephanie Schmitz and Kane-Willis, Kathleen. 2017. *Whitewashed: The African American Opioid Epidemic*. Chicago Urban League. https://www.thechicagourbanleague.org/cms/lib/IL07000264/Centricity/Domain/1/Whitewashed%20AA%20Opioid%20Crisis%2011-15-17_EMBARGOED_%20FINAL.pdf.

Beck, Ulrich. 2000. *The Brave New World of Work*. Cambridge: Polity Press.

Bekker, Sonja, Wilthagen, Ton, Madsen, Per Kongshøj, Zhou, Jianping, Rogowski, Ralf, Keune, Maarten, and Tangian, Andranik. 2008. "Flexicurity: A European Approach to Labour Market Policy." *Intereconomics* 43(2): 68–111.

Bell, Linda and Freeman, Richard. 2001. "The Incentive for Working Hard: Explaining Hours Worked Differences in the US and Germany." *Labour Economics* 8(2): 181–202.

Belsky, Jay and Eggebeen, David. 1991. "Early and Extensive Maternal Employment and Young Children's Socioemotional Development: Children of the National Longitudinal Survey of Youth." *Journal of Marriage and Family* 53(4): 1083–98.

Belsky, Jay and Fearon, R. M. Pasco. 2002. "Early Attachment Security, Subsequent Maternal Sensitivity, and Later Child Development: Does Continuity in Development Depend upon Continuity of Caregiving?" *Attachment and Human Development* 3: 361–87.

Belsky, Jay, Vandell, Deborah, Burchinal, Margaret, Clarke-Stewart, K. Alison, McCartney, Kathleen, Owen, Margaret, and the NICHD Early Child Care Research Network. 2007. "Are There Long-Term Effects of Early Child Care?" *Child Development* 78(2): 681–701.

Benefits.Gov. 2018. *Head Start and Early Head Start.* US Department of Health and Human Services. https://www.benefits.gov/benefits/benefit-details/616.

Bengtson, Vern. 2001. "Beyond the Nuclear Family: The Increasing Importance of Multigenerational Bonds." *Journal of Marriage and Family* 63(1): 1–16.

Ben-Zur, Hasida. 2003. "Happy Adolescents: The Link Between Subjective Well-Being, Internal Resources, and Parental Factors." *Journal of Youth and Adolescence* 32(2): 67–79.

Benz, Marisa and Sidor, Anna. 2013. "Early intervention in Germany and in the USA: A comparison of supporting health services. An overview article." *Mental Health and Prevention* 1: 44-50.

Berger, Lawrence, Hill, Jennifer, and Waldfogel, Jane. 2005. "Maternity Leave, Early Maternal Employment and Child Health and Development in the US." *Economic Journal* 115(501): F29–F47.

Berger, Lawrence M. and Waldfogel, Jane. 2011. "Economic Determinants and Consequences of Child Maltreatment." *OECD Social, Employment and Migration Working Papers.* Working Paper No. 111. http://dx.doi.org/10.1787/5kgf09zj7h9t-en.

Bernal, Raquel and Keane, Michael. 2011. "Child Care Choices and Children's Cognitive Achievement: The Case of Single Mothers." *Labor of Economics* 29(3): 459–512.

Bernstein, Lenny. 2018. "U.S. Life Expectancy Declines Again, A Dismal Trend Not Seen Since World War I." *Washington Post,* November 29. https://www.washingtonpost.com/national/health-science/us-life-expectancy-declines-again-a-dismal-trend-not-seen-since-world-war-i/2018/11/28/ae58bc8c-f28c-11e8-bc79-68604ed88993_story.html?utm_term=.7d7c16abcbc6.

Bertrand, Marianne and Mullainathan, Sendhil. 2004. "Are Emily and Greg More Employable than Lakisha and Jamal? A Field Experiment on Labor Market Discrimination." *American Economic Review* 94(4): 991–1013.

Bhattarai, Abha. 2017. "It's More Expensive than Ever to Raise a Child in the U.S." *Washington Post,* January 10. https://www.washingtonpost.com/news/business/wp/2017/01/10/its-more-expensive-than-ever-to-raise-a-child-in-the-u-s/?utm_term=.eee2b117df10.

Bianchi, Suzanne. 2011. "Family Change and Time Allocation in American Families." *Annals of the American Academy of Political and Social Science* 638(1): 21–44.

Bianchi, Suzanne, Robinson, John, and Milkie, Melissa. 2006. *Changing Rhythms of American Family Life.* New York: Russell Sage Foundation.

Bianchi, Suzanne and Wight, Vanessa. 2010. "The Long Reach of the Job: Employment and Time for Family Life." In Kathleen Christensen and Barbara Schneider (eds.), *Workplace Flexibility: Realigning 20th-Century Jobs for a 21st-Century Workforce.* Ithaca, NY: Cornell University Press.

Bickel, Warren K., Johnson, Matthew W., Koffarnus, Mikhail N., MacKillop, James, and Murphy, James G. "The Behavioral Economics of Substance Use Disorders: Reinforcement Pathologies and Their Repair." *Annual Review of Clinical Psychology* 10: 641–77.

Bird, Robert C. and Brown, Liz. 2018. "The United Kingdom Right to Request as a Model for Flexible Work in the European Union." *American Business Law Journal* 55(1): 53–115.

Bitler, Marianne, Gelbach, Jonah, and Hoynes, Hillary. 2006. "What Mean Impacts Miss: Distributional Effects of Welfare Reform Experiments." *American Economic Review* 96(4): 988–1012.

Bitsko, Rebecca H., Holbrook, Joseph R., Ghandour, Reem M., Blumberg, Stephen J., Visser, Susanna N., Perou, Ruth, and Walkup, John T. 2018. "Epidemiology and Impact of Health Care Provider-Diagnosed Anxiety and Depression among US Children." *Journal of Developmental and Behavioral Pediatrics* 39(5): 395–403.

Bitsko, Rebecca H., Holbrook, Joseph R., Robinson, Lara R., Kaminski, Jennifer W., Ghandour, Reem, Smith, Camille, and Peacock, Georgina. 2016. "Health Care, Family, and Community Factors Associated with Mental, Behavioral, and Developmental Disorders in Early Childhood: United States, 2011–2012." *Morbidity and Morality Weekly Report* 65(9): 221–6. https://www.cdc.gov/mmwr/volumes/65/wr/mm6509a1.htm?s_cid=mm6509a1_w.

Bivens, Josh. 2018. *The Unfinished Business of Health Reform*. Economic Policy Institute. https://www.epi.org/files/pdf/152676.pdf.

Bivens, Josh, Engdahl, Lora, Gould, Eliza, Kroeger, Teresa, McNicholas, Celine, Mishel, Lawrence, Mokhiber, Zane, Shierholz, Heidi, Wilpert, Marni von, Zipperer, Ben, and Wilson, Valerie. 2017. *How Today's Unions Help Working People: Giving Workers the Power to Improve Their Jobs and Unrig the Economy*. Economic Policy Institute. https://www.epi.org/files/pdf/133275.pdf.

Blau, Francine and Grossberg, Adam. 1992. "Maternal Labor Supply and Children's Cognitive Development." *Review of Economics and Statistics* 74(3): 474–81.

Blau, Francine D. and Kahn, Lawrence M. 2013. "Female Labor Supply: Why Is the US Falling Behind?" *National Bureau of Economic Research Working Paper Series*. Working Paper No. 18703. https://www.nber.org/papers/w18702.pdf.

Blewett, Mary. 1983. "Work, Gender and the Artisan Tradition in New England Shoemaking, 1780–1860." *Journal of Social History* 17(2): 221–48.

Block Grants to States for Temporary Assistance for Needy Families, 42 U.S.C. §§ 601–619 (1996).

Blofield, Merike and Filgueira, Fernando. Forthcoming. *Fathers, Families, and the State in the Western World: Social Transformation and Political Responses*.

Blofield, Merike, Joseph, Suad, Deere, Carmen Diana, Eichner, Maxine, Eydal, Guðný Björk, Filgueira, Fernando, Parrenas, Rhacel, Pillai, Neetha, Rosenbluth, Frances, Rostgaard, Tine, et al. 2018. "The Pluralization of Families." In International Panel on Social Progress, *Rethinking Society for the 21st Century: Report of the International Panel on Social Progress*, vol. 3. Cambridge: Cambridge University Press. https://comment.ipsp.org/chapter/chapter-17-pluralization-families#_ftn1.

BlueCross BlueShield. 2018. *Major Depression: The Impact on Overall Health*. https://www.bcbs.com/sites/default/files/file-attachments/health-of-america-report/HoA_Major_Depression_Report.pdf.

Blumin, Stuart M. 1989. *The Emergence of the Middle Class: Social Experience in the American City, 1760–1900*. Cambridge: Cambridge University Press.

Board of Governors of the Federal Reserve System. 2016. *Report on the Economic Well-Being of U.S. Households in 2015*. Federal Reserve Board, Division of Consumer and Community Affairs. https://www.federalreserve.gov/2015-report-economic-well-being-us-households-201605.pdf.

Board of Governors of the Federal Reserve System. 2018. *Report on the Economic Well-Being of U.S. Households in 2017*. Federal Reserve Board, Division of Consumer and Community Affairs. https://www.federalreserve.gov/publications/files/2017-report-economic-well-being-us-households-201805.pdf.

Boddy, Jessica. 2017. "The Forces Driving Middle Aged White People's 'Deaths of Despair.'" *NPR*, March 23. https://www.npr.org/sections/health-shots/2017/03/23/521083335/the-forces-driving-middle-aged-white-peoples-deaths-of-despair.

Bollinger, Christopher, Gonzalez, Luis, and Ziliak, James P. 2009. "Welfare Reform and the Level and Composition of Income." In James P. Ziliak (ed.), *Welfare Reform and Its Long-Term Consequences for America's Poor*. New York: Cambridge University Press.

Boltanski, Luc and Chiapello, Eve. 2005. "The New Spirit of Capitalism." *International Journal of Politics, Culture, and Society* 18(3–4): 161–88.

Bono, Del Emilia, Francesconi, Marco, Kelly, Yvonne, and Sacker, Amanda. 2016. "Early Maternal Time Investment and Early Child Outcomes." *Economic Journal* 126(596): F96–F135.

Bos, Johannes M., Phillips-Fain, Gabriele, Rein, Elena, Weinberg, Emily, and Chavez, Suzette. 2016. *Connecting All Children to High-Quality Early Care and Education: Promising Strategies from the International Community*. American Institutes for Research. https://www.air.org/system/files/downloads/report/High-Quality-Early-Care-and-Education-International-October-2016.pdf.

Bossy, Steve. 2000. "Academic Pressure and Impact on Japanese Students." *McGill Journal of Education* 35(1): 71–89.

Boswell, Wendy, Olson-Buchanan, Julie, and Harris, Brad. 2013. "I Cannot Afford to Have a Life: Employee Adaptation to Feelings of Job Insecurity." *Personnel Psychology* 67(4): 887–915.

Boushey, Heather. 2016. *Finding Time: The Economics of Work–Life Conflict*. Cambridge, MA: Harvard University Press.

Bowlby, John. 1951. *Maternal Care and Mental Health*. Geneva: World Health Organization.

Bowles, Samuel and Park, Yongjin. 2005. "Emulation, Inequality, and Work Hours: Was Thorsten Veblen Right?" *Economic Journal* 115(507): F397–F412.

Boydston, Jeanne. 1990. *Home and Work: Housework, Wages, and the Ideology of Labor in the Early Republic*. New York: Oxford University Press.

Bradley, Robert H., Corwyn, Robert F., McAdoo, Harriette Pipes, and Coll, Cynthia García. 2001. "The Home Environments of Children in the United States, Part I: Variations by Age, Ethnicity, and Poverty Status." *Child Development* 72(6): 1844–67.

Bramlett, Matthew D. and Mosher, William D. 2002. "Cohabitation, Marriage, Divorce, and Remarriage in the United States." *Vital and Health Statistics* 23(22): 1–23. https://www.cdc.gov/nchs/data/series/sr_23/sr23_022.pdf.

Bricker, Jesse, Dettling, Lisa J., Henriques, Alice, Hsu, Joanne W., Jacobs, Lindsay, Moore, Kevin B., Pack, Sarah, Sabelhaus, John, Thompson, Jeffrey, and Windle, Richard A. 2017. "Changes in U.S. Family Finances from 2013 to 2016: Evidence from the Survey of Consumer Finances." *Federal Reserve Bulletin* 103(3). https://www.federalreserve.gov/publications/files/scf17.pdf.

Brooks, Rosa. 2014. "Recline! Why 'Leaning in' Is Killing Us." *Foreign Policy*, February 21. https://foreignpolicy.com/2014/02/21/recline/.

Brooks-Gunn, Jeanne, Han, Wen-Jui, and Waldfogel, Jane. 2002. "Maternal Employment and Child Cognitive Outcomes in the First Three Years of Life: The NICHD Study of Early Child Care." *Child Development* 73(4): 1052–72.

Brooks-Gunn, Jeanne, Han, Wen-Jui, and Waldfogel, Jane. 2010. *First-Year Maternal Employment and Child Development in the First 7 Years*. Boston: Wiley-Blackwell.

Brown, George W. and Harris, Terril. 1978. *Social Origins of Depression: A Study of Psychiatric Disorder in Women*. New York: Routledge.

Brown, Monique J., Thacker, Leroy R., and Cohen, Steven A. 2013. "Association Between Adverse Childhood Experiences and Diagnosis of Cancer." *PLoS One* 8(6).

Brown, Susan. 2011. "Marriage and Child Well-Being: Research and Policy Perspectives." *Journal of Marriage and Family* 72(5): 1059–77.

Brownlee, Elliot. 2000. "Historical Perspectives on U.S. Tax Policy Toward the Rich." In Joel B. Slemrod (ed.), *Does Atlas Shrug? The Economic Consequences of Taxing the Rich*. Cambridge, MA: Harvard University Press.

Brownlee, Elliot. 2016. *Federal Taxation in America: A History*. 3rd ed. New York: Cambridge University Press.

Bruni, Frank. 2015. "Today's Exhausted Superkids." *New York Times*, July 29. https://www.nytimes.com/2015/07/29/opinion/frank-bruni-todays-exhausted-superkids.html.

Bui, Quoctrung and Miller, Claire Cain. 2018. "The Age That Women Have Babies: How a Gap Divides America." *New York Times*, August 4. https://www.nytimes.com/interactive/2018/08/04/upshot/up-birth-age-gap.html.

Burroughs, Charles. 1827. *An Address on Female Education, Delivered in Portsmouth, New-Hampshire, October 26, 1827*. Portsmouth, NH: Childs and March.

Bush, George H. W. 1990. "Message to the House of Representatives Returning Without Approval the Family and Medical Leave Act of 1990, June 29, 1990." In *Public Papers of the Presidents of the United States: George Bush, 1990, Book 1*. Washington, DC: Government Publishing Office.

Butler, Vikki. 2005. *Research Report of Phase One of the Generation 2020 Project*. Barnardo's Cymru. http://www.barnardos.org.uk/report_phase_one_generation2020_project.pdf.

Cabrera, N. J., Shannon, J. D., and Tamis-LeMonda, C. 2007. "Fathers' Influence on Their Children's Cognitive and Emotional Development: From Toddlers to Pre-Kindergarten." *Applied Developmental Science* 11(4): 208–13.

Cain, Glen. 1985. "Comments on Murray's Analysis of the Impact of the War on Poverty on the Labor Market Behavior of the Poor." In *Losing Ground: A Critique*. Special Report No. 38. Institute for Research on Poverty. https://www.irp.wisc.edu/publications/sr/pdfs/sr38.pdf.

Cain Miller, Claire, and Tedeschi, Ernie. 2019. "Single Mothers Are Surging into the Workforce." *New York Times*, May 29. https://www.nytimes.com/2019/05/29/upshot/single-mothers-surge-employment.html

Cajner, Tomaz, Radler, Tyler, Ratner, David, and Vidangos, Ivan. 2017. "Racial Gaps in Labor Market Outcomes in the Last Four Decades and over the Business Cycle." *Finance and Economics Discussion Series*. Series Paper No. 2017-071. https://www.federalreserve.gov/econres/feds/files/2017071pap.pdf.

Calarco, Jessica McCrory. 2018. *Negotiating Opportunities: How the Middle Class Secures Advantages in School*. New York: Oxford University Press.

Campbell, Frances and Ramey, Craig. 1994. "Effects of Early Intervention on Intellectual and Academic Achievement: A Follow-Up Study of Children from Low-Income Families." *Child Development* 65(2): 684–98.

Canada. 2018a. *Canada Child Benefit—How We Calculate Your CCB*. Last modified July 4. https://www.canada.ca/en/revenue-agency/services/child-family-benefits/canada-child-benefit-overview/canada-child-benefit-we-calculate-your-ccb.html.

Canada. 2018b. *Child and Family Benefits Calculator*. Last modified November 20. Available at https://www.canada.ca/en/revenue-agency/services/child-family-benefits/child-family-benefits-calculator.html.

Canada. 2019a. *Employment Insurance Maternity and Parental Benefits*. Government of Canada. Last modified January 18. https://www.canada.ca/en/employment-social-development/programs/ei/ei-list/reports/maternity-parental.html.

Canada. 2019b. *Vacation and general holidays*. Government of Canada. Last modified February 7. Available at https://www.canada.ca/en/employment-social-development/programs/employment-standards/federal-standards/holidays.html.

Carbone, June and Cahn, Naomi. 2014. *Marriage Markets: How Inequality Is Remaking the American Family*. New York: Oxford University Press.

Carbone, June and Cahn, Naomi. Forthcoming. In Julie Novkov and Carol Nackenoff (eds.), *Stated Families, Family Stakes: The Family, the American State, and Political Development*. Lawrence: Kansas University Press.

Carey, Benedict. 2018. "How Suicide Quietly Morphed into a Public Health Crisis." *New York Times*, June 8. https://www.nytimes.com/2018/06/08/health/suicide-spade-bordain-cdc.html.

Carlson, Marcia, McLanahan, Sara, and England, Paula. 2004. "Union Formation in Fragile Families." *Demography* 41(2): 237-61.

Carlson, Marcia, and Berger, Lawrence M. 2013. "What Kids Get from Parents: Packages of Parental Involvement across Complex Family Forms." *Social Service Review* 87(2): 213-49.

Carnegie, Andrew. [1889] 2017. *The Gospel of Wealth*. New York: Carnegie Corporation. https://www.carnegie.org/media/filer_public/0a/e1/0ae166c5-fca3-4adf-82a7-74c0534cd8de/gospel_of_wealth_2017.pdf.

Carson, E. Ann. 2015. *Prisoners in 2014*. US Department of Justice, Bureau of Justice Statistics. https://www.bjs.gov/content/pub/pdf/p14.pdf.

Case, Anne and Deaton, Angus. 2015. "Rising Morbidity and Mortality in Midlife among White, Non-Hispanic Americans in the 21st Century." *PNAS* 112(49): 15078–83. http://www.pnas.org/content/112/49/15078.full.pdf.

Case, Anne and Deaton, Angus. 2017. *Mortality and Morbidity in the 21st Century*. https://www.brookings.edu/wp-content/uploads/2017/03/casedeaton_sp17_finaldraft.pdf.

Casselman, Ben. 2016. "Maybe the Gig Economy Isn't Reshaping Work After All." *New York Times*, June 7. https://www.nytimes.com/2018/06/07/business/economy/work-gig-economy.html.

Center for American Progress. 2018. *The Hidden Cost of a Failing Child Care System*. https://interactives.americanprogress.org/childcarecosts/.

Center for Collegiate Mental Health. 2017. *2016 Annual Report*. https://sites.psu.edu/ccmh/files/2017/01/2016-Annual-Report-FINAL_2016_01_09-1gc2hj6.pdf.

Center on Budget and Policy Priorities. 2016. *Chart Book: TANF at 20*. https://www.cbpp.org/sites/default/files/atoms/files/8-22-12tanf.pdf.

Center on Budget and Policy Priorities. 2017a. *Fact Sheet: Federal Rental Assistance*. https://www.cbpp.org/sites/default/files/atoms/files/4-13-11hous-US.pdf.

Center on Budget and Policy Priorities. 2017b. *Policy Basics: Federal Rental Assistance*. https://www.cbpp.org/research/housing/policy-basics-federal-rental-assistance.

Center on Budget and Policy Priorities. 2018a. *Policy Basics: How Many Weeks of Unemployment Compensation Are Available?* https://www.cbpp.org/sites/default/files/atoms/files/policybasics-uiweeks.pdf.

Center on Budget and Policy Priorities. 2018b. *Policy Basics: The Earned Income Tax Credit*. https://www.cbpp.org/sites/default/files/atoms/files/policybasics-eitc.pdf.

Center on Budget and Policy Priorities. 2018c. *Policy Basics: The Child Tax Credit*. https://www.cbpp.org/sites/default/files/atoms/files/policybasics-ctc.pdf.

Center on Budget and Policy Priorities. 2018d. *Policy Basics: An Introduction to TANF*. https://www.cbpp.org/sites/default/files/atoms/files/7-22-10tanf2.pdf.

Centers for Disease Control and Prevention. 2017. "Quickstats: Suicide Rates, for Teens Aged 15–19 Years, by Sex: United States, 1975–2015." *Morbity and Mortality Weekly Report* 66(30): 816. https://www.cdc.gov/mmwr/volumes/66/wr/mm6630a6.htm#suggestedcitation.

Centers for Disease Control and Prevention. 2018. "Suicide Rates Rising Across the U.S." *CDC Newsroom*, June 7. https://www.cdc.gov/media/releases/2018/p0607-suicide-prevention.html.

Centers for Medicare & Medicaid Services. 2018. *National Health Expenditures; Aggregate and Per Capita Amounts, Annual Percent Change and Percent Distribution: Calendar Years 1960–2017*. https://www.cms.gov/Research-Statistics-Data-and-Systems/Statistics-Trends-and-Reports/NationalHealthExpendData/NationalHealthAccountsHistorical.html.

Chan, Raymond and Joseph, Stephen. 2000. "Dimensions of Personality, Domains of Aspiration, and Subjective Well-Being." *Personality and Individual Differences* 28(2): 347–54.

Charles, Kerwin Kofi, Hurst, Erik, and Schwartz, Mariel. 2018. "The Transformation of Manufacturing and the Decline in U.S. Employment." *National Bureau of Economic Research Working Paper Series*. Working Paper No. 24468. https://www.nber.org/papers/w24468.

Chatterji, Pinka and Markowitz, Sara. 2005. "Does the Length of Maternity Leave Affect Maternal Health?" *Southern Economic Journal* 72(1): 16–41.

Chatterji, Pinka and Markowitz, Sara. 2012. "Family Leave After Childbirth and the Mental Health of New Mothers." *Journal of Mental Health Policy and Economics* 15(2): 61–76.

Chaudry, Ajay and Datta, A. Rupa. 2017. "The Current Landscape for Public Pre-Kindergarten Programs." In *The Current State of Scientific Knowledge on Pre-Kindergarten Effects*. Brookings

Institute and Duke Center for Child and Family Policy. https://www.brookings.edu/wp-content/uploads/2017/04/duke_prekstudy_final_4-4-17_hires.pdf.

Chaudry, Ajay and Wimer, Christopher. 2016. "Poverty is Not Just an Indicator: The Relationship Between Income, Poverty, and Child Well-Being." *Academic Pediatrics* 16(3S): S23–S29.

Cherlin, Andrew J. 2009. *The Marriage-Go-Round: The State of Marriage and the Family in America Today*. New York: Alfred A. Knopf.

Cherlin, Andrew J. 2014. *Labor's Love Lost: The Rise and Fall of the Working-Class Family in America*. New York: Russell Sage Foundation.

Cherlin, Andrew, Ribar, David, and Yasutake, Suzumi. 2016. "Non-Marital First Births, Marriage, and Income Inequality." *American Sociological Review* 81(4): 749–70.

Chetty, Raj. 2016. "Improving Opportunities for Economic Mobility: New Evidence and Policy Lessons." In Federal Reserve Bank of St. Louis and the Board of Governors of the Federal Reserve System (eds.), *Economic Mobility: Research & Ideas on Strengthening Families, Communities & the Economy*. https://www.stlouisfed.org/~/media/files/pdfs/community-development/econmobilitypapers/econmobility_book_508.pdf?la=en.

Chetty, Raj, Grusky, David, Hell, Maximilian, Hendren, Nathaniel, Manduca, Robert, and Narang, Jimmy. 2017. "The Fading American Dream: Trends in Absolute Income Mobility Since 1940." *Science* 356(6336): 398–406.

Chetty, Raj, Hendren, Nathaniel, Jones, Maggie R., and Porter, Sonya R. 2018. "Race and Economic Opportunity in the United States: An Intergenerational Perspective." *National Bureau of Economic Research Working Paper Series*. Working Paper No. 24441. http://www.equality-of-opportunity.org/assets/documents/race_paper.pdf.

Chetty, Raj, Hendren, Nathaniel, Kline, Patrick, Saez, Emmanuel, and Turner, Nicholas. 2014. "Is the United States Still a Land of Opportunity? Recent Trends in Intergenerational Mobility." *National Bureau of Economic Research Working Paper Series*. Working Paper No. 19844. https://www.nber.org/papers/w19844.

Chetty, Raj, Hendren, Nathaniel, Lin, Frina, Majerovitz, Jeremy, and Scuderi, Benjamin. 2016. "Childhood Environment and Gender Gaps in Adulthood." *National Bureau of Economic Research Working Paper Series*. Working Paper No. 21936. https://www.nber.org/papers/w21936.pdf.

Cheuvreux, Marine and Darmaillacq, Corinne. 2014. "Unionisation in France: Paradoxes, Challenges and Outlook." *Trésor-Economics Working Papers*. Working Paper No. 129. https://www.tresor.economie.gouv.fr/Ressources/File/402571.

Chiba, Shuichi, Numakawa, Tadahiro, Ninomiya, Midori, Richards, Misty C., Wakabayashi, Chisato, and Kunugi, Hiroshi. 2012. "Chronic Restraint Stress Causes Anxiety- and Depression-Like Behaviors, Downregulates Glucocorticoid Receptor Expression, and Attenuates Glutamate Release Induced by Brain-Derived Neurotrophic Factor in the Prefrontal Cortex." *Progress in Neuro-Psychopharmacology and Biological Psychiatry* 39(1): 112–19.

Chien, Nina. 2015. "Estimates of Child Care Eligibility and Receipt for Fiscal Year 2012." US Department of Health and Human Services, Office of the Assistant Secretary for Planning and Evaluation. https://aspe.hhs.gov/system/files/pdf/153591/ChildEligibility.pdf.

Child, Maria L. 1866. *The Freedmen's Book*. Boston: Ticknor and Fields.

Child Care Aware of America. 2016a. *Parents and the High Cost of Child Care: 2016 Report*. http://usa.childcareaware.org/wp-content/uploads/2017/01/CCA_High_Cost_Report_01-17-17_final.pdf.

Child Care Aware of America. 2016b. *Parents and the High Cost of Child Care: 2016 Appendices*. http://usa.childcareaware.org/wp-content/uploads/2016/12/CCA_High_Cost_Appendices_2016.pdf.

Child Care Aware of America. 2017a. *Parents and the High Cost of Child Care: 2017 Report*. http://usa.childcareaware.org/wp-content/uploads/2017/12/2017_CCA_High_Cost_Report_FINAL.pdf.

Child Care Aware of America. 2017b. *Parents and the High Cost of Child Care: 2017 Appendices*. http://usa.childcareaware.org/wp-content/uploads/2018/01/2017_CCA_High_Cost_Appendices_FINAL_180112_small.pdf.

Child Trends. 2018. *Key Facts About Teen Births.* https://www.childtrends.org/indicators/teen-births.

Children and Youth Administration. 2018. *General Overview of Day Care Offers and Child-Minding Arrangements of the City of Copenhagen.* City of Copenhagen. https://international.kk.dk/sites/international.kk.dk/files/day_care_offers_2018.pdf.

Children's Bureau. 2018. *Child Maltreatment, 2016.* US Department of Health and Human Services, Administration for Children and Families. https://www.acf.hhs.gov/cb/research-data-technology/statistics-research/child-maltreatment.

Children's Society. 2017. *Good Childhood Report, 2017.* https://www.childrenssociety.org.uk/sites/default/files/the-good-childhood-report-2017_full-report_0.pdf.

Child Trends Databank. 2018. *Children in Working Poor Families.* https://www.childtrends.org/?indicators=children-in-working-poor-families.

Christian, Kate, Morrison, Frederick J. and Bryant, Fred B. 1998. "Predicting Kindergarten Skills: Interactions among Child Care, Maternal Education, and Family Literacy Environments." *Early Childhood Research Quarterly* 13(3): 501–21.

Chua, Amy. 2011. *Battle Hymn of the Tiger Mother.* New York: Penguin Books.

City of East Liverpool, Ohio. 2016. Facebook post, September 8. https://www.facebook.com/cityofeastliverpool/posts/warning-graphic-content!-the-city/879927698809767/.

City of Helsinki. 2019. *Customer Fee Calculator.* https://www.hel.fi/helsinki/en/childhood-and-education/day-care/fees/fee-estimation/?buttonName=&familyIncome=1490&familySize=2&fulltime=fulltime&daysoff=0&submitButton=Calculate.

Clarke-Stewart, Alison and Allhusen, Virginia. 2005. *What We Know About Childcare.* Cambridge, MA: Harvard University Press.

CLASP. 2016. "New TANF Categories Shed Light on State Spending." *CLASP Blog*, August 17. https://www.clasp.org/blog/new-tanf-spending-categories-shine-light-state-spending.

Claxton, Gary, Levitt, Larry, Rae, Matthew, and Sawyer, Bradley. 2018. "Increases in Cost-Sharing Payments Continue to Outpace Wage Growth." *Peterson-Kaiser Health System Tracker.* June 15. https://www.healthsystemtracker.org/brief/increases-in-cost-sharing-payments-have-far-outpaced-wage-growth/#item-start.

Claxton, Gary, Rae, Matthew, Long, Michelle, Damico, Anthony, Foster, Gregory, and Whitmore, Heidi. 2017. *Employer Health Benefits: 2017 Annual Survey.* Henry J. Kaiser Family Foundation and Health Research & Educational Trust. http://files.kff.org/attachment/Report-Employer-Health-Benefits-Annual-Survey-2017.

Clinton, William J. 1996. "Address Before a Joint Session of the Congress on the State of the Union." *American Presidency Project*, January 23. http://presidency.proxied.lsit.ucsb.edu/youtubeclip.php?clipid=53091&admin=42.

Cohan, William. 2015. "Deaths Draw Attention to Wall Street's Grueling Hours." *New York Times*, October 3. https://www.nytimes.com/2015/10/04/business/dealbook/tragedies-draw-attention-to-wall-streets-grueling-pace.html.

Cohen, Elissa, Minton, Sarah, Thompson, Megan, Crowe, Elizabeth, and Giannarelli, Linda. 2016. *Welfare Rules Databook: State TANF Policies as of July 2015.* OPRE Report No. 2016-67. US Department of Health and Human Services, Administration of Children and Families. http://wrd.urban.org/wrd/data/databooks/2015%20Welfare%20Rules%20Databook%20(Final%2009%26%2016).pdf.

Cohen, Patricia. 2017. "Steady Jobs, with Pay and Hours That Are Anything But." *New York Times*, May 31. https://www.nytimes.com/2017/05/31/business/economy/volatile-income-economy-jobs.html.

Cohen, Patricia and Cohen, Jacob. 1996. *Life Values and Adolescent Mental Health.* Mahwah, NJ: Lawrence Erlbaum.

Cohen, Phillip N. 2014. *Enduring Bonds: Inequality, Marriage, Parenting, and Everything Else That Makes Familes Great and Terrible.* Oakland: University of California Press.

Cohen, Phillip N. 2018a. "The Coming Divorce Decline." *SocArXiv Papers.* https://osf.io/preprints/socarxiv/h2sk6/.

Cohen, Phillip N. 2018b. "Wives' Share of Couple Income Update." *Family Inequality Blog*, December 10. https://familyinequality.wordpress.com/2018/12/10/wives-share-of-couple-income-update/.

Cohen, Sheldon, Janicki-Deverts, Denise, Chen, Edith, and Matthews, Karen A. 2010. "Childhood Socioeconomic Status and Adult Health." *Annals of the New York Academy of Sciences* 1186: 37–55.

Cohen, Zachary. 2017. "Congress Passes $700B Defense Bill, Sends to Trump's Desk." *CNN*, November 16. https://www.cnn.com/2017/11/16/politics/ndaa-defense-policy-passes-congress/index.html.

Cohn, Jonathan. 2011. "The Two Year Window." *New Republic*, November 9. https://newrepublic.com/article/97268/the-two-year-window.

Cohn, Jonathan. 2013. "The Hell of American Day Care." *New Republic*, April 15. https://newrepublic.com/article/112892/hell-american-day-care.

Cole, David. 2016. *Engines of Liberty: The Power of Citizens to Make Constitutional Law*. New York: Basic Books.

Collins, Caitlyn. 2019. "The Real Mommy War Is Against the State." *New York Times*, February 9. https://www.nytimes.com/2019/02/09/opinion/sunday/the-real-mommy-war-is-against-the-state.html.

Colorado Department of Health Care Policy and Financing. 2018. *Child Health Plan Plus*. https://www.colorado.gov/hcpf/child-health-plan-plus.

Committee on Child Maltreatment Research, Policy, and Practice for the Next Decade: Phase II and Board on Children, Youth, and Families. 2014. *New Directions in Child Abuse and Neglect Research*. Washington, DC: National Academies Press.

Conger, Rand D., Conger, Katherine J., Elder, Glen H., Lorenz, Frederick O., Simons, Ronald L., and Whitbeck, Les B. 1992. "A Family Process Model of Economic Hardship and Adjustment of Early Adolescent Boys." *Child Development* 63(3): 526–41.

Congressional Budget Office. 1984. *Poverty among Children*. https://www.cbo.gov/sites/default/files/98th-congress-1983-1984/reports/1984_12_03_poverty.pdf.

Congressional Budget Office. 2016. *Trends in Family Wealth, 1987 to 2013*. https://www.cbo.gov/sites/default/files/114th-congress-2015-2016/reports/51846-familywealth.pdf.

Congressional Budget Office. 2018. *The Budget and Economic Outlook: 2018 to 2028*. https://www.cbo.gov/system/files?file=115th-congress-2017-2018/reports/53651-outlook.pdf.

Conley, Dalton. 2008. "Rich Man's Burden." *New York Times*, September 2. http://www.nytimes.com/2008/09/02conley.html.

Connidis, Ingrid Arnet. 1992. "Life Transitions and the Adult Sibling Tie: A Qualitative Study." *Journal of Marriage and Family* 54(4): 972–82.

Consumer Financial Protection Bureau. 2017. *Consumer Experiences with Debt Collection: Findings from the CFPB's Survey of Consumer Views on Debt*. https://s3.amazonaws.com/files.consumerfinance.gov/f/documents/201701_cfpb_Debt-Collection-Survey-Report.pdf.

Conway, Anne, Han, Wen-Jui, Brooks-Gunn, Jeanne, and Waldfogel, Jane. 2017. "First-Year Maternal Employment and Adolescent Externalizing Behavior." *Journal of Child and Family Studies* 26(8): 2237–51.

Cools, Sara, Fiva, Jon H., and Kirkebøen, Lars J. 2015. "Causal Effects of Paternity Leave on Children and Parents." *Scandinavian Journal of Economics* 117(3): 801–28.

Coontz, Stephanie. 2014. "Opinion: The New Instability." *New York Times*, July 26. https://www.nytimes.com/2014/07/27/opinion/sunday/the-new-instability.html.

Cooper, David. 2017. "Another Year of Congressional Inaction Has Further Eroded the Federal Minimum Wage." *Economic Policy Institute*, July 24. https://www.epi.org/publication/another-year-of-congressional-inaction-has-further-eroded-the-federal-minimum-wage/.

Copen, Casey E. 2017. *Condom Use During Sexual Intercourse among Women and Men Aged 15–44 in the United States: 2011–2015 National Survey of Family Growth*. National Health Statistics Report No. 105. https://www.cdc.gov/nchs/data/nhsr/nhsr105.pdf.

Coplan, Robert, Findlay, Leanne, and Schneider, Barry. 2010. "Where Do Anxious Children 'Fit' Best? Childcare and the Emergence of Anxiety in Early Childhood." *Canadian Journal of Behavioural Science* 42(3): 185–93.

Cornman, Stephen Q. 2016. *Revenues and Expenditures for Public Elementary and Secondary School Districts: School Year 2012–13 (Fiscal Year 2013).* NCES Report No. 2015-303. US Department of Education, National Center for Education Statistics. https://nces.ed.gov/pubs2015/2015303.pdf.

Costa, Dora and Steckel, Richard. 1997. "Long Term Trends in Health, Welfare, and Economic Growth in the United States." In Richard H. Steckel and Roderick Floud (eds.), *Health and Welfare During Industrialization.* Chicago: University of Chicago Press. https://www.nber.org/papers/h0076.

Cott, Nancy F. 1977. *The Bonds of Womanhood: "Woman's Sphere" in New England, 1780–1835.* 2nd ed. New Haven, CT: Yale University Press.

Council of Economic Advisers. 2014. *The Economics of Early Childhood Investments.* Executive Office of the President of the United States. https://obamawhitehouse.archives.gov/sites/default/files/docs/the_economics_of_early_childhood_investments.pdf.

Covert, Bryce. 2015. "Motherhood Will Cost You." *Elle*, September 8. http://www.elle.com/culture/news/a30136/motherhood-will-cost-you/.

Covert, Bryce and Israel, Josh. 2017. "Mississippi Is Rejecting Nearly All of the Poor People Who Apply for Welfare." *ThinkProgress*, April 13. https://thinkprogress.org/mississippi-reject-welfare-applicants-57701ca3fb13/.

Crandall-Hollick, Margot L. 2018. *Child and Dependent Care Tax Benefits: How They Work and Who Receives Them.* CRS Report No. R44993. Congressional Research Service. https://fas.org/sgp/crs/misc/R44993.pdf.

Crittenden, Ann. 2001. *The Price of Motherhood.* New York: Henry Holt.

Crouter, Ann and Bumpus, Matthew. 2001. "Linking Parents' Work Stress to Children's and Adolescents' Psychological Adjustment." *Current Directions in Psychological Science* 10(5): 156–9.

Crouter, Ann C., Bumpus, Matthew F., Head, Melissa R., and McHale, Susan M. 2004. "Implications of Overwork and Overload for the Quality of Men's Family Relationships." *Journal of Marriage and Family* 63(2): 404–16.

Cunha, Jesse M. 2014. "Testing Paternalism: Cash versus In-Kind Transfers." *American Economic Journal: Applied Economics* 6(2): 195–230.

Curran, Thomas and Hill, Andrew P. 2017. "Perfectionism Is Increasing over Time: A Meta-Analysis of Birth Cohort Differences from 1989 to 2016." American Psychological Association. https://www.apa.org/pubs/journals/releases/bul-bul0000138.pdf.

Currie, Janet. 2001. "Early Childhood Education Programs." *Journal of Economic Perspectives.* 15(2): 213–38.

Currier, Erin, Biernacka-Lievestro, Joanna, Elliot, Diana, Elmi, Sheida, Key, Clinton, Lake, Walter, and Sattelmeyer, Sarah. 2015. *The Precarious State of Family Balance Sheets.* Pew Charitable Trusts. https://www.pewtrusts.org/-/media/assets/2015/01/fsm_balance_sheet_report.pdf.

Curtin, Sally, Heron, Melonie, Miniño, Arialdi M. and Warner, Margaret. 2018. "Recent Increases in Injury Mortality among Children and Adolescents Aged 10–19 Years in the United States: 1999–2016." *National Vital Statistics Reports* 67(4). https://www.cdc.gov/nchs/data/nvsr/nvsr67/nvsr67_04.pdf.

Curtin, Sally, Ventura, Stephanie, and Martinez, Gladys. 2014. *Recent Declines in Nonmarital Childbearing in the United States.* NCHS Data Brief No. 162. US Department of Health and Human Services, National Center for Health Statistics. https://www.cdc.gov/nchs/data/databriefs/db162.pdf.

Dahl, Molly, DeLeire, Thomas, and Schwabish, Johnathan. 2011. "Estimates of Year-to-Year Variability in Worker Earnings and in Household Incomes from Administrative, Survey, and Matched Data." *Journal of Human Resources* 46(4): 750–74.

Daly, Mary C., Hobijn, Bart, and Pedtke, Joseph H. 2017. *Disappointing Facts about the Black–White Wage Gap.* FRBSF Economic Letter No. 2017–26. Federal Reserve Bank of San Francisco. https://www.frbsf.org/economic-research/files/el2017-26.pdf.

Daniels, Jeff. 2017. "Senate Passes $700 Billion Defense Policy Bill, Backing Trump Call for Steep Increase in Military Spending." *CNBC*, September 18. https://www.cnbc.com/2017/09/18/senate-passes-700-billion-defense-policy-bill-backing-trump-call-for-steep-increase-in-military-spending.html.

Danziger, Sheldon and Gottschalk, Peter. 1985. "The Poverty of Losing Ground." *Challenge* 28(2): 32–8.

Davala, Sarath, Jhabvala, Renana, Standing, Guy, and Mehta, Soumya Kapoor. 2015. *Basic Income: A Transformative Policy for India.* London: Bloomsbury.

Deahl, Jessica. 2017. "Child Care Scarcity Has Very Real Consequences for Working Families." *NPR*, January 3. https://www.npr.org/sections/health-shots/2017/01/03/506448993/child-care-scarcity-has-very-real-consequences-for-working-families.

Deahl, Jessica and Ludden, Jennifer. 2016. "On Your Mark, Give Birth, Go Back to Work." *NPR*, October 4. https://www.npr.org/2016/10/04/495839747/on-your-mark-give-birth-go-back-to-work.

Declercq, Eugene R., Sakala, Carol, Corry, Maureen P., Applebaum, Sandra, and Herrlich, Ariel. 2013. *Listening to Mothers III: New Mothers Speak Out.* Childbirth Connection. http://transform.childbirthconnection.org/wp-content/uploads/2013/06/LTM-III_NMSO.pdf.

Deloitte. 2016. *Parental Leave Survey.* https://www2.deloitte.com/content/dam/Deloitte/us/Documents/about-deloitte/us-about-deloitte-paternal-leave-survey.pdf

Deming, David. 2009. "Early Childhood Intervention and Life-Cycle Skill Development: Evidence from Head Start." *American Economic Journal: Applied Economics* 1(3): 111–34.

Denizet-Lewis, Benoit. 2017. "Why Are More American Teenagers than Ever Suffering from Severe Anxiety?" *New York Times Magazine*, October 11. https://www.nytimes.com/2017/10/11/magazine/why-are-more-american-teenagers-than-ever-suffering-from-severe-anxiety.html.

Department for Business, Innovation and Skills. 2014. *The Fourth Work–Life Balance Employer Survey (2013).* BIS Research Paper No. 184. https://assets.publishing.service.gov.uk/government/uploads/system/uploads/attachment_data/file/398557/bis-14-1027-fourth-work-life-balance-employer-survey-2013.pdf.

Department of Finance. 2019. *Canada's New Parental Sharing Benefit.* Government of Canada. https://www.fin.gc.ca/n18/docs/18-008_6-eng.pdf.

DeRose, Laurie, Lyons-Amos, Mark, Wilcox, W. Bradford, and Huarcaya, Gloria. 2017. "The Cohabitation-Go-Round: Cohabitation and Family Across the Globe." In Social Trends Institute, *World Family Map 2017: Mapping Family Change and Child Well-Being Outcomes.* http://worldfamilymap.ifstudies.org/2017/files/WFM-2017-FullReport.pdf#page=36&zoom=auto,-99,307.

Desilver, Drew. 2013. "Black Unemployment Rate Is Consistently Twice That of Whites." Pew Research Center, August 21. http://www.pewresearch.org/fact-tank/2013/08/21/through-good-times-and-bad-black-unemployment-is-consistently-double-that-of-whites/.

Desilver, Drew. 2017. "Among Developed Nations, Americans' Tax Bills Are Below Average." Pew Research Center, October 24. http://www.pewresearch.org/fact-tank/2017/10/24/among-developed-nations-americans-tax-bills-are-below-average/.

Desmond, Matthew. 2018. "Americans Want to Believe Jobs Are the Solution to Poverty. They're Not." *New York Times Magazine*, September 11. https://www.nytimes.com/2018/09/11/magazine/americans-jobs-poverty-homeless.html.

Desmond, Matthew. 2019. "Dollars on the Margins." *New York Times Magazine*, February 21. https://www.nytimes.com/interactive/2019/02/21/magazine/minimum-wage-saving-lives.html.

Dettling, Lisa J., Hsu, Joanne W., Jacobs, Lindsay, Moore, Kevin B., and Thompson, Jeffrey P. 2017. "Recent Trends in Wealth-Holding by Race and Ethnicity: Evidence from the Survey of Consumer Finances." *FEDS Notes*, September 27. https://doi.org/10.17016/2380-7172.2083.

Deutsche Welle. 2018. Berlin first in Germany to scrap child day care fees. *DW*. July 30. Available at https://www.dw.com/en/berlin-first-in-germany-to-scrap-child-day-care-fees/a-44883019.

Devins, Sabine. 2010. "The midwife: Your best friend in natal care." *The Local*. October 5. https://www.thelocal.de/20101005/30273.

Diener, Ed and Oishi, Shigehiro. 2000. "Money and Happiness: Income and Subjective Well-being Across Nations." In Ed Diener Ed and Eunook M. Suh (eds.), *Culture and Subjective Well-Being*. Cambridge, MA: MIT Press.

Doepke, Matthias and Zilibotti, Fabrizio, 2019. *Love, Money, and Parenting: How Economics Explains the Way We Raise Our Kids*. Princeton, NJ: Princeton University Press.

Doepke, Matthias and Zilibotti, Fabrizio. 2017. "Parenting with Style: Altruism and Paternalism in Intergenerational Preference Transmission." *Econometrica* 85(5): 1331–71.

Dong, M., Giles, W. H., Felitti, V. J., Dube, S. R., Williams, J. E., Chapman, D. P., and Anda, R. F. 2004. "Insights into Causal Pathways for Ischemic Heart Disease: Adverse Childhood Experiences Study." *Circulation* 110(3): 1761–6.

Dooley, David and Prause, Jo Ann. 2002. "Mental Health and Welfare Transitions: Depression and Alcohol Abuse in AFDC Women." *American Journal of Community Psychology* 30(6): 787–813.

Dorfman, Joseph. 1940. "The Economic Philosophy of Thomas Jefferson." *Political Science Quarterly* 55(1): 98–121.

Dornbusch, Sanford, Carlsmith, Merrill, Bushwall, Steven, Ritter, Philip, Leiderman, Herbert, Hastorf, Albert, and Gross, Ruth. 1985. "Single Parents, Extended Households, and the Control of Adolescents." *Child Development* 56(2): 326–41.

Doty, Pamela. 2010. "The Evolving Balance of Formal and Informal, Institutional and non-Institutional Long-Term Care for Older Americans: A Thirty-Year Perspective." *Public Policy and Aging Report* 20(1): 3–9.

Dowd, Nancy. 2018. *Reimagining Inequality: A New Deal for Children of Color*. New York: New York University Press.

DPA. 2018. "Free for all? How Germany plans to tackle its childcare problem." *The Local*. May 28. https://www.thelocal.de/20180528/free-for-all-how-germany-plans-to-tackle-its-childcare-problem.

Drogin, Bob. 1985. "'Got No Choice': The True Victims of Poverty: The Children." *Los Angeles Times*, July 30. http://articles.latimes.com/1985-07-30/news/mn-4195_1_poor-children.

Ducharme, Jamie. 2018. "U.S. Life Expectancy Dropped for the Third Year in a Row: Drugs and Suicide Are Partly to Blame." *Time*, November 29. http://time.com/5464607/us-life-expectancy-2017/.

DuMont, Kimberly, Kirkland, Kristen, Mitchell-Herzfeld, Susan, Ehrhard-Dietzel, Susan, Rodriguez, Monica L., Lee, Eunju, Layne, China, and Greene, Rose. 2011. *A Randomized Trial of Healthy Families New York (HFNY): Does Home Visiting Prevent Child Maltreatment?* https://www.ncjrs.gov/pdffiles1/nij/grants/232945.pdf.

Duncan, Greg J. and Brooks-Gunn, Jeanne (eds.). 1997. *Consequences of Growing Up Poor*. New York: Russell Sage Foundation.

Duncan, Greg J., Hill, Martha S., and Hoffman, Saul D. 1988. "Welfare Dependence Within and Across Generations." *Science* 239(4839): 467–71.

Duncan, Greg J. and Hoffman, Saul D. 1988. "The Use and Effects of Welfare: A Survey of Recent Evidence." *Social Science Review* 62(2): 238–57.

Duncan, Greg J., Yeung, Jean W., Brooks-Gunn, Jeanne, and Smith, Judith R. 1998. "How Much Does Childhood Poverty Affect the Life Chances of Children?" *American Sociological Review* 63(3): 406–23.

Duncan, Greg J., Ziol-Guest, Kathleen M. and Kalil, Ariel. 2010. "Early-Childhood Poverty and Adult Attainment, Behavior, and Health." *Child Development* 81(1): 306–25.

Duvander, Ann-Zofie, Mussino, Eleonora, and Tervola, Jussi. 2016. *Men's Childcare: A Comparative Study of Fathers' Parental Leave Use in Sweden and Finland.* https://cdn.uclouvain.be/public/Exports%20reddot/demo/documents/CQ16_Duvander.pdf.

Dykman, B. M. 1998. "Integrating Cognitive and Motivational Factors in Depression: Initial Tests of a Goal-Orientation Approach." *Journal of Personality and Social Psychology* 74(1): 139–58.

Dynan, Karen, Elmendorf, Douglas, and Sichel, Daniel. 2012. "The Evolution of Household Income Volatility." *B.E. Journal of Economic Analysis & Policy* 12(2): 1–42.

Eagan, Kevin, Stolzenberg, Ellen Bara, Zimmerman, Hilary B., Aragon, Melissa C., Sayson, Hannah Whang, and Rios-Aguilar, Cecilia. 2017. *The American Freshman: National Norms, Fall 2016.* Cooperative Institutional Research Program. https://www.heri.ucla.edu/monographs/TheAmericanFreshman2016-Expanded.pdf.

Ebbert, Ashley M., Infruna, Frank J., and Luthar, Suniya S. 2018. "Mapping Developmental Changes in Perceived Parent–Adolescent Relationship Quality Throughout Middle School and High School." *Development and Psychopathology,* 25:1–16.

ECE Consensus Letter. 2019. *National Institute for Early Education Research.* http://nieer.org/publications/ece-consensus-letter-for-researchers.

Eckenrode, John, Campa, Mary, Luckey, Dennis W., Henderson, Charles R., Cole, Robert, Kitzman, Harriet, Anson, Elizabeth, Sidora-Arcoleo, Kimberly, Powers, Jane, and Olds, David. 2010. "Long-Term Effects of Prenatal and Infancy Nurse Home Visitation on the Life Course of Youths: 19-Year Follow-up of a Randomized Trial." *Archives of Pediatrics and Adolescent Medicine* 164(1): 9–15.

Economic Commission for Europe, Timber Committee. 2016. *Finland: Market Statement.* https://www.unece.org/fileadmin/DAM/timber/country-info/statements/Finland2016.pdf.

Economic Policy Institute and Oxfam America. 2016. *Few Rewards: An Agenda to Give America's Working Poor a Raise.* https://s3.amazonaws.com/oxfam-us/www/static/media/files/Few_Rewards_Report_2016_web.pdf.

Economist. 2012a. "Effective Tax Rates." *Economist,* October 16. https://www.economist.com/graphic-detail/2012/10/16/effective-tax-rates.

Economist. 2018. "Why States in Trump Country Are Considering Medicaid Expansion." *Economist,* October 25. https://www.economist.com/united-states/2018/10/25/why-states-in-trump-country-are-considering-medicaid-expansion.

Economist Intelligence Unit. 2012. *Stating well: Benchmarking Early Education Across the World.* Economist. http://graphics.eiu.com/upload/eb/lienstartingwell.pdf.

Edin, Kathryn and Kefalas, Maria. 2005. *Promises I Can Keep: Why Poor Women Put Motherhood Before Marriage.* Berkeley: University of California Press.

Edin, Kathryn and Lein, Laura. 1997. *Making Ends Meet: How Single Mothers Survive Welfare and Low-Wage Work.* New York: Russell Sage Foundation.

Edin, Kathryn and Nelson, Timothy J. 2013. *Doing the Best I Can: Fatherhood in the Inner City.* Berkeley: University of California Press.

Edin, Kathryn and Reed, Joanna. 2005. "Why Don't They Just Get Married? Barriers to Marriage among the Disadvantaged." *Future Child* 15(2): 117–137.

Edin, Kathryn and Shaefer, H. 2015. *$2.00 a Day: Living on Almost Nothing in America.* Boston: Houghton Mifflin Harcourt.

Éducaloi. 2019. *Maternity, Paternity and Parental Leave.* https://www.educaloi.qc.ca/en/capsules/maternity-paternity-and-parental-leave.

Edwards, Ashley. 2014. *Dynamics of Economic Well-Being: Poverty, 2009–2011.* US Census Bureau. https://www.census.gov/prod/2014pubs/p70-137.pdf.

Edwards, Valerie J., Holden, George W., Felitti, Vincent J., and Anda, Robert F. 2003. "Relationship Between Multiple Forms of Childhood Maltreatment and Adult Mental Health in

Community Respondents: Results from the Adverse Childhood Experiences Study." *American Journal of Psychiatry* 160(8): 1453–60.

Eerola, Essi and Saarimaa, Tuukka. 2017. "Delivering Affordable Housing and Neighborhood Quality: A Comparison of Place- and Tenant-Base Programs." *CESifo Working Papers* (Paper no. 6674). https://www.ifo.de/DocDL/cesifo1_wp6674.pdf

Eisenberg, M. E., Neumark-Sztainer, D., Fulkerson, J. A., and Story, M. 2008. "Family Meals and Substance Use: Is There a Long-Term Protective Association?" *Journal of Adolescent Health* 43(2): 151–6.

Eisenberg, Marla, Olson, Rachel, Neumark-Sztainer, Dianne, Story, Mary, and Bearinger, Linda. 2004. "Correlations Between Family Meals and Psychosocial Well-Being among Adolescents." *Archives of Pediatrics and Adolescent Medicine* 158(8): 792–6.

Ekberg, John, Eriksson, Rickard, and Friebel, Guido. 2013. "Parental Leave: A Policy Evaluation of the Swedish 'Daddy-Month' Reform." *Journal of Public Economics* 97: 131–43.

Ekono, Mercedes, Jiang, Yang, and Smith, Sheila. 2016. *Young Children in Deep Poverty*. Columbia University, National Center for Children in Poverty. http://www.nccp.org/publications/pdf/text_1133.pdf.

Ellis, Bruce J., Essex, Marilyn J., and Boyce, Thomas W. 2005. "Biological Sensitivity to Context: II. Empirical Explorations of an Evolutionary-Developmental Theory." *Development and Psychopathy* 17(2): 303–28.

Ellman, Ira Mark, Kurtz, Paul M., Weithorn, Lois A., Bix, Brian H., Czapanskiy, Karen, and Eichner, Maxine. 2010. *Family Law: Cases, Text, Problems*. 5th ed. New Providence, NJ: LexisNexis.

Ellwood, David and Bane, Mary Jo. 1985. *The Impact of AFDC on Family Structure and Living Arrangements*. Cambridge, MA: Harvard University Press.

Ellwood, David and Jencks, Christopher. 2004. "The Spread of Single-Parent Families in the United States Since 1960." *KSG Faculty Research Working Paper Series*. Working Paper No. RWP 04–008. https://papers.ssrn.com/sol3/papers.cfm?abstract_id=517662##.

Ellwood, David and Summers, Lawrence. 1985. "Poverty in America: Is Welfare the Answer or the Problem?" *National Bureau of Economic Research Working Paper Series*. Working Paper No. 1711. http://www.nber.org/papers/w1711.pdf.

Ely, Richard T. 1886. "Report of the Organization of the American Economic Association." *Publications of the American Economic Association* 1(1): 5–32.

Ely, Richard T. 1910. "The American Economic Association, 1885–1909." *American Economic Association Quarterly*, 3rd Series 11(1): 47–111.

Emmons, William R., Kent, Ana H., and Ricketts, Lowell R. 2018. "A Lost Generation? Long-Lasting Wealth Impacts of the Great Recession on Young Families." *The Demographics of Wealth 2018 Series: How Education, Race and Birth Year Shape Financial Outcomes*. Essay No. 2. https://www.stlouisfed.org/~/media/files/pdfs/hfs/essays/hfs_essay_2_2018.pdf?la=en.

Employment Development Department. 2018. *Calculating Paid Family Leave Benefit Payment Amounts*. State of California. http://www.edd.ca.gov/Disability/Calculating_PFL_Benefit_Payment_Amounts.htm.

Employment Security Department. 2018. *Leave Benefits*. Washington State. https://esd.wa.gov/paid-family-medical-leave/benefits.

Engels, Frederick. [1845] 1975. "The Condition of the Working Class in England." In *Karl Marx, Frederick Engels: Collected Works*, vol. 4. London: Lawrence & Wishart.

Esping-Andersen, Gøsta. 1990. *The Three Worlds of Welfare Capitalism*. Princeton, NJ: Princeton University Press.

Esping-Andersen, Gøsta. 2002. *Why We Need a New Welfare State*. New York: Oxford University Press.

Esping-Andersen, Gøsta. 2009. *The Incomplete Revolution: Adapting to Women's New Roles*. Cambridge: Polity Press.

Esposito, Dawn, Aronowitz, Stanley, Chancer, Lynn, DiFazio, William, and Yard, Margaret. 1998. "The (In) Spectre Returns! Global Capitalism and the Future of Work." *Critical Perspectives on Accounting* 9(1): 7–54.

Essex, Marilyn, Boyce, W. Thomas, Hertzman, Clyde, Lam, Lucia, Armstrong, Jeffrey, Neumann, Sarah, and Kobor, Michael. 2013. "Epigenetic Vestiges of Early Developmental Adversity: Childhood Stress Exposure and DNA Methylation in Adolescence." *Child Development* 84(1): 58–75.

Essex, Marilyn J., Klein, Marjorie H., Cho, Eunsuk, and Kalin, Ned H. 2002. "Maternal Stress Beginning in Infancy May Sensitize Children to Later Stress Exposure: Effects on Cortisol and Behavior." *Biological Psychiatry* 52(8): 776–84.

Essex, Marilyn J., Klein, Marjorie H., Cho, Eunsuk, and Kraemer, Helena C. 2003. "Exposure to Maternal Depression and Marital Conflict: Gender Differences in Children's Later Mental Health Symptoms." *Journal of the American Academy of Child & Adolescent Psychiatry* 42(6): 728–37.

Essex, Marilyn J., Klein, Majorie H., Miech, Richard, and Smider, Nancy A. 2001. "Timing of Initial Exposure to Maternal Major Depression and Children's Mental Health Symptoms in Kindergarten." *British Journal of Psychology* 179(2): 151–6.

Eurofound. 2003. *Overtime in Europe.* European Foundation for the Improvement of Living and Working Conditions. https://www.eurofound.europa.eu/observatories/eurwork/comparative-information/overtime-in-europe.

Eurofound. 2015. *Collective bargaining in Europe in the 21st Century.* European Foundation for the Improvement of Living and Working Conditions. https://www.eurofound.europa.eu/sites/default/files/ef_publication/field_ef_document/ef1548en.pdf.

Eurofound. 2016. *Working Time Developments in the 21st Century: Work Duration and Its Regulation in the EU.* European Foundation for the Improvement of Living and Working Conditions.. https://www.eurofound.europa.eu/sites/default/files/ef_publication/field_ef_document/ef1573en.pdf.

European Commission, EACEA, Eurydice and Eurostat. 2014. *Key Data on Early Childhood Education and Care in Europe: 2014 Edition.* Education, Audiovisual and Culture Executive Agency. https://ec.europa.eu/eurostat/documents/3217494/5785249/EC-01-14-484-EN.PDF/cbdf1804-a139-43a9-b8f1-ca5223eea2a1.

Expatica. 2018. *Finding Childcare in Germany.* Available at https://www.expatica.com/de/living/family/finding-childcare-in-germany-106276/.

Eydal, Guðný Björk and Rostgaard, Tine, eds. 2016. *Fatherhood in the Nordic Welfare States: Comparing Care Policies and Practice.* Bristol: Policy Press.

Fagan, Patrick F. and Hadford, Christina. 2015. *The Fifth Annual Index of Family Belonging and Rejection.* Marriage and Religion Research Institute. https://downloads.frc.org/EF/EF15B28.pdf.

Fairlie, Robert W. and Sundstrom, William A. 1999. "The Emergence, Persistence, and Recent Widening of the Racial Unemployment Gap." *Industrial and Labor Relations Review* 52(2): 252–70.

Fair Work Ombudsman. 2018. *Returning to Work from Parental Leave.* Australian Government. https://www.fairwork.gov.au/leave/maternity-and-parental-leave/returning-to-work-from-parental-leave.

Falk, Gene. 2014. *Temporary Assistance for Needy Families (TANF): Eligibility and Benefit Amounts in State TANF Cash Assistance Programs.* Congressional Research Service. https://fas.org/sgp/crs/misc/R43634.pdf.

FAMIFED. 2018. *Basiskinderbijslag.* Federal Agency for Family Allowances, Belgium. Last modified May 15. http://brussel.famifed.be/nl/gezinnen/kinderbijslagen-en-toeslagen/basiskinderbijslag.

Farber, Henry, Haltiwanger, John, and Abraham, Katharine. 1997. "The Changing Face of Job Loss in the United States, 1981–1995." *Brookings Papers on Economic Activity: Microeconomics* 1997: 55–142.

Farber, Henry S., Herbst, Daniel, Kuziemko, Ilyana, and Naidu, Suresh. 2018. "Unions and Inequality over the Twentieth Century: New Evidence from Survey Data." *National Bureau of Economic Research Working Paper Series*. Working Paper No. 24587. https://www.nber.org/papers/w24587.

Farran, Dale C. and Lipsey, Mark W. 2016. "Evidence for the Benefits of State Prekindergarten Programs: Myth & Misrepresentation." *Behavioral Science & Policy* 2(1): 9–18.

Farrell, Diana and Greig, Fiona. 2016. *Paychecks, Paydays, and the Online Platform Economy: Big Data on Income Volatility*. JP Morgan Chase & Co. Institute. https://www.jpmorganchase.com/corporate/institute/document/jpmc-institute-volatility-2-report.pdf.

Farrington, Robert. 2014. "Too Poor for College, Too Rich for Financial Aid." *Forbes*, June 17. https://www.forbes.com/sites/robertfarrington/2014/06/17/too-poor-for-college-too-rich-for-financial-aid/#319027e16922.

Federal Office for Migration and Refugees. 2015a. *Child Benefit and Other Benefits*. Government of Germany. http://www.bamf.de/EN/Willkommen/KinderFamilie/Kindergeld/kindergeld-node.html.

Feinberg, Lynn and Choula, Rita. 2012. *Understanding the Impact of Family Caregiving on Work*. Fact Sheet No. 271. AARP Public Policy Institute. http://www.aarp.org/content/dam/aarp/research/public_policy_institute/ltc/2012/understanding-impact-family-caregiving-work-AARP-ppi-ltc.pdf.

Feldman, Ruth, Sussman, Amy, and Zigler, Edward. 2004. "Parental Leave and Work Adaptation at the Transition to Parenthood: Individual, Marital, and Social Correlates." *Journal of Applied Developmental Psychology* 25(4): 459–79.

Felitti, Vincent J., Anda, Robert F., Nordenberg, Dale, Williamson, David F., Spitz, Alison M., Edwards, Valerie, Koss, Mary P., and Marks, James S. 1998. "Relationship of Childhood Abuse and Household Dysfunction to Many of the Leading Causes of Death in Adults: The Adverse Childhood Experiences (ACE) Study." *American Journal of Preventative Medicine* 14(4): 245–58.

Fernald, Lia C. H., Gertler, Paul J., and Neufeld, Lynnette M. 2008. "Role of Cash in Conditional Cash Transfer Programmes for Child Health, Growth, and Development: An Analysis of Mexico's *Oportunidades*." *Lancet* 371(9615): 828–37.

Filgueira, Fernando and Rossel, Cecilia. 2017. "Confronting Inequality: Social Protection for Families and Early Childhood Through Monetary Transfers and Care Worldwide." *United Nations Social Policy Series*. No. 226. https://repositorio.cepal.org/bitstream/handle/11362/43158/S1701242_en.pdf?sequence=1&isAllowed=y.

Fine, Sidney. 1956. *Laissez Faire and the General-Welfare State: A Study of Conflict in American Thought, 1865–1901*. Ann Arbor: University of Michigan Press.

Fiorini, Mario and Keane, Michael. 2014. "How the Allocation of Children's Time Affects Cognitive and Noncognitive Development." *Journal of Labor Economics* 32(4): 787–836.

Fiscella, Kevin and Kitzman, Harriet. 2009. "Disparities in Academic Achievement and Health: The Intersection of Child Education and Health Policy." *Pediatrics* 123(3): 1073–80.

Fishback, Price V. 2010. "Social Welfare Expenditures in the United States and the Nordic Countries: 1900–2003." *National Bureau of Economic Research Working Paper Series*. Working Paper No. 15982. http://www.nber.org/papers/w15982.

Fitzgerald, John. 1991. "Welfare Duration and the Marriage Market: Evidence from the Survey of Income and Program Participation." *Journal of Human Resources* 26(3): 545–61.

Floyd, Ife. 2017. *TANF Cash Benefits Have Fallen by More than 20 Percent in Most States and Continue to Erode*. Center on Budget and Policy Priorities. https://www.cbpp.org/sites/default/files/atoms/files/10-30-14tanf.pdf.

Floyd, Ife, Burnside, Ashley, and Schott, Liz. 2018. *Policy Brief: TANF Reaching Few Poor Families*. Center on Budget and Policy Priorities. https://www.cbpp.org/sites/default/files/atoms/files/4-5-17tanf.pdf.

Floyd, Ife, Pavetti, LaDonna, and Schott, Liz. 2017. *TANF Reaching Few Poor Families*. Center on Budget and Policy Priorities. : https://www.cbpp.org/sites/default/files/atoms/files/6-16-15tanf.pdf.

Fogel, Robert William. 1986. "Nutrition and the Decline in Mortality Since 1700: Some Preliminary Findings." In Stanley L. Engerman and Robert E. Gallman (eds.), *Long-Term Factors in American Economic Growth*. Chicago: University of Chicago Press. http://www.nber.org/chapters/c9687.

Fogel, Robert William. 2004. *The Escape from Hunger and Premature Death, 1700–2100: Europe, America, and the Third World*. Cambridge: Cambridge University Press.

Folbre, Nancy. 2001. *The Invisible Heart: Economics and Family Values*. New York: New Press.

Fomby, Paula and Cherlin, Andrew J. 2007. "Family Instability and Child Well-Being." *American Sociological Review* 72(2): 181–204.

Foner, Eric. 1995. *Free Soil, Free Labor, Free Men: The Ideology of the Republican Party Before the Civil War*. New York: Oxford University Press.

Food and Nutrition Service. 2017. *Supplemental Nutrition Assistance Program State Activity Report: Fiscal Year 2016*. US Department of Agriculture. https://fns-prod.azureedge.net/sites/default/files/snap/FY16-State-Activity-Report.pdf.

Food and Nutrition Service. 2018. *Supplemental Nutrition Assistance Program, National View Summary, FY 2015–2018*. US Department of Agriculture. https://fns-prod.azureedge.net/sites/default/files/pd/34SNAPmonthly.pdf.

Fording, Richard, Schram, Sanford, and Soss, Joe. 2011. *Disciplining the Poor: Neoliberal Paternalism and the Persistent Power of Race*. Chicago: University Press of Chicago.

Forget, Evelyn L. 2011. "The Town with No Poverty: The Health Effects of a Canadian Guaranteed Annual Income Field Experiment." *Canadian Public Policy* 37(3): 283–305.

Forster, Diana, Hewlett, Sylvia Ann, Sherbin, Laura, Shiller, Peggy and Sumberg, Karen. 2010. *Off-Ramps and On-Ramps Revisited*. Center for Work-Life Policy,

Forsythe, John. 1939. "Legislative History of the Fair Labor Standards Act." *Law and Contemporary Problems* 6(3): 464–90.

Foster, George G. 1850. *New York by Gas-light: With Here and There a Streak of Sunshine*. New York: Dewitt & Davenport.

Francis, Darlene, Diorio, Josie, Liu, Dong, and Meaney, Michael J. 1999. "Nongenomic Transmission Across Generations of Maternal Behavior and Stress Responses in the Rat." *Science* 286(5442): 1155–58.

Frank, Robert. 1999. *Luxury Fever: Why Money Fails to Satisfy in an Era of Excess*. New York: Free Press.

Frank, Robert. 2011. *The Darwin Economy: Liberty, Competition, and the Common Good*. Princeton, NJ: Princeton University Press.

Frank, Robert, Levine, Adam, and Dijk, Wege. 2014. "Expenditure Cascades." *Review of Behavioral Economics* 1(1–2): 55–73.

Frase, Peter and Gornick, Janet. 2013. "The Time Divide in Cross-National Perspective: The Work Week, Education and Institutions That Matter." *Social Forces* 91(3): 697–724.

Freeman, Richard. 2007. *America Works: The Exceptional U.S. Labor Market*. New York: Russell Sage Foundation.

Friedli, Lynne. 2009. *Mental Health, Resilience and Inequalities*. World Health Organization Regional Office for Europe. http://www.euro.who.int/__data/assets/pdf_file/0012/100821/E92227.pdf.

Friedman, Benjamin. 2015. "Work and Consumption in an Era of Unbalanced Technological Advance." *Journal of Evolutionary Economics* 27(2): 221–37.

Friedman, Milton. [2002] 1962. *Capitalism and Freedom*. Chicago: University of Chicago Press.

Friedman, Susan Hatters, Horwitz, Sarah McCue, and Resnick, Phillip J. 2005. "Child Murder by Mothers: A Critical Analysis of the Current State of Knowledge and a Research Agenda." *American Journal of Psychiatry* 162(9): 1578–87.

Friedman-Krauss, Allison, Barnett, Steven W., and Nores, Milagros. 2016. *How Much Can High-Quality Universal Pre-K Reduce Achievement Gaps?* Center for American Progress. https://cdn.americanprogress.org/wp-content/uploads/2016/04/01115656/NIEER-AchievementGaps-report.pdf.

283

Friedman-Krauss, Allison H., Barnett, Steven, Weisenfeld, G. G., Kasmin, Richard, DiCrecchio, Nicole, and Horowitz, Michelle. 2018. *The State of Preschool 2017: State Preschool Yearbook*. National Institute for Early Education Research. http://nieer.org/wp-content/uploads/2018/07/State-of-Preschool-2017-Full-7-16-18.pdf.

Fry, Richard, Cohn, D'Vera, Livingston, Gretchen, and Taylor, Paul. 2011. *The Old Prosper Relative to the Young: The Rising Age Gap in Economic Well-Being*. Pew Research Center. http://www.pewresearch.org/wp-content/uploads/sites/3/2011/11/WealthReportFINAL.pdf.

Fuller, Bruce, Loeb, Susanna, Strath, Annelie, and Carrol, Bidemi. 2004. "State Formation of the Child Care Sector: Family Demand and Policy Action." *Sociology of Education* 77(4): 337–58.

Furstenberg, Frank J. 1995. "Fathering in the Inner City: Paternal Participation and Public Policy." In William Marsiglio (ed.), *Fatherhood: Contemporary Theory, Research, and Social Policy*. Thousand Oaks, CA: Sage.

Furstenberg, Frank J. 2009. "If Moynihan Had Only Known: Race, Class, and Family Change in the Late Twentieth Century." *Annals of the American Academy of Political and Social Science* 621(1): 94–110.

Galea, Sandro and Vlahov, David. 2002. "Social Determinants and the Health of Drug Users: Socioeconomic Status, Homelessness, and Incarceration." *Public Health Reports* 117(suppl. 1): S135–S145.

Galinsky, Ellen, Howes, Carolee, Kontos, Susan, and Shinn, Marybeth. 1994. *The Study of Children in Family Child Care and Relative Care: Highlights of Findings*. New York: Families and Work Institute.

Gallman, Robert. 2000. "Economic Growth and Structural Change in the Long Nineteenth Century." In Stanley Engerman and Robert Gallman (eds.), *The Cambridge Economic History of the United States*. Cambridge: Cambridge University Press.

Galston, William A. and Kamarck, Elaine C. 2015. *More Builders and Fewer Traders: A Growth Strategy for the American Economy*. Center for Effective Public Management at Brookings. https://www.brookings.edu/wp-content/uploads/2016/06/CEPMGlastonKarmarck4.pdf.

Garber, Judy, Robinson, Nancy S., and Valentiner, David. 1997. "The Relation Between Parenting and Adolescent Depression: Self-Worth as a Mediator." *Journal of Adolescent Research* 12(1): 12–33.

García, Jorge, Heckman, James, Leaf, Duncan, and Prados, María. 2016. "The Life-Cycle Benefits of an Influential Early Childhood Program." *National Bureau of Economic Research Working Paper Series*. Working Paper No. 22993. http://www.nber.org/papers/w22993.pdf.

Gardner, Suzanne. 2019. "The city with the most expensive daycare in Canada is . . . " *Today's Parent*. February 7. Available at https://www.todaysparent.com/kids/daycare/most-expensive-daycare-canada-city-2018/.

Garfinkle, Irwin and McLanahan, Sarah. 1986. *Single Mothers and Their Children: A New American Dilemma*. Baltimore: Urban Institute Press.

Garrison, Marsha. 2014. "The Changing Face of Marriage." In John Eekelaar and Rob George (eds.), *Routledge Handbook of Family Law and Policy*. Abingdon: Routledge.

Gates, Jimmie. 2017. "MDHS Confirms Most New Applicants Rejected for Welfare." *Clarion Ledger*, April 20. http://www.clarionledger.com/story/news/2017/04/20/mdhs-confirms-most-new-applicants-rejected-welfare/100692926/.

Geary, Daniel. 2015. "The Moynihan Report: An Annotated Edition." *Atlantic*, September 14. https://www.theatlantic.com/politics/archive/2015/09/the-moynihan-report-an-annotated-edition/404632/.

Gennetian, Lisa, Wolf, Sharon, Hill, Heather, and Morris, Pamela. 2015. "Intrayear Household Income Dynamics and Adolescent School Behavior." *Demography* 52(2): 455–83.

George Bush for President. 1988. *The George Bush Record on Child Care*. https://dolearchives.ku.edu/sites/dolearchive.drupal.ku.edu/files/files/historyday/originals/hd15_ghwbush_023.pdf.

Germany Trade and Invest. 2019. *Terms of Employment*. Federal Ministry for Economic Affairs and Energy, Government of Germany. https://www.gtai.de/GTAI/Navigation/EN/Meta/about-us.html.

GFI Software. 2015. "Work Email Onslaught: Staff Have Nowhere to Hide, US Study Finds." *GFI Software*, June 24. https://www.gfi.com/company/press/press-releases/2015/06/work-email-onslaught-staff-have-nowhere-to-hide-us-study-finds.

Gibson, Campbell and Lennon, Emily. 1999. "Historical Census Statistics on the Foreign-Born Population of the United States: 1850–1990." *U.S. Census Bureau, Population Division Working Papers*. Working Paper No. 29. https://www.census.gov/population/www/documentation/twps0029/twps0029.html.

Gibson-Davis, Christina, Edin, Kathryn, and McLanahan, Sara. 2005. "High Hopes but Even Higher Expectations: The Retreat from Marriage among Low-Income Couples." *Journal of Marriage and Family* 67(5): 1301–12.

Gilder, George. 1981. *Wealth and Poverty*. New York: Basic Books.

Gilens, Martin. 1996. "'Race Coding' and White Opposition to Welfare." *American Political Science Review* 90(3): 593–604.

Glass, Jennifer, Simon, Robin, and Andersson, Matthew. 2016. "Parenthood and Happiness: Effects of Work–Family Reconciliation Policies in 22 OECD Countries." *American Journal of Sociology* 122(3): 886–929.

Golden, Lonnie. 2015. *Irregular Work Scheduling and Its Consequences*. Briefing Paper No. 394. Economic Policy Institute. https://www.epi.org/files/pdf/82524.pdf.

Golden, Lonnie and Jorgensen, Helene. 2002. *Time after Time: Mandatory Overtime in the U.S. Economy*. Briefing Paper No. 120. Economic Policy Institute. https://www.epi.org/files/page/-/old/briefingpapers/120/bp120.pdf.

Golden, Lonnie and Tesfayi, Gebreselassie. 2007. *Over-Employment Mismatches: The Preference for Fewer Work Hours*. Bureau of Labor Statistics, Monthly Labor Review. https://www.bls.gov/opub/mlr/2007/04/art2full.pdf.

Golden, Lonnie and Wiens-Tuers, Barbara. 2005. "Mandatory Overtime Work in the United States: Who, Where, and What?" *Labor Studies Journal* 30(1): 1–26.

Goldsmith, Belinda. 2010. "French Most Likely to Use All Vacation, Japanese Least: Poll." *Reuters*, August 6. http://www.reuters.com/article/us-vacations-poll-idUSTRE6753LI20100806.

Goldstein, Amy. 2018. "Three Deep Red States Vote to Expand Medicaid." *Washington Post*, November 7. https://www.washingtonpost.com/national/health-science/three-deep-red-states-vote-to-expand-medicaid/2018/11/07/6586ae58-e1dc-11e8-ab2c-b31dcd53ca6b_story.html?noredirect=on&utm_term=.fe12e440c17e.

Goldwater, Barry. 1961. "Letter from Goldwater." *New York Times*, July 23.

Gompers, Samuel. 1881. "The Curse of Tenement-House Cigar Manufacture." In Stuart B. Kaufman,. (ed.), *The Samuel Gompers Papers: The Making of a Union Leader, 1850–86*, vol. 1. Urbana: University of Illinois Press.

Goodman, Peter S. 2017. "The Robots Are Coming, and Sweden Is Fine." *New York Times*, December 27. https://www.nytimes.com/2017/12/27/business/the-robots-are-coming-and-sweden-is-fine.html.

Goodman, Sherryl H. and Gotlib, Ian H. 1999. "Risk for Psychopathology in the Children of Depressed Mothers: A Developmental Model for Understanding Mechanisms of Transmission." *Psychological Review* 106(3): 458–90.

Gordon, Linda. 1994. *Pitied but Not Entitled: Single Mothers and the History of Welfare, 1890–1935*. New York: Free Press.

Gornick, Janet and Meyers, Marcia. 2003. *Families That Work: Policies for Reconciling Parenthood and Employment*. New York: Russell Sage Foundation.

Gornick, Janet C. and Nell, Emily. 2017. "Children, Poverty, and Public Policy: A Cross-National Perspective." *LIS Working Paper Series*. Working Paper No. 701. http://www.lisdatacenter.org/wps/liswps/701.pdf.

Gottschalk, Peter and Moffitt, Robert. 2009. "The Rising Instability of U.S. Earnings." *Journal of Economic Perspectives* 23(4): 3–24.

Graham, Carol. 2017. *Happiness for All? Unequal Hopes and Lives in Pursuit of the American Dream.* Princeton, NJ: Princeton University Press.

Graham, Carol and Pinto, Sergio. 2018. "Unequal Hopes and Lives in the USA: Optimism, Race, Place, and Premature Mortality." *Journal of Population Economics* 32(2): 665–733.

Grall, Timothy. 2013. *Custodial Mothers and Fathers and Their Child Support: 2011.* Current Population Report No. P60-246. US Census Bureau. https://www.census.gov/prod/2013pubs/p60-246.pdf.

Grall, Timothy. 2016. *Custodial Mothers and Fathers and Their Child Support: 2013.* Current Population Report No. P60-255. US Census Bureau. : https://www.census.gov/content/dam/Census/library/publications/2016/demo/P60-255.pdf.

Greenfield, Meg. 1985. "Mirage-Words That We Live By." *Newsweek*, February 11, p. 80.

Greenstein, Robert. 1985. "Losing Faith in Losing Ground: The Intellectual Mugging of the Great Society." *New Republic* 192(12): 12–17.

Greenstein, Robert, Maag, Elaine, Huang, Chye-Ching, Horton, Emily, and Cho, Chloe. 2018. *Improving the Child Tax Credit for Very Low-Income Families.* US Partnership on Mobility from Poverty. https://www.mobilitypartnership.org/improving-child-tax-credit-very-low-income-families.

Greenstein, Theodore. 1993. "Maternal Employment and Child Behavioral Outcomes: A Household Economics Analysis." *Journal of Family Issues* 14(3): 323–54.

Greger, Hanne Klæboe, Myhre, Arne Kristian, Lydersen, Stian, and Jozefiak, Thomas. 2016. "Child Maltreatment and Quality of Life: A Study of Adolescents in Residential Care." *Health and Quality of Life Outcomes* 14(1): 74–91.

Gregg, Paul, Washbrook, Elizabeth, Propper, Carol, and Burgess, Simon. 2005. "The Effects of a Mother's Return to Work Decision on Child Development in the UK." *Economic Journal* 115(501): F48–F80.

Grzywacz, Joseph G., Daniel, Stephanie S., Tucker, Jenna, Walls, Jill, and Leerkes, Esther. 2011. "Nonstandard Work Schedules and Developmentally Generative Parenting Practices: An Application of Propensity Score Techniques." *Family Relations* 60(1): 45–59.

Gupta, Nabanita Datta and Simonsen, Marianne. 2010. "Non-Cognitive Child Outcomes and Universal High Quality Child Care." *Journal of Public Economics* 94(1–2): 30–43.

Gutman, Herbert G. 1973. "Work, Culture, and Society in Industrializing America, 1815–1919." *American Historical Review* 78(3): 531–88.

Guttmacher Institute. 2018. *Contraceptive Use in the United States.* https://www.guttmacher.org/sites/default/files/factsheet/fb_contr_use_0.pdf.

Guttmacher Institute. 2019. *Unintended Pregnancy in the United States.* https://www.guttmacher.org/sites/default/files/factsheet/fb-unintended-pregnancy-us.pdf.

Guzzo, Karen Benjamin. 2014. "Trends in Cohabitation Outcomes: Compositional Changes and Engagement among Never-Married Young Adults." *Journal of Marriage and Family* 76(4): 826–42.

Haas, Linda and Rostgaard, Tine. 2011. "Fathers' Rights to Paid Parental Leave in the Nordic Countries: Consequences for the Gendered Division of Leave." *Community, Work & Family* 14(2): 177–95.

Hacker, Jacob. 2006. *The Great Risk Shift: The Assault on American Jobs, Families, Health Care, and Retirement and How You Can Fight Back.* New York: Oxford University Press.

Hacker, Jacob. 2011. "Understanding Economic Insecurity: The Downward Spiral of the Middle Class." *Communities & Banking* 22(4): 25–8.

Hacker, Jacob and Pierson, Paul. 2010a. "Winner-Take-All Politics: Public Policy, Political Organization, and the Precipitous Rise of Top Incomes in the United States." *Politics and Society* 38(2): 152–204.

Hacker, Jacob and Pierson, Paul. 2010b. *Winner-Take-All Politics: How Washington Made the Rich Richer—and Turned Its Back on the Middle Class.* New York: Simon & Schuster.

Hacker, Jacob and Pierson, Paul. 2016. *American Amnesia: How the War on Government Led Us to Forget What Made America Prosper.* New York: Simon & Schuster.

Hacker, Jacob, Rehm, Phillip, and Schlesinger, Mark. 2010. *Standing on Shaky Ground: Americans' Experience with Economic Insecurity.* Economic Security Index. http://www.economicsecurityindex.org/upload/media/ESI%20report%20final_12%2013.pdf.

Hadfield, Kristin, Amos, Margaret, Ungar, Michael, Gosselin, Julie, and Ganong, Lawrence. 2018. "Do Changes to Family Structure Affect Child and Family Outcomes? A Systematic Review of the Instability Hypothesis." *Journal of Family Theory and Review* 10(1): 87–110.

Haines, Michael. 1981. "Poverty, Economic Stress, and the Family in a Late Nineteenth-Century American City: Whites in Philadelphia, 1880." In Theodore Hershberg (ed.), *Philadelphia: Work, Space, Family, and Group Experience in the Nineteenth Century.* New York: Oxford University Press.

Haines, Michael, Craig, Lee, and Weiss, Thomas. 2003. "The Short and the Dead: Nutrition, Morality, and the 'Antebellum Puzzle' in the United States." *Journal of Economic History* 63(2): 382–413.

Hair, Nicole, Hanson, Jamie, Wolfe, Barbara, and Pollack, Seth. 2015. "Association of Child Poverty, Brain Development, and Academic Achievement." *JAMA Pediatrics.* 169(9): 822–29.

Halfon, Neal, Larson, Kandyce, Son, John, Lu, Michael, and Bethell, Christina. 2016. "Income Inequality and the Differential Effect of Adverse Childhood Experiences in US Children." *Academic Pediatrics* 17(7): S70–S78.

Hall, Lauren A. 2016. *Bridging the Gap: Is Welfare a Parental Leave Alternative for Low-Income Families?* University of Maryland School of Social Work, Ruth Young Center for Families and Children. http://www.familywelfare.umaryland.edu/reports1/childunderone.pdf.

Halligan, Sarah L., Murray, Lynne, Martins, Carla, and Cooper, Peter J. 2007. "Maternal Depression and Psychiatric Outcomes in Adolescent Offspring: A 13-Year Longitudinal Study." *Journal of Affective Disorders* 97(1–3): 145–54.

Hamermesh, Daniel and Stancanelli, Elena. 2015. "Long Workweeks and Strange Hours." *ILR Review* 68(5): 1007–18.

Hamill, Pete. 1969. "The Revolt of the White Lower Middle Class." *New Yorker,.* April 14, pp. 24–9.

Hamilton, Brady E., Martin, Joyce A., Osterman, Michelle J. K., Driscoll, Anne K., and Rossen, Lauren M. 2018. *Births: Provisional Data for 2017.* Vital Statistics Rapid Release No. 004. https://www.cdc.gov/nchs/data/vsrr/report004.pdf.

Han, Wen-Jui and Waldfogel, Jane. 2007. "Parental Work Schedules, Family Process, and Early Adolescents' Risky Behavior." *Children and Youth Services Review* 29(9): 1249–66.

Han, Wen-Jui, Waldfogel, Jane, and Brooks-Gunn, Jeanne. 2001. "The Effects of Early Maternal Employment on Later Cognitive and Behavioral Outcomes." *Journal of Marriage and Family* 63(2): 336–54.

Hansen, Kirstine and Hawkes, Denise. 2009. "Early Childcare and Child Development." *Journal of Social Policy* 38(2): 211–39.

Hardy, Bradley. 2016. "Addressing Income Volatility in the United States: Flexible Policy Solutions for Changing Economic Circumstances." Washington Center for Equitable Growth. October 31. https://equitablegrowth.org/addressing-income-volatility-in-the-united-states-flexible-policy-solutions-for-changing-economic-circumstances/.

Hardy, Bradley. 2017. "Income Instability and the Response of the Safety Net." *Contemporary Economic Policy* 35(2): 312–30.

Hardy, Bradley and Ziliak, James. 2013. "Decomposing Trends in Income Volatility: The 'Wild Ride' at the Top and Bottom." *Economic Inquiry* 52(1): 459–76.

Hari, Johanne. 2018. "We Need New Ways of Treating Depression." *Vox*, June 13. https://www.vox.com/the-big-idea/2018/2/25/16997572/causes-depression-pills-prozac-social-environmental-connections-hari.

Harknett, Kristen and McLanahan, Sara. 2004. "Racial and Ethnic Differences in Marriages After the Birth of a Child." *American Sociological Review* 69(6): 790–811.

Harknett, Kristen and Schneider, Daniel. 2012. "Is a Bad Economy Good for Marriage? The Relationship Between Macroeconomic Conditions and Marital Stability from 1998–2009." *National Poverty Center Working Paper Series*. Working Paper No. 12-06. http://www.npc.umich.edu/publications/u/2012-06%20NPC%20Working%20Paper.pdf.

Harrington, Brad, Van Deusen, Fred and Humberd, Beth. 2011. *The New Dad: Caring, Committed, Conflicted*. Boston College Center for Work and Family. http://www.bc.edu/content/dam/files/centers/cwf/research/publications/researchreports/The%20New%20Dad%202011_Caring%20Committed%20and%20Conflicted.

Harrington, Brad, Van Deusen, Fred, Fraone, Jennifer, and Mazar, Iyar. 2015. *The New Dad: A Portrait of Today's Father*. Boston College Center for Work and Family. https://www.bc.edu/content/dam/files/centers/cwf/research/publications/researchreports/The%20New%20Dad%202015%20presentation_with%20embedded%20video.pdf.

Harris, Kathleen Mullan. 1993. "Work and Welfare among Single Mothers in Poverty." *American Journal of Sociology* 99(2): 317–52.

Harrison, Megan E., Norris, Mark L., Obeid, Nicole, Fu, Maeghan, Weinstangel, Hannah, and Sampson, Margaret. 2015. "Systematic Review of the Effects of Family Meal Frequency on Psychosocial Outcomes in Youth." *Canadian Family Physician* 61(2): e96–e106.

Hart, Betty and Risley, Todd R. 1995. *Meaningful Differences in the Everyday Experience of Young American Children*. Baltimore: Paul H. Brookes.

Hart, Carl. 2013. *High Price: A Neuroscientist's Journey of Self-Discovery That Challenges Everything You Know About Drugs and Society*. New York: HarperCollins.

Hart, Carl. 2014. "Opinion: As with Other Problems, Class Affects Addiction." *New York Times*, March 10. https://www.nytimes.com/roomfordebate/2014/02/10/what-is-addiction/as-with-other-problems-class-affects-addiction.

Harter, Jim. 2018. *Employee Engagement on the Rise in the US*. Gallup. https://news.gallup.com/poll/241649/employee-engagement-rise.aspx.

Harvard Center on the Developing Child. 2007a. *The Impact of Early Adversity on Child Development*. https://46y5eh11fhgw3ve3ytpwxt9r-wpengine.netdna-ssl.com/wp-content/uploads/2015/05/inbrief-adversity-1.pdf.

Harvard Center on the Developing Child. 2007b. *The Science of Early Childhood Development*. https://46y5eh11fhgw3ve3ytpwxt9r-wpengine.netdna-ssl.com/wp-content/uploads/2007/03/InBrief-The-Science-of-Early-Childhood-Development2.pdf.

Harvard Center on the Developing Child. 2013. *The Science of Neglect*. https://46y5eh11fhgw3ve3ytpwxt9r-wpengine.netdna-ssl.com/wp-content/uploads/2015/05/InBrief-The-Science-of-Neglect-3.pdf.

Haskins, Ron. 2004. *Preschool Programs and the Achievement Gap: The Little Train That Could*. Washington, DC: Brookings Institution.

Hayes, Jeff and Hartmann, Heidi. 2018. *Paid Family and Medical Leave Insurance: Modest Costs are a Good investment in America's Economy*. Fact Sheet No. B368. Institute for Women's Policy Research. https://iwpr.org/wp-content/uploads/2018/02/B368_Paid-Leave-Fact-Sheet-1.pdf.

Hays, Sharon. 2003. *Flat Broke with Children: Women in the Age of Welfare Reform*. New York: Oxford University Press.

Heckman, James. 2016. *There's More to Gain by Taking a Comprehensive Approach to Early Childhood Development*. Heckman Equation. https://heckmanequation.org/www/assets/2017/01/F_Heckman_CBAOnePager_120516.pdf.

Heckman, James J., Moon, Seong Hyeok, Pinto, Rodrigo, Savelyev, Peter A., and Yavitz, Adam. 2010. "The Rate of Return to the HighScope Perry Preschool Program." *Journal of Public Economics* 94(1–2): 114–28.

Hedegaard, Holly, Miniño, Arialdi M., and Warner, Margaret. 2018. *Drug Overdose Deaths in the United States, 1999–2017*. NCHS Data Brief No. 329. US Department of Health and Human Services, National Center for Health Statistics. https://www.cdc.gov/nchs/data/databriefs/db329-h.pdf.

Hegewisch, Ariane. 2009. *Flexible Working Policies: A Comparative Review.* Research Report No. 16. Equality and Human Rights Commission, Institute for Women's Policy Research. http://www.equality-ne.co.uk/downloads/426_Flexible-Working-Policies.pdf.

Hegewisch, Ariane and Gornick, Janet C. 2008. *Statutory Routes to Workplace Flexibility in Cross-National Perspective.* Institute for Women's Policy Research. https://iwpr.org/wp-content/uploads/wpallimport/files/iwpr-export/publications/B258%20workplaceflex.pdf.

Hemez, Paul. 2016. *Marriage Rate in the U.S.: Geographic Variation, 2015.* Bowling Green State University, National Center for Family & Marriage Research. https://www.bgsu.edu/content/dam/BGSU/college-of-arts-and-sciences/NCFMR/documents/FP/hemez-marriage-rate-us-geo-2015-fp-16-22.pdf.

Henry J. Kaiser Family Foundation. 2008. *Health Care and the 2008 Elections.* https://www.kff.org/health-costs/issue-brief/health-care-costs-and-election-2008/.

Henry J. Kaiser Family Foundation. 2018. *Fact Sheet: Key Facts about the Uninsured Population.* http://files.kff.org/attachment//fact-sheet-key-facts-about-the-uninsured-population.

Herbst, Chris. 2017. "Are Parental Welfare Work Requirements Good for Disadvantaged Children? Evidence from Age-of-Youngest Child Exemptions." *Journal of Policy Analysis and Management* 36(2): 327–57.

Hertz, Rosanna. 1999. "Working to Place Family at the Center of Life: Dual-Earner and Single-Parent Strategies." *Annals of the American Academy of Political and Social Science* 562(1): 16–31.

Heuveline, Patrick, Timberlake, Jeffrey M., and Furstenberg, Frank F. 2003. "Shifting Childrearing to Single Mothers: Results from 17 Western Countries." *Population and Development Review* 29(1): 47–71.

Hildyard, Kathryn and Wolfe, David. 2002. "Child Neglect: Developmental Issues and Outcomes." *Child Abuse and Neglect* 26(6): 679–95.

Hill, Heather. 2012. "Welfare as Maternity Leave? Exemptions from Welfare Work Requirements and Maternal Employment." *Social Services Review* 86(1): 37–67.

Hill, Heather, Morris, Pamela, Gennetian, Lisa, Wolf, Sharon, and Tubbs, Carly. 2013. "The Consequences of Income Instability for Children's Well-Being." *Child Development Perspectives* 7(2): 85–90.

Hiltonsmith, Robert. 2013. *At What Cost? How Student Debt Reduces Lifetime Wealth.* Demos. https://www.demos.org/sites/default/files/imce/AtWhatCostFinal.pdf.

Himmelweit, Susan. 1995. "The Discovery of 'Unpaid Work': The Social Consequences of the Expansion of 'Work.'" *Feminist Economics* 1(2): 1–19.

Hochschild, Arlie. 2003. *The Commercialization of Intimate Life: Notes from Home and Work.* Berkeley: University of California Press.

Hochschild, Arlie and Machung, Ann. 1989. *The Second Shift: Working Parents and the Revolution at Home.* New York: Penguin Group.

Hogan, Dennis, Eggebeen, David and Clogg, Clifford. 1993. "The Structure of Intergenerational Exchanges in American Families." *American Journal of Sociology* 98(6): 1428–58.

Holder, Mark D. and Coleman, Ben. 2008. "The Contribution of Temperament, Popularity, and Physical Appearance to Children's Happiness." *Journal of Happiness Studies* 9(2): 279–302.

Holmlund, Bertil and Lundborg, Per. 1999. "Wage Bargaining, Union Membership, and the Organization of Unemployment Insurance." *Labor Economics* 6(3): 397–415.

Holzer, Harry J., Schanzenbach, Diane Whitmore, Duncan, Greg J., and Ludwig, Jens. 2007. "The Economic Costs of Poverty in the United States: Subsequent Effects of Children Growing Up Poor." Institute for Research on Poverty. (Discussion Paper No. 1327-07. https://irp.wisc.edu/publications/dps/pdfs/dp132707.pdf.

Home Visiting Evidence of Effectiveness. 2015a. *Implementing Health Access Nurturing Development Services (HANDS) Program: Estimated Costs of Implementation.* US Department of Health and Human Services. https://homvee.acf.hhs.gov/Implementation/3/

Health-Access-Nurturing-Development-Services--HANDS--Program-Estimated-Costs-of-Implementation/37/5.

Home Visiting Evidence of Effectiveness. 2015b. *Implementing Health Access Nurturing Development Services (HANDS) Program: Model Overview.* US Department of Health and Human Services. https://homvee.acf.hhs.gov/Implementation/3/Health-Access-Nurturing-Development-Services--HANDS--Program-Model-Overview/37.

Horowitz, Juliana M., Parker, Kim, Graf, Nikki, and Livingston, Gretchen. 2017. *Americans Widely Support Paid Family and Medical Leave, but Differ over Specific Policies.* Pew Research Center. http://www.pewsocialtrends.org/wp-content/uploads/sites/3/2017/03/Paid-Leave-Report-FINAL_updated-10.2.pdf.

Horton, John Benjamin. 1979. *Not Without Struggle: An Account of the Most Significant Political and Social-Action Changes That Have Occurred in the Lives of Black Kentuckians in the Twentieth Century.* New York: Vantage Press.

Horwitz, Morton J. 1977. *The Transformation of American Law, 1780–1860.* Cambridge, MA.: Harvard University Press.

Hotz, V. Joseph, McElroy, Susan Williams and Sanders, Seth G. 2005. "Teenage Childbearing and Its Life Cycle Consequences: Exploiting a Natural Experiment." *Journal of Human Resources* 40(3): 683–715.

Howard, Kimberly, Martin, Anne, Berlin, Lisa and Brooks-Gunn, Jeanne. 2011. "Early Mother–Child Separation, Parenting, and Child Well-Being in Early Head Start Families" *Attachment and Human Development* 13(1): 5–26.

Huberman, Michael and Minns, Chris. 2007. "The Times They Are Not Changin': Days and Hours of Work in Old and New Worlds, 1870–2000." *Explorations in Economic History* 44(4): 538–67.

Huerta, Maria, Adema, Willem, Baxter, Jennifer, Han, Wen-Jui, Lausten, Mette, Lee RaeHyuck, and Waldfogel, Jane. 2014. "Fathers' Leave and Fathers' Involvement: Evidence from Four OECD Countries." *European Journal of Social Security* 16(4): 308–46.

Hujala, Eeva, Fonsén, Elina, and Elo, Janniina. 2012. "Evaluating the Quality of the Child Care in Finland." *Early Child Development and Care* 182(3–4): 299–314.

Huntington, Clare. 2015. "Postmarital Family Law: A Legal Structure for Nonmarital Families." *Stanford Law Review* 67(1): 167–240.

Huntington, Clare. Forthcoming. "Early Childhood Development and the Replication of Poverty." In Ezra Rosser (ed.), *Holes in the Safety Net: Federalism and Poverty.* Cambridge: Cambridge University Press.

Hurst, James Willard. 1964. *Justice Holmes on Legal History.* New York: Macmillan.

Hutchings, Judy and Lane, Eleanor. 2005. "Parenting and the Development and Prevention of Child Mental Health Problems." *Current Opinion in Psychiatry* 18(4): 386–91.

Ingraham, Christopher and Johnson, Carolyn Y. 2016. "The Story Behind the Photo of Two Heroin Users and Their Four-Year-Old Child." *Independent*, September 10. https://www.independent.co.uk/news/world/americas/heroin-picture-parents-ohio-police-child-a7235621.html.

Institute for Research on Poverty. 1973. *Summary Report: The New Jersey Graduated Work Incentive Experiment.* Mathematica Policy Research. https://www.mathematica-mpr.com/our-publications-and-findings/publications/new-jersey-graduated-work-incentive-experiment-summary-report.

Institute for Research on Poverty. 1976. *The Rural Income Maintenance Experiment.* US Department of Health, Education, and Welfare. https://www.irp.wisc.edu/publications/sr/pdfs/sr10.pdf.

Internal Revenue Service. 2018. *U.S. Individual Income Tax: Personal Exemptions and Lowest and Highest Bracket Tax Rates, and Tax Base for Regular Tax, 1913–2015.* https://www.irs.gov/statistics/soi-tax-stats-historical-table-23.

International Labour Office. 2009. *ILO Database of Conditions of Work and Employment Laws: Maternity Protection.* International Labour Organization. https://www.ilo.org/

wcmsp5/groups/public/---ed_protect/---protrav/---travail/documents/image/wcms_ 146202.pdf.

International Labour Office. 2014. *Maternity and Paternity at Work: Law and Practice Across the World*. International Labour Organization. https://www.ilo.org/wcmsp5/groups/public/---dgreports/---dcomm/---publ/documents/publication/wcms_242615.pdf.

Irving, Shelley K., and Loveless, Tracy A. 2015. *Dynamics of Economic Well-Being: Participation in Government Programs, 2009-2012: Who Gets Assistance?* US Census Bureau. https://www.census.gov/content/dam/Census/library/publications/2015/demo/p70-141.pdf

Isaacs, Julia. 2009. *How Much Do We Spend on Children and the Elderly?* Brookings Center on Children & Families. https://www.brookings.edu/wp-content/uploads/2016/07/1_how_much_isaacs.pdf.

Isaacs, Julia B., Lou, Cary, Hahn, Heather, Hong, Ashely, Quakenbush, Caleb, and Steuerle, C. Eugene. 2018. *Kids' Share, 2018: Report on Federal Expenditures on Children in 2017 and Future Projections*. Urban Institute. https://www.urban.org/sites/default/files/publication/98725/kids_share_2018_0.pdf.

Isaacs, Julia, Edelstein, Sara, Hahn, Heather, Steele, Ellen, and Steuerle, C. Eugene. 2015. *Kids' Share, 2015: Report on Federal Expenditures on Children in 2014 and Future Projections*. Urban Institute. https://www.urban.org/sites/default/files/publication/71431/2000422-Kids-Share-2015-Report-on-Federal-Expenditures-on-Children-Through-2014.pdf.

Jackson, Aurora P., Brooks-Gunn, Jeanne, Huang, Chien-Chung, and Glassman, Marc. 2000. "Single Mothers in Low-Wage Jobs: Financial Strain, Parenting, and Preschoolers' Outcomes." *Child Development* 71(5): 1409–23.

Jacobs, Jerry and Gerson, Kathleen. 2004. *The Time Divide: Work, Family, and Gender Inequality*. Cambridge, MA.: Harvard University Press.

Jacoby, Melissa and Holman, Mirya. 2014. "Financial Fragility, Medical Problems and the Bankruptcy System." In Marion Crain and Michael Sherraden (eds.), *Living and Working in the Shadow of Economic Fragility*. New York: Oxford University Press.

Jefferson, Thomas. 1801. "First Inaugural Address." *The Avalon Project at Yale Law School*. http://avalon.law.yale.edu/19th_century/jefinau1.asp.

Jencks, Christopher. 1985. "How Poor Are the Poor?" *New York Review of Books*, 32(8): 41.

Jencks, Christopher, Smith, Marshall, Acland, Henry, Bane, Mary Jo, Cohen, David, Gintis, Herbert, Heyns, Barbara, and Michelson, Stephanie. 1981. *Inequality: A Reassessment of the Effect of Family and Schooling in America*. New York: Harper Colophon Books.

Jensen, J.J. 2014. "Denmark". In *Ausgewählte Konzepte der fachpraktischen Ausbildung in Europa. Impulse für Deutschland? [Selected approaches towards workplace-based learning and mentoring practices in early childhood teacher education in Europe. Impetus for Germany?]* by Pamela Oberhuemer. München: Deutsches Jugendinstitut. http://www.weiterbildungsinitiative.de/uploads/media/WiFF_Studie_22_Fachpraktische_Ausbildung.p df

Johansson, Thomas. 2011. "Fatherhood in Transition: Paternity Leave and Changing Masculinities." *Journal of Family Communication* 11(3): 165–80.

Johnson, Lyndon B. 1964. "U.S. President Lyndon B. Johnson Visits Ohio University." *Ohio University Library: Digital Initiatives*, May 7. https://media.library.ohio.edu/digital/collection/archives/id/40947/.

Jones, Jacqueline. 1985. *Labor of Love, Labor of Sorrow: Black Women, Work, and the Family from Slavery to the Present*. New York: Basic Books.

Jones, Lauren E., Milligan, Kevin S., and Stabile, Mark. 2015. "Child Cash Benefits and Family Expenditures: Evidence from the National Child Benefit." *National Bureau of Economic Research Working Paper Series*. Working Paper No. 21101. http://www.nber.org/papers/w21101.pdf.

Jones, Robert P., Cox, Daniel, and Navarro-Rivera, Juhem. 2014. *Economic Insecurity, Rising Inequality, and Doubts About the Future: Findings from the 2014 American Values Survey*. Public Religion Research Institute. https://www.prri.org/wp-content/uploads/2014/09/PRRI-AVS-with-Transparancy-Edits.pdf.

Jorgensen, Helene and Appelbaum, Eileen. 2014. *Expanding Federal Family and Medical Leave Coverage: Who Benefits from Changes in Eligibility Requirements?* Center for Economic and Policy Research. http://cepr.net/documents/fmla-eligibility-2014-01.pdf.

Joshi, Ritu, Khadilkar, Suvarna, and Patel, Madhuri. 2015. "Global Trends in Use of Long-Acting Reversible and Permanent Methods of Contraception: Seeking a Balance." *International Journal of Gynecology and Obstetrics* 131(suppl. 1): S60–S63.

Juhl, Pernille. 2018. "Early Childhood Education and Care in Denmark: The Contested Issue of Quality in Children's Everyday Lives." In Susanne Garvis Sivanes Phillipson, and Heidi Harju-Luukkainen (eds.), *International Perspectives on Early Childhood Education and Care: Early Childhood Education in the 21st Century*, vol. 1. New York: Routledge.

Jungmann, Tanja, Brand, Tilman, Dähne, Verena, Herrmann, Peggy, Günay, Hüsamettin, Sandner, Malte and Sierau, Susan. 2015. "Comprehensive evaluation of the Pro Kind home visiting program: A summary of results." *Mental Health and Prevention* 3: 89-97.

Kalleberg, Arne. 2011. *Good Jobs, Bad Jobs: The Rise of Polarized and Precarious Employment Systems in the United States, 1970s to 2000s.* New York: Russell Sage Foundation.

Kamal, Rabah and Cox, Cynthia. 2017. "How Has U.S. Spending on Healthcare Changed over Time?" *Peterson-Kaiser Health System Tracker*, December 20. https://www.healthsystemtracker.org/chart-collection/u-s-spending-healthcare-changed-time/#item-per-capita-pocket-expenditures-grown-since-1970_2017.

Kamerman, Sheila B. and Kahn, Alfred J. 1993. "Home Health Visiting in Europe." *Future of Children* 3(3): 39–52.

Kan, Michelle, Levanon, Gad, Li, Allen, and Ray, Rebecca L. 2018. *Job Satisfaction 2018: A Tighter Labor Market Leads to Higher Job Satisfaction.* Conference Board. https://www.conference-board.org/publications/publicationdetail.cfm?publicationid=8120.

Kang, Shimi. 2015. "How the Wealthy Are Disadvantaged: How Upper and Upper Middle Class Kids Are at Risk." *Psychology Today*, December 1. https://www.psychologytoday.com/us/blog/the-dolphin-way/201512/how-the-wealthy-are-disadvantaged.

Kantor, Jodi. 2014. "Working Anything but 9 to 5." *New York Times*, August 13. https://www.nytimes.com/interactive/2014/08/13/us/starbucks-workers-scheduling-hours.html.

Kantor, Jodi and Streitfeld, David. 2015. "Inside Amazon: Wrestling Big Ideas in a Bruising Workplace." *New York Times*, August 15. https://www.nytimes.com/2015/08/16/technology/inside-amazon-wrestling-big-ideas-in-a-bruising-workplace.html.

Kaplan, Greg, Violante, Giovanni L., and Weidner, Justin. 2014. "The Wealthy Hand-to-Mouth." *Brookings Papers on Economic Activity* 2014(1): 77–153.

Kaplan, Marnie and Mead, Sara. 2017. *The Best Teachers for Our Littlest Learners? Lessons from Head Start's Last Decade.* Bellwether Education Partners. https://bellwethereducation.org/sites/default/files/Bellwether_HeadStartWorkforce.pdf.

Karch, Andrew. 2013. *Early Start: Preschool Politics in the United States.* University of Michigan. https://oapen.org/download?type=document&docid=625245.

Karoly, Lynn A. 2017. *Investing in the Early Years: The Costs and Benefits of Investing in Early Childhood Education in New Hampshire.* RAND. https://www.rand.org/pubs/research_reports/RR1890.html.

Karoly, Lynn A., Ghosh-Dastidar, Bonnie, Zellman, Gail L., Perlman, Michal, and Fernyhough, Lynda. 2008. *Prepared to Learn: The Nature and Quality of Early Care and Education for Preschool-Age Children in California.* RAND. https://www.rand.org/content/dam/rand/pubs/technical_reports/2008/RAND_TR539.pdf.

Karoly, Lynn, Greenwood, Peter, Everingham, Susan, Houbé, Jill, Kilburn, M. Rebecca, Rydell, C. Peter, Sanders, Matthew, and Chiesa, James. 1998. *Investing in Our Children: What We Know and What We Don't Know About the Costs of and Benefits of Early Childhood Interventions.* RAND. https://www.rand.org/content/dam/rand/pubs/monograph_reports/1998/MR898.pdf.

Karoly, Lynn A., Kilburn, Rebecca, and Cannon, Jill S. 2005. *Children at Risk: Consequences for School Readiness and Beyond*. RAND. https://www.rand.org/pubs/research_briefs/RB9144.html.

Kasser, Tim and Ryan, Richard M. 1993. "A Dark Side of the American Dream: Correlates of Financial Success as a Central Life Aspiration." *Journal of Personality and Social Psychology* 65(2): 410–22.

Kasser, Tim and Ryan, Richard M. 1996. "Further Examining the American Dream: Differential Correlates of Intrinsic and Extrinsic Goals." *Personality and Social Psychology Bulletin* 22(3): 280.

Katz, Josh and Goodnough, Abby. 2017. "The Opioid Crisis Is Getting Worse, Particularly for Black Americans." *New York Times*, December 22. https://www.nytimes.com/interactive/2017/12/22/upshot/opioid-deaths-are-spreading-rapidly-into-black-america.html.

Katz, Lawrence and Krueger, Alan B. 2016. "The Rise and Nature of Alternative Work Arrangements in the United States, 1995–2015." *National Bureau of Economic Research Working Paper Series*. Working Paper No. 22667. https://www.nber.org/papers/w22667.pdf.

Katz, Michael B. 1983. *Poverty and Policy in American History*. New York: Academic Press.

Katz, Michael B. 1986. *In the Shadow of the Poorhouse: A Social History of Welfare in America*. New York: BasicBooks.

Katz, Michael B. 1989. *The Undeserving Poor: From the War on Poverty to the War on Welfare*. New York: Pantheon Books.

Katz, Michael. 1996. *In the Shadow of the Poorhouse: A Social History of Welfare in America*. Rev. ed. New York: Basic Books.

Kaye, H. Stephen, Harrington, Charlene, and LaPlante, Mitchell P. 2010. "Long-Term Care: Who Gets It, Who Provides It, Who Pays, and How Much?" *Health Affairs* 29(1): 11–21.

Kearney, Melissa, Hershbein, Brad, and Jácome, Elisa. 2015. *Profiles of Change: Employment, Earnings, and Occupations from 1990–2013*. Hamilton Project. http://www.hamiltonproject.org/assets/legacy/files/downloads_and_links/worker_profiles_changes_earnings_occupations_1990-2013_FINAL.pdf.

Kearney, Melissa and Levine, Phillip. 2014. "Income Inequality and Early Nonmarital Childbearing." *Journal of Human Resources* 49(1): 1–31.

Kearney, Melissa and Levine, Phillip. 2017. "The Economics of Non-Marital Childbearing and the 'Marriage Premium for Children.'" *National Bureau of Economic Research Working Paper Series*. Working Paper No. 23230. https://www.nber.org/papers/w23230.

Kehrer, Kenneth C. 1977. "Findings from the Gary Income Maintenance Experiment: Testimony Before the House Committee on Ways and Means, October 11, 1977." *Mathematica Policy Research Working Papers*. Working Paper No. A-26. https://www.mathematica-mpr.com/our-publications-and-findings/publications/findings-from-the-gary-income-maintenance-experiment-testimony.

Kela. 2015. *Home and Family: Benefits for Families with Children and Housing Benefits*. http://www.kela.fi/documents/10180/1978560/2015_Home_family.pdf.

Kela. 2017. *Benefits for LGBT families*. Last modified April 10. https://www.kela.fi/web/en/rainbow-families.

Kela. 2018a. *Maternity Grant*. Last modified June 13. https://www.kela.fi/web/en/maternity-grant.

Kela. 2018b. *Kela Benefits in Euros 2018*. https://www.kela.fi/documents/12099/6889543/Kela_benefits_in_euros_2018.pdf/23cc6882-1755-442c-bf5e-5f4595d64fbc.

Kela. 2018c. *Study Grant*. Last modified September 3. https://www.kela.fi/web/en/financial-aid-for-students-study-grant.

Kela. 2018d. *Amount and Payment of Child Benefit*. Last modified January 18. https://www.kela.fi/web/en/child-benefit-amount-and-payment.

Kela. 2018e. *Amount and Payment of Child Maintenance Allowance*. Last modified January 1. https://www.kela.fi/web/en/child-maintenance-allowance-amount-and-payment.

Kela/FPA. 2015. *Adequacy of basic social security in Finland 2011–2015*. https://www.julkari.fi/bitstream/handle/10024/126908/WorkingPapers80%20%281%29.pdf?sequence=1

Kelleher, David. 2013. "Survey: 81% of U.S. Employees Check Their Work Mail Outside Work Hours." *GFI TechTalk*, May 20. https://techtalk.gfi.com/survey-81-of-u-s-employees-check-their-work-mail-outside-work-hours/.

Kelley, Florence. 1914. *Modern Industry in Relation to the Family, Health, Education, Morality*. New York: Longmans, Green.

Kelly-Irving, Michelle, Denoit, Lepage, Dedieu, Dominique, Bartley, Mel, Blane, David, Grosclaude, Pascale, Lang, Thierry, and Delpierre, Cyrille. 2013. "Adverse Childhood Experiences and Premature All-Cause Mortality." *European Journal of Epidemiology* 28(9): 721–34.

Kendig, Sarah M. and Bianchi, Suzanne M. 2008. "Single, Cohabiting, and Married Mothers' Time with Children." *Journal of Marriage and Family* 70(5): 1228–40.

Kennedy, Sheela and Bumpass, Larry. 2008. "Cohabitation and Children's Living Arrangements: New Estimates from the United States." *Demographic Research* 19(47): 1663–92.

Kenworthy, Lane. 2019. *Social Democratic Capitalism*. New York: Oxford University Press.

Kenworthy, Lane. 2008. "Slow Income Growth for Middle America." *Lane Kenworthy Blog*, September 3. https://lanekenworthy.net/2008/09/03/slow-income-growth-for-middle-america/.

Kessler-Harris, Alice. 2001. *In Pursuit of Equity: Women, Men, and the Quest for Economic Citizenship in 20th-Century America*. New York: Oxford University Press.

Kessler-Harris, Alice. 2003. *Out to Work: A History of Wage-Earning Women in the United States*. New York: Oxford University Press.

Keyes, Katherine M., Maslowsky, Julie, Hamilton, Ava, and Schulenberg, John. 2015. "The Great Sleep Recession: Changes in Sleep Duration among US Adolescents, 1991–2012." *Pediatrics* 135(3): 460–68.

Keynes, John Maynard. 1930. "Economic Possibilities for Our Grandchildren." In *Essays in Persuasion*. New York: W. W. Norton.

Keys, Benjamin. 2008. "Variable Effects of Earnings Volatility on Food Stamp Participation." In Jolliffe Dean and James Ziliak (eds.), *Income Volatility and Food Assistance in the United States*. Kalamazoo, MI: W. E. Upjohn Institute for Employment Research.

Khan, Sarah and Khan, Rafeeq Alam. 2017. "Chronic Stress Leads to Anxiety and Depression." *Annals of Psychiatry and Mental Health* 5(1): 1091–95.

Khazan, Olga. 2013. "The Secret to Finland's Success with Schools, Moms, Kids—and Everything" *Atlantic*, July 11. https://www.theatlantic.com/international/archive/2013/07/the-secret-to-finlands-success-with-schools-moms-kids-and-everything/277699/.

Kiley, Jocelyn. 2017. "Support for Single Payer Grows among Democrats." Pew Research Center, June 23. http://www.pewresearch.org/fact-tank/2017/06/23/public-support-for-single-payer-health-coverage-grows-driven-by-democrats/.

Kirkland, Kristen and Mitchell-Herzfeld, Susan. 2012. *Evaluating the Effectiveness of Home Visiting Services to Promoting Children's Adjustment to School*. New York State Office of Children and Family Services, Bureau of Evaluation and Research. https://www.pewtrusts.org/~/media/legacy/uploadedfiles/pcs_assets/2013/schoolreadinessexecutivesummarypdf.pdf.

Kitzman Harriet J., Olds, David L., Cole, Robert E., Hanks, Carole A., Anson, Elizabeth A., Arcoleo, Kimberly J., Luckey, Dennis W., Knudtson, Michael D., Henderson, Charles R., and Holmberg, John R. 2010. "Enduring Effects of Prenatal and Infancy Home Visiting by Nurses on Children: Follow-up of a Randomized Trial among Children at Age 12 Years." *Archives of Pediatrics and Adolescent Medicine* 164(5): 412–18.

Klerman, Jacob, Daley, Kelly, and Pozniak, Alyssa. 2014. *Family and Medical Leave in 2012: Technical Report*. Abt Associates. https://www.dol.gov/asp/evaluation/fmla/FMLA-2012-Technical-Report.pdf.

Kluve, Jochen and Tamm, Marcus. 2013. "Parental Leave Regulations, Mothers' Labor Force Attachment and Fathers' Childcare Involvement: Evidence from a Natural Experiment." *Journal of Population Economics* 26(3): 983–1005.

Koball, Heather and Jiang, Yang. 2018a. *Basic Facts about Low-Income Children: Children Under 18 Years, 2016*. Columbia University, National Center for Children in Poverty. http://www.nccp.org/publications/pdf/text_1194.pdf.

Koball, Heather and Jiang, Yang. 2018b. *Basic Facts about Low-Income Children: Children Under 9 Years, 2016*. Columbia University, National Center for Children in Poverty. http://www.nccp.org/publications/pub_1195.html.

Komlos, John. 1987. "The Height and Weight of West Point Cadets: Dietary Change in Antebellum America." *Journal of Economic History* 47(4): 897–927.

Kontos, Susan, Howes, Carollee, Shinn, Marybeth, and Galinsky, Ellen. 1995. *Quality in Family Child Care and Relative Care*. New York: Teachers College Press.

Kottelenberg, Michael J., and Lehrer, Steven F. 2013. "New Evidence on the Impacts of Access to and Attending Universal Childcare in Canada." *NBER Working Series*. Working Paper No. 18785. https://www.nber.org/papers/w18785.

Kottelenberg, Michael J. and Lehrer, Steven F. 2014. "Do the Perils of Universal Childcare Depend on the Child's Age?" *CESifo Economic Studies* 60(2): 338–65.

Krupnick, Matt. 2015. "Low-Income Students Struggle for College, Even in a State That Provides Help." *PBS*, August 18. http://www.pbs.org/newshour/updates/low-income-students-struggle-pay-college-even-state-still-provides-help/.

Kuhn, Peter and Lozano, Fernando. 2008. "The Expanding Workweek? Understanding Trends in Long Work Hours among U.S. Men, 1979–2006." *Journal of Labor Economics* 26(2): 311–43.

Kwong, Tammie. 2014. "Adverse Childhood Experiences (ACEs) and Their Influence on Social Connectedness." *Public Health Theses* (No. 1157). https://elischolar.library.yale.edu/cgi/viewcontent.cgi?referer=https://www.google.com/&httpsredir=1&article=1156&context=ysphtdl.

Lahey, Jessica. 2015. *The Gift of Failure: How the Best Parents Learn to Let Go So Their Children Can Succeed*. New York: HarperCollins.

Lambert, Susan J., Fugiel, Peter J., and Henly, Julia R. 2014. *Precarious Work Schedules among Early-Career Employees in the US: A National Snapshot*. University of Chicago, School of Social Service Administration. https://ssa.uchicago.edu/sites/default/files/uploads/lambert.fugiel.henly_.precarious_work_schedules.august2014_0.pdf.

Lampman, Robert. 1969. *Nixon's Family Assistance Plan*. Institute for Research on Poverty. https://www.irp.wisc.edu/publications/dps/pdfs/dp5769.pdf.

Landau, Elizabeth. 2012. "Cost of Children's Health Care Hitting Families Harder." *CNN*, May 21. https://www.cnn.com/2012/05/21/health/health-care-spending/index.html.

Lapierre, Sylvie, Bouffard, Léandre, and Bastin, Etienne. 1997. "Personal Goals and Subjective Well-Being in Later Life." *International Journal of Aging and Human Development* 45(4): 287–303.

LARC4CO. 2019. *Colorado Is Reducing Unintended Pregnancy*. Accessed June 1 https://static1.squarespace.com/static/5b7afd32c258b45a46558dd1/t/5b91a6bd6d2a7382e3881391/1536272062250/LARC4CO-fact-sheet+rev+09-06-18_2.pdf.

Lareau, Annette. 2011. *Unequal Childhoods: Class, Race, and Family Life*. 2nd ed. Berkeley: University Press of California.

Laughlin, Lynda. 2011. *Maternity Leave and Employment Patterns of First-Time Mothers: 1961–2008*. Current Population Report No. P70-128. US Census Bureau. https://www.census.gov/prod/2011pubs/p70-128.pdf.

Laughlin, Lynda. 2013. *Who's Minding the Kids? Child Care Arrangements*. Current Population Report No. P70-135. US Census Bureau. https://www.census.gov/prod/2013pubs/p70-135.pdf.

Laurie, Bruce. 1989. *Artisans Into Workers: Labor in Nineteenth-Century America*. Chicago: University of Illinois Press.

Layard, Richard. 2005. *Happiness: Lessons from a New Science*. New York: Penguin Press.

Layzer, Jean I. and Burstein, Nancy. 2007. *National Study of Child Care for Low-Income Families: Patterns of Child Care Use among Low-Income Families*. US Department of Health and Human Services, Administration for Children and Families. https://www.acf.hhs.gov/sites/default/files/opre/patterns_cc_execsum.pdf.

Leckman, James and March, John. 2011. "Developmental Neuroscience Comes of Age." *Journal of Child Psychology* 52(4): 333–8.

Lee, Bong Joo and Yoo, Min Sang. 2015. "Family, School, and Community Correlates of Children's Subjective Well-being: An International Comparative Study." *Child Indicators Research* 8(1): 151–75.

Lee, Jacqueline. 2017. "Youth Suicide Rates in Santa Clara County Highest in Palo Alto." *Mercury News*, August 18. https://www.mercurynews.com/2017/03/03/cdc-report-youth-suicide-rates-in-county-highest-in-palo-alto-morgan-hill/

Lee, Meery and Larson, Reed. 2000. "The Korean 'Examination Hell': Long Hours of Studying, Distress, and Depression." *Journal of Youth and Adolescence* 29(2): 249–71.

Lee, Rosalyn D., Fang, Xiangming, and Luo, Feijun. 2013. "The Impact of Parental Incarceration on the Physical and Mental Health of Young Adults." *Pediatrics* 131(4): e1188–e1195.

Lee, Su-Hyun and May, Tiffany. 2018. "Go Home, South Korea Tells Workers, as Stress Takes Its Toll." *New York Times*, July 28. https://www.nytimes.com/2018/07/28/world/asia/south-korea-overwork-workweek.html.

Leff, Mark. 1973. "Consensus for Reform: The Mothers'-Pension Movement in the Progressive Era." *Social Service Review* 47(3): 397–417.

Leinonen, Jenni A., Solantaus, Tytti S., and Punamäki, Raija-Leena. 2002. "The Specific Mediating Paths Between Economic Hardship and the Quality of Parenting." *International Journal of Behavioral Development* 26(5): 423–35.

Leonard, Noelle, Gwadz, Marya, Ritchie, Amanda, Linick, Jessica, Cleland, Charles, Elliott, Luther, and Grethel, Michele. 2015. "A Multi-Method Exploratory Study of Stress, Coping, and Substance Use among High School Youth in Private Schools." *Frontiers in Psychology* 6: 1–16.

Lerner, Sharon. 2015. "The Real War on Families: Why the U.S. Needs Paid Leave Now." *In These Times*, August 18. http://inthesetimes.com/article/18151/the-real-war-on-families.

Lero, Donna S. 2015. *Current Stats on Paternity Leave and Fathers' Use of Parental Leave and Income Support in Canada and Quebec.* Center for Families, Work and Well-Being, University of Guelph. https://www.worklifecanada.ca/cms/resources/files/731/CURRENT_STATS_ON_PATERNITY_LEAVE_AND_FATHERS.pdf

Leve, Leslie D., Kim, Hyoun K., and Pears, Katherine C. 2005. "Childhood Temperament and Family Environment as Predictors of Internalizing and Externalizing Trajectories from Ages 5 to 17." *Journal of Abnormal Child Psychology* 33(5): 505–20.

Levine, Madeline. 2006. *The Price of Privilege: How Parental Pressure and Material Advantage Are Creating a Generation of Disconnected and Unhappy Kids.* New York: HarperCollins.

Levine, Robert A., Watts, Harold, Hollister, Robinson, Williams, Walter, O'Connor, Alice, and Widerquist, Karl. 2005. "A Retrospective on the Negative Income Tax Experiments: Looking Back at the Most Innovate Field Studies in Social Policy." In Karl Widerquist, Michael Anthony Lewis, and Steven Pressmanm (eds.), *The Ethics and Economics of the Basic Income Guarantee.* New York: Ashgate.

Levy, Frank and Temin, Peter. 2007. "Inequality and Institutions in 20th Century America." *National Bureau of Economic Research Working Paper Series.* Working Paper No. 13106. http://www.nber.org/papers/w13106.pdf.

Licht, Walter. 1995. *Industrializing America: The Nineteenth Century.* Baltimore: Johns Hopkins University Press.

Lieberman, Abbie. 2017. *A Tale of Two Pre-K Leaders: How State Policies for Center Directors and Principles Leading Pre-K Programs Differ, and Why They Shouldn't.* New America. https://www.newamerica.org/education-policy/policy-papers/tale-two-pre-k-leaders/.

LIMRA. 2015. *LIMRA Secure Retirement Institute: $30,000 in student loan debt could mean $325,000 in lost retirement savings.* https://www.limra.com/en/newsroom/industry-trends/2015/

limra-secure-retirement-institute-$30000-in-student-loan-debt-could-mean-$325000-in-lost-retirement-savings/

Lino, Mark, Kuczynski, Kevin, Rodriguez, Nestor and Schap, TusaRebecca. 2017. *Expenditures on Children by Families: 2015.* Report No. 1528-2105. US Department of Agriculture, Center for Nutrition Policy and Promotion. https://fns-prod.azureedge.net/sites/default/files/crc2015_March2017_0.pdf.

Livingston, Gretchen. 2015. "For Most Highly Educated Women, Motherhood Doesn't Start Until the 30s." Pew Research Center, January 15. http://www.pewresearch.org/fact-tank/2015/01/15/for-most-highly-educated-women-motherhood-doesnt-start-until-the-30s/.

Livingston, Gretchen. 2018a. "About One-Third of U.S. Children Are Living with an Unmarried Parent." Pew Research Center, April 27. http://www.pewresearch.org/fact-tank/2018/04/27/about-one-third-of-u-s-children-are-living-with-an-unmarried-parent/.

Livingston, Gretchen. 2018b. "Stay-at-Home Moms and Dads Account for About One-in-Five U.S. Parents." Pew Research Center, September 24. http://www.pewresearch.org/fact-tank/2018/09/24/stay-at-home-moms-and-dads-account-for-about-one-in-five-u-s-parents/.

Livingston, James. 2016. *No More Work: Why Full Employment is a Bad Idea.* Chapel Hill, NC: University of North Carolina Press.

LoBue, Vanessa, Nishida, Tracy, Chiong, Cynthia, DeLoache, Judy, and Haidt, Jonathan. 2011. "When Getting Something Good Is Bad: Even Three-Year-Olds React to Inequality." *Social Development* 20(1): 154–70.

Loeb, Susanna, Bridges, Margaret, Bassok, Daphna, Fuller, Bruce, and Rumberger, Russell. 2007. "How Much Is Too Much? The Influence of Preschool Centers on Children's Social And Cognitive Development." *Economics of Education Review* 26(1): 52–66.

Loeb, Susanna, Fuller, Bruce, Kagan, Sharon Lynn, and Carrol, Bidemi. 2004. "Child Care in Poor Communities: Early Learning Effects of Type, Quality, and Stability." *Child Development* 75(1): 47–65.

Lorenzo, George. 2015. "How Does Life for Working Parents in Finland Compare to Those in the U.S.?" *Fast Company*, October 7. https://www.fastcompany.com/3051689/how-does-life-for-working-parents-in-finland-really-compare-to-the-us.

Lowe, Peggy. 2018. "Popular with Voters, More Conservative States Push for Medicaid Expansion." *Marketplace*, December 10. https://www.marketplace.org/2018/12/10/health-care/popular-voters-more-conservative-states-push-medicaid-expansion.

Lower-Basch, Elizabeth and Schmit, Stephanie. 2015. *TANF and the First Year of Life: Making a Difference at a Pivotal Moment.* CLASP. http://www.clasp.org/resources-and-publications/body/TANF-and-the-First-Year-of-Life_Making-a-Difference-at-a-Pivotal-Moment.pdf.

Luby, Joan. 2015. "Poverty's Most Insidious Damage, the Developing Brain." *JAMA Pediatrics* 169(9): 810–11.

Luby, Joan, Belden, Andy, Botteron, Kelly, Marrus, Natasha, Harms, Michael P., Babb, Casey, Nishino, Tomoyuki, and Barch, Deanna. 2013. "The Effects of Poverty on Childhood Brain Development: The Mediating Effect of Caregiving and Stressful Life Events." *JAMA Pediatrics* 167(12): 1135–42.

Ludden, Jennifer. 2016. "How Politics Killed Universal Child Care in the 1970s." *NPR*, October 13. https://www.npr.org/2016/10/13/497850292/how-politics-killed-universal-childcare-in-the-1970s.

Lund, Terese J. and Dearing Eric. 2013. "Is Growing Up Affluent Risky for Adolescents or Is the Problem Growing Up in an Affluent Neighborhood?" *Journal of Research on Adolescence* 23(2): 274–82.

Luthar, Suniya S. 2003. "The Culture of Affluence: Psychological Costs of Material Wealth." *Child Development* 74(6): 1581–93.

Luthar, Suniya S. 2013. "The Problem with Rich Kids." *Psychology Today*, November 5. https://www.psychologytoday.com/us/articles/201311/the-problem-rich-kids.

Luthar, Suniya S. and Barkin, Samuel H. 2012. "Are Affluent Youth Truly 'at Risk'? Vulnerability and Resilience Across Three Diverse Samples." *Developmental Psychopathology* 24(2): 429–49.

Luthar, Suniya S., Barkin, Samuel H., and Crossman, Elizabeth J. 2013. "'I Can, Therefore I Must': Fragility in the Upper-Middle Classes." *Developmental Psychopathology* 25(4, pt. 2): 1529–49.

Luthar, Suniya S. and Becker, Bronwyn E. 2002. "Privileged but Pressured? A Study of Affluent Youth." *Child Development* 73(5): 1593–1610.

Luthar, Suniya S. and D'Avanzo, Karen. 1999. "Contextual Factors in Substance Use: A Study of Suburban and Inner-City Adolescents." *Development and Psychopathology* 11(4): 845–67.

Luttmer, Erzo F. P. 2005. "Neighbors as Negatives: Relative Earnings and Well-Being." *Quarterly Journal of Economics* 120(3): 963–1002.

Lythcott-Haims, Julie. 2015. *How to Raise an Adult: Break Free of the Overparenting Trap and Prepare Your Kid for Success.* New York: Henry Holt.

Maag, Elaine. 2007. *Tax Credits, the Minimum Wage, and Inflation.* Report No. 17. Urban-Brookings Tax Policy Center, Tax Policy Issues and Options. https://www.urban.org/sites/default/files/publication/50696/311401-tax-credits-the-minimum-wage-and-inflation_1.pdf.

Maddison, Angus. 2001. *The World Economy: A Millennial Perspective.* OECD Development Centre Studies. http://theunbrokenwindow.com/Development/MADDISON%20The%20World%20Economy--A%20Millennial.pdf.

Madland, David. 2018. "Wage Boards for American Workers: Industry-Level Collective Bargaining for All Workers." Center for American Progress, April 9. https://www.americanprogress.org/issues/economy/reports/2018/04/09/448515/wage-boards-american-workers/.

Magnuson, Katherine and Duncan, Greg. 2016. "Can Early Childhood Interventions Decrease Inequality of Economic Opportunity?" *Russell Sage Foundation Journal of the Social Sciences* 2(2), 123–41.

Magnuson, Katherine and Waldfogel, Jane. 2005. "Early Childhood Care and Education: Effects on Ethnic and Racial Gaps in School Readiness." *Future of Children* 15(1): 169–96.

Mah, Linda, Szabuniewicz, Claudia, and Fiocco, Alexandra J. 2016. "Can Anxiety Damage the Brain?" *Current Opinion in Psychiatry* 29(1): 56–63.

Main, G. 2014. "Child Poverty and Children's Subjective Well-Being." *Child Indicators Research* 7(3): 451–72.

Malik, Rasheed, Hamm, Katie, Adamu, Maryam, and Morrissey, Taryn. 2016. *Child Care Deserts: An Analysis of Child Care Centers by ZIP Code in 8 States.* Center for American Progress. https://cdn.americanprogress.org/content/uploads/2016/10/01070626/ChildcareDeserts-report3.pdf.

Manning, Wendy. 2015. "Cohabitation and Child Wellbeing." *Future Child* 25(2): 51–66.

Manning, Wendy and Smock, Pamela. 1999. "New Families and Nonresident Father–Child Visitation." *Social Forces* 78(1): 87–116.

Manning, Wendy and Smock, Pamela. 2000. "'Swapping' Families: Serial Parenting and Economic Support for Children." *Journal of Marriage and Family* 62(1): 111–22.

Manning, Wendy, Stewart, Susan, and Smock, Pamela. 2003. "The Complexity of Fathers' Parenting Responsibilities and Involvement with Nonresident Children." *Journal of Family Issues* 24(5): 645–67.

Margo, Robert. 2000. "The Labor Force in the Nineteenth Century." In Stanley L. Engerman and Robert E. Gallman (eds.), *The Cambridge Economic History of the United States*, Volume II: *The Long Nineteenth Century.* Cambridge: Cambridge University Press.

Martin, Joyce, Hamilton, Brady, Sutton, Paul, Ventura, Stephanie, Menacker, Fay, and Kirmeyer, Sharon. 2006. "Births: Final Data for 2004." *National Vital Statistics Reports* 55(1). https://www.cdc.gov/nchs/data/nvsr/nvsr55/nvsr55_01.pdf.

Martinez, G., Daniels, K. and Chandra, A. 2012. "Fertility of Men and Women Aged 15–44 Years in the United States: National Survey of Family Growth, 2006–2010." *National Health Statistics Report* 12(51).

Massachusetts Bureau of Statistics of Labor. 1870. *Second Annual Report of the Bureau of Statistics of Labor Embracing the Account of its Operations and Inquiries from March 1, 1870, to March 1, 1871.* Boston: Wright and Potter.

Massachusetts Bureau of Statistics of Labor. 1873. *Fourth Annual Report of the Bureau of Statistics of Labor Embracing the Account of Its Operations and Inquirings from March 1, 1872, to March 1, 1873.* Boston: Wright and Potter.

Matthaei, Julie A. 1982. *An Economic History of Women in America: Women's Work, the Sexual Division of Labor, and the Development of Capitalism.* New York: Schocken Books.

Matthews, Dylan. 2015. "Selling Plasma to Survive: How over a Million American Families Live on $2 per Day." *Vox*, September 2. https://www.vox.com/2015/9/2/9248801/extreme-poverty-2-dollars.

Matthews, Dylan. 2016a. "Sweden Pays Parents for Having Kids—and It Reaps Huge Benefits. Why doesn't the US?" *Vox*, May 23. https://www.vox.com/2016/5/23/11440638/child-benefit-child-allowance.

Matthews, Dylan. 2016b. "'If the Goal Was to Get Rid of Poverty, We Failed': The Legacy of the 1996 Welfare Reform." *Vox*, June 20. https://www.vox.com/2016/6/20/11789988/clintons-welfare-reform.

Maume, David. 2006. "Gender Differences in Taking Vacation Time." *Work and Occupations* 33(2): 161–90.

Maye, Adewale. 2019. *No-Vacation Nation, Revisited.* Center for Economic and Policy Research. Available at http://cepr.net/images/stories/reports/no-vacation-nation-2019-05.pdf.

Mayer, Gerald. 2004. "Union Membership Trends in the United States." Congressional Research Service. https://digitalcommons.ilr.cornell.edu/cgi/viewcontent.cgi?referer=http://www.pewresearch.org/&httpsredir=1&article=1176&context=key_workplace.

Mayer, Jane. 2016. *Dark Money: The Hidden History of the Billionaires Behind the Rise of the Radical Right.* New York: Doubleday.

Mayer, Susan. 1997. *What Money Can't Buy: Family Income and Children's Life Chances.* Cambridge, MA: Harvard University Press.

McCluskey, Martha T. 2003. "Efficiency and Social Citizenship: Challenging the Neoliberal Attack on the Welfare State." *Indiana Law Journal* 78(3): 783–874.

McEwen, Bruce S. 2006. "Protective and Damaging Effects of Stress Mediators: Central Role of the Brain." *Dialogues in Clinical Neuroscience* 8(4): 367–81.

McGee, Rob, Williams, Sheila, and Nada-Raja, Shyamala. 2001. "Low Self-Esteem and Hopelessness in Childhood and Suicidal Ideation in Early Adulthood." *Journal of Abnormal Child Psychology* 29(4): 281–91.

McGuinness, Teena M. and Schneider, Kristina. 2007. "Poverty, Child Maltreatment, and Foster Care." *Journal of the American Psychiatric Nurses Association* 13(5): 296–303.

McLanahan, Sara. 1985. "Charles Murray and the Family." In *Institute for Research on Poverty, Losing Ground: A Critique.* Special Report No. 38. https://www.irp.wisc.edu/publications/sr/pdfs/sr38.pdf.

McLanahan, Sara. 2004. "Diverging Destinies: How Children Are Faring Under the Second Demographic Transition." *Demography* 41(4): 607–27.

McLanahan, Sara. 2009. "Fragile Families and the Reproduction of Poverty." *Annals of the American Academy of Political and Social Science* 621(1): 111–31.

McLanahan, Sara. 2011. "Family Instability and Complexity After a Nonmarital Birth: Outcomes for Children in Fragile Families." In Marcia J. Carlson and Paula England (eds.), *Social Class and Changing Families in an Unequal America.* Stanford, CA: Stanford University Press.

McLanahan, Sara and Sandefur, Gary. 1994. *Growing Up with a Single Parent: What Hurts, What Helps.* Cambridge, MA: Harvard University Press.

McLoyd, Vonnie C. 1989. "Socialization and Development in a Changing Economy: The Effects of Paternal Job And Income Loss on Children." *American Psychologist* 44(2): 293–302.

McLoyd, Vonnie C., Jayaratne, Toby Epstein, Ceballo, Rosario, and Borquez, Julio. 1994. "Unemployment and Work Interruption among African American Single Mothers: Effects on Parenting and Adolescent Socioemotional Functioning." *Child Development* 65(2): 562–89.

Mears, Daniel P. and Siennick, Sonja E. 2016. "Young Adult Outcomes and the Life-Course Penalties of Parental Incarceration." *Journal of Research in Crime and Delinquency* 53(1): 3–35.

Medalia, Carla and Jacobs, Jerry. 2008. "Working Time for Married Couples in 28 Countries." In Ronald Burke and Cary Cooper (eds.), *The Long Work Hours Culture: Causes, Consequences and Choices.* Bingley: Emerald Group. https://www.google.com/url?sa=t&rct=j&q=&esrc= s&source=web&cd=1&ved=2ahUKEwjvkdLUj8PiAhVBT98KHRsABE0 QFjAAegQIABAC&url=https%3A%2F%2Fsociology.sas.upenn.edu%2Fsites %2Fsociology.sas.upenn.edu%2Ffiles%2Fworking%2520time%2520in%252028 %2520countries%2520website%2520version.doc&usg =AOvVaw3vLpIWQyV48TVJzW76CVUi.

Meier, Ann, Musick, Kelly, Flood, Sarah, and Dunifon, Rachel. 2016. "Mothering Experiences: How Single-Parenthood and Employment Shift the Valence." *Demography* 53(3): 649–74.

Menlo-Atherton High School. 2015. "Teen Sleep in Action." *TriVocis* 62(8). http:// www.mabearspta.org/wp-content/uploads/2015/04/TrivocisMay2015Final.pdf.

Merelli, Annalisa. 2016. "The US' Terrifying Parenting Pay Gap, by the Numbers." *Quartz*, June 22. https://qz.com/713013/the-biggest-cost-of-raising-children-is-earnings-lost-when-parents-dont-work/.

Merikangas, Kathleen Ries, He, Jian-Ping, Brody, Debra, Fisher, Prudence W., Bourdon, Karen, and Koretz, Doreen S. 2010. "Prevalence and Treatment of Mental Disorders among U.S. Children in the 2001–2004 NHANES." *Pediatrics* 125(1): 75–81.

Merrill, Michael. 1995. "Putting 'Capitalism' in Its Place: A Review of Recent Literature." *William and Mary Quarterly* 52(2): 315–326.

Mesman, Judi, van Ijzendoorn, Marinus, and Bakermans-Kranenburg, Marian. 2012. "Unequal in Opportunity, Equal in Process: Parental Sensitivity Promotes Positive Child Development in Ethnic Minority Families." *Child Development Perspectives* 6(3): 239–50.

Mettler, Suzanne. 2011. *The Submerged State: How Invisible Government Policies Undermine American Democracy.* Chicago: University of Chicago Press.

Milkie, Melissa A., Nomaguchi, Kei M., and Denny, Kathleen E. 2015. "Does the Amount of Time Mothers Spend with Children or Adolescents Matter?" *Journal of Marriage and Family* 77(2): 355–72.

Milkie, Melissa, Raley, Sara B., and Biachi, Suzanne M. 2009. "Taking on the Second Shift: Time Allocations and Time Pressures of U.S. Parents with Preschoolers." *Social Forces* 88(2): 487–517.

Miller, Claire Cain. 2015. "When Family-Friendly Policies Backfire." *New York Times*, May 26. https://www.nytimes.com/2015/05/26/upshot/when-family-friendly-policies-backfire.html.

Miller, Claire Cain. 2018. "The Relentlessness of Modern Parenting." *New York Times*, December 25. https://www.nytimes.com/2018/12/25/upshot/the-relentlessness-of-modern-parenting.html.

Miller, Daniel P., Waldfogel, Jane, and Han, Wen-Jui. 2012. "Family Meals and Child Academic and Behavioral Outcomes." *Child Development* 83(6): 2104–20.

Milligan, Kevin and Stabile, Mark. 2011. "Do Child Tax Benefits Affect the Well-Being of Children? Evidence from Canadian Child Benefit Expansions." *American Economic Journal: Economic Policy* 3(3): 175–205.

Millsap, Adam. 2017. "The Opioid Problem Is an Employment Problem." *Forbes*, July 3. https://www.forbes.com/sites/adammillsap/2017/07/03/the- opioid-problem-is-an-employment-problem/#7b45e8ff3073.

Mills-Koonce, W. Roger, Willoughby, Michael T., Zvara, Bharathi, Barnett, Melissa, Gustafsson, Hanna, Cox, Martha J., and the Family Life Project Key Investigators. 2015. "Mothers' and Fathers' Sensitivity and Children's Cognitive Development in Low-Income, Rural Families." *Journal of Applied Developmental Psychology* 38: 1–10.

Ministry of Children and Social Affairs. 2018a. *Daycare and Daycare Centers.* https:// www.borger.dk/familie-og-boern/Boernepasning/Dagpleje-vuggestue-boernehave-og-privat-pasning.

Ministry of Children and Social Affairs. 2018b. *Grants and Own Payment*. http://
    socialministeriet.dk/arbejdsomraader/dagtilbud/tilskud-og-egenbetaling.

Ministry of Economic Affairs and Employment. 2001. *Employment Contracts Act*. Finland. https://
    www.finlex.fi/en/laki/kaannokset/2001/en20010055.pdf.

Ministry of Economic Affairs and Employment. 2011. *Working Hours Act*. Finland. https://
    www.finlex.fi/fi/laki/kaannokset/1996/en19960605_20100991.pdf.

Ministry of Education. 2019. *Financial Support for Child Care*. Ontario. Available at https://
    www.ontario.ca/page/child-care-subsidies.

Ministry of Education and Culture. 2009. *Universities Act 558/2009*. Finland. http://www.finlex.fi/
    fi/laki/kaannokset/2009/en20090558.pdf.

Ministry of Education and Culture. 2018. *Customer Fees for Early Childhood Education*. Finland.
    https://minedu.fi/varhaiskasvatusmaksut.

Ministry of Employment and the Economy. 2016. *The Annual Holidays Act*. Finland, Labor and Trade
    Department. https://tem.fi/documents/1410877/2918981/The+Annual+Holidays+Act/
    9bd1fbbc-2a16-4937-bf2f-beefc55ccca4.

Ministry of Social Affairs. 2017. *Parental Leave*. Republic of Estonia. Last modified November
    6. https://www.sm.ee/en/parental-leave.

Ministry of Labor. 2019a. "Family Medical Leave." *Your Guide to the Employment Standards
    Act*. Ontario. Available at https://www.ontario.ca/document/your-guide-employment-
    standards-act-0/family-medical-leave#section-10.

Ministry of Labor. 2019b. *Information for Employees About Hours of Work and Overtime
    Pay*. Ontario. Available at https://www.labour.gov.on.ca/english/es/pubs/hours/
    infosheet.php.

Ministry of Social Affairs and Health. 2013. *Child and Family Policy in Finland*. Finland, Ministry of
    Social Affairs and Health. http://www.congreso.es/docu/docum/ddocum/dosieres/sleg/
    legislatura_10/spl_78/pdfs/41.pdf.

Mishel, Lawrence. 2013. *The Vast Majority of Wage Earners Are Working Harder, and for Not Much
    More: Trends in U.S. Work Hours and Wages Over 1979–2007*. Issue Brief No. 348. Economic
    Policy Institute. https://www.epi.org/files/2013/ib348-trends-us-work-hours-wages-1979-
    2007.pdf.

Mishel, Lawrence, Bernstein, Jared, and Shierholz, Heidi. 2009. *The State of Working America,
    2008/2009*. Ithaca, NY: Cornell University Press.

Mishel, Lawrence, Bivens, Josh, Gould, Elise, and Shierholz, Heidi. 2012. *The State of Working
    America*. 12th ed. Ithaca, NY: ILR Press.

Mishel, Lawrence and Eisenbrey, Ross. 2015. *How to Raise Wages: Policies That Work and Policies
    That Don't*. Briefing Paper No. 391. Economic Policy Institute. https://www.epi.org/files/
    2015/bp391.pdf.

Mishel, Lawrence and Schieder, Jessica. 2017. *CEO Pay Remains High Relative to the Pay of Yypical
    Workers and High-Wage Earners*. Economic Policy Institute. https://www.epi.org/files/pdf/
    130354.pdf.

Mishel, Lawrence, Schmitt, John and Shierholz, Heidi. 2013. "Assessing the Job Polarization
    Explanation of Growing Wage Inequality." *Economic Policy Institute Working Papers*. Working
    Paper   No.   295.   https://www.epi.org/files/2012/wp295-assessing-job-polarization-
    explanation-wage-inequality.pdf.

Mississippi Department of Human Services. 2018. *Temporary Assistance for Needy Families*. http://
    www.mdhs.ms.gov/economic-assistance/tanf/.

Mistry, Rashmita S., Lowe, Edward D., Benner, Aprile D. and Chien, Nina. 2008. "Expanding
    the Family Economic Stress Model: Insights from a Mixed-Methods Approach." *Journal of
    Marriage and Family* 70(1): 196–209.

Mistry, Rashmita, Vandewater, Elizabeth, Huston, Aletha, and McLoyd, Vonnie. 2002. "Economic
    Well-Being and Children's Social Adjustment: The Role of Family Process in an Ethnically
    Diverse Low-Income Sample." *Child Development* 73(3): 935–51.

Mocan, Naci. 2007. "Can Consumers Detect Lemons? An Empirical Analysis of Information Asymmetry in the Market for Child Care." *Journal of Population Economics* 20(4): 743–80.

Moffitt, Robert. 2003. "The Temporary Assistance for Needy Families Program." In Robert Moffitt (ed.), *Means-Tested Transfer Programs in the United States.* Chicago: University of Chicago Press.

Moffitt, Robert. 2015. "The Deserving Poor, the Family, and the U.S. Welfare System." *Demography* 52(3): 729–49.

Moiduddin, Emily, Aikens, Nikki, Tarullo, Louisa, West, Jerry, and Xue, Yange. 2012. *Child Outcomes and Classroom Quality in FACES 2009.* OPRE Report 2012-37a. US Department of Health and Human Services, Administration for Children and Families. https://www.acf.hhs.gov/sites/default/files/opre/faces_2009.pdf.

Mojtabai, R., Olfson, M., and Han, B. 2016. "National Trends in the Prevalence and Treatment of Depression in Adolescents and Young Adults." *Pediatrics* 138(6).

Mondale, Walter F. 2010. *The Good Fight: A Life in Liberal Politics.* New York: Scribner.

Mongeau, Lillian. 2016. "Why Oklahoma's Public Preschools Are Some of the Best in the Country." *Hechinger Report,* February 2. https://hechingerreport.org/why-oklahomas-public-preschools-are-some-of-the-best-in-the-country/.

Morduch, Jonathan and Schneider, Rachel. 2013. *Spikes and Dips: How Income Uncertainty Affects Households.* US Financial Diaries. https://static1.squarespace.com/static/53d008ede4b0833aa2ab2eb9/t/53d6e12ae4b0907fe7bedf6f/1410469662568/issue1-spikes.pdf.

Morduch, Jonathan and Schneider, Rachel. 2017. *The Financial Diaries: How American Families Cope in a World of Uncertainty.* Princeton, NJ: Princeton University Press.

Morgan, Kimberly. 2001. "A Child of the Sixties: The Great Society, the New Right, and the Politics of Federal Child Care." *Journal of Policy History* 13(2): 215–50.

Morris, Pamela A., Hill, Heather D., Gennetian, Lisa A., Rodrigues, Chris, and Wolf, Sharon. 2015. "Income Volatility in U.S. Households with Children: Another Growing Disparity between the Rich and the Poor?" *IRP Discussion Paper Series.* No. 1429-15. https://www.irp.wisc.edu/wp/wp-content/uploads/2018/05/dp142915.pdf.

Morsy, Leila and Rothstein, Richard. 2016. *Mass Incarceration and Children's Outcomes: Criminal Justice Policy Is Education Policy.* Economic Policy Institute. https://www.epi.org/files/pdf/118615.pdf.

Mosher, W. D. and Jones, J. 2010. "Use of Contraception in the United States: 1982–2008." *Vital and Health Statistics* 23(29). https://www.cdc.gov/nchs/data/series/sr_23/sr23_029.pdf.

Moynihan, Daniel. 1965. *The Negro Family: The Case for National Action.* US Department of Labor, Office of Policy Planning and Research. http://web.stanford.edu/~mrosenfe/Moynihan's%20The%20Negro%20Family.pdf.

Mullainathan, Sendhil and Shafir, Eldar. 2013. *Scarcity: Why Having Too Little Means So Much.* New York: Times Books.

Muris, Peter. 2002. "Parental Rearing Behaviors and Worry of Normal Adolescents." *Psychological Reports* 91(2): 428–30.

Muris, Peter, Meesters, Cor, and Brake, Anneke van. 2003. "Assessment of Anxious Rearing Behaviors with a Modified Version of 'Egna Minnen Betraffande Uppfostran' Questionnaire for Children." *Journal of Psychopathology and Behavioral Assessment* 25(4): 229–37.

Muris, Peter and Merckelbach, Harald. 1998. "Perceived Parental Rearing Behaviour and Anxiety Disorders Symptoms in Normal Children." *Personality and Individual Differences* 25(6): 1199–1206.

Murphey, David, Bandy, Tawana, and Moore, Kristen A. 2012. *Frequent Residential Mobility and Young Children's Well-Being.* Research Brief No. 2012-02. Child Trends. https://www.childtrends.org/wp-content/uploads/2012/01/Child_Trends-2012_02_14_RB_Mobility.pdf.

Murphy, Sherry L., Xu, Jiaquan, Kochanek, Kenneth D., and Arias, Elizabeth. 2018. *Mortality in the United States, 2017*. NCHS Data Brief No. 328. US Department of Health and Human Services, National Center for Health Statistics. https://www.cdc.gov/nchs/data/databriefs/db328-h.pdf.

Murray, Charles. 1994. *Losing Ground: American Social Policy, 1950–1980*. New York: Basic Books.

Murray, Charles. 2012. *Coming Apart: The State of White America, 1960–2010*. New York: Crown Forum.

National Alliance for Caregiving and AARP Public Policy Institute. 2015. *Caregiving in the U.S.: 2015 Report*. http://www.aarp.org/content/dam/aarp/ppi/2015/caregiving-in-the-united-states-2015-report-revised.pdf.

National Center for Children in Poverty. 2018a. *Basic Needs Budget Calculator*. Columbia University. http://www.nccp.org/tools/frs/budget.php.

National Center for Children in Poverty. 2018b. *United States Demographics of Poor Children*. Columbia University. http://www.nccp.org/profiles/US_profile_7.html.

National Center for Educational Statistics. 2018. *Preschool and Kindergarten Enrollment, 2017*. https://nces.ed.gov/programs/coe/indicator_cfa.asp.

National Center for Health Statistics. 2017. "Quarterly Provisional Estimates for Selected Birth Indicators, 2015–Quarter 4, 2016." *NCHS Vital Statistics Rapid Release*. Last modified May 17. https://www.cdc.gov/nchs/products/vsrr/natality.htm.

National Center for Health Statistics. 2019. *Percentage Births to Unmarried Mothers by State*. Centers for Disease Control and Prevention. Last modified January 15. https://www.cdc.gov/nchs/pressroom/sosmap/unmarried/unmarried.htm.

National Center on Addiction and Substance Abuse. 2011. *National Survey of American Attitudes on Substance Abuse XVI: Teens and Parents*. National Center on Addiction and Substance Abuse at Columbia University. https://www.centeronaddiction.org/download/file/fid/1282.

National Conference of State Legislatures. 2016. *State Family and Medical Leave Laws*. http://www.ncsl.org/research/labor-and-employment/state-family-and-medical-leave-laws.aspx.

National Home Visiting Resource Center. 2018. *Data Supplement: 2017 Home Visiting Yearbook, An Overview*. https://www.nhvrc.org/wp-content/uploads/NHVRC_Data-Supplement-Summary_FINAL.pdf.

National Institute of Child Health and Human Development. 2006. *The NICHD Study of Early Child Care and Youth Development: Findings for Children up to Age 4½ Years*. US Department of Health and Human Services, National Institutes of Health. https://www.nichd.nih.gov/publications/pubs/documents/seccyd_06.pdf.

National Low Income Housing Coalition. 2016. Housing Spotlight: The Long Wait for a Home. https://nlihc.org/sites/default/files/HousingSpotlight_6-1.pdf.

National Scientific Council on the Developing Child. 2007. *The Science of Early Childhood Development*. Harvard University, Center on the Developing Child. http://developingchild.harvard.edu/resources/the-science-of-early-childhood-development-closing-the-gap-between-what-we-know-and-what-we-do/.

National Scientific Council on the Developing Child. 2009. "Young Children Develop in an Environment of Relationships." *National Scientific Council on the Developing Child Working Paper Series*. Working Paper No. 1. Harvard University, Center on the Devloping Child. http://developingchild.harvard.edu/wp-content/uploads/2004/04/Young-Children-Develop-in-an-Environment-of-Relationships.pdf.

National Scientific Council on the Developing Child. 2012. "The Science of Neglect: The Persistent Absence of Responsive Care Disrupts the Developing Brain." *National Scientific Council on the Developing Child Working Paper Series* Working Paper No. 12. Harvard University, Center on the Developing Child. http://developingchild.harvard.edu/wp-content/uploads/2012/05/The-Science-of-Neglect-The-Persistent-Absence-of-Responsive-Care-Disrupts-the-Developing-Brain.pdf.

National Sleep Foundation. 2018. *Teens and Sleep*. https://www.sleepfoundation.org/sleep-topics/teens-and-sleep.

National Transfer Accounts. 2016. *Data Sheet*. http://www.ntaccounts.org/doc/repository/NTA%20Data%20Sheet%202016.pdf.

Nation's Report Card. 2018. *2015 Math and Reading Assessments: State Score Changes*. https://www.nationsreportcard.gov/reading_math_2015/#reading/state/scores?grade=4.

Nelson, Charles, Fox, Nathan, and Zeanah, Charles. 2014. *Romania's Abandoned Children: Deprivation, Brain Development, and the Struggle for Recovery*. Cambridge, MA: Harvard University Press.

Nelson, Margaret K. 2010. *Parenting Out of Control: Anxious Parents in Uncertain Times*. New York: New York University Press.

Nepomnyaschy, Lenna and Waldfogel, Jane. 2007. "Paternity Leave and Fathers' Involvement with Their Young Children." *Community, Work, and Family* 10(4): 427–53.

Neumark, David and Postlewaite, Andrew. 1998. "Relative Income Concerns and the Rise in Married Women's Employment." *Journal of Public Economics* 70(1): 157–83.

Newport, Frank. 2017. "Majority Want Government to Ensure Healthcare Coverage." Gallup, December 8. http://news.gallup.com/poll/223391/majority-government-ensure-healthcare-coverage.aspx.

New Republic. 1968. "T.R.B. from Washington." *New Republic* 158(17): 4.

New York State. 2018. *Paid Family Leave: Information for Employees*. https://paidfamilyleave.ny.gov/paid-family-leave-information-employees.

New York Times. 1869. "Over-work of Children in Our Factories." *New York Times*. October 6.

New York Times. 1969. "Poll Supports Aid to Child Centers." *New York Times*, July 13.

New York Times. 1976. "'Welfare Queen' Becomes Issue in Reagan Campaign." *New York Times*, February 15.

NICHD Early Child Care Research Network. 1997. "Poverty and Patterns of Child Care." In Greg J. Duncan and Jeanne Brooks-Gunn (eds.), *Consequences of Growing Up Poor*. New York: Russel Sage Foundation.

NICHD Early Child Care Research Network. 2003. "Does Amount of Time Spent in Child Care Predict Socioemotional Adjustment During the Transition to Kindergarten?" *Child Development* 74(4): 976–1005.

Nickerson, Carol, Schwarz, Norbert, Diener, Ed, and Kahneman, Daniel. 2003. "Zeroing in on the Dark Side of the American Dream: A Closer Look at the Negative Consequences of the Goal for Financial Success." *Psychological Science* 14(6): 531–36.

Niemiec, Christopher P., Ryan, Richard M. and Deci, Edward L. 2009. "The Path Taken: Consequences of Attaining Intrinsic And Extrinsic Aspirations in Post-College Life." *Journal of Research of Personality* 43(3): 291–306.

Nixon, Richard. 1969a. "Address to the Nation on Domestic Programs." *American Presidency Project*, August 8. https://www.presidency.ucsb.edu/documents/address-the-nation-domestic-programs.

Nixon, Richard. 1969b. "Statement Announcing the Establishment of the Office of Child Development. April 9, 1969." In *Public Papers of the Presidents of the United States: Richard M. Nixon, 1969*. Washington DC: Government Publishing Office.

Nixon, Richard. 1971a. "Annual Message to the Congress on the State of the Union." *American Presidency Project*, January 22. https://www.presidency.ucsb.edu/documents/annual-message-the-congress-the-state-the-union-1.

Nixon, Richard. 1971b. Economic Opportunity Amendments of 1971—Veto Message (S. Doc. No. 92-48). *Congressional Record* 92d Cong., 1st sess. vol. 117, pt. 35, pp. 46057–46059. December 10. https://www.gpo.gov/fdsys/pkg/GPO-CRECB-1971-pt35/pdf/GPO-CRECB-1971-pt35-3.pdf.

North Carolina Department of Health and Human Services. 2016. *Work First: Income and Budgeting*. https://www2.ncdhhs.gov/info/olm/manuals/dss/csm-95/man/WF114.pdf.

North Carolina Division of Child Development and Early Education. 2016. *Summary of the North Carolina Child Care Law and Rules.* North Carolina Department of Health and Human Services. http://ncchildcare.nc.gov/pdf_Forms/summary_ncchildcare_laws_rules.pdf.

North Carolina Division of Child Development and Early Education. 2017. *North Carolina Early Childhood and Administration Credentials.* North Carolina Health and Human Services. Aceessed December14. http://ncchildcare.nc.gov/providers/credent.asp.

Novak, William J. 1996. *The People's Welfare: Law and Regulation in Nineteenth-Century America.* Chapel Hill: University of North Carolina Press.

NPR and Marist. 2018. *NPR/Marist Poll January 2018: Picture of Work.* http://maristpoll.marist.edu/nprmarist-poll-results-january-2018-picture-of-work/.

NPR, Robert Wood Johnson Foundation, and Harvard T. H. Chan School of Public Health. 2016. *Child Care and Health in America.* https://www.npr.org/documents/2016/oct/Child-Care-and-Development-Report-2016.pdf.

NPR Staff. 2016. "'I Wasn't There to Help': Dad with Newborn Struggles with Lack of Leave." *NPR,* October 5. https://www.npr.org/2016/10/05/496536123/i-wasnt-there-to-help-dad-with-newborn-struggles-with-lack-of-leave.

O'Connor, Julia S., Orloff, Ann Shola, and Shaver, Sheila. 1999. *States, Markets, Families: Gender, Liberalism and Social Policy in Australia, Canada, Great Britain, and the United States.* Cambridge: Cambridge University Press.

OECD. 2000. *Early Childhood Education and Care Policy in Finland.* http://www.oecd.org/finland/2476019.pdf.

OECD. 2006. *Starting Strong II: Early Childhood Education and Care.* http://www.oecd.org/edu/school/startingstrongiiearlychildhoodeducationandcare.htm.

OECD. 2009. *Society at a Glance, 2009: OECD Social Indicators.* https://www.oecd-ilibrary.org/docserver/soc_glance-2008-en.pdf?expires=1549939922&id=id&accname=guest&checksum=D0D415D147195EA933A4E6B020A2DFCB.

OECD. 2010. *Education Today, 2010: The OECD Perspective.* http://www.oecd.org/berlin/46299897.pdf.

OECD. 2011. *Doing Better for Families, 2011.* https://www.oecd.org/els/soc/47701118.pdf.

OECD. 2012. *Education at a Glance: OECD Indicators, 2012.* https://www.oecd-ilibrary.org/docserver/eag-2012-en.pdf?expires=1541181918&id=id&accname=guest&checksum=172296D889B136C179ECAA503033DD3D/.

OECD. 2013. *SF3.4: Family Violence.* https://www.oecd.org/els/soc/SF3_4_Family_violence_Jan2013.pdf.

OECD. 2014a. *PF1.3: Family Cash Benefits.* http://www.oecd.org/els/soc/PF1_3_Family_Cash_Benefits_Jul2013.pdf.

OECD. 2014b. *Social Expenditure Update: Social Spending Is Falling in Some Countries, but in Many Others It Remains at Historically High Levels.* https://www.oecd.org/els/soc/OECD2014-SocialExpenditure_Update19Nov_Rev.pdf.

OECD. 2015a. *How's Life? 2015: Measuring Well-Being.* http://www.keepeek.com/Digital-Asset-Management/oecd/economics/how-s-life-2015_how_life-2015-en.

OECD. 2015b. *How's Life? 2015: Measuring Well-Being—Chapter 4, Figure 4.32. Children's Life Satisfaction.* http://dx.doi.org/10.1787/888933259880.

OECD. 2015c. *How's Life? 2015: Measuring Well-Being—Chapter 4, Figure 4.25. Children Feeling Pressured by Schoolwork.* http://dx.doi.org/10.1787/888933259816.

OECD. 2016a. *PISA 2015 Results: Excellence and Equity in Education, Volume I.* http://dx.doi.org/10.1787/9789264266490-en.

OECD. 2016b. *Education at a Glance, 2016: OECD Indicators.* https://www.oecd-ilibrary.org/docserver/eag-2016-en.pdf?expires=1542654206&id=id&accname=guest&checksum=173729D8F19142A1551FB8F9D9AF1D1A/.

OECD. 2016c. *LMF2.2: Patterns of Employment and the Distribution of Working Hours for Couples with Children.* httsps://www.oecd.org/els/family/LMF-2-2-Distribution-working-hours-couple-households.pdf.

OECD. 2016d. *LMF1.2: Maternal Employment Rates.* https://www.oecd.org/els/family/LMF_1_2_Maternal_Employment.pdf.

OECD. 2016e. *Starting Strong, IV: Early Childhood Education and Care, Country Note: Finland.* https://www.oecd.org/edu/school/ECECDCN-Finland.pdf.

OECD. 2016f. *PF3.2: Enrolment in Childcare and Pre-School.* http://www.oecd.org/els/soc/PF3_2_Enrolment_childcare_preschool.pdf.

OECD. 2016g. *PF3.3: Informal Childcare Arrangements.* http://www.oecd.org/els/family/PF3-3-Informal-childcare-arrangements.pdf.

OECD. 2016h. *PH3.3 Recipients and Payment Rates of Housing Allowances.* https://www.oecd.org/els/family/PH3-3-recipients-payment-rates-housing-allowances.pdf

OECD. 2016i. *Back to Work: Denmark—Improving the Re-employment Prospects of Displaced Workers.* http://www.oecd.org/employment/back-to-work-denmark-9789264267503-en.htm.

OECD. 2016j. *Social Spending Stays at Historically High Levels in Many OECD Countries.* http://www.oecd.org/els/soc/OECD2016-Social-Expenditure-Update.pdf.

OECD. 2017a. *PISA 2015 Results (Volume III): Students' Well-Being.* http://www.oecd-ilibrary.org/education/pisa-2015-results-volume-iii_9789264273856-en.

OECD. 2017b. *Life Satisfaction.* http://www.oecdbetterlifeindex.org/topics/life-satisfaction/.

OECD. 2017c. *PF1.6: Public Spending by Age of Children.* http://www.oecd.org/els/family/PF1_6_Public_spending_by_age_children.xlsx.

OECD. 2017d. *PF2.1: Key Characteristics of Parental Leave Systems.* http://www.oecd.org/els/soc/PF2_1_Parental_leave_systems.pdf.

OECD. 2017e. *Education at a Glance, 2017: OECD Indicators.* https://www.oecd-ilibrary.org/education/education-at-a-glance-2017_eag-2017-en.

OECD. 2017f. *PF3.4: Childcare Support.* Last modified August 27. https://www.oecd.org/els/soc/PF3_4_Childcare_support.pdf.

OECD. 2017g. *Level of GDP per Capita and Productivity.* http://stats.oecd.org/Index.aspx?DataSetCode=PDB_LV#.

OECD. 2017h. *OECD Employment Outlook, 2017.* https://read.oecd-ilibrary.org/employment/oecd-employment-outlook-2017_empl_outlook-2017-en#page1.

OECD. 2017i. *Net Replacement Rates for Six Family Types: Initial Phase of Unemployment.* http://www.oecd.org/els/soc/NRR_Initial_EN.xlsx.

OECD. 2017j. *OECD Employment Outlook, 2017—Statistical Annex.* http://www.oecd.org/els/emp/employment-outlook-statistical-annex.htm.

OECD. 2017k. *PF1.1: Public Spending on Family Benefits.* http://www.oecd.org/els/soc/PF1_1_Public_spending_on_family_benefits.pdf.

OECD. 2018a. *SF3.1: Marriage and Divorce Rates.* https://www.oecd.org/els/family/SF_3_1_Marriage_and_divorce_rates.pdf.

OECD. 2018b. *SF1.3: Further Information on the Living Arrangements of Children.* http://www.oecd.org/els/soc/SF_1_3_Living-arrangements-children.pdf.

OECD. 2018c. *Education at a Glance, 2018.* https://www.oecd-ilibrary.org/education/education-at-a-glance_19991487.

OECD. 2018d. *Education Finance Indicators: Proportions of Public and Private Expenditure on Educational Institutions.* https://stats.oecd.org/index.aspx?queryid=79391.

OECD. 2018e. *Education Finance Indicators: Annual Expenditure per Student by Educational Institutions by Expenditure Type.* https://stats.oecd.org/index.aspx?queryid=79397.

OECD. 2018f. *LFS by Age and Sex—Indicators.* https://stats.oecd.org/Index.aspx?DataSetCode=LFS_SEXAGE_I_R.

OECD. 2018g. *HC1.2: Housing Costs Over Income.* https://www.oecd.org/els/family/HC1-2-Housing-costs-over-income.pdf.

OECD. 2018h. *Education Spending.* https://data.oecd.org/eduresource/education-spending.htm#indicator-chart.

OECD. 2018i. *Gross Domestic Product (GDP).* https://data.oecd.org/gdp/gross-domestic-product-gdp.htm.

306

REFERENCES

OECD. 2018j. *Population.* https://data.oecd.org/pop/population.htm#indicator-chart.
OECD. 2018k. *Working Age Population.* https://data.oecd.org/pop/working-age-population.htm.
OECD. 2018l. *Minimum Relative to Average Wages of Full-Time Workers.* Accessed May 24. http://stats.oecd.org/Index.aspx?DatasetCode=MIN2AVE.
OECD. 2018m. *OECD Employment Outlook, 2018.* http://dx.doi.org/10.1787/888933779390.
OECD. 2018n. *Tax Revenue.* https://data.oecd.org/tax/tax-revenue.htm.
OECD. 2018o. *Key Policies to Promote Longer Working Lives: County Note, 2007 to 2017, Denmark.* https://www.oecd.org/els/emp/Denmark%20Key%20policies_Final.pdf.
OECD. 2018p. *PF3.2: Enrolment in Childcare and Pre-School.* https://www.oecd.org/els/soc/PF3_2_Enrolment_childcare_preschool.pdf.
OECD. 2019a. *Hours Worked.* https://data.oecd.org/emp/hours-worked.htm.
OECD. 2019b. *Level of GDP per Capita and Productivity.* https://data.oecd.org/lprdty/gdp-per-hour-worked.htm.
OECD. 2019c. *Social Expenditure—Aggregated Data.* https://stats.oecd.org/Index.aspx?DataSetCode=SOCX_AGG.
OECD. 2019d. *Employment Rate by Age Group.*https://data.oecd.org/emp/employment-rate-by-age-group.htm.
Offer, Shira and Schneider, Barbara. 2011. "Revisiting the Gender Gap in Time-Use Patterns: Multitasking and Well-Being among Mothers and Fathers in Dual-Earner Families." *American Sociological Review* 76(6): 809–33.
Office of Adolescent Health. 2016. *Trends in Teen Pregnancy and Childbearing: Teen Births.* US Department of Health and Human Services. https://www.hhs.gov/ash/oah/adolescent-development/reproductive-health-and-teen-pregnancy/teen-pregnancy-and-childbearing/trends/index.html.
Office of Family Assistance. 2014a. *Characteristics and Financial Circumstances of TANF Recipients, Fiscal Year 2012.* U.S. Department of Health and Human Services, Administration for Children & Families. Available at http://www.acf.hhs.gov/programs/ofa/resource/characteristics-and-financial-circumstances-appendix-fy2012.
Office of Family Assistance. 2014b. *TANF Financial Data—FY 2013.* US Department of Health and Human Services, Administration for Children and Families. https://www.acf.hhs.gov/ofa/resource/tanf-financial-data-fy-2013.
Office of Family Assistance. 2017. *TANF Financial Data—FY 2015.* US Department of Health and Human Services, Administration for Children and Families. https://www.acf.hhs.gov/ofa/resource/tanf-financial-data-fy-2015.
Office of the Assistant Secretary for Planning and Evaluation. 2018. *U.S. Federal Poverty Guidelines Used to Determine Financial Eligibility for Certain Federal Programs.* US Department of Health and Human Services. https://aspe.hhs.gov/poverty-guidelines.
Oishi, Shingehiro and Kesebir, Selin. 2015. "Income Inequality Explains Why Economic Growth Does Not Always Translate to an Increase in Happiness." *Psychological Science* 26(10): 1630–38.
Olds, David, Henderson, Charles R., Cole, Robert, Eckenrode, John, Kitzman, Harriet, Luckey, Dennis, Pettitt, Lisa, Sidora, Kimberly, Morris, Pamela, and Powers, Jane. 1998. "Long-Term Effects of Nurse Home Visitation on Children's Criminal and Antisocial Behavior: 15-Year Follow-up of a Randomized Controlled Trial." *Journal of the American Medical Association* 280(14): 1238–44.
Olds, David L., Kitzman, Harriet, Cole, Robert, Robinson, JoAnn, Sidora, Kimberly, Luckey, Dennis W., Henderson, Charles R., Hanks, Carole, Bondy, Jessica, and Holmberg, John. 2004. "Effects of Nurse Home-Visiting on Maternal Life Course and Child Development: Age 6 Follow-up of a Randomized Trial." *Pediatrics* 114(6): 1550–1559.
Olds, David L., Kitzman, Harriet, Hanks, Carole, Cole, Robert, Anson, Elizabeth, Sidora-Arcoleo, Kimberly, Luckey, Dennis W., Henderson, Charles R., Holmberg, John, and Tutt, Robin A. 2007. "Effects of Nurse Home Visiting on Maternal and Child Functioning: Age-9 Follow-up of a Randomized Trial." *Pediatrics* 120(4): e832–e845.

Olen, Helanie. 2017. "Even the Insured Often Can't Afford Their Medical Bills." *Atlantic*, June 18. https://www.theatlantic.com/business/archive/2017/06/medical-bills/530679/.

Olivetti, Claudia and Petrongolo, Barbara. 2017. "The Economic Consequences of Family Policies: Lessons from a Century of Legislation in High-Income Countries." *Journal of Economic Perspectives* 31(1): 205–30.

O'Neill, June A., Bassi, Laurie A., and Wolf, Douglas A. 1987. "The Duration of Welfare Spells." *Review of Economics and Statistics* 69(2): 241–8.

Øresunddirekt. 2018. *Parental Leave When Working in Denmark*. https://www.oresunddirekt.se/in-english/in-english/family-parenting-in-denmark/parental-leave-when-you-work-in-denmark.

Orloff, Ann Shola. 2006. "From Maternalism to 'Employment for All': State Policies to Promote Women's Employment Across the Affluent Democracies." In Jonah Levy (ed.), *The State After Statism: New State Activities in the Age of Liberalization*. Cambridge, MA: Harvard University Press.

Oswalt, Sara B., Lederer, Alyssa M., Chestnut-Steich, Kimberly, Day, Carol, Halbritter, Ashlee, and Ortiz, Dugeidy. 2018. "Trends in College Students' Mental Health Diagnoses and Utilization of Services, 2009–2015." *Journal of American College Health*. https://www.tandfonline.com/doi/pdf/10.1080/07448481.2018.1515748?needAccess=true.

Owens, Judith. 2014. "Insufficient Sleep in Adolescents and Young Adults: An Update on Causes and Consequences." *Pediatrics* 134(3): e921–e932.

Pager, Devah. 2007. *Marked: Race, Crime, and Finding Work in an Era of Mass Incarceration*. Chicago: University of Chicago Press.

Panos, Robert J., Astin, Alexander W., and Creager, John A. 1967. *National Norms for Entering College Freshmen—Fall 1967*. American Council on Education. https://www.heri.ucla.edu/PDFs/pubs/TFS/Norms/Monographs/NationalNormsForEnteringCollege-Freshmen1967.pdf.

Pao, Maureen. 2016. "U.S. Parents Are Sweating and Hustling to Pay for Child Care." *NPR*, October 22. https://www.npr.org/2016/10/22/498590650/u-s-parents-are-sweating-and-hustling-to-pay-for-child-care.

Parcel, Toby and Menaghan, Elizabeth. 1994. "Early Parental Work, Family Social Capital, and Early Childhood Outcomes." *American Journal of Sociology* 99(4): 972–1009.

Parke, Ross D., Coltrane, Scott, Duffy, Sharon, Buriel, Raymond, Dennis, Jessica, Powers, Justina, French, Sabine, and Widaman, Keith F. 2004. "Economic Stress, Parenting, and Child Adjustment in Mexican American and European American Families." *Child Development* 75(6): 1632–56.

Parker, Kim, Horowitz, Juliana, Bell, James, Livingston, Gretchen, Schwarzer, Steve, and Patten, Eileen. 2015. *Family Support in Graying Societies: How Americans, Germans and Italians Are Coping with an Aging Population*. Pew Research Center. http://www.pewresearch.org/wp-content/uploads/sites/3/2015/05/2015-05-21_family-support-relations_FINAL.pdf.

Parker, Kim and Patten, Eileen. 2013. *The Sandwich Generation: Rising Financial Burdens for Middle-Aged Americans*. Pew Research Center. http://www.pewresearch.org/wp-content/uploads/sites/3/2013/01/Sandwich_Generation_Report_FINAL_1-29.pdf.

Parker, Kim and Stepler, Renee. 2017. "As U.S. Marriage Rate Hovers at 50%, Education Gap in Marital Status Widens." Pew Research Center, September 14. http://www.pewresearch.org/fact-tank/2017/09/14/as-u-s-marriage-rate-hovers-at-50-education-gap-in-marital-status-widens/.

Parker, Kim and Wang, Wendy. 2013a. "Americans' Time at Paid Work, Housework, Child Care, 1965 to 2011." In *Modern Parenthood: Roles of Moms and Dads Converge as They Balance Work and Family*. Pew Research Center, March 13. http://www.pewsocialtrends.org/2013/03/14/chapter-5-americans-time-at-paid-work-housework-child-care-1965-to-2011/.

Parker, Kim and Wang, Wendy. 2013b. "Balancing Work and Family Life." In *Modern Parenthood: Roles of Moms and Dads Converge as They Balance Work and Family*. Pew Research Center. http://www.pewsocialtrends.org/wp-content/uploads/sites/3/2013/03/FINAL_modern_parenthood_03-2013.pdf.

Parkes, Alison, Sweeting, Helen, and Wight, David. 2016. "What Shapes 7-Year-Olds' Subjective Well-Being? Prospective Analysis of Early Childhood and Parenting Using the Growing Up in Scotland Study." *Social Psychiatry and Psychiatric Epidemiology* 51(10): 1417–28.

Pascal, Chris, Bertram, Tony, Delany, Sean, and Nelson, Carol. 2013. *A Comparison of International Childcare Systems*. United Kingdom Department for Education, Centre for Research in Early Childhood. http://www.crec.co.uk/DFE-RR269.pdf.

Patients' Perspectives on Health Care in the United States: A Look at Seven States & the Nation. NPR, Robert Wood Johnson Foundation, and Harvard T. H. Chan School of Public Health. https://www.rwjf.org/content/dam/farm/reports/surveys_and_polls/2016/rwjf427031.

Patnaik, Ankita. 2015. "Parental Leave Policies and Their Consequences for Inequality." Cornell University, Cornell Theses and Dissertations.

Patnaik, Ankita. Forthcoming 2019. "Reserving Time for Daddy: The Consequences of Fathers' Quotas." *Journal of Labor Economics.* https://papers.ssrn.com/sol3/papers.cfm?abstract_id=3225239.

Patten, Eileen and Parker, Kim. 2012. *A Gender Reversal on Career Aspirations: Young Women Now Top Young Men in Valuing a High-Paying Career.* Pew Research Center. http://www.pewsocialtrends.org/files/2012/04/Women-in-the-Workplace.pdf.

Patterson, James T. 2009. *America's Struggle Against Poverty in the Twentieth Century.* Cambridge, MA: Harvard University Press.

Paxson, Christina and Waldfogel, Jane. 2003. "Welfare Reforms, Family Resources, and Child Maltreatment." *Journal of Policy Analysis and Management* 22(1): 85–113.

Payne, Keith. 2017. *The Broken Ladder: How Inequality Affects the Way We Think, Live, and Die.* New York: Viking.

Pear, Robert. 1996. "Senate Passes Welfare Measure, Sending It for Clinton's Signature." *New York Times,* August 2. http://www.nytimes.com/1996/08/02/us/senate-passes-welfare-measure-sending-it-for-clinton-s-signature.html.

Pennington, Bill. 2017. "They Can Hit 400-Foot Homers, but Playing Catch? That's Tricky." *New York Times,* April 1. https://www.nytimes.com/2017/04/01/sports/baseball/they-can-hit-400-foot-homers-but-playing-catch-thats-tricky.html.

Peralta, Katherine. 2014. "College Grads Taking Many Low-Wage Jobs: The Unskilled See Hunt for Work Get Even Tougher." *Boston Globe,* March 10. https://www.bostonglobe.com/business/2014/03/09/college-grads-taking-low-wage-posts-displace-less-educated/BW0af4pRxHj3huC4QfGFfM/story.html.

Perlow, Leslie and Porter, Jessica. 2009. "Making Time Off Predictable—and Required." *Harvard Business Review* 87(10): 102–9.

Perou, Ruth, Bitsko, Rebecca H., Blumberg, Stephen J., Pastor, Patricia, Ghandour, Reem M., Gfroerer, Joseph C., Hedden, Sarra L., Crosby, Alex E., Visser, Susanna N., Schieve, Laura A., et al. 2013. "Mental Health Surveillance among Children—United States, 2005–2011." *Supplements* 62(02): 1–35. https://www.cdc.gov/mmwr/preview/mmwrhtml/su6202a1.htm.

Perry, Mark. 2016. "New US Homes Today Are 1,000 Square Feet Larger than in 1973 and Living Space per Person Has Nearly Doubled." *AEIdeas,* June 5. http://www.aei.org/publication/new-us-homes-today-are-1000-square-feet-larger-than-in-1973-and-living-space-per-person-has-nearly-doubled/.

Perry-Jenkins, Maureen, Goldberg, Abbie E., Pierce, Courtney P. and Sayer, Aline G. 2007. "Shift Work, Role Overload, and the Transition to Parenthood." *Journal of Marriage and Family* 69(1): 123–38.

Petito, Fausta and Cummins, Robert A. 2000. "Quality of Life in Adolescence: The Role of Perceived Control, Parenting Style, and Social Support." *Behaviour Change* 17(3): 196–207.

Petre, Jonathan. 2016. "Teenagers' Stress and Anxiety Levels Are at an All-Time High with Middle-Class Children the Worst Affected." *Daily Mail,* August 6. https://www.dailymail.co.uk/

health/article-3727507/Teenagers-stress-anxiety-levels-time-high-middle-class-children-worst-affected.html.

Pew Research Center. 2008. "Who Wants to Be Rich?" Pew Research Center, April 30. http://www.pewsocialtrends.org/2008/04/30/who-wants-to-be-rich/#.

Pew Research Center. 2015a. *Raising Kids and Running a Household: How Working Parents Share the Load.* http://assets.pewresearch.org/wp-content/uploads/sites/3/2015/11/2015-11-04_working-parents_FINAL.pdf.

Pew Research Center. 2015b. *Parenting in America: Outlook, Worries, Aspirations Are Strongly Linked to Financial Situation.* http://www.pewresearch.org/wp-content/uploads/sites/3/2015/12/2015-12-17_parenting-in-america_FINAL.pdf.

Pew Research Center. 2016a. "On Views of Race and Inequality, Blacks and Whites Are Worlds Apart." Available at http://assets.pewresearch.org/wp-content/uploads/sites/3/2016/06/ST_2016.06.27_Race-Inequality-Final.pdf.

Pew Research Center. 2016b. "U.S. Teen Birth Rate Has Fallen Dramatically over Time." Pew Research Center, April 29. http://www.pewresearch.org/ft_16-04-29_teenbirths_longterm_640/.

Pew Research Center. 2017. "A Third of Americans Live in a Household with Three or More Smartphones." Pew Research Center, May 25. http://www.pewresearch.org/fact-tank/2017/05/25/a-third-of-americans-live-in-a-household-with-three-or-more-smartphones/.

Pfeffer, Fabian T. and Schoeni, Robert F. 2016. "How Wealth Inequality Shapes Our Future." *RSF: Russell Sage Foundation Journal of the Social Sciences* 2(6): 2–23.

Philips, Deborah and Adams, Gina. 2001. "Child Care and Our Youngest Children." *Future of Our Children* 11(1): 35–51.

Phillips, Deborah and Zigler, Edward. 1987. "The Checkered History of Federal Child Care Regulation." *Review of Research in Education* 14: 3–41.

Phillips, Julie A., Robin, Ashley V., Nugent, Colleen N., and Idler, Ellen L. 2010. "Understanding Recent Changes in Suicide Rates among the Middle-aged: Period or Cohort Effects?" *Public Health Reports* 125(5): 680–8.

Phillips, Meredith. 2011. "Parenting, Time Use, and Disparities in Academic Outcomes." In Greg J. Duncan and Richard J. Murnane (eds.), *Withering Opportunity? Rising Inequality, Schools, and Children's Life Chances.* New York: Russell Sage Foundation.

Pifer, Alan and Chisman, Forrest (eds.). 1985. *The Report of the Committee on Economic Security of 1935; and Other Basic Documents Relating to the Development of the Social Security Act.* Washington, DC: National Conference on Social Welfare.

Piketty, Thomas and Saez, Emmanuel. 2007. "How Progressive Is the U.S. Federal Tax System? A Historical and International Perspective." *Journal of Economic Perspectives* 21(1): 3–24.

Piketty, Thomas and Saez, Emmanuel. 2013. *U.S. Income Series.* http://elsa.berkeley.edu/~saez/TabFig2012prel.xls.

Piketty, Thomas and Saez, Emmanuel. 2019. *U.S. Income Series.* http://elsa.berkeley.edu/~saez/TabFig2017prel.xls.

Piketty, Thomas, Saez, Emmanuel, and Stantcheva, Stefanie. 2014. "Optimal Taxation of Top Labor Incomes: A Tale of Three Elasticities." *American Economic Association* 6(1): 230–71.

Piketty, Thomas, Saez, Emmanuel, and Zucman, Gabriel. 2018. "Distributional National Accounts: Methods and Estimates for the United States." *Quarterly Journal of Economics* 133(2): 553–609.

Pimpare, Stephen. 2004. *The New Victorians: Poverty, Politics, and Propaganda in Two Gilded Ages.* New York: New Press.

Pingle, Jonathan. 2003. "What if Welfare Had No Work Requirements? The Age of Youngest Child Exemption and the Rise in Employment of Single Mothers." *Finance and Economic Discussion Series Working Papers.* Working Paper No. 2003-57. Board of Governors of the Federal Reserve System. https://www.federalreserve.gov/pubs/feds/2003/200357/200357pap.pdf.

Plemmons, Gregory, Hall, Matthew, Doupnik, Stephanie, Gay, James, Brown, Charlotte, Browning, Whitney, Casey, Robert, Freundlich, Katherine, Johnson, David P., Lind, Carrie, et al. 2018. "Hospitalization for Suicide Ideation or Attempt: 2008–2015." *Pediatrics* 141(6).

Pölkki, Pirjo L. and Vornanen, Riitta H. 2016. "Role and Success of Finnish Early Childhood Education and Care in Supporting Child Welfare Clients: Perspectives from Parents and Professionals." *Early Childhood Education Journal* 44(6): 581–94.

Pope, Denise, Brown, Maureen and Miles, Sarah. 2015. *Overloaded and Underprepared: Strategies for Stronger Schools and Healthy, Successful Kids.* San Francisco: Jossey-Bass.

Posey, Kirby G. 2016. *Household Income: 2015.* American Community Survey Brief No. ACSBR/15-02. US Department of Commerce, US Census Bureau. https://www.census.gov/content/dam/Census/library/publications/2016/acs/acsbr15-02.pdf.

Poutré, Alain, Rorison, Jamey, and Voigh, Mamie. 2017. *Limited Means, Limited Options: College Remains Unaffordable for Many Americans.* Institute for Higher Education Policy. http://www.ihep.org/sites/default/files/uploads/docs/pubs/limited_means_limited_options_report_final.pdf.

Praag, H.M. van. 2004. "Can Stress Cause Depression?" *Progress in Neuro-Psychopharmacology & Biological Psychiatry* 28(5): 891–907.

Presser, Harriet. 2003. *Working in a 24/7 Economy: Challenges for American Families.* New York: Russell Sage Foundation.

Pressman, Steven. 2011. "Policies to Reduce Child Poverty: Child Allowances versus Tax Exemptions for Children." *Journal of Economic Issues* 45(2): 323–32.

Price, Joseph. 2010. *The Effect of Parental Time Investments: Evidence from Natural Within-Family Variation.* BYU Research. http://byuresearch.org/home/downloads/price_parental_time_2010.pdf.

Proceedings of the Conference on the Care of Dependent Children. 1909. Washington, DC: Government Printing Office. https://ia801403.us.archive.org/28/items/proceedingsconf01statgoog/proceedingsconf01statgoog.pdf.

Putnam, Robert. 2000. *Bowling Alone: The Collapse and Revival of American Community.* New York: Simon & Schuster.

Putnam, Robert. 2015. *Our Kids: The American Dream in Crisis.* New York: Simon & Schuster.

Putnam, Robert D., Frederick, Carl B., and Snellman, Kaisa. 2012. *Growing Class Gaps in Social Connectedness among American Youth: 1975–2009.* Harvard Kennedy School of Government, Saguaro Seminar: Civic Engagement in America. https://hceconomics.uchicago.edu/sites/default/files/file_uploads/Putnam-etal_2012_Growing-Class-Gaps.pdf.

Quart, Alissa. 2013. "Opinion: Crushed by the Cost of Child Care." *New York Times*, August 17. https://opinionator.blogs.nytimes.com/2013/08/17/crushed-by-the-cost-of-child-care/.

Quart, Alissa. 2018. *Squeezed: Why Our Families Can't Afford America.* New York: Ecco Press.

Quinn, Mattie. 2017. "Universal Pre-K Is Hard to Find and Harder to Fund." *Governing.* February. http://www.governing.com/topics/education/gov-universal-pre-kindergarten.html.

Radel, Laura, Baldwin, Melinda, Crouse, Gilbert, Ghertner, Robin, and Waters, Annette. 2018. *Substance Use, the Opioid Epidemic, and the Child Welfare System: Key Findings from a Mixed Methods Study.* US Department of Health and Human Services, Office of the Assistant Secretary for Planning and Evaluation. https://aspe.hhs.gov/system/files/pdf/258836/SubstanceUseChildWelfareOverview.pdf.

Raikes, Helen, Torquati, Julia, Wang, Cixin, and Shjedstad, Brinn. 2012. "Parent Experiences with State Child Care Subsidy Systems and Their Perceptions of Choice and Quality in Care Selected." *Early Education and Development* 23(4): 558–82.

Ramey, Garey and Ramey Valerie. 2010. *The Rug Rat Race.* http://econweb.ucsd.edu/~vramey/research/Rugrat.pdf.

Rapee, Ronald. 1997. "Potential Role of Childrearing Practices in the Development of Anxiety and Depression." *Clinical Psychology Review* 17(1): 47–67.

Raphael, T. J., Angell, Isabel, and Hall, Amber. 2017. "Finland's Guaranteed Basic Income Is Working to Tackle Poverty." *Kera News*, May 6. https://www.keranews.org/post/finlands-guaranteed-basic-income-working-tackle-poverty.

Raschke, Christian. 2016. "The Impact of the German Child Benefit on Household Expenditures and Consumption." *German Economic Review* 17(4): 438–77.

Ratcliffe, Susan. 2015. *Child Poverty and Adult Success*. Urban Institute. https://www.urban.org/sites/default/files/publication/65766/2000369-Child-Poverty-and-Adult-Success.pdf.

Raub, Amy, Earle, Alison, Chung, Paul, Batra, Priya, Schickedanz, Adam, Bose, Bijetri, Jou, Judy, Chorny, Nicolas de Guzman, Wong, Elizabeth, Franken, Daniel, and Heymann, Jody. 2018. *Paid Leave for Family Illness: A Detailed Look at Approaches Across OECD Countries.* WORLD Policy Analysis Center. https://www.worldpolicycenter.org/sites/default/files/WORLD%20Report%20-%20Family%20Medical%20Leave%20OECD%20Country%20Approaches_0.pdf.

Raworth, Kate. 2017. *Doughnut Economics: Seven Ways to Think Like a 21st-Century Economist.* White River Junction, VT: Chelsea Green.

Ray, Rebecca, Gornick, Janet C., and Schmitt, John. 2010. "Who Cares? Assessing Generosity and Gender Equality in Parental Leave Policy Designs in 21 Countries." *Journal of European Social Policy* 20(3): 196–216.

Ray, Rebecca, Sanes, Milla, and Schmitt, John. 2013. *No-Vacation Nation Revisited.* Center for Economic and Policy Research. http://cepr.net/documents/publications/no-vacation-update-2013-05.pdf.

Reagan, Ronald. 1981. "Inaugural Address." *American Presidency Project*, January 20. http://www.presidency.ucsb.edu/ws/?pid=43130.

Reagan, Ronald. 1982. "Radio Address to the Nation on Taxes, the Tuition Tax Credit, and Interest Rates, April 24, 1982." *American Presidency Project*, April 24. http://presidency.proxied.lsit.ucsb.edu/ws/index.php?pid=42445.

Reagan, Ronald. 1986. *Address before a Joint Session of Congress on the State of the Union.* February 4. https://www.reaganlibrary.gov/research/speeches/20486a.

Reardon, Sean. 2013a. "Opinion: No Rich Child Left Behind." *New York Times*, April 27. https://opinionator.blogs.nytimes.com/2013/04/27/no-rich-child-left-behind/?mtrref=undefined&assetType=opinion&login=email.

Reardon, Sean. 2013b. "The Widening Income Achievement Gap." *Educational Leadership* 70(8): 10–16.

Reardon, Sean and Portilla, Ximena. 2016. "Recent Trends in Income, Racial, and Ethnic School Readiness Gaps at Kindergarten Entry." *AERA Open* 2(3): 1–18.

Redford, Jeremy, Desrochers, Donna, and Mulvaney Hoyer, Kathleen. 2017. *The Years Before School: Children's Non-parental Care Arrangements From 2001-2012.* NCES Report No. 2017-096. US Department of Education, National Center for Education Statistics. https://nces.ed.gov/pubs2017/2017096.pdf

Reeves, Richard V. and Krause, Eleanor. 2018. "Raj Chetty in 14 Charts: Big Findings on Opportunity and Mobility We Should All Know." *Brookings*. https://www.brookings.edu/blog/social-mobility-memos/2018/01/11/raj-chetty-in-14-charts-big-findings-on-opportunity-and-mobility-we-should-know/.

Reeves, Richard V., Sawhill, Isabel V., and Krause, Eleanor. 2016. "The Most Educated Women Are the Most Likely to Be Married." *Brookings*. https://www.brookings.edu/blog/social-mobility-memos/2016/08/19/the-most-educated-women-are-the-most-likely-to-be-married/.

Reich, Robert. 1984. "Whatever Happened to the Welfare Ideal?" *New York Times*,. January 1. http://www.nytimes.com/1984/01/01/books/whatever-happened-to-the-welfare-ideal.html?pagewanted=all.

Renzetti, Claire M. 2009. *Economic Stress and Domestic Violence*. National Online Resource Center on Violence Against Women. https://vawnet.org/sites/default/files/materials/files/2016-09/AR_EconomicStress.pdf.

Repetti, Rena and Wood, Jenifer. 1997. "Effects of Daily Stress at Work on Mothers' Interactions with Preschoolers." *Journal of Family Psychology* 11(1): 90–108.

Repo, Katja. 2010. "Families, Work and Home Care: Assessing the Finnish Child Home Care Allowance." *Barn* 1: 43–61.

Reynolds, Alan. 2007. *Has U.S. Income Inequality Really Increased?* Cato Institute Policy Analysis No. 586. https://object.cato.org/sites/cato.org/files/pubs/pdf/pa586.pdf.

Reynolds, Arthur, Ou, Suh-Ruu, and Temple, Judy A. 2018. "A Multicomponent, Preschool to Third Grade Preventative Intervention and Educational Attainment at 35 Years of Age." *JAMA Pediatrics* 172(3): 247–56.

Rhode Island Department of Labor and Training. 2018. *Temporary Disability Insurance/Temporary Caregiver Insurance.* http://www.dlt.ri.gov/tdi/.

Ridge, Tess. 2011. "The Everyday Costs of Poverty in Childhood: A Review of Qualitative Research Exploring the Lives and Experiences of Low-Income Children in the UK." *Children and Society* 25: 73–84.

Riis, Jacob. 1890. *How the Other Half Lives; Studies among the Tenements of New York.* New York: Charles Scribner's Sons.

Riley, Matilda and Riley, John. 1993. "Connections: Kin and Cohort." In Vern Bengtson and W. Andrew Achenbaum (eds.), *The Changing Contract Across Generations.* New York: Aldine de Gruyter.

Ripley, Amanda. 2013. *The Smartest Kids in the World and How They Got That Way.* New York: Simon & Schuster.

Rippeyoung, Phyllis and Noonan, Mary. 2012. "Is Breastfeeding Truly Cost Free? Income Consequences of Breastfeeding for Women." *American Sociological Review* 77(2): 244–67.

Robila, Mihaela and Krishnakumar, Ambika. 2006. "Economic Pressure and Children's Psychological Functioning." *Journal of Child and Family Studies* 15(4): 433–41.

Rodgers, Daniel T. 2011. *Age of Fracture.* Cambridge, MA: Harvard University Press.

Roelofs, Jeffrey, Meesters, Cor, Huurne, Mijke ter, Bamelis, Lotte, and Muris, Peter. 2006. "On the Links Between Attachment Style, Parental Rearing Behaviors, and Internalizing and Externalizing Problems in Non-Clinical Children." *Journal of Child and Family Studies* 15(3): 331–44.

Roeters, Anne, Lippe, Tanja van der, and Kluwer, Esther S. 2010. "Work Characteristics and Parent–Child Relationship Quality: The Mediating Role of Temporal Involvement." *Journal of Marriage and Family* 72(5): 1317–28.

Rogers, Katie. 2016. "Life Expectancy in U.S. Declines Slightly, and Researchers Are Puzzled." *New York Times.* December 8. Available at https://www.nytimes.com/2016/12/08/health/life-expectancy-us-declines.html.

Rohwedder, Susann and Wenger, Jeffrey. 2015. *The Fair Labor Standards Act: Worker Misclassification and the Hours and Earnings Effects of Expanded Coverage.* RAND Labor and Population. https://www.rand.org/content/dam/rand/pubs/working_papers/WR1100/WR1114/RAND_WR1114.pdf.

Romig, Kathleen. 2018. *Social Security Lifts More Americans above Poverty than Any Other Program.* Center on Budget and Policy Priorities: Policy Futures. https://www.cbpp.org/sites/default/files/atoms/files/10-25-13ss.pdf.

Roosevelt, Franklin. 1944. *State of the Union Address to Congress, January 11, 1944.* http://www.fdrlibrary.marist.edu/archives/address_text.html.

Rose, Elizabeth. 2010. *The Promise of Preschool: From Head Start to Universal Pre-Kindergarten.* New York: Oxford University Press.

Rose, Julie L. 2016. *Free Time.* Princeton, NJ: Princeton University Press.

Rosenfeld, Jake. 2014. *What Unions No Longer Do.* Cambridge, MA: Harvard University Press.

Rosenthal, Jack. 1971. "President Vetoes Child Care Plan as Irresponsible." *New York Times,* December 10.

Ross-Brown, Sam and Teuscher, Amanda. 2015. "Why the DOL's New Overtime Rule Is Such a Big Deal." *American Prospect,* September 3. http://prospect.org/article/why-dols-new-overtime-rule-such-big-deal.

Rossin-Slater, Maya, Ruhm, Christopher, and Waldfogel, Jane. 2013. "The Effects of California's Paid Family Leave Program on Mothers' Leave-Taking and Subsequent Labor Market Outcomes." *Journal of Policy Analysis and Management* 32(2): 224–45.

Roth, William. 1976. "The Politics of Daycare: The Comprehensive Child Development Act of 1971." *Institute for Research on Poverty Discussion Papers* No. 369-76. https://www.irp.wisc.edu/publications/dps/pdfs/dp36976.pdf.

Rothstein, Bo. 1992. "Labor–Market Institutions and Working-Class Strength." In Sven, Steinmo, Kathleen Thelen, and Frank Longstreth (eds.), *Structuring Politics: Historical Institutionalism in Comparative Analysis.* Cambridge: Cambridge University Press.

Rothstein, Richard. 2017. *The Color of Law: A Forgotten History of How Our Government Segregated America.* New York: Liveright.

Ruhm, Christopher. 2000. "Parental Leave and Child Health." *Journal of Health Economics* 19(6): 931–60.

Ruhm, Christopher. 2008. "Maternal Employment and Adolescent Development." *Labour Economics* 15(5): 958–83.

Ruhm, Christopher and Waldfogel, Jane. 2011. "Long-Term Effects of Early Childhood Care and Education." *IZA Discussion Papers.* No. 6149. http://ftp.iza.org/dp6149.pdf.

Ryan, Camille and Bauman, Kurt. 2016. *Educational Attainment in the United States: 2015.* US Department of Commerce, US Census Bureau. https://www.census.gov/content/dam/Census/library/publications/2016/demo/p20-578.pdf.

Ryan, Mary P. 1981. *Cradle of the Middle Class: The Family in Oneida County, New York, 1790–1865.* Cambridge: Cambridge University Press.

Ryan, Richard M., Sheldon, Kennon M., Kasser, Tim, and Deci, Edward L. 1996. "All Goals Are Not Created Equal: An Organismic Perspective on the Nature of Goals and Their Regulation." In Peter M. Gollwitzer and John A. Bargh (eds.), *The Psychology of Action: Linking Cognition and Motivation to Behavior.* New York: Guilford Press.

Ryan, William. 1965. "Savage Discovery: The Moynihan Report." *Nation,* November 22, pp. 380–4.

Saad, Lydia. 2012. "Stay-at-Home Moms in US Lean Independent, Lower-Income." *Gallup, Politics,* April 19. http://www.gallup.com/poll/153995/stay-home-moms-lean-independent-lower-income.aspx.

Sacks, Vanessa, Murphey, David, and Moore, Kristin. 2014. *Adverse Childhood Experiences: National and State-Level Prevalence.* Child Trends Research Brief No. 2014-28. Child Trends. https://www.childtrends.org/wp-content/uploads/2014/07/Brief-adverse-childhood-experiences_FINAL.pdf.

Saez, Emmanuel. 2015. *Striking It Richer: The Evolution of Top Incomes in the United States (Updated with 2013 Preliminary Estimates).* https://eml.berkeley.edu/~saez/saez-UStopincomes-2015.pdf.

Salkind, Neil J. and Haskins, Ron. 1982. "Negative Income Tax: The Impact on Children from Low-Income Families." *Journal of Family Issues* 3(2): 165–80.

Sampson, Robert and Laub, John. 1994. "Urban Poverty and the Family Context of Delinquency: A New Look at Structure and Process in a Classic Study." *Child Development* 65(2): 523–40.

Samuelson, Paul. 1968. "Negative Income Tax." *Newsweek,* June 10, p. 76.

Sanders, Matthew R. 2008. "Triple P-Positive Parenting Program as a Public Health Approach to Strengthening Parenting." *Journal of Family Psychology* 22(4): 506–17.

Sanders, Matthew R., Markie-Dadds, Carol, Tully, Lucy A., and Bor, William. 2000. "The Triple P-Positive Parenting Program: A Comparison of Enhanced, Standard, and Self-Directed Behavioral Family Intervention for Parents of Children with Early Onset Conduct Problems." *Journal of Consulting and Clinical Psychology* 68(4): 624–40.

Santiago, Catherine DeCarlo, Wadsworth, Martha E., and Stump, Jessica. 2011. "Socioeconomic Status, Neighborhood Disadvantage, and Poverty-Related Stress: Prospective Effects on Psychological Syndromes among Diverse Low-Income Families." *Journal of Economic Psychology* 32: 218–30.

Santorum, Rick. 2005. *It Takes a Family: Conservatism and the Common Good.* Wilmington, DE: ISI Books.

Sarkadi, Anna, Kristiansson, Robert, Oberklaid, Frank, and Bremberg, Sven. 2008. "Fathers' Involvement and Children's Developmental Outcomes: A Systematic Review of Longitudinal Studies." *Acta Pædiatrica* 97(2): 153–8.

Schawbel, Dan. 2014. "Why Millennials Should Get Used to Work–Life Imbalance." *Time Money*, October 29. http://time.com/money/3545722/millennials-work-life-balance/.

Scheiber, Harry. 1997. "Review: Private Rights and Public Power: American Law, Capitalism, and the Republican Polity in Nineteenth-Century America." *Yale Law Journal* 107(3): 823–61.

Schelling, Thomas C. [1978] 2006. *Micromotives and Macrobehavior*. New York: W. W. Norton.

Schmidt, Stefanie. 1999. "Long-Run Trends in Workers' Beliefs About Their Own Job Security: Evidence from the General Social Survey." *Journal of Labor Economics* 17(S4): S127–S141.

Schmidtbauer, Ashely. 2014. "The In-Betweeners of a Broken System." *Huffpost Blog*, April 15. https://www.huffingtonpost.com/ashley-schmidtbauer-/in-betweeners-working-poor_b_ 5121188.html?utm_hp_ref=@working_poor.

Schmit, Stephanie, Matthews, Hannah, Smith, Sheila, and Robbins, Taylor. 2013. *Investing in Young Children: A Fact Sheet on Early Care and Education, Participation, Access, and Quality*. Center for Law and Social Policy (CLASP) and National Center for Children in Poverty (NCCP). https://files.eric.ed.gov/fulltext/ED547124.pdf.

Schmit, Stephanie and Walker, Christina. 2016. *Disparate Access: Head Start and CCDBG Data by Race and Ethnicity*. Center for Law and Social Policy (CLASP). http://ccf.ny.gov/files/ 1914/5625/2696/Disparate-Access.pd.pdf.

Schmitt, Glenn R., Reedt, Louis, and Blackwell, Kevin. 2017. *Demographic Differences in Sentencing: An Update to the 2012 Booker Report*. US Sentencing Commission. https:// www.ussc.gov/sites/default/files/pdf/research-and-publications/research-publications/ 2017/20171114_Demographics.pdf.

Schochet, Leila. 2017. *The Importance of Child Care Safety Protections*. Center for American Progress. https://cdn.americanprogress.org/content/uploads/2017/10/27133918/ ChildSafety-brief.pdf

Schoen, Cathy, Radley, David, and Collins, Sara R. 2015. *State Trends in the Cost of Employer Health Insurance Coverage, 2003–2013*. Commonwealth Fund. https:// www.commonwealthfund.org/sites/default/files/documents/___media_files_ publications_issue_brief_2015_jan_1798_schoen_state_trends_2003_2013.pdf.

Schor, Juliet. 1992. *The Overworked American: The Unexpected Decline of Leisure*. New York: Basic Books.

Schor, Juliet. 1998. *The Overspent American: Upscaling, Downshifting, and the New Consumer*. New York: Basic Books.

Schore, Allan. 2017. "All Our Sons: The Developmental Neurobiology and Neuroendocrinology of Boys at Risk." *Infant Mental Health Journal* 38(1): 15–52.

Schott, Liz, Floyd, Ife, and Burnside, Ashley. 2018. *How States Use Funds Under the TANF Block Grant*. Center on Budget and Policy Priorities. https://www.cbpp.org/sites/default/files/ atoms/files/1-5-17tanf.pdf.

Schraedley, Pamela K., Gotlib, Ian H., and Hayward, Chris. 1999. "Gender Differences in Correlates of Depressive Symptoms in Adolescents." *Journal of Adolescent Health* 25(2): 98–108.

Schram, Sanford F., Soss, Joe, and Fording, Richard C. (eds.). 2003. *Race and the Politics of Welfare Reform*. Ann Arbor: University of Michigan Press.

Schreyer, Inge and Oberhuemer, Pamela. 2017. "Denmark: Key Contextual Data." In Pamela Oberhuemer and Inge Schreyer (eds.), *Workforce Profiles in Systems of Early Childhood Education and Care in Europe*. http://www.seepro.eu/English/pdfs/DENMARK_Key_ Data.pdf.

Schrobsdorff, Susanna. 2016. "Teen Depression and Anxiety: Why the Kids Are Not Alright." *TIME Health*, October 27. http://time.com/4547322/american-teens-anxious-depressed-overwhelmed/.

Schulman, Karen and Blank, Helen. 2016. *Red Light Green Light: State Child Care Assistance Policies, 2016.* National Women's Law Center. https://nwlc.org/wp-content/uploads/2016/10/NWLC-State-Child-Care-Assistance-Policies-2016-final.pdf.

Schulte, Brigid. 2014. *Overwhelmed: Work, Love, and Play When No One Has the Time.* New York: Sarah Crichton Books.

Schulte, Brigid. 2015. "Making Time for Kids? Study Says Quality Trumps Quantity." *Washington Post,* March 28. https://www.washingtonpost.com/local/making-time-for-kids-study-says-quality-trumps-quantity/2015/03/28/10813192-d378-11e4-8fce-3941fc548f1c_story.html?utm_term=.26b0be01e114.

Schulte, Brigid and Durana, Alieza. 2016. *The New America Care Report.* New America and Better Life Lab. https://na-production.s3.amazonaws.com/documents/FINAL_Care_Report.pdf.

Schultz, Connie. 2013. "Review: Sheryl Sandberg's 'Lean In' Is Full of Good Intentions, but Rife with Contradictions." *Washington Post,* March 1. https://www.washingtonpost.com/opinions/review-sheryl-sandbergs-lean-in-is-full-of-good-intentions-but-rife-with-contradictions/2013/03/01/3380e00e-7f9a-11e2-a350-49866afab584_story.html?noredirect=on&utm_term=.3fa493a41e03.

Schwartz, Christine. 2010. "Earnings Inequality and the Changing Association Between Spouses' Earnings." *American Journal of Sociology* 115(5): 1524–57.

Schwartz, Christine and Mare, Robert. 2005. "Trends in Educational Assortative Marriage from 1940 to 2003." *Demography* 42(4): 621-646.

Schweinhart, Lawrence, Weikart, David, and Larner, Mary. 1986. "Consequences of Three Preschool Curriculum Models Through Age 15." *Early Childhood Research Quarterly.* 1(1): 15–45.

Schweizer, Valerie. 2018. *Marriage Rate in the U.S.: Geographic Variation, 2017.* Family Profiles (No. FP-18-20). National Center for Family and Marriage Research. https://www.bgsu.edu/content/dam/BGSU/college-of-arts-and-sciences/NCFMR/documents/FP/schweizer-geo-var-marriage-rate-fp-18-20.pdf.

Scott, Eugene. 2018. "Some of Those Hit Hardest by the Opioid Epidemic Are Not Rural, White Americans." *Washington Post,* March 2. https://www.washingtonpost.com/news/the-fix/wp/2018/03/02/some-of-those-hit-hardest-by-opioid-epidemic-are-not-rural-white-americans/?noredirect=on&utm_term=.ea9472e9e9dd.

Scott, Stephen. 2012. "Parenting Quality and Children's Mental Health: Biological Mechanisms and Psychological Interventions." *Current Opinion in Psychiatry* 25(4): 301–6.

Scruggs, Lyle. 2002. "The Ghent System and Union Membership in Europe, 1970–1996." *Political Research Quarterly* 55(2): 275–97.

Sedlak, Andrea J., Mettenburg, Jane, Basena, Monica, Petta, Ian, McPherson, Karla, Greene, Angela, and Li, Spencer 2010. *Fourth National Incidence Study of Child Abuse and Neglect (NIS-4): Report to Congress, Executive Summary.* US Department of Health and Human Services, Administration for Children and Families. https://www.acf.hhs.gov/sites/default/files/opre/nis4_report_exec_summ_pdf_jan2010.pdf.

Self, Robert. 2012. *All in the Family: The Realignment of American Democracy Since the 1960s.* New York: Hill & Wang.

Sellers, Charles. 1991. *The Market Revolution: Jacksonian America, 1815-1846.* New York: Oxford University Press.

Sen, Biaskha. 2010. "The Relationship Between Frequency of Family Dinner and Adolescent Problem Behaviors After Adjusting for Other Family Characteristics." *Journal of Adolescence* 33(1): 187–96.

Senate Committee on Education and Labor. 1885. *Report of the Committee of the Senate upon the Relations Between Labor and Capital, and Testimony Taken by the Committee.* 48th Congress. https://babel.hathitrust.org/cgi/pt?id=hvd.hj1eew;view=1up;seq=7.

Senate Committee on Finance. 1935. *Hearings before the Committee on Finance.* 74th Congress. : https://www.ssa.gov/history/pdf/s35contents.pdf.

Shaefer, Luke H., Collyer, Sophie, Duncan, Greg, Edin, Kathryn, Garfinkel, Irwin, Harris, David, Smeeding, Timothy M., Waldfogel, Jane, Wimer, Christopher, and Yoshikawa, Hirokazu. 2018. "A Universal Child Allowance: A Plan to Reduce Poverty and Income Instability among Children in the United States." *RSF: The Russell Sage Foundation Journal of the Social Sciences* 4(2): 22–42.

Shafer, Kevin and Qian, Zhenchao. 2010. "Marriage Timing and Educational Assortative Mating." *Journal of Comparative Family Studies* 41(5): 661–91.

Shapiro, Isaac and Trisi, Danilo. 2017. *Child Poverty Falls to Record Low, Comprehensive Measure Shows Stronger Government Policies Account for Long-Term Improvement.* Center on Budget and Policy Priorities. https://www.cbpp.org/sites/default/files/atoms/files/10-5-17pov.pdf.

Shattuck, Rachel M. and Kreider, Rose M. 2013. *Social and Economic Characteristics of Currently Unmarried Women with a Recent Birth: 2011.* American Community Survey Report No. ACS-21. US Department of Commerice, US Census Bureau. https://www2.census.gov/library/publications/2013/acs/acs-21.pdf.

Shaw, Daniel S., Keenan, Kate, Vondra, Joan I., Dellaquadri, Eric, and Giovannelli, Joyce. 1997. "Antecedents of Preschool Children's Internalizing Problems: A Longitudinal Study of Low-Income Families." *Journal of the American Academy of Child & Adolescent Psychiatry* 36(12): 1760–7.

Sheldon, Kennon M. and Kasser, Tim. 1995. "Coherence and Congruence: Two Aspects of Personality Integration." *Journal of Personality and Social Psychology* 68(3): 531–43.

Sheldon, Kennon M. and Kasser, Tim. 1998. "Pursuing Personal Goals: Skills Enable Progress, but Not All Progress Is Beneficial." *Personality and Social Psychology Bulletin* 24(12): 1319–31.

Sheldon, Kennon M., Ryan, Richard M., Deci, Edward L., and Kasser, Tim. 1995. "The Independent Effects of Goal Contents and Motives on Well-Being: It's Both What You Pursue and Why You Pursue It." *Personality and Social Psychology Bulletin* 30(4): 475–86.

Shonkoff, Jack and Garner, Andrew. 2012. "Technical Report: The Lifelong Effects of Early Childhood Adversity and Toxic Stress." *Pediatrics* 129(1): e232–e246.

Shonkoff, Jack and Phillips, Deborah. 2000. *From Neurons to Neighborhoods: The Science of Early Childhood Development.* Washington, DC: National Academy Press.

Sidora-Arcoleo, Kimberly, Anson, Elizabeth, Lorber, Michael, Cole, Robert, Olds, David, and Kitzman, Harriet. 2010. "Differential Effects of a Nurse Home-Visiting Intervention on Physically Aggressive Behavior in Children." *Journal of Pediatric Nursing* 25(1): 35–45.

Sigle-Rushton, Wendy. 2010. "Men's Unpaid Work and Divorce: Reassessing Specialization and Trade in British Families." *Feminist Economics* 16(2): 1–26.

SimpleTax. 2019. *Tax Calculator.* Accessed April 22. Available at https://simpletax.ca/calculator.

Skinner, Curtis, and Oschorn, Susan. 2012. *Paid Family Leave: Strengthening Families and Our Future.* Columbia University, National Center for Children in Poverty. http://www.nccp.org/publications/pdf/text_1059.pdf.

Skocpol, Theda. 1992. *Protecting Soldiers and Mothers: The Political Origins of Social Policy in the United States.* Cambridge, MA: Belknap Press.

Slaughter, Anne-Marie. 2012. "Why Women Can't Have It All." *Atlantic,* July–August. https://www.theatlantic.com/magazine/archive/2012/07/why-women-still-cant-have-it-all/309020/.

Smaldone, A., Honig, J. C., and Byrne, M. W. 2007. "Sleepless in America: Inadequate Sleep and Relationships to Health and Well-Being of Our Nation's Children." *Pediatrics* 119(suppl. 1): S29–S37.

Smeeding, Timothy. 2005. "Government Programs and Social Outcomes: The United States in Comparative Perspective." *Luxembourg Income Study Working Paper Series.* (Working Paper No. 426. http://www.lisdatacenter.org/wps/liswps/426.pdf.

Smith, Adam. [1902] 1776. *The Wealth of Nations: Part Two.* New York: P. F. Collier and Son.

Smith, Adam. 1817. *The Theory of Moral Sentiments: An Essay.* Philadephia: Anthony Finley.

Smith, Judith and Brooks-Gunn, Jeanne. 1997. "Correlates and Consequences of Harsh Discipline for Young Children." *Archives of Pediatrics and Adolescent Medicine* 1997(151): 777–86.

Smith, Judith R., Brooks-Gunn, Jeanne, and Klebanov, Pamela K. 1997. "Consequences of Living in Poverty for Young Children's Cognitive and Verbal Ability and Early School Achievement." In Greg J. Duncan and Jeanne Brooks-Gunn (eds.), *Consequences of Growing Up Poor*. New York,: Russel Sage Foundation.

Smith, Liz. 2018. "Here's How Much Americans Have in Their Savings Accounts." *Business Insider*, February 8. https://www.businessinsider.com/how-much-the-average-american-has-in-their-savings-account-2018-2.

Smith, Peggy. 2004. "Elder Care, Gender, and Work: The Work–Family Issue of the 21st Century." *Berkeley Journal of Employment and Labor Law* 25(2): 351–400.

Smolensky, Eugene and Gootman, Jennifer. 2003. *Working Families and Growing Kids: Caring for Children and Adolescents*. Washington, DC: National Academy Press.

Snyder, Ashley H., Weisman, Carol S., Liu, Guodong, Leslie, Douglas and Chuang, Cynthia H. "The Impact of the Affordable Care Act on Contraceptive Use and Costs Among Privately Insured Women." *Women's Health Issues* 28(3): 219–223.

Solnick, Sara J. and Hemenway, David. 1998. "Is More Always Better? A Survey on Positional Concerns." *Journal of Economic Behavior & Organization* 37(3): 373–83.

Solomon-Fears, Carmen. 2014. *Nonmarital Births: An Overview*. Congressional Research Service. https://fas.org/sgp/crs/misc/R43667.pdf.

Soss, Joe, Fording, Richard C., and Schram, Sanford F. 2008. "The Color of Devolution: Race, Federalism, and the Politics of Social Control." *American Journal of Political Science* 52(3): 536–53.

Soss, Joe, Schram, Sanford F., Vartanian, Thomas P., and O'Brien, Erin. 2003 "The Hard Line and the Color Line: Race, Welfare, and the Roots of Get-Tough Reform." In Sanford F. Schram, Joe Soss, and Richard C. Fording (eds.), *Race and the Politics of Welfare Reform*. Ann Arbor: University of Michigan Press.

Sowell, Thomas. 2010. *The Real Public Service*. Creators. https://www.creators.com/read/thomas-sowell/05/10/the-real-public-service-

Sparrow, James T. 2011. *Warfare State: World War II Americans and the Age of Big Government*. New York: Oxford University Press.

Spencer, Herbert. 1852. *Essays: Scientific, Political, and Speculative*, vol. 1. London: Williams & Norgate. http://oll.libertyfund.org/titles/spencer-essays-scientific-political-and- speculative-vol-1--5.

Squires, David and Anderson, Chloe. 2015. *U.S. Health Care from a Global Perspective: Spending, Use of Services, Prices, and Health in 13 Countries*. Commonwealth Fund. http://www.commonwealthfund.org/~/media/files/publications/issue-brief/2015/oct/1819_squires_us_hlt_care_global_perspective_oecd_intl_brief_v3.pdf.

Stanca, Lucca. 2012. "Suffer the Little Children: Measuring the Effects of Parenthood on Well-Being Worldwide." *Journal of Economic Behavior and Organization* 81(3): 742–50.

Stancyzk, Alexandra B. 2016. "The Dynamics of Household Economic Circumstances Around a Birth." *Washington Center for Equitable Growth Working Paper Series*. http://cdn.equitablegrowth.org/wp-content/uploads/2016/09/30112707/10042016-WP-income-volatility-around-birth.pdf.

Stanford Department of Psychiatry and Behavioral Sciences' Center for Youth Mental Health and Wellbeing. 2016. *Understanding the Mental Health Needs and Concerns of Youth and Their Parents: An Exploratory Investigation, Major Themes and Findings*. https://med.stanford.edu/content/dam/sm/psychiatry/documents/CntrforYouth/MajorThemesFindingsFinalReport.pdf.

Stanford Research Institute and Mathematica Policy Research. 1978. *The Seattle-Denver Income Maintenance Experiment: Midexperimental Labor Supply Results and a Generalization to the National Population*. https://babel.hathitrust.org/cgi/pt?id=mdp.39015015286308;view=1up;seq=5.

Stanley, Amy Dru. 1996. "Home Life and the Morality of the Market." In Melvyn Stokes and Stephen Conway (eds.), *The Market Revolution in America: Social, Political, and Religious Expressions, 1800–1880*. Charlottesville: University Press of Virginia.

Stanley, Amy Dru. 1998. *From Bondage to Contract: Wage Labor, Marriage, and the Market in the Age of Slave Emancipation.* Cambridge: Cambridge University Press.

Stanley, Megan, Floyd, Ife, and Hill, Misha. 2016. *TANF Cash Benefits Have Fallen by More than 20% in Most States and Continue to Erode.* Center on Budget and Policy Priorities. https://www.cbpp.org/sites/default/files/atoms/files/10-30-14tanf.pdf.

Stansell, Christine. 1986. *City of Women: Sex and Class in New York, 1789–1860.* New York: Knopf.

State of New Jersey Department of Labor and Workforce Development. 2018. *Benefit Calculation and Duration of Benefits.* https://www.nj.gov/labor/fli/worker/state/FL_SP_calculating_benefits.html.

Statistics Canada. 2019. *Table 11-10-0028-01: Single-earner and dual-earner census families by number of children.* Available at https://www150.statcan.gc.ca/t1/tbl1/en/tv.action?pid=1110002801&pickMembers%5B0%5D=1.16.

Statistics Finland. 2018a. *010—Household Income: Structure by Stage of Life Cycle, 1989–2016.* http://pxnet2.stat.fi/PXWeb/pxweb/en/StatFin/StatFin__tul__tjt/statfin_tjt_pxt_010.px/table/tableViewLayout2/?rxid=4b281bf4-46ac-410e-8c6b-f2a217304488.

Statistics Finland. 2018b. *001—Household Consumption Expenditure by Type of Household, 1985–2016.* http://pxnet2.stat.fi/PXWeb/pxweb/en/StatFin/StatFin__tul__ktutk/statfin_ktutk_pxt_001.px/?rxid=4b281bf4-46ac-410e-8c6b-f2a217304488.

Steckel, Richard. 1990. "Poverty and Prosperity: A Longitudinal Study of Wealth Accumulation, 1850–860." *Review of Economics and Statistics* 72(2): 275–85.

Steensland, Brian. 2008. *The Failed Welfare Revolution: America's Struggle over Guaranteed Income Policy.* Princeton, NJ: Princeton University Press.

Stein, Elizabeth M., Gennuso, Keith P., Ugboaja, Donna C., and Remington, Patrick L. 2017. "The Epidemic of Despair among White Americans: Trends in the Leading Causes of Premature Death, 1999–2015." *American Journal of Public Health* 107(10): 1541–7.

Steinbuch, Yaron. 2016. "Mother of 'Heroin Boy' Is a Crack-Smoking Stripper." *New York Post,* September 14. https://nypost.com/2016/09/14/mom-of-heroin-boy-says-she-wants-her-son-back/.

Stephan, Catherine. 2017. *Ins-and-outs of the Danish Flexicurity Model.* BNP Paribas, Economic Research Department. http://economic-research.bnpparibas.com/Views/DisplayPublication.aspx?type=document&IdPdf=30102.

Sterling, Dorothy. 1984. *We Are Your Sisters: Black Women in the 19th Century.* New York: W. W. Norton.

Stewart-Brown, Sarah L. and Schrader-Mcmillan, Anita. 2011. "Parenting for Mental Health: What Does the Evidence Say We Need to Do? Report of Workpackage 2 of the DataPrev project." *Health Promotion International* 26(1): i10–i28.

Stockholm International Peace Research Institute. 2018. *SIPRI Military Expenditure Database, 2018.* https://www.sipri.org/databases/milex.

Stokes, Bruce. 2011. "The Happiest Countries in the World." *Atlantic,* June 8. https://www.theatlantic.com/business/archive/2011/06/the-happiest-countries-in-the-world/240103/.

Stolberg, Sheryl Gay, and Pear, Robert. 2008. "Bush Speaks in Defense of Markets." *New York Times.* Nov 13. https://www.nytimes.com/2008/11/14/business/economy/14bush.html.

Stoltzfus, Eli. 2015. "Access to Dependent Care Reimbursement Accounts and Workplace-Funded Childcare." *Beyond the Numbers* 4(1): 1–6. https://www.bls.gov/opub/btn/volume-4/pdf/access-to-dependent-care-reimbursement-accounts-and-workplace-funded-childcare.pdf.

Stone, Chad, Trisi, Danilo, Sherman, Arloc, and Taylor, Roderick. 2018. *A Guide to Statistics on Historical Trends in Income Inequality.* Center on Budget and Policy Priorities. https://www.cbpp.org/sites/default/files/atoms/files/11-28-11pov_0.pdf.

Stone, Lyman. 2018. "American Women Are Having Fewer Children than They'd Like." *New York Times,* February 13. https://www.nytimes.com/2018/02/13/upshot/american-fertility-is-falling-short-of-what-women-want.html.

Stone, Pamela. 2007. *Opting Out? Why Women Really Quit Careers and Head Home*. Berkley: University of California Press.

Storrie, Kim, Ahern, Kathy, and Tuckett, Anthony. 2010. "A Systematic Review: Students with Mental Health Problems—A Growing Problem." *International Journal of Nursing Practice* 16(1): 1–6.

Strasser, Julia, Borkowski, Liz, Couillard, Megan, Allina, Amy and Wood, Susan. 2016. *Long-Acting Reversible Contraception: Overview of Research & Policy in the United States*. Jacobs Institute of Women's Health. https://publichealth.gwu.edu/sites/default/files/downloads/projects/JIWH/LARC_White_Paper_2016.pdf.

Strazdins, Lyndall, Korda, Rosemary J., Lim, Lynette L-Y, Broom, Dorothy H., and D'Souza, Rennie M. 2004. "Around-the-Clock: Parent Work Schedules and Children's Well-Being in a 24-h Economy." *Social Science and Medicine* 59(7): 1517–27.

Surowiecki, James. 2014. "The Cult of Overwork." *New Yorker*, January 27. http://www.newyorker.com/magazine/2014/01/27/the-cult-of-overwork.

Sverke, Magnus, Hellgren, Johnny, and Näswall, Katharina. 2002. "No Security: A Meta-Analysis and Review of Job Insecurity and Its Consequences." *Journal of Occupational Health Psychology* 7(3): 242–64.

Swartz, Teresa. 2009. "Intergenerational Family Relations in Adulthood: Patterns, Variations, and Implications in the Contemporary United States." *Annual Review of Sociology* 35: 191–212.

Swedish Institute. 2019. *Parental Leave*. https://sweden.se/quickfact/parental-leave/.

Synder, Ashey H., Weisman, Carol S., Liu, Guodong, Leslie, Douglas, and Chuang, Cynthia H. 2018. "The Impact of the Affordable Care Act on Contraceptive Use and Costs among Privately Insured Women." *Women's Health Issues* 28(3): 219–23.

Tach, Laura, Mincy, Ronald, and Edin, Kathryn. 2010. "Parenting as a 'Package Deal': Relationships, Fertility, and Nonresident Father Involvement among Unmarried Parents." *Demography* 47(1): 181–204.

Taguma, Miho, Litjens, Ineke, and Makowiecki, Kelly. 2012. *Quality Matters in Early Childhood Education and Care: Finland 2012*. OECD. https://www.oecd.org/education/school/49985030.pdf.

Tanaka, Sakiko and Waldfogel, Jane. 2007. "Effects of Parental Leave and Work Hours on Fathers' Involvement with Their Babies: Evidence from the Millennium Cohort Study." *Community, Work and Family* 10(4): 409–26.

Tarokh, Leila, Saletin, Jared M., and Carskadon, Mary A. 2016. "Sleep in Adolescence: Physiology, Cognition and Mental Health." *Neuroscience and Biobehavioral Reviews* 70: 182–8.

Tavernise, Sabrina. 2012. "Education Gap Grows Between Rich and Poor, Studies Say." *New York Times*, February 9. http://www.nytimes.com/2012/02/10/education/education-gap-grows-between-rich-and-poor-studies-show.html.

Tax Policy Center. 2018. *Historical Highest Marginal Income Tax Rates*. Urban Institute and Brookings Institution. https://www.taxpolicycenter.org/statistics/historical-highest-marginal-income-tax-rates.

Taylor, Paul, Funk, Cary, and Clark, April. 2007. *Generation Gap in Values, Behaviors as Marriage and Parenthood Drift Apart, Public Is Concerned About Social Impact*. Pew Research Center. http://www.pewresearch.org/wp-content/uploads/sites/3/2007/07/Pew-Marriage-report-6-28-for-web-display.pdf.

Taylor, Paul, Livingston, Gretchen, and Motel, Seth. 2011. *In a Down Economy, Fewer Births*. Pew Research Center. http://assets.pewresearch.org/wp-content/uploads/sites/3/2011/10/REVISITING-FERTILITY-AND-THE-RECESSION-FINAL.pdf.

Taylor, Ronald D., Budescu, Mia, Gebre, Azeb, and Hodzic, Irma. 2014. "Family Financial Pressure and Maternal and Adolescent Socioemotional Adjustment: Moderating Effects of Kin Social Support in Low Income African American Families." *Journal of Child and Family Studies* 23(2): 242–54.

Team Fix. 2015. "Who Said What and What it Meant: The Fourth GOP Debate, Annotated." *Washington Post*. November 10. https://www.washingtonpost.com/news/the-fix/wp/2015/11/10/well-be-annotating-the-gop-debate-here/?utm_term=.cfa4d0355292.

Thakrar, Ashish P., Forrest, Alexandra D., Maltenfort, Mitchell G., and Forrest, Christopher B. 2018. "Child Morality in the US and 19 OECD Comparator Nations: A 50-Year Time-Trend Analysis." *Health Affairs* 37(1): 140–9.

The Second Expert Group for Evaluation of the Adequacy of Basic Social Security. 2015. *Adequacy of Basic Social Security in Finland 2011-2015*. Kela Fpa Working Papers (Working paper no. 80/2015). https://www.julkari.fi/bitstream/handle/10024/126908/WorkingPapers80%20%281%29.pdf?sequence=1

Thévenon, Olivier and Institut national d'études démographiques (INED). 2014. *Family Policies: France (2014)*. PERFAR. https://www.perfar.eu/policy/family-children/france.

Thompson, Derek. 2012. "How America Spends Money: 100 Years in the Life of the Family Budget." *Atlantic*, April 5. https://www.theatlantic.com/business/archive/2012/04/how-america-spends-money-100-years-in-the-life-of-the-family-budget/255475/.

Thompson, Derek. 2013. "The Workforce Is Even More Divided by Race than You Think." *Atlantic*, November 6. https://www.theatlantic.com/business/archive/2013/11/the-workforce-is-even-more-divided-by-race-than-you-think/281175/.

Thomson, Elizabeth, Hanson, Thomas, and McLanahan, Sara. 1994. "Family Structure and Child Well-Being: Economic Resources vs. Parental Behaviors." *Social Forces* 73(1): 221–42.

Tierney, John. 2013. "The Rational Choices of Crack Addicts." *New York Times*, September 16. https://www.nytimes.com/2013/09/17/science/the-rational-choices-of-crack-addicts.html.

Tomlins, Christopher L. 1993. *Law, Labor, and Ideology in the Early American Republic*. New York: Cambridge University Press.

Topping, Alexandra. 2017. "Finland: The Only Country Where Fathers Spend More Time with Kids than Mothers." *Guardian*, December 5. https://www.theguardian.com/lifeandstyle/2017/dec/04/finland-only-country-world-dad-more-time-kids-moms.

Tough, Paul. 2012. *How Children Succeed: Grit, Curiosity, and the Hidden Power of Character*. New York: Houghton Mifflin Harcourt.

Tracy, Melissa, Zimmerman, Frederick, Galea, Sandro, McCauley, Elizabeth, and Stoep, Ann Vander. 2008. "What Explains the Relation Between Family Poverty and Childhood Depressive Symptoms?" *Journal of Psychiatric Research* 42(14): 1163–75.

Trattner, Walter. 1970. *Crusade for the Children: A History of the National Child Labor Committee and Child Labor Reform in America*. Chicago,: Quadrangle Books.

Trattner, Walter. 1974. *From Poor Law to Welfare State: A History of Social Welfare in America*. New York: Free Press.

Traub, Amy, Hiltonsmith, Robert, and Draut, Tamara. 2016. *The Parent Trap: The Economic Insecurity of Families with Young Children*. Demos. https://www.demos.org/sites/default/files/publications/Parent%20Trap.pdf.

Truslow Adams, James. [1931] 2012. *The Epic of America*. New Brunswick: First Transaction.

Trustees of Princeton University. 2019. *About the Fragile Families and Child Wellbeing Study*. https://fragilefamilies.princeton.edu/about.

Tsao, Tsu-Yu, Konty, Kevin, Van Wye, Gretchen, Barbot, Oxiris, Hadler, James, Linos, Natalia, and Bassett, Mary. 2016. "Estimating Potential Reductions in Premature Mortality in New York City from Raising the Minimum Wage to $15." *American Journal of Public Health* 106(6): 1036–41.

Twenge, Jean. 2014. "Time Period and Birth Cohort Differences in Depressive Symptoms in the U.S., 1982–2013." *Social Indicators Research* 121(2): 437–54.

Twenge, Jean and Donnelly, Kristin. 2016. "Generational Differences in American Students' Reasons for Going to College, 1971–2014: The Rise of Extrinsic Motives." *Journal of Social Psychology* 156(6): 620–9.

Twenge, Jean, Gentile, Brittany, DeWall, Nathan, Ma, Debbie, Lacefield, Katharine, and Schurtz, David R. 2010. "Birth Cohort Increases in Psychopathology among Young Americans, 1938–2007: A Cross-Temporal Meta-Analysis of the MMPI." *Clinical Psychology Review* 30(2): 145–54.

Twenge, Jean M. and Park, Heejung. 2017. "The Decline in Adult Activities among U.S. Adolescents, 1976–2016." *Child Development* 90(2): 1–17.

Twenge, J. M., Campbell, W. K., and Freeman, E. C. 2012. "Generational Differences in Young Adults' Life Goals, Concern for Others, and Civic Orientation, 1966–2009." *Journal of Personality and Social Psychology* 102(5): 1045–62.

UNICEF. 2007. *Child Poverty in Perspective: An Overview of Child Well-Being in Rich Countries.* United Nations Children's Fund, Innocenti Research Centre. https://www.unicef.org/media/files/ChildPovertyReport.pdf.

UNICEF. 2012. *Measuring Child Poverty: New League Tables of Child Poverty in the World's Rich Countries.* United Nations Children's Fund, Innocenti Research Centre. https://www.unicef-irc.org/publications/pdf/rc10_eng.pdf.

UNICEF. 2013. *Child Well-Being in Rich Countries: A Comparative Overview.* United Nations Children's Fund, Innocenti Research Centre. https://www.unicef-irc.org/publications/pdf/rc11_eng.pdf.

Upstream USA. 2019. *Delaware CAN.* https://www.upstream.org/campaigns/delaware-can/.

US Bureau of Labor Statistics. 2014. *Women in the Labor Force: A Databook.* BLS Report No. 1049. https://www.bls.gov/cps/wlf-databook-2013.pdf.

US Bureau of Labor Statistics. 2017. *Table 32. Leave Benefits: Access, Private Industry Workers, March 2017.* US Department of Labor. https://www.bls.gov/ncs/ebs/benefits/2017/ownership/private/table32a.pdf.

US Bureau of Labor Statistics. 2018a. *News Release: Union Members—2017.* US Department of Labor. Last modified January 19. https://www.bls.gov/news.release/pdf/union2.pdf.

US Bureau of Labor Statistics. 2018b. *News Release: Employment Characteristics of Families—2017.* US Department of Labor. https://www.bls.gov/news.release/pdf/famee.pdf.

US Bureau of Labor Statistics. 2018c. *Table 6: Employment Status of Mothers with Own Children Under 3 Years Old by Single Year of Age of Youngest Child and Marital Status, 2016–2017 Annual Averages.* US Department of Labor. https://www.bls.gov/news.release/famee.t06.htm.

US Census Bureau. 1990. *Table 4: Population, 1790 to 1990.* https://www.census.gov/population/censusdata/table-4.pdf.

US Census Bureau. 2016a. *Poverty Thresholds by Size of Family and Number of Children.* https://www.census.gov/data/tables/time-series/demo/income-poverty/historical-poverty-thresholds.html.

US Census Bureau. 2016b. *Dynamics of Economic Well-Being: Poverty, 2009–2012, Table 3: People in Poverty 2 or More Months by Selected Characteristics—2009 to 2012.* https://www.census.gov/data/tables/time-series/demo/income-poverty/poverty-dynamics-09-12.html.

US Census Bureau. 2017a. *POV-01: Age and Sex of All People, Family Members and Unrelated Individuals Iterated by Income-to-Poverty Ratio and Race.* https://www.census.gov/data/tables/time-series/demo/income-poverty/cps-pov/pov-01.html.

US Census Bureau. 2017b. *POV-28: Income Deficit or Surplus of Families and Unrelated Individuals by Poverty Status.* https://www.census.gov/data/tables/time-series/demo/income-poverty/cps-pov/pov-28.html.

US Census Bureau. 2018a. *Table F-10: Presence of Children Under 18 Years Old, All Families by Median and Mean Income—1974 to 2017.* https://www2.census.gov/programs-surveys/cps/tables/time-series/historical-income-families/f10ar.xls.

US Census Bureau. 2018b. *Poverty Thresholds for 2016 by Size of Family and Number of Related Children Under 18 Years.* https://www2.census.gov/programs-surveys/cps/tables/time-series/historical-poverty-thresholds/thresh16.xls.

US Census Bureau. 2018c. *Table B17024: Age by Ratio of Income to Poverty Level in the Past 12 Months. Universe: Population for Whom Poverty Status Is Determined.—2017 American Community Survey 1-Year Estimates.* https://factfinder.census.gov/faces/tableservices/jsf/pages/productview.xhtml?pid=ACS_17_1YR_B17024&prodType=table.

US Census Bureau. 2018d. *POV-01: Age and Sex of All People, Family Members and Unrelated Individuals Iterated by Income-to-Poverty Ratio and Race.* Current Population Survey, Annual Social and Economic Supplement. https://www2.census.gov/programs-surveys/cps/tables/pov-01/2018/pov01_100_1.xls.

US Census Bureau. 2018e. *POV-28: Income Deficit or Surplus of Families and Unrelated Individuals by Poverty Status.* Current Population Survey, Annual Social and Economic Supplement. https://www2.census.gov/programs-surveys/cps/tables/pov-28/2018/pov28_001_1.xls.

US Congress. 1935. *Congressional Record.* 74th Cong., 1st sess. Vol. 79, pt. 6, pg. 5862 (statement of Rep. Claude Fuller).

US Department of Commerce. 2015. *2015 Characteristics of New Housing.* https://www.census.gov/construction/chars/pdf/c25ann2015.pdf.

US Department of Health and Human Services. 2002. *Trends in the Well-Being of America's Children & Youth, 2001.* https://aspe.hhs.gov/report/trends-well-being-americas-children-and-youth-2001.

US Department of Health and Human Services. 2015. *Child Care and Development Fund (CCDF) Program: Proposed Rule.* 80 Fed. Reg. 80466, 45 C.F.R. pt. 98. https://www.gpo.gov/fdsys/pkg/FR-2015-12-24/pdf/2015-31883.pdf.

US Department of Health and Human Services. 2017. "QuickStats: Suicide Rates, for Teens Aged 15–19 Years, by Sex—United States, 1975–2015." *Morbidity and Mortality Weekly Report* 66(30): 816.

US Department of Health and Human Services. 2018. *2018 HHS Poverty Guidelines.* https://www.acf.hhs.gov/sites/default/files/ocs/2018_hhs_poverty_guidelines.pdf.

US Department of Labor. 2016. *Handy Reference Guide to the Fair Labor Standards Act.* https://www.dol.gov/whd/regs/compliance/hrg.htm.

US Department of Labor. 2017. *FMLA Frequently Asked Questions.* https://www.dol.gov/whd/fmla/fmla-faqs.htm.

US Department of the Treasury. 2019. *Tax Guide 2018: For Individuals.* Publication No. 17. Internal Revenue Service. https://www.irs.gov/pub/irs-pdf/p17.pdf.

US Government Accountability Office. 2015. *Contingent Workforce: Size, Characteristics, Earnings and Benefits.* http://www.gao.gov/assets/670/669899.pdf.

US Government Accountability Office. 2016. *Child Care: Access to Subsidies and Strategies to Manage Demand Vary Across States.* https://www.gao.gov/assets/690/681652.pdf.

US Health Resources and Services Administration. 2019. *Maternal, Infant, and Early Childhood Home Visiting Program.* https://mchb.hrsa.gov/sites/default/files/mchb/MaternalChildHealthInitiatives/HomeVisiting/pdf/home-visiting-infographic-2017.pdf.

USA.gov. 2019. *Find Affordable Rental Housing.* Last modified Feb. 4. https://www.usa.gov/finding-home#item-37252.

Van Giezen, Robert. 2013. "Paid Leave in Private Industry over the Past 20 Years." *Beyond the Numbers* 2(18). https://www.bls.gov/opub/btn/volume-2/paid-leave-in-private-industry-over-the-past-20-years.htm.

Vance, J. D. 2016. *Hillbilly Elegy: A Memoir of a Family and Culture in Crisis.* New York: HarperCollins.

Vandell, Deborah and Ramanan, Janaki. 1992. "Effects of Early and Recent Maternal Employment on Children from Low-Income Families." *Child Development* 63(4): 938–49.

Vandell, Deborah and Wolfe, Barbara. 2000. *Child Care Quality: Does It Matter and Does It Need to Be Improved?* Institute for Research on Poverty, Special Report No. 78. https://pdfs.semanticscholar.org/4722/d210ea739a7c0eae6de63f55eccb57a27671.pdf.

VanHeuvelen, Tom. 2018. "Moral Economies or Hidden Talents? A Longitudinal Analysis of Union Decline and Wage Inequality, 1973–2015." *Social Forces* 97(2): 495–529.

Vantaa. 2018. *Determining Early Childhood Education's Customer Fees as of August 1, 2018.* https://www.vantaa.fi/instancedata/prime_product_julkaisu/vantaa/embeds/vantaawwwstructure/142280_523048_Maksutiedote_en_20181101.pdf.

Veblen, Thorstein. 1899. *The Theory of the Leisure Class.* Project Gutenberg. http://www.gutenberg.org/files/833/833-h/833-h.htm.

Ventura, Stephanie J., Hamilton, Brady E., and Mathews, T. J. 2014. "National and State Patterns of Teen Births in the United States, 1940–2013." *National Vital Statistics Reports* 63(4). https://www.cdc.gov/nchs/data/nvsr/nvsr63/nvsr63_04.pdf.

Vericker, Tracy, Macomber, Jennifer, and Golden, Olivia. 2010. *Infants of Depressed Mothers Living in Poverty: Opportunities to Identify and Serve.* Urban Institute. http://www.urban.org/sites/default/files/publication/29086/412199-Infants-of-Depressed-Mothers-Living-in-Poverty-Opportunities-to-Identify-and-Serve.PDF.

Villena-Rodán, Benjamín and Ríos-Aguilar, Cecilia. 2011. "Causal Effects of Maternal Time-Investment on Children's Cognitive Outcomes." *Centro de economía aplicada, Universidad de Chile, Working Paper Series.* Working Paper No. 285. https://econpapers.repec.org/paper/edjceauch/285.htm.

Vine, Michaela, Stoep, Ann Vander, Bell, Janice, Rhew, Isaac C., Gudmundsen, Gretchen, and McCauley, Elizabeth. 2012. "Associations Between Household and Neighborhood Income and Anxiety Symptoms in Young Adolescents." *Depression and Anxiety* 29(9): 824–32.

Vogel, Cheri A., Xue, Yange, Moiduddin, Emily M., Carlson, Barbara Lepidus, and Kisker, Ellen Eliason. 2010. *Early Head Start Children in Grade 5: Long-Term Followup of the Early Head Start Research and Evaluation Project Study Sample.* OPRE Report No. 2011-8. Mathematica Policy Research. https://www.acf.hhs.gov/sites/default/files/opre/grade5.pdf.

Votruba-Drzal, Elizabeth, Coley, Rebekah Levine, Koury, Amanda S., and Miller, Portia. 2013. "Center-Based Child Care and Cognitive Skills Development: Importance of Timing and Household Resources." *Journal of Educational Psychology* 105(3): 821–38.

WABC. 2018. "Officers Pry 1-Year-Old from Brooklyn Mom's Arms During Arrest; Police Investigating." *ABC 7*, December 10. https://abc7ny.com/society/officers-pry-1-year-old-from-moms-arms-during-arrest/4868592/.

Walburg, Vera, Goehlich, Maja, Conquet, Marlene, Callahan, Stacey, Scholmerich, Axel and Chabrol, Henri. 2010. "Breast feeding initiation and duration: comparison of Frenchand German mothers." *Midwifery* 26: 109-115.

Wade, Roy, Shea, Judy A., Rubin, David, and Wood, Joanne. 2014. "Adverse Childhood Experiences of Low-Income Urban Youth." *Pediatrics* 134(1): e13–e20.

Waldfogel, Jane. 2002. "Childcare, Women's Employment, and Child Outcomes." *Journal of Population Economics* 15(3): 527–48.

Waldfogel, Jane. 2006. *What Children Need.* Cambridge, MA: Harvard University Press.

Waldfogel, Jane, Danziger, Sandra, Danziger, Sheldon, and Seefeldt, Kristin. 2001. "Welfare Reform and Lone Mothers' Employment in the US." *Center for Analysis of Social Exclusion Discussion Paper Series.* CASE Paper No. 47. London School of Economics. http://eprints.lse.ac.uk/6437/1/Welfare_Reform_and_Lone_Mothers'_Employment_in_the_US.pdf.

Waldfogel, Jane, Han, Wen-Jui, and Brooks-Gunn, Jeanne. 2002. "The Effects of Early Maternal Employment on Child Cognitive Development." *Demography* 39(2): 369–92.

Waldfogel, Jane and Washbrook, Elizabeth. 2011. "Early Years Policy." *Child Development Research.* http://eprints.lse.ac.uk/43728/1/Early%20years%20policy(lsero).pdf.

Waldinger, Robert. 2015. "What Makes a Good Life? Lessons from the Longest Study on Happiness." *TEDx*, November. https://www.ted.com/talks/robert_waldinger_what_makes_a_good_life_lessons_from_the_longest_study_on_happiness?language=en.

Walker, Christina and Matthews, Hannah. 2016. "Declining TANF Child Care Spending Underscores Need for Major Child Care Investment." *CLASP Blog*, August 30. https://www.clasp.org/blog/declining-tanf-child-care-spending-underscores-need-major-child-care-investment.

Wallace, Kelly. 2017. "The 'Fifth Trimester': When New Moms Return to Work." *CNN*, April 6. https://www.cnn.com/2017/04/06/health/fifth-trimester-working-mom-resources-parenting/index.html.

Wang, Wendy. 2015. "The Link Between a College Education and a Lasting Marriage." Pew Research Center, December 4. http://www.pewresearch.org/fact-tank/2015/12/04/education-and-marriage/.

Wang, Wendy and Parker, Kim. 2014. *Record Share of Americans Have Never Married: As Values Economics, and Gender Patterns Change.* Pew Research Center. http://www.pewresearch.org/wp-content/uploads/sites/3/2014/09/2014-09-24_Never-Married-Americans.pdf.

Wang, Wendy, Parker, Kim, and Taylor, Paul. 2013. *Breadwinner Moms: Mothers Are the Sole or Primary Provider in Four-in-Ten Households with Children; Public Conflicted about the Growing Trend.* Pew Research Center. http://www.pewresearch.org/wp-content/uploads/sites/3/2013/05/Breadwinner_moms_final.pdf.

Warren, Elizabeth and Tyagi, Amelia Warren. 2003. *The Two-Income Trap: Why Middle-Class Parents Are Going Broke.* New York: Basic Books.

Warwick, Liz. 2004. "Dr. Michael Meany: More Cuddles, Less Stress!" *Bulletin of the Centre of Excellence for Early Childhood Development* 4(2): 2.

Washbrook, Elizabeth, Christopher Ruhm, Jane Waldfogel, and Wen-Jui Han. 2011. "Public Policies, Women's Employment after Childbearing, and Child Well-Being." *B.E. Journal of Economic Analysis and Policy* 11(1): 1–42.

Washbrook, Elizabeth, Jane Waldfogel, Christopher Ruhm, and Wen-Jui Han. 2008. *The Timing of Mothers' Employment after Childbirth.* Bureau of Labor Statistics, Monthly Labor Review. https://www.bls.gov/opub/mlr/2008/article/timing-of-mothers-employment-after-childbirth.htm. Figure 1.

Weber, Lauren. 2013. "Why Dads Don't Take Paternity Leave: More Companies Offer New Fathers Paid Time Off, but Many Fear Losing Face Back at the Office." *Wall Street Journal*, June 12. https://www.wsj.com/articles/SB10001424127887324049504578541633708283670.

Weeks, Kathi. 2011. *The Problem with Work: Feminism, Marxism, Antiwork Politics, and Postwork Imaginaries.* Durham, NC: Duke Univeristy Press.

Weinberger, A. H., Gbedemah, M., Martinez, A. M., Nash, D., Galea, S., and Goodwin, R. D. 2018. "Trends in Depression Prevalence in the USA from 2005 to 2015: Widening Disparities in Vulnerable Groups." *Psychological Medicine* 48(8): 1308–15.

Weiss, Michael J. Salomon and Wagner, Sheldon H. 1998. "What Explains the Negative Consequences of Adverse Childhood Experiences on Adult Health? Insights from Cognitive and Neuroscience Research." *American Journal of Preventative Medicine* 14(4): 356–60.

Welti, Kate and Manlove, Jennifer. 2018. *Estimated Reductions in Unintended Pregnancy among Delaware Title X Family Planning Clients After a Contraceptive Access Intervention.* Child Trends. https://www.childtrends.org/estimated-reductions-in-unintended-pregnancy-among-delaware-title-x-family-planning-clients-after-a-contraceptive-access-intervention.

West, Rachel. 2017. "For the Cost of the Tax Bill, the U.S. Could Eliminate Child Poverty. Twice." *Talk Poverty*, December 12. https://talkpoverty.org/2017/12/12/u-s-eliminate-child-poverty-cost-senate-tax-bill/.

Western, Bruce. 1997. *Between Class and Market: Postwar Unionization in the Capitalist Democracies.* Princeton, NJ: Princeton University Press.

Western, Bruce and Rosenfeld, Jake. 2011. "Unions, Norms, and the Rise in U.S. Wage Inequality." *American Sociological Review* 76(4): 513–37.

Whitebrook, Marcy, McLean, Caitlin, Austin, Lea, and Edwards, Bethany. 2018. *Early Childhood Workforce Index.* Center for the Study of Child Care Employment. http://cscce.berkeley.edu/files/2018/06/Early-Childhood-Workforce-Index-2018.pdf.

White House Working Group on the Family. 1986. *The Family: Preserving America's Future: A Report to the President.* https://catalog.hathitrust.org/Record/002585656.

Whitehurst, Grover (Russ). 2017. "Will Tax Reform Provide More Support for Children and Their Families? Follow the Money." *Evidence Speaks Reports* 2(27). https://www.brookings.edu/wp-content/uploads/2017/10/follow-the-money-report1.pdf.

Wight, Vanessa, Raley, Sara and Bianchi, Susan. 2008. "Time for Children, One's Spouse and Oneself among Parents Who Work Nonstandard Hours." *Social Forces* 87(1): 243–71.

Wilcox, Bradford and DeRose, Laurie. 2017. "In Europe, Cohabitation Is Stable . . . Right?" *Brookings Institute*, March 27. https://www.brookings.edu/blog/social-mobility-memos/2017/03/27/in-europe-cohabitation-is-stable-right/.

Wilcox, William Bradford and Marquardt, Elizabeth. 2010. *When Marriage Disappears: The New Middle America*. National Marriage Project and Institute for American Values. http://stateofourunions.org/2010/SOOU2010.pdf.

Wildsmith, Elizabeth, Manlove, Jennifer, and Cook, Elizabeth. 2018. "Dramatic Increase in the Proportion of Births Outside of Marriage in the United States from 1990 to 2016." Child Trends. https://www.childtrends.org/publications/dramatic-increase-in-percentage-of-births-outside-marriage-among-whites-hispanics-and-women-with-higher-education-levels.

Wilkinson, Richard and Pickett, Kate. [2009] 2010. *The Spirit Level: Why Greater Equality Makes Societies Stronger*. New York: Bloomsbury Press.

Williams, Joan and Boushey, Heather. 2010. *The Three Faces of Work–Family Conflict: The Poor, the Professionals, and the Missing Middle*. Center for American Progress. https://cdn.americanprogress.org/wp-content/uploads/issues/2010/01/pdf/threefaces.pdf.

Williams, Lynn M. and Towell, Pat. 2016. *Fact Sheet: Selected Highlights of the FY2017 National Defense Authorization Act (H.R. 4909, S. 2943)*. CRS Report No. R44497. Congressional Research Service. https://fas.org/sgp/crs/natsec/R44497.pdf.

Williams, Matt. 2017. *TANF at 20 in Mississippi: A Path Out of Poverty or a Shrinking Safety Net?* Mississippi Low-Income Child Care Initiative. http://www.mschildcare.org/wp-content/uploads/2019/02/2017-TANF-AT-20_1.5.16.pdf.

Wilson, Valerie. 2015. "Black Unemployment Is Significantly Higher than White Unemployment Regardless of Educational Attainment." Economic Policy Institute, December 15. https://www.epi.org/publication/black-unemployment-educational-attainment/.

Wilson, Valerie and Rodgers, William M. 2016. *Black–White Wage Gaps Expand with Rising Wage Inequality*. Economic Policy Institute. https://www.epi.org/files/pdf/101972.pdf.

Wilson, William Julius. 1987. *The Truly Disadvantaged: The Inner City, the Underclass, and Public Policy*. Chicago: University of Chicago Press.

Wilson, William Julius. 1996. *When Work Disappears: The World of the New Urban Poor*. New York: Vintage Books.

Winton, Richard. 2019. "Mystery Parent Paid $6.5 Million to Get Kids into Top Universities as Part of Admissions Scandal." *Los Angeles Times*, March 25. https://www.latimes.com/local/lanow/la-me-college-admissions-bribe-fixer-20190324-story.html

Wogan, J. B. 2016. "How Are States Using Welfare Funding? Often, Not to Help People Work." *Governing*, October 26. http://www.governing.com/topics/health-human-services/gov-welfare-work-state-spending.html.

Wolf, Sharon, Magnuson, Katherine A., and Kimbro, Rachel T. 2017. "Family Poverty and Neighborhood Poverty: Links with Children's School Readiness Before and After the Great Recession." *Children and Youth Services Review* 79: 368–84.

Wolff, Edward N. 2017. "Household Wealth Trends in the United States, 1962 to 2016: Has Middle Class Wealth Recovered?" *National Bureau of Economic Research Working Paper Series*. Working Paper No. 24085. http://www.nber.org/papers/w24085.

Wood, Joanne N., Medina, Sheyla P., Feudtner, Chris, Luan, Xianqun, Localio, Russell, Fieldston, Evan S., and Rubin, David M. 2012. "Local Macroeconomic Trends and Hospital Admissions for Child Abuse, 2000–2009." *Pediatrics* 130(2): e358–e364.

World Bank. 2018. *Mortality Rate, Under-5 (per 1,000 Live Births)*. World Bank. https://data.worldbank.org/indicator/SH.DYN.MORT?locations=US.

World Bank. 2019. *Adolescent Fertility Rate (Births per 1,000 Women Ages 15–19)*. https://data.worldbank.org/indicator/SP.ADO.TFRT.

World Health Organization. 2004. *The Importance of Caregiver–Child Interactions for the Survival and Healthy Development of Young Children: A Review*. http://apps.who.int/iris/bitstream/10665/42878/1/924159134X.pdf.

World Health Organization. 2018. *Global Health Estimates 2016: Disease Burden by Cause, Age, Sex, by Country and by Region, 2000–2016*. https://www.who.int/healthinfo/global_burden_disease/estimates/en/index1.html.

Wright, Lesley. 2011. "Franks Pushes Tax-Exemption Bill." *The Arizona Republic*. May 23.

Wrigley, Julia and Dreby, Joanna. 2005. "Fatalities and the Organization of Child Care in the United States, 1985–2003." *American Sociological Review* 70(5): 729–57.

Yahoo-ABC News Network. 2017. "Constituent Loses His Temper at Rep. Tom MacArthur Over Health Care." *ABC News*, May 11. https://abcnews.go.com/Politics/video/constituent-loses-temper-rep-tom-macarthur-health-care-47338603.

Yeung, W. Jean, Linver, Miriam, and Brooks-Gunn, Jeanne. 2002. "How Money Matters for Young Children's Development: Parental Investment and Family Processes." *Child Development* 73(6): 1861–79.

Yoshikawa, Hirokazu. 1995. "Long-Term Effects of Early Childhood Programs on Social Outcomes and Delinquency." *Future of Children* 5(3): 51–75.

Yoshikawa, Hirokazu, Weiland, Christina, Brooks-Gunn, Jeanne, Burchinal, Margaret, Espinosa, Linda, Gormley, William, Ludwig, Jens, Magnuson, Katherine, Phillips, Deborah, and Zaslow, Martha. 2013. *Investing in Our Future: The Evidence Base on Preschool Education*. Society for Research in Child Development and Foundation for Child Development. https://www.fcd-us.org/assets/2016/04/Evidence-Base-on-Preschool-Education-FINAL.pdf.

Zarrett, Nicole and Lerner, Richard. 2008. *Ways to Promote the Positive Development of Children and Youth*. Research-to-Results Brief No. 2008-11. Child Trends. https://www.childtrends.org/wp-content/uploads/01/Youth-Positive-Devlopment.pdf.

Zernike, Kate. 2011. "Retreat of the 'Tiger Mother.'" *New York Times*, January 14. http://www.nytimes.com/2011/01/16/fashion/16Cultural.html.

Zhang, T. Y., Chrétien, P., Meaney, M. J., and Gratton, A. 2005. "Influence of Naturally Occurring Variations in Maternal Care on Prepulse Inhibition of Acoustic Startle and the Medial Prefrontal Cortical Dopamine Response to Stress in Adult Rats." *Journal of Neuroscience* 25(6): 1493–1502.

Zhang, Tie-Yuan, Bagot, Rose, Parent, Carine, Nesbitt, Cathy, Bredy, Timothy W., Caldji, Christian, Fish, Eric, Anisman, Hymie, Szyf, Moshe, and Meaney, Michael J. 2006. "Maternal Programming of Defensive Responses Through Sustained Effects on Gene Expression." *Biological Psychology* 73(1): 72–89.

Zhang, Tie-Yun and Meaney, Michael J. 2010. "Epigenetics and the Environmental Regulation of the Genome and Its Function." *Annual Review of Psychology* 61(1): 439–66.

Zhang, Tie-Yun, Parent, Carine, Weaver, Ian, and Meany, Michael J. 2004. "Maternal Programming of Individual Differences in Defensive Responses in the Rat." *Annals of the New York Academy of Sciences* 1032: 85–103.

Zilberstein, Karen. 2016. "Parenting in Families of Low Socioeconomic Status: A Review with Implications for Child Welfare Practice." *Family Court Review* 54(2): 221–31.

Ziliak, James P., Hardy, Bradley, and Bollinger, Christopher. 2011. "Earnings Volatility in America: Evidence from Matched CPS." *Labour Economics* 18(6): 742–54.

Zoorob, Michael J. and Salemi, Jason L. 2017. "Bowling Alone, Dying Together: The Role of Social Capital in Mitigating the Drug Overdose Epidemic in the United States." *Drug and Alcohol Dependence* 173(1): 1–9.

INDEX

For the benefit of digital users, indexed terms that span two pages (e.g., 52–53) may, on occasion, appear on only one of those pages.

Page numbers followed by *f* refer to figures.